T0294861

Money and Banking:
The American Experience

The George Edward Durell Foundation
Winchester, Virginia

GEORGE MASON UNIVERSITY PRESS
Fairfax, Virginia

Library of Congress Cataloging-in-Publication Data

Money and banking : the American experience.
p.   cm.
"The George Edward Durell Foundation, Winchester, Virginia."
Includes bibliographical references and index.
1. Money—United States—History—Congresses.   2. Banks and
banking—United States—History—Congresses.   I. George Edward
Durell Foundation.
HG501.M66   1994   332.1'0973—dc20   94–36742 CIP

ISBN 0–913969–74–5 (cloth : alk. paper)

Contents

Introduction

by Clifford F. Thies

There was a time, not so long ago, when the study of monetary history was an honorable part of economics. Then came the Keynesian revolution. Keynesian economics taught, among other things, that all we had to do was fit econometric models to the quarterly data of the post-World War II economy in order to estimate the parameters necessary for monetary and fiscal policy decisions. The distant past was irrelevant to estimation of these parameters because of structural changes. Subjects such as free banking, the legal tender cases and silver agitation became forgotten.

Today, with the complete breakdown of the monetary regime that was put into place during the 1930s, interest in monetary history has revived. Economists are interested precisely in the "structure" of money and banking: what *is* money, and what *are* banks? Because these fundamental questions had formerly seemed satisfactorily answered, they were not seen as interesting. Money was what the Federal Reserve defined it to be, and banks were what the several regulatory agencies involved defined them to be. But, with new technologies, overwhelming market forces, and changes in law and regulation, the answers we had taken for granted have been revealed to be inadequate.

This volume presents ten articles concerning the American experience in money and banking originally presented at the 1990 Durell Conference on Money and Banking. The articles, as a set, span the period from the founding of the country to, more or less, the present. Individually, they range from a presentation of an overview of the entire period to a case study of a particular chain of banks that failed during the Great Depression. The unifying theme of these articles is their consideration of the legal and economic underpinnings of money and banking during the several monetary regimes found in the history of the United States.

Inherently Unstable

Kevin Dowd opened the conference with what may be termed the "new history" of banking in the United States. According to the received history, banks are inherently unstable, and therefore in need of special government regulation and protection. They are inherently unstable because they only carry fractional reserves (i.e., banks have liquid assets equal to only a fraction of their deposits). Normally, banks can operate with fractional reserves because withdrawals from deposit accounts are at least approximately matched by contributions into the same. Internal clearing allows banks to economize on liquidity, and increase their investment in assets having greater earning power. But, this higher return comes at a price; the risk of a run on the bank.

Because they operate with fractional reserves, when there is a run on the bank, banks are forced to suspend redemption. A run on the bank forces suspension whether or not the particular bank involved is solvent (that is, has total assets the value of which exceed total liabilities). Bank panics occur when suspensions of some banks raise concerns for the liquidity of banks in general, precipitating many runs on the bank. Thus, bank panics are self-fulfilling prophesies of insolvency, and irrational insofar as solvent banks—in the absence of bank panic—would be able to continue to make good on their promise to redeem deposits. Government deposit insurance put an end to bank panics because it removed the concern of depositors for bank safety. With government deposit insurance, banks would only be closed by bank regulators because of insolvency.

In part, the received history is based on the folklore of "wild cat" banking during the free banking era, from the early 19th century to the Civil War. "Wild cat" banks were so named because they were located deep in the woods, where only the wild cats roamed. Because of their remote location, people were reluctant to present their banknotes for redemption. "Wild cat" banks not only allowed unscrupulous bankers to defraud the public, they engendered paper money-financed speculative booms, that were followed by bank panics, the collapse of stock, bond and real estate prices, and recession.

Notice that, implicit in the received history is the belief that people used to be incredibly naive. Why else would they accept the paper of unknown and far-away banks; and, not just occasionally, but to such an extent as to have recurrent macroeconomic impact.

The actual history of free banking was quite different. Yes, there were some "wild cat" banks during this period, but these were the exception to the rule. Free banks were, for the time, very stable. Banknotes of all but the strongest banks tended to circulate only within the immediate vicinity of the bank. Even the banknotes of strong banks passed at a discount in distant cities, reflecting the cost of redemption. Redemption, including the possibility of a run on the bank, motivated bankers to consider liquidity and riskiness as well as profitability.

The bank failures that occurred during the free banking era could often be explained by two simple facts: Free banks were required to carry state bonds as collateral for the banknotes they issued. And, a number of state government found themselves financially embarrassed during this period. In those states where the state government was financially stable, free banks did well. Indeed, it was because free banking was generally successful that it was adopted by most states prior to the Civil War, and incorporated into the federal legislation providing for the chartering of national banks.

A mirror image to the actual history of the stability of free banks (contrasting to the folklore of inherent stability) is the actual history of failure of government deposit insurance (contrasting to the folklore of its success). From New York State's early 19th century "safety fund," to Oklahoma's early 20th century "guaranty fund," to the Federal Savings and Loan Insurance Corporation, government deposit insurance has proven itself to be an unmitigated disaster.

Government deposit insurance has always turned the problems of embezzlement, insider dealing and fraud endemic to banking, into conflagrations of crime and corruption. In the failure of the Federal Savings and Loan Insurance Corporation, outright criminal activity accounted for much of the losses put to taxpayers and depositors.[1] Political scandal forced the retirement of the Speaker of the House of Representatives, the Chairman of the House Banking Committee, and other ranking congressmen. The U.S. Senate went so far as to admonish one of its members.[2]

Government deposit insurance has led to such disastrous results because it immunizes the public from losses due to bank failure, thereby cutting short market discipline over risk-taking. It attempts to use the government's regulatory power as a substitute for market discipline. Yet history shows that when regulations are directly contrary to private interests, and the stakes are high enough, that the integrity of the regulatory process will be compromised. Just as locks keep honest people honest, regulation *can* be used to suppress fraud when it is in the self-interest of bankers to act prudently, and in so doing complement market discipline.

Dowd's analysis ranges broadly, considering several constitutional issues and the role of public choice. The silence of the U.S. Constitution, for example, on the issue of whether Congress could grant corporate charters was resolved by Chief Justice Marshall's ruling in *McCulloch v. Maryland,* which invoked the "necessary and proper" clause of the Constitution and the "sovereignty" of government. The more immediate action and reaction was to allow the charter of the Second Bank of the United States to stand, and to spur the populist attack against that bank that we associate with Andrew Jackson.

A History of Trial and Error

The received history was simple enough: In response to various problems in money and banking, regulatory powers over the same were enlarged and centralized. The major pieces of legislation include the money and banking acts of the 1860s, the Federal Reserve Act of 1913, and the money and banking acts of the 1930s. Together, these gave us a uniform and "elastic" currency, along with federally-chartered, supervised and guaranteed banks. With all the parts finally put into place, runs on the bank were ended, as were bank panics, suspensions, and the recurrent cycle of speculative boom and bust. In addition, the path was cleared for sustainable, non-inflationary economic growth with full employment. This is why, economically–speaking, the 1930s marked the end of history.

But, there is no such simple theme to the new history. Each monetary regime requires its own analysis. The new history is neither Hamiltonian (i.e., it does not favor assertion of the power of the federal government in the area of money and banking) nor Jacksonian (i.e., it does not favor the assertion of the power of state government to restrict branching across or within states). The several monetary regimes found in the history of the United States are little more than a series of historical accidents. For those who find these matters curious, it is a rich history. But, for those who merely want to know how to fix what went wrong in the failure of the latest monetary regime, it can indeed be frustrating.

At the time of the founding, the granting of a corporate charter required an act of the legislature. It usually involved the granting of monopoly privilege, and subjected the receiver to special taxes. In banking, especially, states jealously guarded access to the market. "Free banking" opened access to all who could meet the pre-specified conditions. It turned incorporating as a bank into a simple filing with the Secretary of State (or some other state official).[3] But, while free banking in the United States opened up the market in banking in one way, it limited the market in other ways.

In the United States, free banking was also unit banking. This was true not only in the states that adopted free banking legislation, but also in the national bank system put into place during the 1860s. The ability of banks to branch, as well as to cooperate in other ways, was denied. Populist sentiment combined with the self-interest of local bankers to make a formidable political alliance. It is hard to believe that legislators could have failed to see the dangers involved in unit banking, especially for the agricultural and mining regions of the country. Perhaps the regulations imposed on free banks, as well as government deposit insurance, were designed to make unit banks safe.

While much of the focus of the new history of the antebellum period concerns free banking, the experience of a number of other state banking systems are notable: Virginia, for example, with its branch banking system; and, Ohio, with its mutual guarantee banking system. That the received history made short shrift of these episodes is understandable: Branch banking and mutual guarantee systems were quite safe, and do not contribute much to the thesis that continuing failures of unregulated banks led inexorably to the most recent monetary regime.

The Nationalization of Money

The new history of money and banking has turned many former positions on their head. Many proponents of *laissez-faire* have also been proponents of "hard money" (i.e., a gold standard), and of "100 percent" banking. Concerning fractional reserve banking, the more radical argument has been that anything less than 100 percent reserve banking constitutes fraud, and on that basis should be suppressed by government.

Going back some time in history, paper money gained circulation because it was more convenient to exchange warehouse receipts for precious metals stored by gold- and silversmiths, than to exchange the metals themselves. As the story goes, fractional reserve banking was born in the discovery by certain gold- and silversmiths that they could issue a multiple amount of these receipts than they had of the metal on hand. These receipts were fraudulent insofar as they represented that more metal was being warehoused than was actually the case. But that was a long, long time ago. The argument that negotiable paper is fraudulent unless backed 100 percent by its redemption media is, today (when there is no claim of 100 percent reserves), merely part of the larger issue of limited liability.

In the west, at about the same time that this country was founded, concern arose for the relief of those who, even with a good faith effort, could not repay their debts. The alternatives of being sold into slavery, or of languishing in debtor's prison, were no longer acceptable. Bankruptcy became adopted. While the specifics have varied, bankruptcy involves the admission on the part of the debtor of his inability to repay his debts as promised, and the forced liquidation or seizure of his assets by creditors (save those assets excluded from bankruptcy), according to their priorities of claim as specified by contract.

In the language of finance, debt is a contingent claim. Specifically, debt is a put option issued by creditors to debtors, covering the assets of the debtor. Its value is the higher of the liquidation value of the assets of the debtor, and the redemption value of the debt. The only real distinction between put options such as are issued against shares of corporate stock, and debt, is the judgement required for determination of the debtor's "good faith" effort to repay, and (related to this) the concern for one's moral turpitude resulting from recourse to bankruptcy. The connection that some make between fraud and fractional reserve banking is made clear by the similar arguments made against relief of indebtedness through bankruptcy.

If debt is a contingent claim, why do certain liabilities—for example, banknotes—gain currency? In part, the answer is that these options are sufficiently "in the money" (that is, have collateral value sufficiently in excess of their redemption value) that the issuer is near certain to redeem them. This would, of course, be the case with the liabilities of 100 percent reserve banks. These reserves perfectly secure the liability. This could also be the case with collateral other than the redemption media. In such a case, the collateral and liability would not be perfectly matched, and there would be a chance of the value of the collateral falling to less than that of the liability. Nevertheless, if the value of the collateral is sufficiently in excess of the liability such a fluctuation in value would be unlikely.

The other part of the answer to why the liabilities of some gain currency, is that a sufficient part of the public accepts these liabilities as a medium of exchange. To be sure, this involves some circular reasoning.

How can anyone be the first to accept something as money when, to be recognized as money, it must be generally accepted as money. But, rather than being a vicious circle, this is better characterized as an historical helix: The acceptance of the liability by some is what leads to the acceptance by others. Those who initially accept the liability are, presumably, in a position to know that it is near certain to be redeemed. Those who later come to accept it do so, perhaps, only because of the expectation that they will be able to pass it on in exchange.

Government has played at least two roles in the process by which paper money gains currency: First, its decision as to what it will accept influences others in their similar decisions. Second, its coercive powers over those subject to it make tenuous any money other than its own. Money, like political power, comes out of the barrel of a gun.

As Gregory B. Christiansen points out, the decision of the federal government to accept the banknotes of the First Bank of the United States, greatly helped that bank's liabilities enter into circulation as money. Gary M. Pecquet discusses how the government of the Confederate States of America was able put its treasury notes into circulation by getting the state governments of the Confederacy to accept them in payment of taxes. Richard H. Timberlake similarly mentions that the limited amounts of U.S. Treasury notes issued prior to the Civil War were accepted in payment of taxes by the federal government. These are three instances of the government influencing what becomes accepted as money through its decision as to what it will accept. Timberlake then goes on to discuss how the federal government was able, with the issue of greenbacks, and the legal tender cases that resulted, to simply force its money onto the country.

In 1862, with the Civil War underway, Congress authorized the first issue of United States notes, or greenbacks, that were to be "lawful money" and legal tender for all debts, public and private.[4] This act was headed for the Supreme Court the moment President Lincoln signed it. The great irony of the legal tender cases was that it was Salmon P. Chase, as Lincoln's secretary of the treasury, who pushed the act through Congress; and, it was also Chase, as chief justice, speaking for a four-to-three majority in *Hepburn v. Griswold,* who declared the legal tender acts to be unconstitutional. Creditors, he said, "...are as fully entitled to the protection of this constitutional provision [the takings clause of the 5th Amendment] as holders of any other description of property."

On the very day of this decision, President Grant sent two nominations to the Senate to fill vacancies on the Supreme Court. Both nominees were on record as favoring the constitutionality of the legal tender acts. The reconstituted court immediately called up two cases, *Knox v. Lee* and *Parker v. Davis,* the facts of which were similar to *Hepburn.* The two new members joined the three dissenting justices in *Hepburn* to decide that the legal tender acts were indeed constitutional.

The Golden Rule

While Chase's ruling that the legal tender acts were unconstitutional was overturned, his decision in *Bronson v. Rodes*—that debt contracts that provided by specific reference for payment in gold or silver coin were enforceable—was not. This led to the standardization of the gold clause in long-term bonds and mortgages. The gold clause provided for repayment in gold coin of the United States as of the date of the contract. It was designed to protect the creditor from suspension, devaluation, or switch to silver.[5] While there is some evidence that the market valued the protection afforded by the gold clause, the inviability of the gold clause was always in doubt. In 1893, for example, when the Treasury's gold reserve fell to near its legal minimum, rumors spread that the gold clause had been declared invalid.

The test of the inviability of the gold clause came in 1933 when, in the middle of the Great Depression, President Franklin D. Roosevelt decided to devalue the dollar, and to negate the loss that would, as a result, be suffered by debtors, by voiding the gold clause.[6] The next year, the Supreme Court, in a five-to-four vote, upheld the voiding of the gold clause. In 1939, the Court extended its ruling to void all forms of debt-indexation. After having forced its paper money onto the nation, the federal government prohibited the use of any other as a standard of value in debt contracts.[7] In 1977, the Gold Clause Resolution was repealed.[8] The non-flood of debt-indexation that followed could be because of the dependence of debt-indexation on the will of the Congress.[9]

The ban of debt-indexation has not been the only instance of the monopolization of money by the government. Both in the sense of medium of exchange and standard of value, there have been numerous prohibitions. Scrip money, issued by many private companies as well as by state and local governments, has been kept from evolving into a general medium of exchange by laws banning the issuance of private currency.[10] A nascent money and banking system based on grain futures was ended by the intervention of the state of Illinois.[11] The failure of the even more exotic, labor money standard attempted by the American anarchist Josiah Warren in conjunction with his Time Stores and the Long Island community of Modern Times, might have had something to do with its having been unenforceable.[12]

The above discussion questions the argument that gold and government-issued fiat currency are natural because they have been used as money. Gold became money (and silver was de-monetized) due to bungled attempts to institute bimetal standards.[13] The allure of gold is due to the fact that gold was, for a time, the symbol of 19th century economic liberalism. Yet, close examination demonstrates that the symbolism is and was always misplaced. Gold became money, and was maintained as money, due to a series of interventions in the market process.

The Constitution grants Congress the power to "coin money, [and] regulate the value thereof." As J. Huston McCulloch notes, in his discussion of Timberlake's paper, this provision was intended to sustain a functioning bimetal standard. Because of Gresham's Law,[14] the affixing of an official exchange rate between gold and silver will inevitably lead to the circulation of only one of the metals. Specifically, whichever metal is undervalued will be the one that will circulate. However, both metals might circulate if the official exchange rate is periodically changed so as to keep it close to the market rate.

Such periodic changes would not constitute "takings" repulsive to (the intent of) the 5th Amendment *as long as* they were not applied retroactively to extant contracts.[15] That is, debtors would be allowed to deliver the cheaper of gold or silver according to their official exchange rate at the time of the contract.

Given the possibility that any commodity might dramatically increase in value, a bimetal standard allows the debtor to repay with the cheaper of the two metals and thereby avoid the burden of repaying with the dear one. If bankruptcy is costly, this could easily be mutually advantageous to debtors and creditors compared to a monometal standard. But, it is hard to imagine how a bimetal standard could be mutually advantageous compared to indexation.[16] By relating debt payments to an average of the prices of many commodities, indexation stabilizes the burden of debt. This is why economists have long advocated indexation.[17]

It must be remembered that the Roosevelt administration did not abrogate the gold clause in order to lower the purchasing power value of debt below the levels prevailing at the time of contracting. It did so in order to return the purchasing power of debt to something like those levels. In other words, Roosevelt attempted to relieve debtors of the onerous burdens caused by the breakdown of the gold standard and massive deflation of the Great Depression.

That no harm was done to creditors was specifically noted by the Supreme Court. Speaking for the Court, Chief Justice Charles Evan Hughes stated "We think that the reasonable import of the promise is that it was intended to assure one who lent his money to the government and took its bond that he would not suffer loss through depreciation in the medium of payment." Yet, in spite of the substantive content of this ruling, the Court soon decided that any form of indexation was contrary to public policy. The dogma of sovereignty replaced reasoned consideration of what was the intent of the gold clause. Thus, the stage was set for the ruination of creditors by the post-World War II inflation, and the transformation of conventional debt into speculations on the future course of monetary policy.

Instead of insulating money from government, the gold standard exposed money to the monetary decisions of every government in the world. Following its defeat of France in the Franco-Prussian War of 1870, the government of Prussia switched from a silver standard to a gold standard. As a result of the appreciation of gold against silver, France, the other members of the Latin Union, and the United States were forced to reduce the monetary role of silver, in order to minimize the loss on their large holdings of the white metal. This contributed to a further appreciation of gold against silver. Deflation increased the burdens of those who had contracted debts denominated in gold, with the result of bankruptcies and depressed economic conditions all around the world.[18]

The movement of prices during the late 19th century was mild compared to what happened after World War I. Anna J. Schwartz writes of the attempt by Benjamin Strong, of the New York Federal Reserve Bank, to restore the pre-war gold standard during the 1920s, an attempt that was ended so spectacularly by its success. As England, France, Germany, and other countries resumed convertibility, the world demand for gold reserves increased. Yet, there was not enough gold to support the prices that had only been partially returned to their pre-war level by the immediate post-war deflation.

Since the supply of gold was insufficient, gold flowed out of the holdings of the Federal Reserve. The Fed responded by "immunizing" these outflows, not by reducing the U.S. money supply. By the late 1920s, the amount of "free gold" in the Fed had fallen to near zero. By the late 1920s, it would have been clear to an astute observer that the United States would be forced either to devalue or to deflate.[19]

A true gold standard would have required the Federal Reserve to reduce the money supply during the gold outflows of the 1920s. This policy would have gradually reduced prices to their pre-war levels. Alternately, once the massive deflationary forces of the Great Depression became obvious, the Hoover administration could have urged across-the-board cuts in wages and prices so as to minimize the impact on employment and production.[20] Another alternative—Irving Fisher's—would have been to adjust the gold content of the dollar so that a dollar would always be constant in terms of its purchasing power.

The solution eventually implemented by President Roosevelt was to bring about a "reflation" of prices through devaluation, abrogation of the gold clause, expansion of the money supply, cartelization of U.S. industry through the National Recovery Administration, the Wagner Act, and a number of regulatory agencies, and federal social insurance. Thus, the bungled attempt to fix both the gold content of the dollar and the price level, resulted in a catastrophic collapse of the world monetary order, and ushered in a massive and still growing increase in government. In the prophetic words of Justice James C. McReynolds, in the dissent from the Court's decision in the Gold Clause cases,

> "The Constitution as many of us have understood it, the instrument that has meant so much to us, is gone. The guarantees heretofore supposed to protect against arbitrary action have been swept away. The powers of Congress have been so enlarged that now no man can tell their limitations."

In a word, the new history of money and banking is enormous. Because of the tendency to attribute inflation, depression, even war, and who knows what else, to poorly designed monetary regimes, it might be said that, according to the new history, the love of monetary policy is the root of all evil. Yet, we know that among those who have been responsible for setting monetary policy have been intelligent and dedicated public servants.[21] How could they have made such costly mistakes? The received history of money and banking was much easier to grasp: Problems in money and banking were due to monetary policy-makers not having enough power. The new history argues that even with intelligent and dedicated public servants, monetary policy-making is fraught with danger.

Charles W. Calomiris, in his comment on Schwartz' paper, argues for rules that will induce better central bank decision-making. Included among these rules are flexibility, accountability and credibility. On its face, this sounds like an impossible combination as, for example, rules seem to be the opposite of flexibility. Yet this is precisely what commercial bankers do. Accountable to the market, commercial bankers take in deposits and make loans, using their judgment to recognize credit worthiness. In this process, they create liquidity. The rule by which they operate is simple—maximize profits. This "bottom line" rule captures the totality of cost and benefit in whatever environment commercial bankers find themselves.

According to the inherent instability hypothesis, the rule of profit-maximization in competitive, commercial banking leads to problems such as recurrent breakdown of the payments system. Accordingly, a generation ago, economists accepted that commercial bankers were to be subject to regulation by central bankers. They disagreed, however, as to the appropriate degree of flexibility to be allowed central bankers. One side advocated greater flexibility for central bankers, and the other less. Calomiris could be interpreted as arguing that, with the appropriate incentives and controls, central bankers should be allowed greater flexibility.

The market to which commercial bankers are accountable is very broad, and includes depositors, other creditors, investors, and insurers, the accounting profession, bond rating agencies, the stock market, investment bankers, other commercial bankers, and regulatory agencies. In addition to being external to the commercial bank, the members of this market have clearly defined interests, which induces economic monitoring and timely foreclosure. In contrast, the market to which central bankers are accountable is not well defined.[22] Ultimately, because they share in the sovereignty of government, central bankers are not accountable.

In *The Economic Consequences of the Peace*, John Maynard Keynes made a scathing attack on the Treaty of Versailles through which the victorious powers sought to subjugate the defeated powers following World War I. According to Keynes, every provision of the treaty was "permeated with ruthlessness and pitilessness, in which no breath of human sympathy can be detected, which flies in the face of everything that binds man to man, which is a crime against humanity itself, against a suffering and tortured people."[23] While many of his specific warnings did not come to pass, the attempt to exact reparations from Germany and her allies, without allowing them access to foreign markets, clearly set the stage for later problems.

Twenty-five years later, with the end of World War II in sight, representatives of the allied governments met in Bretton Woods, New Hampshire, to draw up plans for the reconstitution of world trade and finance. Under Keynes' leadership, the Bretton Woods' agreement provided for the freeing of international trade, restoration of fixed exchange rates (linked indirectly to gold through the U.S. dollar), and the reconstruction of war-torn economies. The economic consequences of these arrangements were completely different from the consequences of the peace treaty following World War I. Until it became obvious that the United States could not be trusted with supplying the world with a stable currency, this monetary regime financed a long period of sustained, non-inflationary economic growth, and this in spite of the burdens of the cold war.

The new history of money and banking reconsiders the past freed of the prejudices associated with the inherent instability hypothesis. This facilitates a more complete accounting of the complexity and unevenness in this history. It should not replace the demonization of the private sector in money and banking with a alternate demonization of the public sector. Instead, by admitting to the costliness of mistakes in the design of the monetary order, it makes possible an appreciation of monetary regimes that, at least for a particular time and place, were successful.

Notes

1. In the form of reduced interest on deposits due to increased deposit insurance premiums.

2. To be sure, this Senator had already announced his retirement.

3. During the 19th century, states, one by one, allowed incorporation via a simple filing for business in general, requiring special licenses for only certain kinds of business. Since then, the kinds of business for which special licenses are required has tended to grow.

4. Except for customs duties and interest on the public debt, both of which were payable in coin.

5. Prior to 1900, when the United States was put officially onto a monometal gold standard, the United States had been officially on a bimetal standard; however, due to "the Crime of '73," coinage of silver was restricted. Through 1896, and the defeat of William Jennings Bryan, there was concern that silver agitation would restore silver to full monetary status, which—given the market value of silver—would have precipitated a switch to silver.

6. Most foreign governments that had issued bonds payable in U.S. gold coin similarly repudiated. France was the major exception. France continued to

honor the gold clause in its bonds until 1937, when the Chamber of Deputies abrogated the gold clause.

7. See J. Huston McCulloch, "The Ban on Indexed Bonds." *American Economic Review* 70 (December 1980) pp. 1018–1021.

8. Repeal, in itself, did not revive the gold clauses in pre-1933 contracts, but novations have re-invigorated certain of these gold clauses. For example, rent paid on a 99 year lease in Seattle was adjusted upon transfer of the lease consequent to a corporate restructuring.

9. For an entirely different analysis of the non-flood of debt-indexation following repeal, see Stuart Weiner, "Why are so few financial assets indexed to inflation." *Federal Reserve Bank of Richmond Economic Review,* May 1983, pp. 3–18.

10. Richard H. Timberlake, "Private Production of Scrip-Money in the Isolated Community." *Journal of Money, Credit and Banking* 19 (November 1987) pp. 437–447.

11. Jeffrey C. Williams, "Fractional Reserve Banking in Grain," *Journal of Money, Credit and Banking* 16 (November 1984) pp. 488–496.

12. This currency was redeemable either in bushels of corn or hours of labor, at the option of the issuer.

13. Ludwig von Mises, *Human Action,* 3rd revised edition, New Haven: Yale University Press, 1963, pp. 471–473.

14. While named for Sir Thomas Gresham, who advised Queen Elizabeth of England on the subject in the 16th century, the "law" was first developed by Nicole Oresme, Bishop of Lisieux, advisor to Charles the Fifth of France, in 1366. It was also developed by Copernicus of Thorn, advisor to Sigismund the First of Poland, in 1526.

15. McCulloch describes the 1834 change in the official ratio as "the Crime of '34" because it incorporated such an *ex post facto provision.* Even so, Justice McReynolds, in his impassioned dissent in the Gold Clause cases, said that "The purpose [of the 1834 change] was to restore the use of gold as currency—not to force up prices or destroy obligations. . . No injury was done to creditors;. . ."

16. Or, to a specific commodity in which one of the parties has an exposure, and which hedges against the exposure.

17. The arguments for indexation were first made by Irving Fisher, William Stanley Jevons and Alfred Marshall.

18. A generation later, new discoveries perhaps induced by the profitability of gold-mining sparked a rebound of prices.

19. Barrie Wigmore, "Was the Bank Holiday of 1933 Caused by a Run on the Dollar?" *Journal of Economic History* 47 (September 1988) pp. 739–755.

20. Instead, Hoover exhorted business to "neither raise nor lower wages."

21. This is not intended to include those who have been so compromised by sectarian interests, "constituent service," and political pragmatism as to have no real allegiance to the public interest.

22. Furthermore, it is not clear that central bankers should be made directly accountable to the democratic branches of government.

23. John Maynard Keynes, *The Economic Consequences of the Peace.* London: Macmillan, 1919. p. 233.

Money and Banking:
The American Experience

by Kevin Dowd

> Even granted the market failures that we and many other econo-
> mists had attributed to a strictly *laissez–faire* policy in money and
> banking, the course of events encouraged the view that turning to
> government as an alternative was a cure that was worse than the
> disease. . . . Government failure might be worse than market
> failure.

Milton Friedman and Anna Schwartz[1]

Introduction

The time has come for a radical revision of the United States
monetary history. It used to be generally accepted that the banking
system required extensive government involvement to protect it from
its own "inherent" instability. For a long time even economists who
were otherwise sympathetic to *laissez-faire* accepted this view and
believed that the banking industry was an exception to the general
rule that markets work better when left alone. Those who held this
view felt that it was supported by the experience of U.S. monetary
history. Everyone "knew" that free banking before the Civil War had
caused chaos, for example, and that the institution of the Federal
Deposit Insurance Corporation in the 1930s had stabilized the banking system in the post-War period. But apart from leading them to feel
that it was borne out by U.S. history, the view that banking was
inherently unstable also indicated what researchers could expect
when they studied history, and thereby colored their main findings.
Their findings, in turn, lent support to the theoretical view that
unregulated banking is unstable.

Both the theory and the historical interpretation are now under attack. Since Fredriech Hayek rediscovered free banking in 1976, a great deal of work has been done which suggests that *laissez-faire* in banking ought to be highly stable and that traditional fears of its "inherent" instability are, at the very least, much exaggerated.[2] If free banking is stable, however, then historical experiences of banking instability must be due to the absence of free banking, and one has a clear prediction to test against the historical evidence: Banking instability must be due to government involvement. The prediction that free banking is stable runs against the "stylized facts" that people have traditionally drawn from U.S. monetary history, but the traditional interpretation of U.S. monetary experience has itself come under attack. Work by Rockoff (1974), Rolnick and Weber (1984, 1985, 1986) and others suggests that "free banking" in the antebellum period was actually quite successful, while Sylla (1972) indicated that many of the problems of the National Banking System period can be traced to legislative restrictions and Timberlake (1984) showed how clearinghouse associations evolved to help private banks cope with those restrictions. Work by Benston (1986), Benston et al (1986) and Kaufman (1988) and others also indicated that U.S. banking was much more stable in the days before the F.D.I.C. than had been generally realized, and work by Kane (1985) and Calomiris (1989a, b, 1990) suggests that deposit insurance actually *de*stabilized the banking system. Recent research by Gorton (1986) and Miron (1988) also suggests that the founding of the Fed destabilized the U.S. banking system. The revision of U.S. monetary history is only beginning, but the evidence accumulated so far appears to be consistent with what free banking theory leads us to expect, and there are no obvious discrepancies to explain.[3] The boot is now on the other foot, as it were, and the revised historical record presents proponents of the traditional view with serious problems. If banking is inherently unstable, then why was "free banking" not a complete disaster, and why was U.S. banking apparently more stable before the F.D.I.C., and the Federal Reserve than it was after? And looking further afield, if free banking is unstable, why did relatively unregulated banking appear to work so well in the past in countries like Scotland, Canada, China, and Sweden, and others besides?[4]

The Constitution and the Money Power

The Constitution granted Congress very limited monetary powers: it allowed Congress only to authorize the coining of gold or silver money and to "regulate" (*i.e.*, specify) the dollar value of those coins. It also gave Congress authority to borrow on the credit of the United States, but this power was intended as a fiscal power rather than a monetary one (Timerlake, 1990, p. 305). Since the constitutional settlement was based on the principle that the powers of the federal government were delegated powers, it was also reasonable to conclude that a "strict" interpretation of Congressional powers was called for—that powers not expressly granted to Congress were prohibited to it—and that all other powers (*i.e.*, sovereignty) remained with the people or the states[5] (see *e.g.*, Holzer 1981, pp. 5–7, 199–200). The very limited powers—monetary and otherwise—of the Congress were thus further hemmed in by the "strict" interpretation of the Constitution and the pre-existing rights of the people and the states.

But it was not long before Congress began to break free of these constraints and expand its powers. In 1790 controversy arose over whether Congress had authority to charter a national bank. Supporters of the proposal pointed to fiscal and other advantages for it, and they managed to get the bill passed despite the objections of opponents who argued that the measure was unconstitutional. Opponents were sufficiently strong, nonetheless, that they were able to block the renewal of the Bank's charter when it came due in 1811, and the charter subsequently lapsed. In 1816, however, another bank was set up— the Second Bank of the United States—and the issue of its constitutionality went to the Supreme Court in 1819. In a famous ruling, Chief Justice Marshall defended the Bank's constitutionality as a fiscal arm of the government by invoking the "necessary and proper" clause (Article 1, Section 10) of the Constitution (and supporters of the Bank proceeded to use the Bank's fiscal legitimacy to defend its various other actions).[6] Significantly, Marshall also defended the constitutionality of the Bank by going outside the powers explicitly granted to Congress and invoking the nebulous concept of federal "sovereignty" that was supposed to have been repudiated when the United States was founded. In so doing, he legitimized the "loose" construction of the Constitution over the "strict" one, and what decided the constitutionality of federal actions was no longer whether the Constitution specifically *allowed* the federal government to do what it proposed to do, but whether the Constitution had not *explicitly prohibited* it. This ruling provided the basis on which Congress for its own (*i.e.,* political) reasons could later lay claim to a wide range of monetary powers which were not provided for in the Constitution.[7] It was to be a long time before Congress would lay claim to these powers, nonetheless, and in the meantime the opponents of the Second Bank were able to prevent the renewal of its charter which then lapsed in 1836. For the next generation the federal government made no further attempts to charter banks or regulate banking, and banking legislation was left entirely to the states.

In the meantime, many banks were set up under the separate legal systems of different states. The procedures for setting up state banks were inherited from colonial times. To establish a bank required a charter from the legislature, and state legislatures had the right to grant charters as and when they chose. A typical charter would give the shareholders some form of limited liability (usually fixed at twice the value of subscribed capital) and placed restrictions on the ratio of notes to capital. The lack of freedom of entry in the banking industry meant that charters involved a degree of monopoly privilege—and were therefore valuable—and state legislatures normally sold them for financial favors (*e.g.,* cheap loans). More significantly, charters usually restricted banks to operate only in the county (and sometimes, the state) where they were chartered, and often restricted banks to one office only. This restriction would have helped prop up the value of charters—and hence, what the legislature could get for them—by restricting competition at the local level. It also had two other effects that were to be highly significant:

The first effect was to weaken—and therefore destabilize—the banking system by restricting banks' freedom to branch. Restricting branching increased banks' vulnerability by limiting their scope for diversifying their risks. It also made it more difficult for a bank office to borrow, and it hindered the development of note and deposit clearing systems which would have helped discipline over-issue and maintain the value of bank money at par. Branching restrictions created a system of "unit banks" that was to be a major—if not *the* major—source of weakness in the American banking system throughout its later history.

The second consequence was to create a powerful group with a vested interest in maintaining restrictions against bank competition.

Since branch banking was a threat to the local monopoly privileges enjoyed by unit bankers, the latter had a strong incentive to lobby against branching concessions, and they were to defeat such concessions time and time again. *A very damaging combination thus emerged from the early bank charters: a system of weak banks was established together with a powerful pressure group that had an incentive to lobby against attempts to deal with the cause of their weakness.* Nor did the damage stop there. The same group also had an interest in promoting measures to protect the unit banks, and the unit banking lobby could (and did) use the very weakness of unit banks to support the case for their protection. Particularly important among these protection measures in later years was the establishment of state-sponsored liability insurance schemes to discourage bank runs, but (as related below) these schemes usually had the opposite effect to that intended and weakened the banks even more.

U.S. "Free Banking"

The federal withdrawal from banking legislation in 1836 left the field entirely to the states, and a number of them then proceeded to enact "free banking" laws. The first states were Michigan in 1837 and New York and Georgia in 1838, and over the following years many others followed suit. These laws varied from state to state, but a typical "free banking" law had the following features:[8]

- Anyone could set up a "free bank" who could raise the capital to do so, provided a minimum capital requirement was met.
- "Free bank" note issues were to be secured with holdings of specified bonds which were to be deposited with the state authorities. The usual bonds specified were state (and sometimes federal) ones.
- The notes of "free banks" were to be redeemable on demand, on penalty of liquidation, and note holders had first claim on the assets of a failed bank.
- The shareholders were normally allowed some form of limited liability, usually fixed at twice the value of the capital subscribed.

The key provisions are the first two. The first established free entry into the banking system, subject only to a minimum size constraint, while the second provision promoted the demand for state debt, and hence raised the prices that states could get for it. While the earlier charter system had raised revenue for the states by selling charters, the new "free banking" system raised revenue by creating a captive market for state debt. (The charter system continued in operation, by the way, and chartered banks operated side by side with "free" ones.)

The "free banking" experiences of different states varied considerably, but they were reasonably successful on the whole. Recent work indicates that "free banking" was much more successful than traditional accounts had indicated (see *e.g.*, Rockoff, 1974); Rolnick and Weber, 1984, 1985, 1986). Noteholder losses were comparatively low, for example, and there is no evidence of bank run contagion under "free banking" (see, *e.g.*, Rolnick and Weber, 1986, pp. 885–6). The comparative success of "free banking" is also indicated by the way it was imitated. There was an initial spurt of "free banking" laws in the late 1830's, and the successes of "free banking" encouraged a number of states to switch to it in the 1850's, and more than half the states in the Union had adopted "free banking" by the eve of the Civil War.

The question arises, nonetheless, why some experiences with "free banking" were more successful than others. Part of the reason seems to lie with differences in states' legal frameworks, and "free banking" appears to have been more successful in states where branch-banking laws were more liberal.[9] Several "free banking" experiments also failed because states undermined checks against over-issue by intervening to order the banks to suspend convertibility (*e.g.*, Michigan, in its first "free banking" experiment). But the main reason for the varying success of "free banking" appears to have been the combination of the bond deposit provision and the soundness of different states' finances.[10] The failures of "free banks" tended to be clustered, and the evidence indicates that these clusters occurred when there were large falls in the prices of state bonds (see the Rolnick-Weber work cited earlier). These price falls destroyed much of the banks' net worth since it undermined the value of their assets while their liabilities remained relatively stable in value. The banks would then fail so they could pass on some of the losses to their creditors. The large falls in the prices of state debt, in turn, were caused by those states' precarious fiscal positions. In apparently every case, the large falls in bond prices that occurred were associated with speculation that the states in question would default on their debts. Indiana defaulted in 1841, for instance, and it was not alone. Where states' finances were sound, on the other hand, there were no major problems with "free banking." The evidence indicates, therefore, that the main cause of the falling bond prices that put most of the failed "free banks" out of business was fiscal. It was the combination of the bond deposit provision and the fiscal instability of some states that was the root cause of most of the "free bank" failures. The "free bank failures" were a case of government rather than market failure.

The National Banking System

The onset of the Civil War brought the federal government back into business of regulating banking. Within a year, large unvoluntary loans to the government weakened the banks and obliged them to suspend convertility, and the Treasury soon began to issue notes itself. (The U.S. was to remain on the inconvertible greenback standard until 1879). Still searching for more funds to fight the War, the Federal government then decided to raise more revenue from the banks by adopting the bond deposit provision at the federal level. A new system of federal regulation—the National Banking System— was thus established as a war measures act. Apart from raising revenue, it also had the subsidiary objective of "unifying" the currency by eliminating the variety of state bank notes which often fluctuated in value against each other.[11] Under the new system, any group of five or more could form a note-issuing bank provided they met (quite stringent) capital standards, and provided that their note issues were secured by deposits of United States bonds. (The collateral requirement raised the demand U.S. bonds, of course, and ensured that the Treasury would get a higher price for them.) The Treasury would have first lien on the assets of a failed bank, but the Treasury also guaranteed the notes of national banks, and shareholders were to have double-liability. The national banks were also to observe a 25 percent minimum reserve ratio between their holdings of eligible reserves and their liabilities (which also increased the demand for federal debt, since federal debt counted as eligible reserves). The national banks were also to pay taxes of 1 percent on their notes and one-half percent of their deposits, and arrangements were made for state banks to switch over to national charters. As the state banks did not switch over fast enough, another act in 1865 killed off the state banks' note issues by imposing a prohibitive tax on 10 percent of them.

The National Banking System had a variety of serious defects:

- It discouraged branch-banking by requiring that a bank only carry on business at the place named on its certificate of association. The unit banking lobby had won again, and the U.S. banking system continued to be plagued by the problems of small unit size.
- The restriction it imposed on the note issue seriously stunted the development of American banking because the U.S. economy was still at the stage where the note issue was an important source of profit for a bank, and without it many banks could not make enough profit to survive. To make matters worse, until 1875 there was also a limit on the total amount of national banknotes that could be issued, and the geographical distribution of permits severely penalized the South and West. Restrictions on the note issued operated as entry barriers, and they retarded not only the development of non-note-issuing national banks, but also the development of state banks that could no longer afford a note issue, (Sylla, 1972).
- Since the bond deposit provision tied the note issue to the price (and availability) of federal government debt, the note issue was forced to contract as the federal government ran surpluses from the end of the Civil War until 1893, and because it used the surpluses to buy back its debt and bid up its price. U.S. debt fell from more than $2,300 million in 1866 to less than $600 million in 1892-3 (Sylla, 1972, pp. 254-5). Ironically, this constraint became increasingly effective just as the ceiling to the total note issue was being lifted, so the abolition of the ceiling had little real effect. The prices of United States bonds had risen by then to well above par, and as national banks could only issue notes up to 90 percent of the par value of bond holdings it was therefore no longer profitable to issue notes anyway (Sylla, 1972, p. 244).
- Finally, the restrictions on the note issue often prevented the supply of notes responding to meet an increase in the demand for them (i.e., the note issue was highly inelastic). This problem was particularly acute in the Spring and Fall when seasonal factors led to increased demands for notes which legal restrictions made it difficult for the banks to satisfy. Even if the banking system could produce the notes

to satisfy normal seasonal requirements, there was always the danger that something could spark off a speculative run for notes which the banking system could not meet.

• There was always a possibility that people might decide to run and demand notes just in case a shortage developed and a major banking crisis might result:

A series of acute financial crises occurred in fairly quick succession—1873, 1884, 1890, 1893, 1907. Crises occurred on most of these occasions in London as well, but they were nothing like as stringent. Money rates in New York rose to fantastic heights as compared with London, and . . . there took place in three out of five cases (1873, 1893 and 1907) widespread suspensions of cash payments, either partial or complete, with currency at a premium over claims on bank accounts (Smith, 1936, p. 133).

Over time, however, the banks gradually evolved means to handle these problems. A clearinghouse system arose which provided banks with a form of mutual guarantee which helped in part to overcome the vulnerability which derived from restrictions against branching (*i.e.,* it gave banks a means to exploit some of the scalar economics they could have obtained by branching, had it been allowed). Clearinghouses functioned like private lenders of last resort, though they had no legal privileges and were subject to all the disciplines of the market. If a bank wanted a loan in a crisis, it would apply to the clearinghouse and submit to examination. If its application was accepted, the clearinghouse made its own resources (*i.e.,* the resources of member banks) available to it, and sent a clear signal to the market that the bank was sound. If the application was rejected, on the other hand, the clearinghouse sent out an equally clear signal that depositors had better close their accounts before it was too late. The clearinghouse signals were credible on the market because the clearinghouse stood ready to back them up with its own resources. The result was that sound banks were protected and unsound banks thrown to the wolves, and the newly purged banking system had the confidence of the public. Membership rules (*e.g.,* capital adequacy requirements, accounting procedures and rules for support operations) were determined by the member banks themselves, and members chose to submit to these restrictions even though they were sometimes burdensome because they could expect more support from the clearinghouse in a crisis than non-members could.[12]

Clearinghouses also helped to overcome the effects of restrictions on the note issue by the issue of clearinghouse loan certificates (see Timberlake, 1984). These had their origin in the crisis of 1857 when the clearing banks in New York agreed to accept certificates from their Clearing Association to economize on precious reserves. These certificates contributed to the system's liquidity at the very time when liquidity was most needed, and their role gradually expanded over time until they became a form of surrogate currency. The public accepted them because they were backed by the clearinghouse—and implicitly, therefore, by the clearing banks as a group, and there was never really any doubt that the banks as a group were sound. By the 1907 crisis hundreds of millions of dollars' worth of clearinghouse certificates were issued and willingly accepted by the public, and while there was some doubt about their legality, their usefulness was understood and the authorities decided not to prosecute. Once the public realized that they could have as much currency as they desired—even if it was surrogate currency—the "panic" demand for currency would fall, and the additional currency would then be retired. Clearinghouse certificates provided the public with the reassurance that they could get whatever currency they wanted, and most people no longer had any reason to demand currency once they had that reassurance.

The Founding of the Federal Reserve

There had been controversy over banking reform for years, but the controversy sharpened in a very definite way after the crisis of 1907. It was clear that there needed to be some facility for the issue of emergency currency, and while the usefulness of clearinghouse certificates was widely recognized, their dubious legality also gave rise to considerable disquiet. Congress responded with an interim measure—the Aldrich-Vreeland Act—to authorize a (legal) issue of emergency currency, and set up a National Monetary Commission to report on longer-term banking reform. Many U.S. economists were also impressed with the way in which European central banks were (apparently) able to handle their liquidity crises, and they tended to draw the conclusion that the greater financial stability of the European economies was due to their central banks. The alternative conclusion—that the greater vulnerability of the U.S. financial system to crisis was due to other peculiarities in the U.S. system, such as the restrictions on branching—does not appear to have been taken seriously. The Commission eventually accepted these views, and its report recommended the establishment of an American central bank—a Federal Reserve System consisting of 12 regional Reserve Banks and a Reserve Board in Washington which would co-ordinate the policies of the different Reserve Banks. Congress accepted these recommendations and the Federal Reserve System came into operation in 1914.

The question still arises, however, why did Congress establish a central bank instead of abolishing the legislative restrictions which served to aggravate the crisis? Part of the explanation arises from a distrust of "private" emergency currency and a widespread feeling that the issue of emergency currency needed to be put on a more "official" basis. Yet, as Timberlake (1984, p. 13) observes, the fear that clearinghouses provided a dangerous form of emergency currency

> flies in the face of the clearinghouse system's actual performance. The most extraordinary fact associated with the several clearinghouse episodes between 1857 and 1907 is that the losses from all the various note issues, spurious and otherwise, *were neglibible!* . . . Few of the economists who analyzed clearinghouse operations even noted in passing this astonishing record, and none used it as an argument for continuing the system (own emphasis).

One must also bear in mind that central banking was highly fashionable in contemporary intellectual circles, and American economists were fascinated with its apparent success in Europe. The American experiences with less regulated banking systems in the antebellum period were by now regarded as a clear failure, and virtually no-one wanted to turn the clock back to the days before the National Banking System. In any case, *laissez-faire* was regarded as anachronistic, and the general climate of opinion increasingly preferred interventionist "solutions." Political factors also militated against trying to remove restrictions on the banks. To have relaxed the restrictions imposed by National Banking legislation would have reduced the revenues the federal government could obtain from the banking system, and forced Congress either to cut programs or find alternative sources of funding elsewhere. Establishing the Fed seemed to be a cheaper way—cheaper for the government—to provide the U.S. banking system with the elastic currency it needed.

The Federal Reserve and the U.S. Banking System

The establishment of the Fed supplanted the earlier quasi-automatic mechanism for providing emergency currency with a managed system whose success depended on the manager's discretion. The new system also differed from the old in its incentive structure. The old clearinghouse officials were customers of the banks, and their wellbeing ultimately depended on their ability to satisfy their clients. On the other hand, the Federal Reserve System now had a monopoly over the provision of emergency currency, and its privileged position prevented market forces from ensuring that emergency currency would be provided as and when required. The new system thus hinged on discretion, and there were only weak incentives for Federal Reserve officials to get their discretionary decisions "right."

The big test came in the early 1930's. A variety of factors helped to undermine public confidence in the banking system and encourage the public to convert (commercial bank) deposits into (Federal Reserve) notes which were perceived to be safer. The Federal Reserve had been set up to deal with exactly this kind of crisis, and the solution was for the Fed to print the additional currency that the public desired to hold. Instead of providing that currency, however, the Fed blamed the crisis on bad bank management and was otherwise paralyzed by indecision and doubt. It failed to provide the leadership which the system required and which its privileges ensured that only it could provide, and the crisis duly escalated into waves of bank failures that had catastrophic effects on real economic activity. The failure of the Fed to support the U.S. banking system is also borne out by a counterfactual experiment carried out by Gorton (1986). He examines the impact of the Fed by predicting what would have happened had the pre-Fed regime continued in operation after 1914, and his results indicate that while a panic would have occurred in December 1929, the "failure and loss percentages would have been an *order of magnitude* lower" in the absence of the Fed (p. 29, my italics). This result suggests there may have been a downturn in the early 1930's, but nothing like the disaster that actually occurred. An assessment of the Fed's performance in the period before the Second World War by Miron (1988) also concludes that the Fed's impact on the economy was destabilizing. He finds that the rate of output growth and the inflation rate both became substantially more volatile, while the average rate of growth of output actually fell (pp. 290–1). His analysis also indicates that these changes cannot be dismissed as coincidental, but ought to be attributed to the founding of the Fed, and these conclusions hold even if one ignores the period of the Great Depression. This latter result indicates, therefore, the Fed not only destabilized the U.S. economy in the 1930's, but destabilized it throughout its early period of operation.

Yet relatively few people at the time saw the Fed as having failed to stem the banking crisis. Many blamed the stock market crash or the inherent volatility of the capitalist system, and the Fed itself pushed the line that it had done what it could given its decentralized decision-making structure and its own limited and unclear powers. Congress accepted the Fed's arguments, and the old confederated Federal Reserve structure was replaced by a much more centralized one under a strengthened Board of Governors, and the Fed's regulatory powers were increased. The Fed had turned the disasters of the 1930's to its own advantage by persuading Congress to extend its hegemony over the American banking system.

After a long lag, the Fed's hegemony was increased further still by the Depository Institutions Deregulation and Monetary Control Act of 1980. Congress had set out to deregulate the financial system, but the Fed managed to push successfully for a major simultaneous extension to its own powers:

> Fed officials in their testimony to congressional committees persistently and doggedly advanced one major theme: the Fed had to have more power—to fight inflation, to prevent chaos in the financial industry from deregulation, and to act as an insurance institution for failing banks who might drag other institutions down with them. By misdirection and subterfuge, the Fed inveigled an unwary Congress into doing its bidding (Timberlake, 1985, p. 101).

The history of the Fed is an object lesson in public choice economics. The Fed consistently pursued its own private interests above everything else, and it played the political game ruthlessly to deflect the blame when things went wrong and to advance its own prestige and power whenever it could. And as Timberlake notes,

> Its 70-year history as a bureaucratic institution confirms the inability of Congress to bring it to heel. Whenever its own powers are at stake, the Fed exercises an intellectual ascendancy over Congress that consistently results in an extension of Fed authority. This pattern reflects the dominance of bureaucratic expertise for which there is no solution as long as the [Fed] continues to exist (1986, p. 759).

The Federal Reserve and the Development of Fiat Currency

When it was founded, the intention was that the Fed should operate subject to the discipline of the gold standard. Yet within a year the First World War had broken out and all the major combatants had abandoned gold. The Fed was still nominally subject to the gold standard, but it now had considerable room for manoeuvre as it was the only player left in the gold standard game. The founders of the Fed had not anticipated this development, and the Fed had no clear idea what to do with the large gold flows that entered the U.S. during the war. In earlier days, the gold inflows would have led to higher prices, but it seemed pointless to allow this to happen when none of the other major countries was on the gold standard, so the Fed tried instead to sterilize the inflows to reduce their impact on the economy, and it continued with this policy in the 1920's, but the new gold standard collapsed in the international financial crisis of 1931. The United States also abandoned the gold standard shortly after (1933), and then returned two years later at the depreciated rate of exchange of $35 per ounce.

After the Second World War a modified gold standard was established—the gold exchange standard in which the United States pegged the price of gold at $35 per ounce and other countries pegged their currencies to the dollar. This system produced some inflation but it seemed otherwise to work tolerably well until the 1960's. The Fed was effectively trying to expand at a rate faster than was compatible with the fixed gold price, and it could only continue with this policy by running down its gold stocks. As these stocks continued to run down, the gold reserve requirements—the gold reserves the Fed was obliged to hold against reserves and notes—threatened to become binding and limit the Fed's ability to expand money supply further. Congress responded by abolishing them and what remained of the discipline of the gold exchange standard was eroded further. A consequence was to weaken the Fed's ability to resist the government at the very time when the Fed was coming under increasing pressure to accommodate the heavy spending of the Johnson Administration. The Fed offered only limited resistance to this pressure, and the gold shortage intensified and led to the eventual abandonment of the gold exchange system in the early 1970's. The Fed's accommodating monetary policies also produced higher inflation, and the collapse of the discipline against excessive monetary growth gave the authorities free reign to embark on a wild career of monetary expansion. What followed over the next two decades was a series of monetary binges followed by mornings after in which a short-lived attempt would be made to bring inflation back down, but which would end as the temptation to expand again eventually won out. As Timberlake (1986, p. 753) observed,

> money stocks and price level fluctuations behaved similarly to a remorseful but irresolute alcoholic and his bottle. A period of monetary drunkenness would be followed by a weeping and wailing and gnashing of teeth and a return to monetary austerity. Then rationalizations would appear: "High interest rates are hurting the fragile economics recovery." . . . "We need monetary relief from _____." (Here, the reader can furnish his favorite scapegoat policy, such as "monetarism".) With a happy gasp, the bottle would reappear again.

The cycle of monetary binges continues with no sign of any end, and the authorities still resist attempts to restore monetary discipline with the same determination that a drunk resists a drying-out program.

It is important to understand why. The inconvertible currency gives the monetary authorities enormous discretion over the monetary system, and from their point of view this discretion can be very useful to have. It gives them a lever, for example, that they can use to try to manipulate the economy for electoral purposes. (Whether they succeed is another matter, however.) Just as important, the *existence* of that discretion puts the authorities under very considerable political pressure to *use* it. If the political process grants the authorities the means to lower interest rates, for instance, those who stand to benefit from lower interest will apply pressure to have interest rates lowered. Had the authorities no control over interest rates, on the other hand, low-interest rate lobbyists would be wasting their time and this pressure would never have arisen. Even if the authorities perceive the "right" course of action and desire to pursue it, democratic processes can make virtue very costly in political terms. The authorities are effectively "captured" by private-interest groups which manipulate them (and thence, their discretionary powers) for their own ends. In the old days, the commitment to redeem the currency with gold or silver provided the government with a certain degree of protection against these pressures—not to mention protecting the value of the currency the private sector used—but the political process gradually undermined this guarantee and then destroyed it altogether. An automatic monetary system was thus replaced by a politicized one, and politicized systems have never been able to deliver monetary stability for long.

Liability Insurance

The problems caused by liability insurance are a recurring issue in U.S. monetary history. An agency is set up by the government which guarantees those who hold bank notes and/or deposits against loss in the event that the bank fails, and the usual justification is that it is to protect banks against the "danger" of runs. Liability insurance provides this protection (at least in the short run), but it also has more subtle effects. The most important of these is to create moral hazard: by removing the concerns of depositors' (and noteholders) for the safety of the bank, it eliminates an important mechanism—the threat of a run—which would otherwise discourage bank management from taking "excessive" risks. A bank can then take risks in the knowledge that it will reap the benefits if the risks pay off, but that it can pass the losses to the insuring agency if they do not. Their protection against loss also means that depositors will be concerned only about the interest they are promised (and not about the risks a bank takes), so a bank that takes more risks can easily obtain more funds simply by raising its interest rates. In the process it also puts pressure on the more conservative banks to raise their interest rates, so risk-taking is rewarded while prudence is penalized. More risks are then taken, and bank safety is undermined. The moral hazard created by insurance is intensified further as a bank's net worth falls. As the bank's capital value falls, managers and shareholders have less to lose from further risk-taking, but they still have everything to gain. This perverse incentive structure encourages ever-greater risk-taking as an institution's net worth falls, and wipes out entirely any incentive to behave prudently when the capital value becomes zero or negative. If the insuring agency is to avoid large losses, it is therefore important that these "zombie" institutions be closed down before they can inflict too much damage on their insurers. A policy to close down institutions that have little or nothing left to lose—an effective failure resolution policy—is essential if insurance premiums are to be kept down without busting the insurance agency.

The problem is to find some way to contain the moral hazard. One way to do that is to discourage banks' risk-taking by charging risk-related premiums. An insurance agency can also do that by imposing capital requirements (to give shareholders something to lose) and by imposing capital interest rate ceilings (to restrict banks' ability to obtain funds to gamble with). To the extent that the moral hazard still remains, the insurance agency *might* also restrict banks' lending activities, although such measures can be counter-productive since they also restrict banks' freedom to diversify risks. To carry out any of these functions, an insurance agency would also need to be able to monitor banks' activities, of course, and it would also have to monitor to know when an institution had become so weak that it ought to be closed down. A "successful" insurance scheme—one that did a reasonable job of controlling moral hazard at relatively low cost—would therefore monitor banks effectively, discourage excessive risk-taking by various means, and close down zombie institutions relatively quickly. A "bad" scheme, on the other hand, would let moral hazard get out of control and both undermine the safety of the banking system and eventually destroy the net worth of the insurance agency itself.

Antebellum Liability Insurance Schemes

U.S. experience bears these points out. The first liability insurance scheme was set up in New York in 1829, and others followed in Vermont (1831), Indiana (1834), Michigan (1836), Ohio (1845) and Iowa (1858) (Calomiris, 1989a). These schemes fell into two basic types. Those in New York, Michigan and Vermont were versions of safety fund systems in which insurance payments depended on the fund's accumulated reserves, and the fact that reserves were limited (and vulnerable) meant that the insurance cover lacked credibility. These schemes also made little attempt to handle moral hazard problems—monitoring was usually carried out by state officials who had relatively little at stake, and there were few attempts to control risk-taking—and all three schemes eventually failed. The other schemes were based on the mutual insurance principle that made each bank liable for the others' losses. The schemes had membership rules to control risk-taking (*e.g.,* capital adequacy) and monitoring was left to the banks. These features "aligned the incentive and authority to regulate, and made insurance protection credible through unlimited

liability among banks" (Calomiris, 1990, p. 8). All three schemes were
reasonably successful.

It is important to note the role of the unit banking lobby in the
establishment of liability insurance. As Calomiris (1990, pp. 4–5)
writes,

> it was the desire to preserve unit banking, and the political influ-
> ence of unit bankers, that gave rise to the perceived need for
> deposit insurance, both in the antebellum period, and in the twen-
> tieth century. It was understood early on . . . that branching . . .
> provided an alternative stabilizer to liability insurance. But unit
> banks and their supporters successfully directed the movement for
> banking reform toward creating government insurance funds. All
> six antebellum states that enacted liability insurance were unit-
> banking states. In the antebellum branch-banking South neither
> government insurance, nor urban clearing houses, developed.
> Similarly, the eight state insurance systems created from 1908 to
> 1917 were all in unit-banking states.

The National Banking System put an end to the state systems of
liability insurance. The main attraction of membership to many banks
had been the relatively low cost of issuing notes. (The alternative was
to issue notes under a "free bank" charter, but the bond collateral
requirement made that relatively expensive.) The introduction of the
federal tax on state-chartered banknotes made those issues unworth-
while, and these banks either gave up the note issue entirely and
switched to uninsured state charters or else they adopted national
charters and subjected themselves to the regulations of the National
Banking System. The new federal regulations thus drove out the state
insurance systems and aborted any further developments in them.
The state systems of note and deposit insurance were replaced by the
federal government's guarantee of the notes of National Banks, and
the greater part of bank liabilities—deposits—was now uninsured.

Deposit Insurance in the Early Twentieth Century

State insurance made a comeback in the early years of the twentieth century. The repeated crises of the National Banking System
helped promote demands for an extension to branch-banking to make
banks safer. This pressure intensified in the aftermath of the 1907
crisis, but the unit banking lobby managed to fight off branching ex-
tensions and divert the political drive for safer banking into new
schemes for state deposit insurance. Eight schemes were subsequently introduced in the succeeding years, as noted earlier, and all in

unit-banking states. These schemes failed to heed the lessons of earlier experience:

> Supervisory authority was placed in government, not member bank hands, and often its use or disuse was politically motivated. Furthermore, the number of banks insured [was] many more than in the antebellum systems (often several hundred), and this further reduced the incentive for a bank to monitor and report the misbehavior of its neighbor banks, since the payoff from detection was shared with so many, and the cost of monitoring was private (Calomiris 1990, p. 9).

These schemes also made little attempt to control moral hazard and there were inordinate delays in closing down insolvent institutions. Not surprisingly, all of them eventually failed.

The evidence also indicates that they destabilized state banking systems (Calomiris, 1989b, p. 40) while their perceived political alternative, branch-banking, had the opposite effect (Benston, 1986, pp. 14–17). To quote Calomiris again, states that allowed branch-banking saw "much lower failure rates—reflecting the unusually high survivability of branching banks—and responded well to the agricultural crises [of the 1920's] by consolidating and expanding branching systems, where this was allowed" (1990, p. 11). Many contemporaries understood the effects of branch banking, and many states responded by relaxing the restrictions against it. From 1924 to 1939, for example, the number of states that allowed branch-banking in some form doubled from 18 to 36 (Calomiris, *loc. cit.*). The push for branch-banking also made itself felt at the federal level, and there was the usual conflict between unit- and branch-bankers. The result was a legislative compromise—the McFadden Act (1927)—which gave national banks very limited branching power but reaffirmed other restrictions against branch-banking.

Federal Deposit Insurance

The bank collapses of the early 1930's gave renewed impetus to the view that banks were unstable because they were vulnerable to runs and Congress responded in the Banking Act of 1933[13] by authorizing the establishment of a system of federal deposit insurance.[14] The new Federal Deposit Insurance Corporation (F.D.I.C.) then came into operation the next year along with a sister organization for the thrifts, the Federal Savings and Loan Insurance Corporation (F.S.L.I.C.). Congress apparently recognized the potential moral hazard problems involved, and it sought to deal with them by restricting banks' (and thrifts') permitted range of activities. It also gave the federal insurance agencies extensive regulatory powers, and, as already noted, it increased the supervisory powers of the Federal Reserve.

The new regulatory regime appeared to work reasonably effectively until the 1970's. It then began to unravel with a vengeance. When the Federal Reserve began to reduce monetary growth rates in the late 1970's, the soaring interest rates that accompanied the new policy undermined the net worth of the banking system and made deposit interest rate ceilings an increasingly damaging constraint to the banks. (The same factors hurt the thrifts even more.) The pressure eased as interest rates declined, but the deregulation that followed the passage of the Depository Institutions Deregulation and Monetary Control Act (1980) and the Garn-St. Germain Act (1982) let the moral hazard genie out of his bottle. The removal of most of the earlier constraints against institutions' exploiting moral hazard had predictable results: They took more risks, and their net worth declined.

In theory, the regulatory authorities might have been able to contain the damage had they intervened to close down weak institutions before they got out of hand, but they were overwhelmed by the scale of the problem, and the measures they took to stay afloat in the short term only aggravated it in the longer run. A kind of regulatory accelerator effect took over, and the regulatory apparatus that had managed to contain the moral hazard problem earlier now served instead to magnify it even more. Since an energetic failure resolution policy would have been expensive and depleted the insuring corporations' limited reserves, they tended to resort to foreclosures only as a last resort. They preferred instead to arrange "mergers"—and often paid handsomely to get them—or simply overlooked problems until they could no longer be ignored. (One has to bear in mind the sheer scale of the problem they were dealing with, and their limited resources meant that they could seldom carry out more than the most cursory "examinations.") An energetic failure resolution policy would also have required that the insurance corporations petition Congress for more funds, and they would then have had to acknowledge the magnitude of the problem and accept much of the blame for it. Ironically, the insurance corporations were now playing the same game *vis a vis* Congress and the executive that their zombie institutions were playing with them. With nothing more to lose, they were playing for time and gambling wildly with the other people's money. The *insurance corporations* were now the zombie institutions, and the *government* didn't have an appropriate failure resolution policy to deal with *them*. For their part, there was little incentive on the part of anyone in government to blow the whistle and come to grips with the problem. Whoever did so would have had to recommend a solution to the crisis—and then take the political flak for what resolution of the crisis would cost. It was easier to ignore the problem and hope that someone else would pick up the poisoned chalice. The government was now acting like a zombie itself at the public expense. Losses so far accumulated amount to about half a *trillion* dollars—the scale of the thrift bailout alone dwarfs all previous federal bailouts put together— and losses continue to grow at a staggering rate. If ever there was a clear-cut case of government failure, this was surely it. A system that had been set up to counter an (imaginary) *market* failure—had ended up producing *government* failure on an unprecedented scale. And the ultimate irony was that the roots of the most costly public finance disaster in U.S. history lay in the unit banking system which had been set up in the first place to raise revenue for the government.

Conclusion: Market Success, Government Failure, and the Interventionary Ratchet Effect

Three points particularly stand out in the U.S. monetary history. The first is that banking was generally successful when left in relative peace by the government. While there has never been full-blown *laissez-faire* in American banking, American experience does nonetheless indicate that banking under the appropriate legal framework can be quite stable without any "support" from the government. There is nothing in U.S. experience to suggest that *laissez-faire* in banking does not work, and much to indicate that it does. The most obvious historical example here is the experience of "free banking" in the antebellum period. It is now reasonably well established that "free banking" was much more successful then was earlier appreciated, and it is in any case difficult to explain why it should have been so widely copied had it been a failure. There *were* problems with some "free banking" episodes, but those problems can be plausibly attributed to specific government interventions, the usual one being the combination of the bond deposit provision and the fiscal instability of some states. The experience of U.S. banking in 50 years after the Civil War also seems to give some indication of the way in which the banking system can stabilize itself in the absence of a government-sponsored lender of last resort. Banks observed high capital ratios to preserve the confidence of their customers, and market forces penalized those banks that allowed their capital values to fall too low. The clearinghouse system also evolved during the same period to provide banks with crisis loans and to issue emergency currency during a crisis. The problems that afflicted U.S. banking during this period can also be attributed to government intervention, this time in the form of the restrictive provisions of the National Banking Acts. Banks achieved whatever stability they did during this period *despite* government interference, not *because* of it, and this conclusion is supported by the way in which the banking system was destabilized further when the banks' own crisis-management procedures were replaced by the Federal Reserve.

The second theme that stands out is government failure. Virtually all major monetary and banking problems in the U.S. history appear to have their root cause in government interference of some sort. The major historical banking problems—banking instability before the Civil War, banking instability, recurrent financial crisis, the inelastic currency, and the stunted growth of U.S. banking after the Civil War; the banking instability of the 1920's and the banking collapses of the 1930's, and the failures of historical and contemporary liability insurance schemes—can all be traced to a great or lesser extent to government interference in banking. And the major monetary problem, inflation, can be traced—in the War of Independence, the War of 1812, the Civil War, and more recently in peacetime—to the government's refusal to submit to the fiscal discipline that a sound money requires. Government interference also seems to be responsible for the major instances of general economic instability. As Milton Friedman wrote,

> In almost every instance, major instability . . . has been produced
> or at the very least, greatly intensified by monetary instability.
> Monetary instability in its turn has generally arisen either from
> governmental intervention or from controversy about what governmental
> monetary policy should be. The failure of government
> to provide a stable monetary framework has thus been a major if
> not the major factor accounting for our severe inflations and
> depressions. Perhaps the most remarkable feature of the record is

the adaptability and flexibility that the private economy has so frequently shown under such extreme provocation (Friedman, 1960, p. 9).

It is important to stress that these government failures had a cumulative dynamic of their own. Time and again, government intervention would produce undesirable (and usually unintended) side-effects. These side-effects would provoke demands for further intervention, so that government would intervene yet again, and new problems would arise that seemed to require still more intervention. Each time intervention produced more problems, and each time the preferred solution was yet more intervention. *This interventionary ratchet effect is the central theme of American monetary history.* It was driven by the interaction of the problems posed by previous government failure and a political process that was captured by powerful interest groups who manipulated it for their own ends. Not only were these groups able to channel the drive for reform into directions that left their powers and privileges intact, or augmented them further, but they were also able to influence the very perception of the problem to be dealt with, and in the process they often managed to get special-interest propaganda elevated to the rank of received analysis.

Two instances of this interventionary ratchet are particularly important in U.S. monetary history. The first is the dynamic interplay of unit banking, banking instability, and liability insurance. Unit banking arose in the first place because entry into the banking industry was not free. The Constitutional settlement had confirmed the rights of states to control bank chartering, and states used their chartering powers to raise revenue—and more revenue could be raised if local competition was reduced by imposing branching restrictions. A powerful interest group was thus created which had a strong interest in maintaining the restrictions, and it was able again and again to block branching concessions. These restrictions severely weakened the U.S. banking system, and the unit-banking lobby was able to use the weakness of the banks to argue for protection in the form of liability insurance. It was no accident that liability insurance was usually introduced in unit-banking states, and that states with branch-banking seldom saw any need for it. The "protection" was usually counterproductive, unfortunately, and it ended up destabilizing the banking system further. In the process of pushing for these measures, the unit-banking/liability insurance lobby also had a critical influence on the way in which the debate was conducted, and lobbying mythology became accepted as conventional wisdom. So branching became anti-competitive, banking inherently unstable, and deposit insurance was a means of stabilizing the banking system. Muddled economics served as a smokescreen that distracted attention from the failures of earlier policies and pushed policy-makers towards the additional interventions the lobbyists wanted.

The other outstanding example of the ratchet effect is provided by the history of the Federal Reserve. The origins of the Fed lay in the instability that arose from the legal restrictions of the National Banking System. Yet rather than abolish those restrictions or leave the banking system as it was, Congress decided instead to establish the Fed to put the issue of emergency currency on an official basis. In doing so, it supplanted a system that had proven itself in practice and divorced the integrity of the banking system from the self-interest of those responsible for protecting it. It also created a pressure group—the Federal Reserve itself—that not only had its own private interests (*i.e.*, power and prestige), but was also uniquely placed to lobby Congress to further those interests. The new System failed in the early 1930's, but the Fed was able to divert the blame and use the opportunity created by the emergency to obtain more power. A major theme in Federal Reserve history is the way it has used its own intellectual superiority over Congress to divert legislative reforms for its own ends, and even to use the consequences of its own mistakes as an argument for an extension of its powers. For its part, the government has sometimes found the Fed a convenient scapegoat—it can blame an "independent" Fed for raising interest rates, for example. The government also found the Fed a very convenient source of revenue, but in the process it undermined the discipline of the gold standard and paved the way for the inflation of the last 25 years. Thus one set of problems led to another. The instability of the National Banking system led to the Fed, and the Fed itself destabilized both the banking system and the economy, and then turned into an engine of inflations.

What is to be done? If markets work, and governments fail, then what is required is to take the government out of the monetary system. Several issues need to be addressed. The first is to find some means to guarantee the value of the currency. Such a guarantee was provided in the past by the gold bimetallic standards, but there is no necessary reason why either of these in particular should be restored.

We might wish to tie the value of the currency to a broader basket of goods, for example, and have an indirectly convertible commodity standard in which each dollar-denominated bank liability had a guaranteed value equal to that of a specified commodity-basket, but was redeemed in terms of medium of redemption that was specified by the contract under which it was issued (see *e.g.*, Yeager, 1985, or Dowd, 1989, chapters 4 and 7). We then need to design a program to take the government completely out of the banking system. The deposit insurance agencies, the Federal Reserve, and any other regulatory bodies (*e.g.*, the Comptroller of the Currency) would all be abolished, and banks would be free to do as they wished subject only to the discipline of an unregulated market-place. The phasing of such a program needs to be very carefully designed, however, if one is to avoid destabilizing the banking system in the interim before the banking system has had time to adjust to the new regime. Many banks have come to depend on the protection of deposit insurance and a lender of last resort, and most of them would need time to prepare themselves for the new regime—one doesn't wish to kick out the props before giving the banks time to stop leaning on them. Congress would also have to pay off its deposit insurance debts before moving to a *laissez-faire* system, and a large number of zombie institutions that the insurance corporations are keeping open will have to be closed down, but Congress will have to take these measures in any case. Congress must complete these tasks and then withdraw entirely from the banking system.

The last problem is how to *keep* the government out of the monetary system. Here again American history is very instructive. The only monetary powers the Constitution gave the federal government were the powers to specify the precious metal content of the dollar and authorize coinage, and *nothing else*. Yet since then the federal government has chartered its own banks, regulated the banking system, issued its own inconvertible currency, levied forced loans from the banks, rewritten legal tender laws, expropriated private holdings of gold, and demonetized both the precious metals. The federal government has taken the very limited monetary power granted it by the Constitution and turned it into a monetary despotism. The solution, therefore, is to eliminate altogether the limited monetary powers that the Constitution grants the federal government. What is required is a constitutional amendment that provides for a total separation between government and the monetary system. That such an express prohibition on government intervention in the monetary system might work is indicated by the success of the First Amendment in outlawing censorship. This Amendment states, categorically, that "Congress shall make no law . . . abridging freedom of speech, or of the press." These freedoms have been challenged many times—usually on the basis of an alleged overriding "public interest" (*i.e.*, government convenience)—but even sympathetic judges had to strike these measures down as they were unable to get past the "no law" provision. The "free money" amendment must be equally unambiguous:

> To accomplish its purpose, that amendment cannot be a half-way measure. Either the government can possess monetary power, or it cannot—and if it cannot, the constitutional amendment must sweep clean. *The few monetary powers delegated to Congress in the Constitution must be abolished, any reserved state monetary powers must be eliminated, and an express prohibition must be erected against any monetary role for government.* Strong medicine, perhaps, but the disease has very nearly killed the patient (Holzer, 1981, p. 202, own italics).

Notes

1. Quoted from Friedman and Schwartz (1986, p. 39).

2. See, for example, White (1984), Selgin (1988), Dowd (1989) and Glasner (1989).

3. See also Selgin (1989a).

4. See White (1984) for Scotland, Schuler (1990) for Canada, Selgin (1989b) for China, and Jonung (1985) for Sweden. Dowd (1991) will provide a collection of papers on some of these and other experiences of (relatively) free banking.

5. Significantly, the Constitution also stripped the states of the right they had previously enjoyed as colonies to emit "bills of credit" (*i.e.*, notes). The colonies had frequently abused their note issue privileges, and the founding fathers hoped to prevent such abuses in the future. One might also note, incidentally, that if the states did not enjoy the right to issue notes they could not delegate such powers to the federal government. The ban on state note issues implicitly extended to the federal government as well.

6. The absurdity of these claims was forcibly pointed out by Henry Clay in the Senate, "It is mockery," he said, "worse than usurpation, to establish (the Bank) for a lawful object, and then extend it to other objects which are not lawful. . . . You may say to this organization, we cannot authorize you to discount—to emit paper—to regulate commerce, etc. No! Our book has no precidents of that kind. But then we can authorize you to collect the revenue, and, while occupied with that, you may do whatever else you please!" (Quoted in Timberlake, 1990, p. 307).

7. The federal government began to claim these powers at the start of the Civil War. Apart from the power to charter and regulate banking (which is discussed below), the federal government also claimed the power to pass legal tender laws and, eventually to outlaw monetary contracts with gold clauses altogether. For more on the evolution of these powers, see Holzer (1981).

8. For more on the details of the 'free banking' laws, see Rockoff (1974), Rolnick and Weber, or Dowd (1989).

9. For example, Calomiris (1990, p. 4) notes that branch-banking helped promote banking stability in the ante-bellum South – an observation which implies that restrictions on branch-banking would have been one factor behind instability elsewhere.

10. Dowd (1989, chapter five) elaborates somewhat further on this explanation of the 'free banking' failures.

11. The multiplicity of small note-issuing banks meant that notes often circulated at a discount far away from their banks of issue. The discount arose because the notes of distant banks were often unfamiliar, and the public had difficulty assessing the reputation of the issuers. This problem seems to have resulted from branch-banking restrictions: in countries where branch-banking was allowed (e.g., Scotland or Canada), a small number of note-issuing banks emerged whose notes were recognized everywhere.

12. One might also note that the banks managed well anyway. For example, Benston et al (1986, pp. 52-70, 74) note how banks used to reassure the public of their soundness by observing relatively high capital ratios. The shareholders' capital was thus used as a performance bond to persuade depositors of the banks' good faith. Their evidence suggests that the public was generally reassured, and bank failure rates were not much different from the failure rates of businesses in general.

13. The year earlier Congress had passed the 1932 National Banking Act (the Glass-Steagall Act) separating commercial and investment banking. While later writers have until recently seen this measure as a public-spirited attempt to promote banking stability, this interpretation was heavily criticized by White (1983). It now appears that the Act was no more than an (another) attempt to cartelize the banking industry (see, e.g., Shughart, 1988).

14. This Act too was motivated by public-choice considerations (i.e., private interest). Shughart (1988) and Benston (1986, esp. p. 20) give good accounts of the background to the Act.

References

Benston, George J. (1986) "Federal Regulation of Banking: Historical Overview," chapter one in George G. Kaufman and Roger C. Kormendi (eds.) *Deregulating Financial Services: Public Policy in Flux*, Cambridge, MA: Ballinger.

Benston, George J. *et alia* (1986) *Perspectives on Safe and Sound Banking: Past, Present, and Future*, Cambridge, MA and London: MIT Press.

Calomiris, Charles W. (1989a) "Deposit Insurance: Lessons from the Record," Federal Reserve Bank of Chicago *Economic Perspectives*, May–June, 10–30.

Calomiris, Charles W. (1989b) "Do 'Vulnerable' Economies Need Deposit Insurance?: Lessons from the U.S. Agricultural Boom and Bust of 1920's," working paper WP–89–18, Federal Reserve Bank of Chicago, October.

Calomiris, Charles W. (1990) "Is Deposit Insurance Necessary? A Historical Perspective," forthcoming in *Journal of Economic History*.

Dowd, Kevin (1989) *The State and the Monetary System*. Oxford: Philip Allan and New York: St. Martin's Press.

Dowd, Kevin (1991) *The Experience of Free Banking*, editor, forthcoming volume, London: Routledge.

Friedman, Milton (1960) *A Program for Monetary Stability*, New York: Fordham University Press (1983 reprint).

Friedman, Milton and Anna J. Schwartz (1986) "Has Government Any Role in Money?" *Journal of Monetary Economics* 17, 37–62.

Glasner, David (1989) *Free Banking and Monetary Reform*, Cambridge and New York: Cambridge University Press.

Gorton, Gary (1986) "Banking Panics and Business Cycles," working paper WP–86–9, Federal Reserve Bank of Philadelphia, March.

Holzer, Henry M. (1981) *Government's Money Monopoly: Its Source and Scope, and How to Fight It*, New York: Books in Focus.

Jonung, Lars (1985) "The Economics of Private Money: The Experience of Private Notes in Sweden 1831–1902," unpublished paper prepared for the Monetary History Study Group.

Kane, Edward J. (1985) *The Gathering Crisis in Federal Deposit Insurance*, Cambridge, MA: MIT Press.

Kaufman, George G. (1988) "The Truth About Bank Runs," chapter two in Catherine England and Thomas Huertas (eds.) *The Financial Services Revolution: Policy Directions for the Future*. Boston: Kluwer Academic Publishers and Washington, DC: Cato Institute.

Miron, Jeffrey A. (1988) "The Founding of the Fed and the Destabilization of the Post-1914 U.S. Economy," chapter ten in Marcello de Cecco and Alberto Giovannini (eds.), *A European Central Bank? Perspectives on Monetary Unification After Ten Years of the EMS*. Cambridge: Cambridge University Press.

Rockoff, Hugh (1974) "The Free Banking Era: A Reexamination," *Journal of Money, Credit and Banking* 6, 141–67.

Rolnick, Arthur J. and Warren E. Weber (1984) "The Causes of the Free Bank Failures: A Detailed Examination," *Journal of Monetary Economics* 14, 267–91.

Rolnick, Arthur J. and Warren E. Weber (1985) "Banking Instability and Regulation in the U.S. Free Banking Era," Federal Reserve Bank of Minneapolis *Quarterly Review*, Summer, 2–9.

Rolnick, Arthur J. and Warren E. Weber (1986) "Inherent Instability in Banking: the Free Banking Experience," *Cato Journal* 5, 877–90.

Schuler, Kurt (1990) "Free Banking in Canada," forthcoming in K. Dowd (ed.) *The Experience of Free Banking*, London: Routledge, 1991.

Selgin, George A. (1988) *The Theory of Free Banking: Money Supply Under Competitive Note Issue*, Totowa, NJ: Rowman and Littlefield.

Selgin, George A. (1990) "Legal Restrictions, Financial Weakening, and the Lender of Last Resort," *Cato Journal* 9, pp. 429–59.

Selgin, George A. (1989b) "Free Banking in Foochow," forthcoming in K. Dowd (ed.) *The Experience of Free Banking*, London: Routledge, 1991.

Shughart, William F. (1988) "A Public Choice Perspective of the Banking Act of 1933," chapter five in Catherine England and Thomas Huertas (eds.) *The Financial Services Revolution: Policy Directions for the Future*. Boston: Kluwer Academic Publishers and Washington, DC: Cato Institute.

Smith, Vera C. (1936) *The Rationale of Central Banking*, London: P.S. King.

Sylla, Richard (1972) "The United States 1863–1913," in Rondo Cameron (ed.) *Banking and Economic Development: Some Lessons of History*, New York: Oxford University Press.

Timberlake, Richard (1984) "The Central Banking Role of Clearinghouse Associations," *Journal of Money, Credit, and Banking* 16, 1–15.

Timberlake, Richard (1985) "Legislative Construction of the Monetary Control Act of 1980," *American Economic Review* 75, Papers and Proceedings 97–102.

Timberlake, Richard (1986) "Institutional Evolution of Federal Reserve Hegemony," *Cato Journal* 5, 743–63.

Timberlake, Richard (1989) "The Government's License to Create Money," *Cato Journal* 9, pp. 301–21.

White, Eugene N. (1983) *The Regulation and Reform of the American Banking Industry*, Princeton: Princeton University Press.

White, Lawrence H. (1984) *Free Banking in Britain: Theory, Experience, and Debate 1800–1845*, Cambridge: Cambridge University Press.

Yeager, Leland B. (1985) "Deregulation and Monetary Reform," *American Economic Review* 75, Papers and Proceedings, 103–7.

The Political Origin and Judicial Sanction of Legal Tender Paper Money in the United States

by Richard H. Timberlake*

> Clearly there is no need of making coin a legal tender at any specified weight. If governments would confine their legislation to fixing by enactment the fineness of the precious metal and the number of grains that shall constitute each piece of a given name, they may safely leave the maintenance of the coinage, . . . and the value of the pieces to be regulated [to] individual interest and action.
>
> —William Brough

The U.S. Constitution grants neither state nor federal governments a license to create legal tender paper money. Yet every Federal Reserve note contains the statement: "This note is legal tender for all debts, public and private." No one questions the authority that vests these notes with the characteristic of a forced currency, *i.e.*, that, as currency, they must be accepted in fulfillment of all public and private obligations. To one who looks to the U.S. Constitution for norms or guidance on monetary practices, the present-day system is inexplicable and anomalous. A key constitutional principle with respect to money is violated, and the implied constitutional prohibition of governmental issues of paper money is flouted (Christiansen, 1988; Siegan, 1987). Were the monetary provisions in the Constitution at some stage rendered obsolete by technical changes in the payments system? Were some sections at odds with others, such that one provision had to be abandoned in order that another part would operate

*I am indebted to the George Edward Durell Foundation for financial assistance that helped make this work possible. I also thank colleagues and associates, particularly George Selgin, Larry White, Hugh McCulloch, John Robbins, and my wife Hildegard for many helpful suggestions.

properly? Were there basic flaws in the different clauses, such that a monetary system based on all the principles could not work? Or were the constitutional norms rendered inoperative through political expediency, monetary misconceptions, and judicial misinterpretations? To answer these questions the investigator must examine the political and judicial arguments and attitudes that developed during the era when *full* legal tender paper money first appeared by act of Congress and obtained Supreme Court acceptance.

Congress first authorized legal tender United States notes (greenbacks) in February 1862, and additional issues in July 1862 and January 1863. The Supreme Court found the notes unconstitutional in 1869–70, but reversed itself in 1871 and declared that the notes issued during the Civil War were legal tender for all debts *ex ante* as well as *ex post*. In 1884 the Court ruled that the notes were also legal tender in time of peace. The events, arguments and constitutional interpretations that led to this monetary revolution over 100 years ago have lessons for both the jurist and the economist who wish to know the proper constitutional basis for money in U.S. policy.

Government Note Issues

On several occasions prior to 1860, Congress authorized the U.S. Treasury to issue Treasury notes (Dunbar, 1897; Timberlake, 1978). These notes were usually issued in small quantities and in large denominations for only one year, were interest-bearing, not re-issuable and, most important, were a tender only for federal government dues and payments. By way of contrast, the United States notes of the Civil War era were issued in massive quantities, were not interest-bearing, became indefinitely reissuable, were legal tender for all debts public *and private,* and for debts made both *before and after* the dates at which the acts became law (Table 1). Even though both forms of paper money served as hand-to-hand currency and as bank reserves. United States notes clearly differed in kind and not just in degree from the earlier Treasury notes.

Wesley C. Mitchell in his comprehensive monograph, *A History of the Greenbacks,* examined critically the initiation of the legal tender measures in Congress, and especially the arguments that furthered their passage. Mitchell drew his account from Representative Elbridge G. Spaulding's *History of the Legal Tender Paper Money.*

Table 1
Characteristics of Federal Government Note Issue,
1812–1861 and 1862–1865

Treasury Notes, 1812–1861	United States Notes, 1862–1865
Legal tender only for government dues and payments.	Fully legal tender for all debts public and private, ex post and ex ante.
Interest-bearing (for the most part).	Non-interest bearing.
Issued for one year after which time interest payments ceased.	Issued for indefinite period—in practice, forever.
Not reissuable when received at Treasury.	
Issued in limited quantities average amount outstanding $5 to $10 million.	Issued in massive quantities, $400 million in circulation in 1865, plus $50 million other legal tender currency.
Large denominations.	All denominations.

Spaulding was the principal architecture of the first legal tender act and of the two subsequent acts.

The first legal tender bill came into existence as a provision in the first national bank bill. In late 1861, as the fiscal necessities of the Treasury burgeoned, Salmon P. Chase suggested in his *Report* to Congress the possibility and desirability of a government-sponsored currency. Chase demeaned state bank notes for being of questionable constitutionality and for representing "loans without interest from the people to the banks." He suggested that the "advantages of this loan be transferred . . . from the banks, representing only the stock-holders, to the Government representing the aggregate interests of the whole people" (Spaulding, 8–9).

Spaulding repeated Chase's pejorative remarks about banking practices as an introduction to a bill he was sponsoring that would collect the state-chartered banks into a national system for issuing national bank notes, *and* provide for a Treasury issue of United States notes redeemable in coin on demand. Both these note systems would be governmentally monitored, regulated, and controlled. The government would ensure itself a monopoly of note issue by taxing state bank notes out of existence (*ibid.,* 9–10).

Spaulding then wrote Chase a letter asking him to draw up a bank bill that would incorporate the features they both found so desirable. But Chase reciprocated, delegating Spaulding, who was Chairman of a Sub-committee of the Committee on Ways and Means in the House of Representatives, to make up the bill for him. Upon reflection, Spaulding came to the conclusion that a bank bill would take too long to get through Congress to be of much help in meeting current government payments. He thereupon "drafted a legal tender Treasury note section to be added to the bank bill, hoping, . . . that [notes] might be made available . . . while the bank bill was put into operation . . ." (ibid., 11–12).

Upon still more "mature" reflection, Spaulding concluded that a comprehensive bill would take too long. The state banks had just suspended specie payments (due largely to U.S. Treasury fiscal policies—although Spaulding did not admit or refer to this fact). He therefore "changed the legal tender section, intended originally to accompany the bank bill, into a separate bill, . . . and on his own motion introduced it into the House by unanimous consent on the 30th of December 1861" (ibid., 14). The bill was almost rejected by the Committee on Ways and Means; but one congressman on the committee, who opposed it, voted for it just so it could get before the full House for debate.

Spaulding's original and all important argument for the bill was its "necessity." "The bill before us," he declared, "is a war measure of necessity, and not of choice. . . ." Yet on the next page, and in the same speech, he stated: "We have the alternative [that is, the choice], either to go into the [securities] market and sell our bonds for what they will command, or to pass this bill, or to find some better mode . . . to raise means to carry on the war" (ibid., 29–31).

When bankers, who met with House and Senate committees at the Treasury Department, spelled out two alternatives to legal tender paper money— "a policy of vigorous taxation and selling [government] bonds at their market value," Spaulding replied that "selling bonds below par was more objectionable than issuing paper money. . . . Thus," noted Mitchell, "the argument for the legal-tender bill was shifted from the ground of necessity to that of expediency" (Mitchell, 49).

The subsequent debates in the House and Senate emphasized congressional aversion to selling government securities below par. Of course, "below par" meant below some governmentally stipulated par value and par rate of interest. If the bonds sold at a discount in the market, this fact simply meant that investors in the market differed from Congress and the Treasury on the appropriate risk-adjusted yield.

In spite of their anti-bank and not-below-par prejudices, many congressmen were uncomfortable with the clear-cut unconstitutionality of the legal tender measure. To counter this notion, Spaulding and other supporters of the bill hit upon the "necessary and proper" clause in the Constitution that Chief Justice Marshall had invoked so notoriously in *McCulloch v. Maryland*. "The degree of [a law's] necessity," Spaulding claimed, thereby giving a future Supreme Court comfortable words with which to fashion a pragmatic decision, "is a question of *legislative discretion*, not of judicial cognizance" (Spaulding, 35).

Congress's power "to borrow money" also entered the debate here. The Constitution gives Congress the express power "to *borrow* money, on the credit of the United States," meaning the fiscal power to authorize the selling of securities for money that will then be used to buy goods and services for appropriate use by government agencies. Senators Howard and Sherman argued that the express power to borrow money implied the power to make Treasury notes a legal tender. But Senator Collamer countered with the conclusive argument that "where there is an express power to do a thing [borrow money], there can be no implied power to do the same thing [create money]" (*ibid.*, 107; Mitchell, 54).

This denial has even more to support it. The Constitution was silent on certain issues, and such points allow reasonable debate. But when the framers specified precise powers for Congress or the Executive or the Supreme Court, they arrived at the principles they expounded after lengthy and exhaustive debate. They surely did not intend to leave the scope of such powers to be decided by future legislative and judicial pragmatists.

The legal tender bill worked its way through Congress by a process of reluctant acceptance. The House Ways and Means Committee was evenly divided on it, but allowed it to go out of Committee to the full House. That body, however, treated the issue as if the Committee had recommended it (Barrett, 326).

Chase was just as reasonable for getting the bill through Congress as were its congressional promoters. As Congress debated and almost stalled on the bill, the committee on Ways and Means asked Chase "to communicate . . . his opinion as to the propriety and necessity of [the bill's] immediate passage by Congress." Chase replied that it was impossible at that time (late January 1862) "to procure sufficient *coin* for disbursements; and it has, therefore, become indispensably necessary that we should resort to the issue of United States notes." Since some people would not accept the notes if they were payment only for government dues, he argued, everyone should be *forced* to accept them to prevent "discrimination" (Spaulding, 45–46). Needless to say, if the notes were made full legal tender, the Treasury would not need to disburse *any* coin. By this time some of the older form of limited tender Treasury notes were in circulation, and since they suffered no lack of acceptability the case of full legal tender notes was weakened further.

Chase was ill-fitted for the Treasury post (Barrett, 333). His anti-bank prejudice was patent. When banker groups recommended that Chase use the banks for governmental deposits and transactions, and that he leave specie in the banks when the banks made loans to the government, he absolutely refused (*ibid.*, 347). Yet, by a simple amendment to the Independent Treasury Act of 1846, the Treasury could have enlisted the suspended banks as government depositories. Not only Chase, but Spaulding and other congressmen objected to this readily available remedy (Spaulding, 175).

Barrett pointed out that in early 1862 people could deposit various government issues already authorized, such as demand notes, in Treasury and sub-treasury offices for five per cent certificates of deposit. This system was so popular that Congress wanted to raise the limits on the CDs from $25 million to $100 million or more. Unfortunately the rate of interest the government paid on the CDs was at the discretion of the Secretary of the Treasury. When Chase observed the popularity of the CDs, he reduced the rate to four percent(!) and "attempted, unsuccessfully, to force holders of loanable funds to convert to 5–20 bonds." According to Barrett, if the Treasury had used the demand notes, which were not full legal tender, as a monetary reserve, it could have floated loans that "would have net the government more than the entire amount of legal tender notes authorized by the [three legal tender] acts" (*ibid.*, 330–332).

Chase's fiscal "strategy" virtually guaranteed failure and, ultimately, recourse to *fiat* paper money. He first sold bonds to the banks for "coin," then locked up the coin in the Treasury. The banks thereupon suspended specie payments because the Treasury now had the gold that had been their reserves. The Treasury then stopped redeeming its notes because Chase wanted to keep the gold in the Treasury. Because banks could no longer furnish any more coin for bonds they bought but had to resort to irredeemable bank notes, Chase assailed bank-issued currency and advocated its replacement with irredeemable, fully legal tender, government-issued paper money. Chase's final letter to Congress on the matter stated: "The legal tender clause is a necessity, . . . and I support it earnestly" (Spaulding, 59, 65; Newcomb, 161).

Don Barrett, Wesley Mitchell, and Simon Newcomb all found the legal tender provision unnecessary for several reasons. Taxation had not even been tried in spite of the sentiment that the general public was "ready" to be taxed. Second, the six percent bonds that the Treasury was marketing remained nearly at par value as late as the summer of 1862, six months after the oratorical hyperbole in Congress (Newcomb, 161). Congress debated the legal tender bill for six weeks after the "pressing necessity" argument first appeared and before the act was passed. Even then, several other financial devices, including the demand notes, continued to tide the government over this period. Only a few greenbacks appeared prior to May 1862 (Barrett, 349–353; Mitchell, 73).

Many congressman tried to wash their hands of the legal tender taint by promising themselves and their colleagues that the bill would provide legal tender only for the duration of the war. Spaulding was one of them. The provision was clearly constitutional as a war measure, he wrote in 1868 to Hugh McCulloch, who was Secretary of the Treasury at the time. "I am equally clear that as a peace measure it is unconstitutional. No one would now think of passing a legal tender act making the promises of the Government . . . a legal tender in payment of 'all debts public and private.' Such a law [in time of peace] could not be sustained for one moment" (Spaulding, Appendix, 24–25. Also, pp. 103 and 202–203).

Legal Tender Cases

When the war finally ended, $400 million of greenbacks and $50-plus million of other legal tender currency, primarily demand notes, were in circulation. Chase resigned as Secretary of the Treasury in 1864, and, after an interim appointment, Lincoln in March 1865 appointed Hugh McCulloch to the post. McCulloch was a professional banker of note from Indiana.

Because government expenditures declined precipitously while tax revenues continued unabated, fiscal surpluses appeared in Treasury receipts. With these surplus balances, McCulloch was able to begin a policy of greenback retirement. Congress at first supported his policy with a resounding resolution in December 1865. By April 1866, however, Congress was having second thoughts on the matter. It limited cancellation and retirement of the notes to $10 million in the ensuing six months and $4 million per month thereafter. Finally, in February 1868, Congress suspended altogether any further retirements of the greenbacks (Dunbar, 199–201). Since the amount outstanding at the time of the "freeze" was $356 million, the experience seemed to prove that any reduction of the outstanding legal tender in excess of 11 percent of the existing stock was not politically feasible. Congressmen, who had once supported the legal tender acts as temporary and reversible, were now retired, dead, defeated, or for "practical" purposes had changed their minds.

The legal tender provision was also getting its day in court, both in state courts and in the Supreme Court. Irwin Unger reported that the constitutionality of the legal tender provision came before the state courts some 16 times between 1863 and 1870. The decisions of the courts reflected a pronounced political bias: Of the 70 state court justices who ruled on the cases, all but one Republican judge upheld the legal tender clause, while every Democratic judge except two pronounced the clause unconstitutional (Siegan, 34; Unger, 175).

If this result seems anomalous in view of later Democratic penchants for easy money and lots of it, it is because traditional Democratic policy at that time still had the Jacksonian momentum of hard money running through it. Republicans, on the other hand, not only had a "national" bank principle in their heritage, but were also in command of the political machinery in both the Congress and the Presidency.

Andrew Johnson, Lincoln's successor, retained McCulloch as Secretary of the Treasury. But Ulysses S. Grant, upon becoming President in 1868, appointed George Boutwell, a former Governor of Massachusetts and a prominent congressman, to the Treasury post. Whereas McCulloch had favored continuous retirement of the greenbacks and an early resumption of specie payments, both Boutwell and Grant were pragmatists. Boutwell, an extreme radical Republican, was very much opposed to McCulloch. He favored a policy of "growing up to specie" (Timberlake, 1978, ch. 7). That is, he wanted to maintain a monetary status quo and let natural growth in real output gradually reduce the price level to the point at which pre-war parity between gold and the dollar would allow the gold standard to become operational.

While Congress and the President were Republican, five of the eight Supreme Court justices were Democrats. This label also applied (at times) to the Chief Justice, who was by this time none other than Salmon P. Chase. Even though he had been Secretary of the Treasury under Lincoln and a Lincoln appointee to the Court, Chase aspired to the Presidency as a Democrat. In fact, Chase in everyone's book "seemed to change his politics to suit his ambitions (McCulloch, 180; Unger, 175).

The first legal tender case to reach Supreme Court was *Hepburn v. Griswold.* The decision dealt only with the constitutionality of the legal tender acts as applied to debts incurred before February 25, 1862, the date the first legal tender act was signed into law. By a 5–3 vote the Court denied the constitutionality of the act for debts contracted before the law was passed, but left moot the question of their constitutionality for debts contracted after passage (Unger, 174; Kemp, ch. 5). The majority decision argued that: (1) the power to bestow legal-tender quality on the notes was not incident to the coinage power; that is, issuing the notes did not require that they be made legal tender in the mode of gold and silver coins. They were not coined, but printed and issued as paper currency. (2) The war power requiring large expenditures of money was no more necessary for the issue of notes than any other governmental power to spend money. In so deciding the Court observed that some notes had circulated that were not full legal tender. Yet these notes had not passed at a discount relative to the full legal tender issues. Therefore, the greenbacks would have served the government's purposes just as well if they had been made a tender only for payments to the government in the mode of the former Treasury notes. (3) Because the legal tender feature impaired the obligation of contracts, it violated the constitutional proscription against "bills of credit" (Article I, Section 10, clause 1) and the Fifth Amendment: "Nor shall any person be deprived of life, liberty, or property without due process of law" (Siegan, 30–32; Breckenridge, 128–129; Hepburn, 275–290).

The Court decided the case in 1869 but delayed announcing the decision until early 1870. By the time the decision was made public, one justice (Crier) who had voted with the majority had retired. Therefore, the final decision as accounted was 4–3.

The *Hepburn* decision caused no appreciable uneasiness in financial circles. "Businessmen," Unger wrote, "received the decision with surprising calm." Few pre-1862 debts were still outstanding, long-term private obligations totalled only $350 million. The price of gold did not react either way (Unger, 175).

Nonetheless, the Grant Administration and the Republican Congress were deeply disturbed. They felt that the Court ruling threatened to de-stabilize the monetary status quo; it seemed as well to be a contrived Democratic attempt to repudiate the Republican Party's war policies. Grant thereupon appointed two new justices to the Court whose opinions on legal tender were well known from their decisions in state court cases (Unger, 177–178; McCulloch, 173). The erstwhile minority on this question thereupon became a majority. On a motion from the Attorney General for further argument on the constitutionality of legal tender cases still undecided, the Court in 1871, in the cases of *Knox v. Lee* and *Parker v. Davis,* reconsidered and subsequently reversed its previous position by holding that U.S. notes were legal tender for debts contracted both before and after February 25, 1862 (Dunne, 77–81; Siegan, 32–34; Breckenridge, 131–132).

The five-to-four majority of the Court that now sanctioned government issues of legal tender notes based its decision on essentially the same arguments that had appeared in Congress nine years earlier. The Court cases and decisions, as Unger observed, "had become miniature political contests . . . Republican jurists felt compelled to defend a major item of Republican wartime legislation; Democratic opposition reflected the party's traditional hostility to paper money and expanded federal function—biases the judges did not abandon as readily as did the party's active politicians" (Unger, 175).

Justice Strong, one of Grant's new appointees, wrote the majority opinion. He based the decision on the "expediency of voiding the legal tender currency." Since passage of the acts, all debts had been contracted "on the understanding that they might be discharged in legal tenders." If the notes were now found invalid as legal tender, "The government would become the instrument of the grossest injustice; all debtors [would be] loaded with an obligation it was never contemplated they should assume . . ." (*ibid.,* 178).

Unger in retrospect of 95 years sympathized with this decision, but it is invalid on several counts. First, the Supreme Court is not supposed to adjudicate on the basis of "expediency." Justice and expediency are not synonymous. Second, even if the majority felt compelled to be expedient, it could have distinguished easily between pre-1862 debts and post-1862 debts and thereby satisfied the criteria of both expediency and justice. All the Court had to do was to reaffirm the *Hepburn* decision of 1870, and apply the principle implied by the very existence of a contract: that a debt is payable in whatever the contract stipulates, or in whatever is legal tender at the time the contract is drawn. In neglecting this constitutional implication, the Court itself became an "instrument of the grossest injustice." Its decision denied the whole reason for the existence of contracts—that is, their ability to reduce uncertainty by describing and defining ahead of time the means for satisfying the contract when it becomes due. If a contract is payable in whatever is legal tender at the time of payment, it loses its very reason for existence. It fails to protect the creditor who was party to it, and, at worst, becomes an instrument of expropriation.

Besides the new majority of the Court, several congressmen and Treasury officials treated this issue at one time or another. Boutwell, for example, stated emphatically that "Every contract . . . is to be performed in the currency of the country *at the time the contract is liquidated.* The power to decide the quantity and quality of that currency is an essential incident of sovereignty" (Boutwell, 71).

Some congressmen addressed the issue at the time of the first legal tender debate. Roscoe Conkling of New York, for example, protested the legal tender clause as unconstitutional for what it would do to the real value of a contractual credit (Spaulding, 65). Simon Newcomb, the astronomer and political economist, also raised the same objection (Newcomb, pp. 94, 180); as did Hugh McCulloch, Boutwell's predecessor in the Treasury (McCulloch, 178). Boutwell, however, was a "party man," as the title to his book testifies. He reiterated in a few pages all the arguments that his fellows had made in the congressional debates: That the legal tender clause was "necessary and proper," and that resumption of specie redemption for the notes in 1879 negated the impropriety of their full legal tender quality (Boutwell, 70–74).

"Necessary and proper," as the Supreme Court interpreted it, could have been used to support *any* policy. Hepburn, in his review of the cases, correctly reasoned: If Congress had the power claimed by the Supreme Court majority, it could have issued *fiat* paper notes unceasingly and paid off its bonded indebtedness with them no matter how much the notes depreciated. "Why then," Hepburn asked, "should the government continue paying interest on the bonds when the principle might be paid in a day?" Hepburn, 266).

The Court added yet another interpretation to its *Knox* decision—one that Spaulding had included in his indefatigable campaign for the notes: that the decision of their issue was "political" and not "judicial," that the decision depended on *Congress's* estimate of the urgency of the express power it chose to exercise as "necessary and proper," and that Congress's decision was not subject to judicial review (Hepburn, 261–262). Yet, the Court paradoxically did review the case. If it believed its own ruling, it should have said so right away and left the rest of its arguments unrecorded. It is not, however, a proper subordinate decision, as the majority's behavior in presenting other arguments makes plain. When the "necessary" actions that Congress legislates prove, as in the legal tender debates to be nothing more than economic misinterpretations and political prejudices, the case for judicial or perhaps economic review, is even more compelling.

In the third legal tender case, *Julliard v. Greenman* argued in 1884, the Court held that Congress's legal tender power was constitutional in time of peace as well as war. This reactionary decision reached into the dust-bin of history and came up with the sixteenth century notion of the state's prerogative of sovereignty as the excuse for declaring the greenbacks valid. "Congress, as the legislature of a sovereign nation," the *Julliard* decision went,

> being expressly empowered by the constitution to . . . borrow money on the credit of the United States and to coin money and regulate the value thereof . . . and being clearly [!] authorized as incidental to the exercise of those great powers to emit bills of credit, . . . and to provide a national currency for the whole people . . ., and the power to make the notes of the government a legal tender in payment of private debts being one of the powers belonging to other civilized [?] nations, and not expressly withheld from Congress by the constitution, we are

irresistibly impelled to the conclusion that the impressing upon the Treasury notes of the United States the quality of being a legal tender in payment of private debts is an *appropriate* means, . . . consistent with the letter and spirit of the constitution, and *therefore . . . 'necessary and proper'* for carrying into execution the [foregoing] powers vested by this constitution in the *government* of the United States [*Julliard v. Greenman*, 110 U.S. 421 (1884].

In a few words the reasoning in the decision went along with the following lines:

(1) The federal government through the Congress has the right to *borrow* "money."

(2) It has, therefore, the right to *issue* paper money, "circulating notes," for the money borrowed. (This argument is a semantic misapplication. *Borrow* and *issue* are two different words with distinct meanings that both the framers and all Supreme Court Justices could easily comprehend.)

(3) Congress also has the power to coin metallic currency and declare the value thereof.

(4) Because Congress has both the power to issue "circulating notes," which are currency [(1) and (2)], and the power to impress gold or silver coin as a legal tender (3), Justice Gray concluded, "under the two powers, taken together [sic], Congress is authorized to establish a national currency, either in coin, or in paper, and to make that currency lawful money for all purposes. (*ibid.* Also, Hunt, 137).

The legal construction of "taking the two powers together" appeared in several juridical briefs in support of the *Julliard* decision (Hunt, 137; Thayer, 96). If one "puts together" the two money clauses, the result is: "The Congress Shall have power to coin [paper] money/on the credit of the United States/and regulate the value thereof." Clearly, this "power" is an absurd distortion of what the Framers thought, said, and wrote. No man who attended the Constitutional Convention in 1787 would have endorsed this construction, or even tolerated it as arguable (Siegan, 21–28).

In retrospect, Hugh McCulloch commented that the *Julliard* decision "covered the whole ground of controversy between those who [thought] that Congress possessed no power not expressly granted by the Constitution, . . . and those who [thought] that all power not absolutely prohibited, belonged to Congress, to be exercised whenever a majority of both branches and the President should consider the exercise of it necessary or expedient. . . ." McCulloch's final observation was that the decision "relieves Congress from what have heretofore been considered well defined restrictions, and clothes a republican government with imperial power" (McCulloch, 178–179).

Criticism of the Legal Tender Cases

The monetary system in the middle 1880's, at the time of the third legal tender decision, was not teetering on the brink of instability. Resumption of specie payments had been an unqualified success; the stock of the U.S. notes was frozen, this time permanently, at $346.7 million, which was slightly less than three percent below the freeze value of 1868; and the silver question seemed reasonably well settled through passage of the Bland-Allison Act of 1878. The gold standard was also working smoothly and in no immediate danger of any internal or external disequilibria. Given these auspices, what might the Supreme Court have ruled in 1884 to maintain both the integrity of the Constitution and the ongoing monetary and economic equilibrium?

First, the Court could have declared the greenbacks unconstitutional as a forced tender for private debts, but constitutional as tender for all payments due the government. Congress could then have enacted a law ordering the Treasury to convert all the greenbacks into the older form of Treasury notes before reissuing them. The Treasury notes would have been simply another form of *limited* legal tender government currency similar to national bank notes and silver currency, and kept at par with the gold dollar by the Treasury's $100-plus million gold balance. Such a currency policy would have had no more effect on the economy than the successful resumption of specie payments five years earlier. Anyone who did not want the notes could have redeemed them for gold at any Treasury office.

By ruling in this manner, the Court would also have avoided sanctioning any "*ex post facto* Law or Law impairing the obligation of Contracts" [Article I, Section 10]. Since most of the contracts in force at the time of the legal tender decisions had been made after the Legal Tender Acts were passed, payments in depreciated paper currency would have resulted in no grave injustices nor financial disequilibrium. The terms in every contract should have determined each case and thereby minimized real injustices due to inflation (Brough, 135).

Juridical analysts may have honestly felt that the federal government had the sovereign powers over the monetary system that their brethren on the Supreme Court had adjudicated. They may also have thought that such a power was no longer dangerous in view of the fact that the legal tender notes were frozen, the gold standard was operational, and the "guidance of human wisdom" was a feature of the age. In any case, legal scholars appeared in print to rationalize intellectually the latter two legal tender decisions.

One of the more eminent of these was an article by James Bradley Thayer in the *Harvard Law Review* in 1887. Thayer based his approval of the Supreme Court's rulings on Congress's powers to "borrow money on the credit of the United States," to "coin" money, and to "regulate" commerce. He "put together" the two money clauses. He wore out "necessary and proper." He did not distinguish between government "bills of credit" that were a tender only for payments to and from the government, and the full legal tender "bills of credit" that were legal tender for all private contracts. He claimed that only the states were prohibited from making anything except gold or silver a tender in payment of debt. He played with the meanings of the words "money" and "regulate," and concluded that the framers had given Congress a sovereign power to furnish a legal tender paper currency, similar in extent to the "power which had frequently been exercised by those legislative bodies [Parliament?] with which the framers of the instrument were most familiar, . . . [and one that] is included in that complete control over money and the currency which is given to Congress [sic]." Thayer argued that the "break-down" of the banking system—by which he meant the Chase-Treasury generated suspension of specie payments—made the issue of government paper money "necessary," and that such currency had to be full legal tender to provide the office of a medium of exchange. "Necessary and proper," among other things, meant "natural and suitable," "reasonably well," "better," "useful," "appropriate," and, citing Marshall's opinion in *McCulloch*, "most eligible." Thayer, too, justified the issue of notes as a means of "borrowing money," when in fact all economists recognize such issues of *fiat* paper money as a seigniorage tax (Thayer, 90–97). Since Congress already had the power to tax directly by straightforward fiscal methods, it could not have been given the power to tax by subterfuge.

Another legal apologist for the Court's decisions was Alva R. Hunt, who wrote a comprehensive treatise on the legal aspects of money in courts of law. Hunt argued that, "The power to issue money and declare the extent to which it shall be current is, from the necessity of having a stable and uniform standard, an attribute of sovereignty. A power assumed very early in the history of civilized governments." Hunt cited William Blackstone, the renowned English jurist, to the effect that giving money "authority" and making it "current" were part of the "King's prerogative" (Hunt, 61–62).

This opinion seems to contradict the colonists' rationale for separating from England and establishing a constitutional republic in the first place. Surely the framers were not looking back to the sovereign kings of England for guidance! Rather much to the contrary.

Furthermore, to entrust a sovereign to provide a stable and uniform standard provides a temptation no sovereign has ever resisted. For such a duty also implies a power to debase the currency and tax by unlimited seigniorage. True, every piece of governmental paper currency is identical to every other piece, but the *real* value of the typical sovereign's currency is anything but uniform and stable over time. Furthermore, the same desirable uniformity would appear and did appear in privately issued currency, including coins, in the few cases where such currency was allowed. Even inferentially one should be no more surprised at uniformity in monetary media than uniformity in dozens of other conventional items routinely produced and used in everyday life—*e.g.,* containers, books, pens, chair and table heights, lights, playing cards, and building bricks—in short, in any usuage where uniformity reduces costs [White, 1989, 178].

Hunt also blessed the clearing of debts with whatever is legal tender at the time of payment (Hunt, 63). When taken to its extreme, as in the case of hyper-inflation, this dictum as much as says that the government is its "sovereign prerogative" over the currency may dilute the real value of a debt to nothing, or promote it to infinity.

Hunt cited numerous cases on the legal tender question from state court decisions between 1864 and 1867. Virtually all of them allowed greenbacks to serve as surrogates for gold without any reference to the real values of the debts contracted. One decision stated that only by virtue of law were either gold coins or greenbacks a legal tender. Therefore, both *had* to be "exactly equivalent for the purpose of payment." The premium on gold at this time (1866) was a value "men voluntarily choose to give for [it]," and therefore, Hunt concluded, could have no bearing on the legality of the case (Hunt, 105. *Brown v. Welch,* 26 Ind. 116).

Hunt argued that in the *Hepburn* decision the Supreme Court ". . . made its comparison between the wrong things. It compared the declared or nominal value of legal tender notes with the market value of the bullion in a coined dollar. The declared value the government controls, while the value of bullion is controlled by the law of supply and demand. If declared values had been compared," Hunt continued, "(and it seems absurd to compare equals), it would have been found that . . . $1,400 in 1857 was equivalent to $1,400 in 1868 [!]" (Hunt, 114). With economic sophistication of this magnitude making decisions in courts of law, it is difficult to understand how the government could ever be bothered with a national debt or with any other economic problems. It could simply legislate all of them out of existence.

The Scholars React

And what of economists who first reviewed congressional arguments over the greenbacks, Wesley Mitchell and Don Barrett, could find no economic justification for their issue as full legal tender. Indeed, both gave cogent arguments for not issuing them. McCulloch and Hepburn, who were both bankers and appointed Treasury officials at different times, also were opposed to the legalization of the notes and their currency for *ex ante* debts.

A political scientist, S.P. Breckenridge, in 1903 traced the entire evolution of legal tender through the ages. Her monograph was an outgrowth of a seminar class in political economy presided over by J. Lawrence Laughlin, a prominent economist of the time at the University of Chicago. In her survey Breckenridge treated the evolution of the legal tender quality from the time of the Plantagenets in England to the Legal Tender Acts and court cases in the United States. Her conclusion was that, . . .

> The Private individual, the creditor, was by a compulsory act of government, through the agency of the courts . . ., forced to share with the government, or bear for it, the cost of the conflict then being waged. By an extraordinary departure from both legislative and judicial precedents, an act as tyrannical as any act of Henry

VIII in [his] dealing with coins, found legislative and executive
support and judicial sanction. It was fitting that the law based on
the doctrine of the prerogative prevailing in the time of the Tudors
[the Case of the Mixt Monies] should be invoked to sustain such
legislation (Breckenridge, 155).

The monetary status quo prior to 1914 may have lulled economists
and other scholars into the false notion that the legal tender issue was
no longer relevant to monetary security. As an adjunct to the gold
standard, the nascent Federal Reserve System promised to make the
monetary system work more smoothly, and to do so on the solid basis
of a monetary standard written in gold. Over the following decades,
however, especially in the 1930's, another momentous sea-change in
monetary practices took place. After 1934 gold was prohibited altogether for domestic monetary use. Federal Reserve notes—latter day
greenbacks—became the legal tender medium. While some economists, such as Walter Spahr and other gold standard "extremists"
objected, the large majority of economists accepted the change both
as necessary and desirable. Managed money, they held, was necessary
to mitigate boom and bust. Under a gold standard, the "guidance of
human wisdom" could not function because the monetary system was
on a defective automatic pilot. The few economists and historians
who treated the legal tender issue at all looked at the Supreme Court
decisions and found them both valid and good because the decisions
enlarged Congress's hands-on control of the monetary system.

Bray Hammond was one banking historian who reviewed the
evolution of monetary control from self-regulating specie standard to
a politically controlled central bank. Hammond interpreted the
money clauses in the Constitution as implying that the framers
wanted the federal government, and not the state governments, to
control the money supply. The Federal government, he argued, had
"responsibilities imposed upon it by the Constitution" to regulate the
supply of money, whatever that money happened to be. Wrapping all
of Congress's express powers into one package—lay and collect taxes,
regulate commerce, coin money, fix standards of weights and measures, plus everything else that was "necessary and proper,"—according to Hammond, substantiated Congress's powers over the monetary
system. The judicial argument that supports this interpretation,
Hammond admitted, leads to the "anomaly of the monetary function
being considered ... with little attention to what the Constitution says

about [money], but with attention chiefly to what the Constitution says about interstate commerce" [!] (Hammond, 109–113).

Hammond's arguments, including the reference to the interstate commerce clause, simply parroted the earlier Supreme Court decisions. Neither Hammond nor others who used this argument ever addressed the question of why a document as profoundly reasoned as the Constitution would provide principles for monetary policy by implication from the clauses on interstate commerce. What is to say that interstate commerce was not based on the norms in the clauses on money, or for that matter to the clauses dealing with firearms?

Gerald Dunne agreed with Hammond's principal contention—that the Constitution's main purpose, rather than limiting severely the monetary powers of the state and federal governments, was to provide sovereign federal controls over the supply of money (Dunne, "Preface," and 24 note). Dunne approved of the *Knox v. Lee* decision that overturned *Hepburn* and made the Legal Tender Acts constitutional for all time. He cited Justice Bradley's argument, in which Bradley supported the Acts by reference to the Case of Mixt Monies in England in 1601 (Dunne, 78). Yet, as Dunne had noted earlier, the Case of the Mixt Monies was simply a means by which a conquering government (England) imposed an expropriatory tax on an occupied territory (Ireland). It was in no way a case involving justice between litigants with equal rights (Dunne, 78, 99; Breckenridge, 25). Far from being an expression of royal sovereignty, it was an example from Roman times of: "Vae victis!" ("Woe to the vanquished"!)—straightforward expropriation of a subject people.

Dunne observed that "judicial appraisal of legal tender began by considering it as a provisional wartime expedient and closed by investing it with a legitimacy that was both permanent and beyond judicial control" (Dunne, 83). He extended this observation in his conclusions. Justices Strong and Bradley in the *Knox v. Lee* and *Parker v. Davis* cases, he claimed, reached the heart of the matter in their recognition that "the government and only the government can declare what money shall be, emit it, enforce it, and protect [sic] it. In short, power is power. Within its limits, the government is, *ipso facto,* absolute, and the possibility of its abuse is simply irrelevant to the question of its existence" (Dunne, 100; Hunt, 101 note). But what *are* the limits on government? Dunne did not begin to answer this question.

Besides his acceptance of the English Court's ruling in the case of the Mixt Monies, Dunne claimed justification for such an absolute governmental authority in the practical experience of the market place! "People in markets think in terms of dollars as dollars rather than units of some fluctuating and variable metallic content," Dunne observed. If the government changes the monetary rules in midgame, it is beyond "even the great powers of the Supreme Court [sic] to put the situation right again. Hence, the Court stays its hand when faced with the blunt consequences of rending the fabric of the economic going concern by invalidating the new monetary rules after they have been assimilated as practical facts of life" (Dunne, 101).

An even later treatise by James Willard Hurst, *A Legal History of Money in the United States,* picked up on Congress's alleged prerogative of sovereignty and the legislature's consequent powers over the money supply. The legal tender power, Hurst claimed, "served the general interest in ready conduct of market transaction and in ready government allocations of economic resources . . . ." One "contribution" that legal tender status gave to money tokens was the help it provided in determining the quantity of money; a second "contribution" was its "help" in promoting "the practical acceptance of given money tokens" (Hurst, 40–43).

Hurst found no constitutional problem with any of the federal government's assumptions of monetary powers, except the Court's validation of legal tender notes in peacetime by its ruling in the *Julliard* decision. However, he concluded that Congress and the Court "did not go beyond the limit, in light of the indicated [?] constitutional intent that the national government *fully control the system of money* and that it enjoy broad authority to promote a truly national economy" (Hurst, 195–196). One can only editorialize here: Nonsense. Nothing in the Constitution remotely supports either of these contentions.

Conclusion

Up until the time of the Civil War, almost no one had seriously considered interpreting the money clauses in the Constitution in any light except that of prohibiting state and federal issues of currency on the basis of discretionary authority. "To coin money" meant to provide the technical facilities for minting coins. "Regulate the value thereof" meant only to specify a weight of fine gold or silver as equal to a number of the units of account, which were dollars. "Regulate," while it may have been a questionable choice for the proper verb, did not mean "determine the supply of money," either of precious metal money or of paper. Indeed, the very act of adopting a specie standard precluded the idea or possibility that "regulate the value" meant anything more profound than simply "specify the weight." The specie standard by its very nature is self-regulating, as all the framers knew or sensed. Clearly, a self-regulating system is incompatible with any kind of policy-inspired manipulation. The only regulation implied by "regulate" was the small-scale kind of housekeeping change in the specifications of the units of account that would keep both precious metals current as money. This problem was inherent and chronic in the management of bimetallic standards (Timberlake, 1988).

The first and second Banks were *not* examples of governmental monetary agencies, as Bray Hammond and later observers have alleged. Both these institutions emerged to assist Congress to fulfill its fiscal powers. Not only were they not vested with either express or implied powers to control the quantity of money, but the debates on their creation explicitly denied them such license. In the circumstances of their existence the Bank's directors were able to assume some unauthorized monetary controls, but no grant of such powers appears anywhere in their charters, nor by any implied understanding between their directors and the government (Timberlake, 1978, 213–214).

The Civil War witnessed an unhealthy shift in political divisions that not many observers have stressed. All the Southern Congressmen, who were primarily Democrats and opposed to national banks and paper money, left the Federal Congress to become a part of the Confederate Congress. This exodus left the remaining Federal Congress overwhelmingly influenced by Whig-Republicans, who could bring out of mothballs all of their pet schemes for a national bank and paper money with assurance of favorable results. By way of contrast, the Confederate government, in four years of war against an adversary with five times its real resources, found "no necessity" to issue full legal tender notes. Rather its notes took the form of the usual Treasury notes of the pre-1860 type—legal tender only for payments due to and receivable from the Confederate government.

Had the monetary ideological make-up of Congress stayed constant after 1860, full legal tender U.S. notes would never have appeared. Even so, most congressmen reluctantly granted their existence under only highly qualified conditions. Those with this mind-set were to express in retrospect what might be called "counterfactual regret:" "I would never have voted for the legal tender bill if I had known that the notes would become a permanent part of the circulation . . . ." Some voted for them only until the war would be over. Others voted for them thinking that a future Supreme Court would declare them unconstitutional, or that some future executive administration would take the heat for their retirement. Still others presumed naively that the Treasury would be able to redeem them for coin as they were issued, and as Chase had at first implied. Nevertheless, both the reasoning available at the time and future economic analysis proved beyond any question that the full legal tender quality of the notes—for all debts public and private, *ex post* and *ex ante*—was decidedly unnecessary.

The inflation of 1862–1865 and the corresponding decline in the real value of fixed dollar claims had repercussions that were bound to be tested in the courts. The Supreme Court's last two decisions, which were the only two that endured, were opprobrious juridical contrivances. The Justices' arguments worked over the words of the Constitution and, by means of semantic legerdemain, twisted many of its meanings completely around. The Justices used the same arguments that the politicians had used in the congressional debates. Indeed, little else could have been expected; for the Justices who made up the court majority were federal politicians vindicating Republican Party policies first and foremost. As Dunne noted innocently: "The sovereign itself . . . is not only participant but also referee in the game of getting and spending" (Dunne, 5). It is not strange, as Hammond fatuously observed, that "changes in [federal] statues and [Supreme Court] jurisprudence have strengthened the Constitution's ban on issues of money by individual states *but have nullified completely the original intent* that the federal government should have no power to make anything but the precious metals legal tender"? (Hammond, 109). Who could expect that a Supreme Court—an ongoing political institution composed of self-interested mortals—would swear fealty to a Constitution that offered no *quid pro quo* when real political prizes were at stake right now?

The Court's most questionable decision was to grant the validity of the legal tender on the grounds that it was a cumulative sum of

Congress's other express powers, including the power to regulate interstate commerce. If this argument is valid, it means for its own negation. Otherwise, it would have had no reason for existence in the first place.

The legal-historical journalists of the twentieth century, who followed the Supreme Court's rationale, accepted the common notion that the monetary system will not manage itself. Therefore, someone must manage it. Therefore, the framer's principles must be altered to allow for governmental control over the money supply. Indeed, the judicial activists go further and allege that the framers had this notion in mind from the beginning!

Neither is it so, nor is it necessary. The framers knew what they were doing. They were setting up a simple monetary system under the Rule of Law that would regulate itself. Their system would work no matter how many unchartered commercial banks issued currency and deposits. As long as banking enterprises obeyed the rules prohibiting force and fraud and were subject to the pressures of free and open competition, they needed no more regulation than blacksmiths or cart-wrights (White, 1984; Selgin, 1988).

One may wonder, in reviewing monetary history from the time of the founding fathers to the present, just where we went wrong. Where was the Achilles's heel in polity that allowed the legislature, executive and judiciary the opportunity to break the Rule of Law in the first place?

Robert Greenfield and Leland Yeager have recently proposed a norm for monetary policy that suggests an answer to this question. They wish to separate the unit of account from the medium of exchange. The unit of account in the United States is the dollar, while the medium of exchange is the one-dollar Federal Reserve note. Greenfield and Yeager argue that it is only an accident of polity that has the two things synonymous in people's minds. For the practical purpose of getting the government (in the guise of the Federal Reserve System) out of any policy-making role, Greenfield and Yeager prescribe that Congress specify the unit-of-account dollar to be of a value equal to a market price index made up of a limited array of staple, conventional, basic commodities—items that would ideally mirror an all-markets average of prices. The government would not involve itself in keeping this price index constant by manipulating the quantity of money, nor by other means. It would leave this function to dealers and arbitrageurs in financial and commodity markets (Greenfield and Yeager, 302–315. See also, White, 1984).

The Greenfield and Yeager analysis and prescription, when regressed to the money clauses of the Constitution, serve to illustrate what the framers, if they had been omniscient, should have done, and what the fatal weakness in Congress's monetary powers turned out to be. "Regulate the value" of gold and silver coins in analogous, with obvious qualifications, to the specification of the unit of account in the Greenfield and Yeager model. The framers put this provision in the same clause that had Congress providing a system of weights and measures. Unfortunately, they also allowed Congress the power to "coin money"—the currency that it "regulates." Coining money is analogous to producing the medium of exchange in the Greenfield and Yeager system. However, it is no more necessary for establishing a viable and stable monetary system than is a provision for Congress to "coin" weights and measures into five-pound bobs and yardsticks. Apparently, the prevailing sentiment at the time of the Constitutional Convention was an uneasiness that private coin smiths might not do an effective job, or that the prevalence of Spanish-produced coins in use at the time sullied the prestige of the fledgling U.S. government.

Without the coinage power, Congresses would have had no reason to debase the coinage and to monopolize currency production in their ongoing quest for seigniorage. Likewise, Supreme Courts would have had no opportunity nor incentive to validate Congress's transgressions of its constitutional limits. The framers thought they had provided effective checks and balances; but they reckoned without the deviousness of the self-interested political opportunists who came to inhabit the federal government. Once Congress, the Executive, and the Supreme Court had stretched and distorted constitutional principles to validate the greenbacks, the Rule of Law for money as well as for other key institutions was dangerously jeopardized.

Notes

1. The anti-bank sentiment in Chase's *Report* appeared again and again both in his communications to Congress and in the debates over the legal tender bills.

2. Mitchell emphasized the absurdity of "necessity" in the presence of clear alternatives.

3. Barrett noted that Chase was one of Lincoln's chief rivals for the presidency, and was appointed to the cabinet in the interest of preserving party unity. Furthermore, he was "spurred on by his own notion that the administration in general would fare better in his hands than in the President's." In 1868 he coveted the *Democratic* nomination for President, even though Lincoln had appointed him Chief Justice of the Supreme Court in 1864. All accounts agree that Chase's ambition had no limit.

4. Using the suspended banks as Treasury depositories would have meant only a simple amendment to the Independent Treasury Act passed in 1846. But Spaulding objected, saying only, "I do not think it would be wise to adopt that policy at this time" (Spaulding, p. 175).

5. Letter to Hugh McCulloch, Secretary of the Treasury, Dec. 9, 1868.

6. For evidence that his argument on "sovereignty" is invalid, see Timberlake, 1990, 315–320.

7. In probabilistic terms, experience suggests that debts are much more likely to be reduced in real value than increased, probably because the government is itself most often a major debtor, and also because debtors are more numerous and politically active than creditors.

8. Much of what Hurst asserts about "legal tender status" suggests that he does not distinguish appropriately between the *acceptability* of money and the *value* of money. (p. 44).

References

Barrett, Don C. "The Supposed Necessity of Legal Tender Paper," Quarterly *Journal of Economics,* 16 May, 1902.

Boutwell, George. *Why I Am a Republican.* Philadelphia: W.S. Fortescue & Co., 1884.

Breckenridge, S.P. *Legal Tender.* New York: Greenwood Press, 1969.

Brough, William. *The Natural Law of Money.* New York: Greenwood Press, 1969. Originally published New York: G.P. Putnman's Sons, 1896.

Christainsen, Gregory. "Fiat Money and the Constitution: A Historical Review." In *Political Business Cycles,* Thomas D. Willett, ed., Durham: Pacific Institute and Duke University Press; 1988.

Dunbar, Charles. *Laws of the United States Relating to Currency, Finance and Banking from 1789 to 1896.* New York: Augustus Kelley, 1969. Originally published Boston: Ginn and Co., 1897 [1891].

Dunne, Gerald T. *Monetary Decisions of the Supreme Court.* New Brunswich: Rutgers University Press, 1960.

Greenfield, Robert L. and Leland B. Yeager. "A Laissez-Faire Approach to Monetary Stability." *Journal of Money, Credit and Banking.* 15, 3, August 1983, pp. 302–315.

Hammond, Bray. *Banks and Politics in America.* Princeton, New Jersey: Princeton University Press, 1957.

Hepburn, A. Barton. *A History of Currency in the United States.* Rev. Ed. New York: Macmillan, 1924.

Hunt, Alva R. *A Treatise on the Law of Tender, and Bringing Money into Court.* St. Paul: Frank P. Dufrensne, 1903.

Hurst, James Willard. *A Legal History of Money in the United States, 1774–1970.* Lincoln, Nebraska: University of Nebraska Press, 1973.

Kemp, Arthur. *The Legal Qualities of Money.* New York: Pageant Press, Inc., 1956.

McCulloch, Hugh. *Men and Measures of Half a Century.* New York: Charles Scribner's Sons, 1900.

Mitchell, Wesley C. *A History of the Greenbacks.* Chicago: University of Chicago Press, 1903.

Newcomb, Simon. *Examination of Our Financial Policy during the Southern Rebellion.* New York: Greenwood Press, 1969. (First published, New York: D. Appleton Co., 1865).

Selgin, George. *The Theory of Free Banking.* Totowa, New Jersey: Rowan and Littlefield, 1988.

Siegan, Bernard H. *The Supreme Court's Constitution.* New Brunswick, New Jersey: Transaction Books, 1987.

Spaulding, Elbridge G. *History of the Legal Tender Paper Money Issued during the Great Rebellion being a Loan without Interest and a National Currency.* Westport, Conn.: Greenwood Press, 1971. (First published, Buffalo, New York: Express Printing Co., 1869.

Thayer, James Bradley. "Legal Tender." *Harvard Law Review.* I, 73, 1887–1888. pp. 73–97.

Timberlake, Richard H. *The Origins of Central Banking in the United States.* Cambridge, Massachusetts: Harvard University Press, 1978.

Timberlake, Richard H. *Independent Institute Policy Studies.* "Gold Standard Policy: An Illusory Means for Achieving Individual Liberty." 1988.

Timberlake, Richard H. "The Government's License to Create Money," *CATO Journal,* vol. 9, No. 2, Fall 1989, pp. 301–321.

Unger, Irwin. *The Greenback Era.* Princeton University Press, 1964.

White, Lawrence H. "Competitive Payments Systems and the Unit of Account." *American Economic Review,* vol. 74, No. 1, September 1984, pp. 699–712.

White, Lawrence H. *Competition and Currency.* New York: New York University Press, 1989.

Comment: The Crime of 1834

by J. Huston McCulloch

In this paper, "The Political Origin and Judicial Sanction of Legal Tender Paper Money in the United States," Richard H. Timberlake cogently argues that the second and third legal tender decisions (*Knox v. Lee,* 1872, and *Julliard v. Greenman,* 1884) were in error to reverse the first legal tender decision (*Hepburn v. Griswold,* 1870), which had held that the *ex post facto* character of the 1862 legal tender laws, which had made greenbacks legal tender for obligations incurred before their own date of passage, was constitutional.

However, I think Timberlake is wrong to single out the Civil War as the first exercise of this power. In fact, the episode in American experience in which *ex post facto* legal tender originally got its foot in the door was, I would argue, the dimly remembered adjustment of the mint ratio in 1834.

The monetary legislation of 1792 provided for the free and unlimited minting of silver "dollars" containing 1/1.293 troy ounce of silver, and of gold "eagles" containing 1/1.939 troy ounce of gold, as well as full-bodied fractional silver and gold coins, and a double eagle. The law went on to provide that one full-weight gold eagle would be "lawful tender by their respective weights. The U.S. was thus on a bimetallic standard with a mint price for silver of $1.293, a mint price for gold of $19.39, and a mint ratio of 15:1.

The market prices of the two metals subsequently hovered between the ratios of 15:1 and 16:1, so that in practice only silver circulated, and only silver was used to discharge debts.[1] In 1834 it was resolved to force gold into circulation by changing the mint ratio to 16:1. This was accomplished by maintaining the silver content of the "dollar," while raising the mint price of gold to $20.67.[2]

The law went on to provide that "said gold coins shall be receivable in *all* payments, when of full weight, according to their respective values" (emphasis added). Since the market value of gold in 1834 was only about 15.74 times that of silver, this meant that there was an immediate 1.6% expropriation of the existing interests of creditors.[3] This differential was hardly enough to get excited over at the time. Its significance was that it set the precedent that Congress could, if it wished, retroactively change the terms of debt contracts by defining as legal tender something different from what had been understood at the time the debt was incurred.

And this precedent did not lie idle. In the second legal tender decision, President Grant's freshly appointed majority in fact pointed to this episode, and argued (as paraphrased by Breckenridge, p. 93), "that no one could claim that herein was to be found a violation of the obligation of contracts."

Let it be known for all time, that I, for one, do claim that this action *was* a violation, of the obligation of contracts! It may have amounted to only petty theft, but theft it was, and it should never be forgotten that it set the stage for the grand larceny that was to follow. It deserves to go down in monetary history as the Crime of 1834.[4]

A bimetallic currency, with both gold and silver full-bodied coins circulating at a fixed ratio, cannot be expected to function forever, or even for long. Although the relative value of the two metals stayed between 15:1 and 16:1 throughout the nineteenth century to 1873 (Shaw, chart facing p. 179), it was approximately 12:1 in the Middle Ages (Shaw, ch. 1), and was 4:1 or even lower in ancient Ugarit, circa 1200 B.C. (Schaeffer, 1957, xxxvi). Today silver is about $5.12 ounce, while gold is about $370 per ounce, which makes the ratio in excess of 70:1. Whether a bimetallic currency can function at all for more than a moment if the world price ratio is continuously changing is debatable, but that does not concern us here. At best, functional bimetallism requires a mint ratio that is changed periodically to keep up with the world price ratio of gold and silver. The Constitution thus gave Congress, along with the authority to coin money, the power to "regulate the value thereof."

Even if both metals do not actually circulate, a case can be made for bimetallic debt contracts that protect debtors against the downside risk of an increase in the value of a single metal. Creditors would demand a premium for granting this protection, but with diminishing absolute risk aversion, this may well be less than borrowers would be willing to pay, making a bimetallic debt standard mutually advantageous. The government may wish to introduce such a provision into its own debt instruments, and it would be no interference with the freedom of contract if it also announced that all contracts would thenceforth be understood by the government's courts to be payable bimetallically at a uniform rate (barring an explicit monometallic clause). Such "standardization" would increase the liquidity of these debt instruments and could be generally beneficial. Even so, it would be desirable to keep this option "near the money" by periodically changing the conventional bimetallic ratio to keep up with the actual world price ratio, just as the New York Stock Exchange periodically changes the exercise price on new stock options as the underlying stock price changes.

If in 1834 legislation had merely specified that the new gold coins would be receivable for their respective dollar values, when of full weight, for all payments contracted *after* date of passage of the legislation (unless otherwise specified by the parties involved), but that *prior* contracts (including existing bank deposits and old bank notes) were to be discharged on the old standard, there would have been no expropriation of creditors, no precedent for the later legal tender paper money, and no Crime of 1834.

To Breckenridge, it was "most unfortunate that the first alteration made by law in the metallic coins of the country partook of the nature of a debasement." In fact, what matters for the obligation of contracts is whether a substantial change is retroactive, and not whether it is an increase or decrease in the mint price. An appreciation in terms of either metal would in fact be a violation of the debtors' rights if applied retroactively.

As a practical matter, it actually makes most sense to alter the mint ratio by means of devaluation in terms of the non-circulating metal, since the appreciating in terms of the circulating metal would impose the great cost and commercial inconvenience of immediately retiring and reminting the entire existing specie coinage. Such repeated devaluations would tend to create an upward trend in the price level, but as long as they were not retroactive, this would not expropriate the holders of long-term debt.

In this light, the better known "Crime of '73" (1873, that is) much maligned by the later bimetallists, was indeed criminal, but only insofar as it *ex post facto enhanced* the claims of creditors, by requiring contracts written before 1873 to be discharged exclusively in gold (after Resumption), rather than bimetallically as contracted. At the time, the world price ratio had been below 16:1 for so long, and the paper dollar was so depreciated relative to either metal, that the silver option was not a big issue. However, just a few months after the U.S. legislation, Germany began selling silver, and the bottom dropped out of the silver market. At some point in time well before gold Resumption in 1879, therefore, the silver option would have been worth using. Justice required that pre-1873 debts (and *only* pre-1873 debts) should have retained this option, and later that it should have been restored.

The "Crime of '34" had the very unfortunate additional consequence of creating the presumption than any return to bimetallism in the 1890's would automatically be accompanied by silver becoming legal tender for all debts contracted prior to the proposed bimetallic legislation, and not just for debts contracted prior to 1873 and subsequent to the new law. Since the bimetallists of the 1890's wanted to restore the 1834 ratio of 16:1, and since the market ratio in the 1890's was 27:1 or less, their program would have amounted to a 40 percent or greater expropriation of creditors.[5] If it had instead been understood that the re-introduction of bimetallism would leave prior debts unaffected, foreign capital inflows would not have been interrupted by the agitation. The debate would have been free to swing on the true issues of the relative merits and feasibility of a bimetallic currency and/or debt standard, and of the appropriate mint ratio. It would immediately have been seen that restoring a ratio of 16:1 would have been simply a tremendous inconvenience for all concerned, since it would have entailed a 70 percent jump in prices, with no relief for existing debtors. Furthermore, the *prospective* option protection for *new* debtors at a ratio so far from the market ratio would have been virtually nil.

The Constitutional Question

I turn now to the issue of the constitutionality of *ex post facto* legal tender legislation. Although I am not a lawyer, I would like to offer a few observations on Timberlake's position.

As Timberlake emphasizes, the Supreme Court in the second and third legal tender cases, along with its sycophantic historians, relied heavily on the totally irrelevant argument that throughout history, *ex post facto* legal tender powers have been part of the sovereign power of the state in all civilized nations.

Throughout history, these same civilized nations have also exercised the equally traditional sovereign powers of locking up dissidents, or torturing confessions out of suspects, and of persecuting religious and ethnic minorities. Imperial Rome, Tudor England, and Bourbon France are undeniably part of our own nation's cultural and political heritage. However, the United States is not Imperial Rome, Tudor England, or Bourbon France. What differentiates the United States from these admittedly highly civilized countries is that the United States has a functioning written Constitution that sharply limits the powers of its government, itself largely inspired by the abuses of these very regimes. The outrages these autocratic governments may have committed in the past are therefore no more relevant for what the government of the United States may not do than are the more recent atrocities of Nazi Germany or Soviet Russia.

The constitutionality of the Legal Tender Acts therefore rests not on historical precedent in other countries, but rather on what the Constitution actually says. Here, it seems to me, unfortunately, that Timberlake and the Court in *Hepburn v. Griswold* (as paraphrased by Timberlake) have somewhat overstated the case against constitutionality, particularly insofar as they rely on the provisions of Section 10 of Article I which prohibits the emission of bills of credit, making anything but gold and silver a tender in payment of debts, and impairing the obligation of contracts. In fact, Section I.10 merely restricts the *states* from these activities. The same section also prohibits states from entering into treaties or coining money, powers which the federal government indisputably was given. Barring the states from emitting bills of credit, from making anything but gold or silver a tender, or from impairing the obligation of contracts, therefore does not even implicitly bar the federal government from these same actions. Section I.9, which lists analogous powers denied to the federal government, does not mention any of these items.

Timberlake is on sounder ground when he invokes the prohibition of *ex post facto* laws, which are denied *both* to Congress (in Section I.9) *and* to the states (in Section I.10). This prohibition was presumably intended primarily to prevent laws imposing criminal penalties from being retroactively enforceable. Nevertheless, the retroactivity of the legal tender acts to debts incurred prior to their date of passage was clearly equally *ex post facto* action.

Timberlake is also correct to point out that retroactivity with respect to private debts furthermore served no wartime purpose. Temporarily or permanently defaulting on existing government bonds, (which in itself does not appear to be unconstitutional) and/or issuing temporarily inconvertible Treasury notes in convenient, quasi-monetary denominations, payable at the government's "earliest convenience," might have helped the war effort, but these measures would not have necessitated capriciously impairing the obligation of private contracts.[6]

Also pertinent to constitutionality is the Fifth Amendment, which provides that "No person shall . . . be deprived of . . . property without due process of law; nor shall private property be taken for public use without just compensation." This is not to say that the government cannot deprive people of property, since taxes (certain of which are clearly condoned in Section I.8) do this all the time. Conceivably the government could levy a 10 percent tax on gold and silver coins, by requiring old ones to be turned in for new ones on a 9 for 10 basis. It perhaps could also tax existing debts, by requiring that 10 percent of the interest or even of the principal be turned over to the government instead of to the creditor. But there is no justification in the taxation power for expropriating 10 percent of the amount due to the creditor and turning this over to the *debtor.*

Although Section I.9 does not expressly prohibit Congress from emitting bills of credit, Brough (1896–1969, 130–133) points out that this power was actually in the first draft of Section I.8, and was expressly *deleted* by the Constitutional Convention.[7] To Brough, this meant that "there is no reason to doubt that it was the intention of the framers of the Constitution to withhold from Congress the power of making paper-money a legal tender." However, Breckenridge (1903/1969, ch. 8) shows that there was not a consensus on this issue, and despite her lack of sympathy for legal tender, concludes that "the reasoning [at the Constitutional Convention] seems to have amounted to this: to prohibit the legal-tender quality being attached to bills of credit implies that such bills will be emitted; but it is not desirable that such bills be emitted; nor is it expedient to go to the extreme of saying that they never shall be put forth. Silence on the subject is, therefore, the safest policy."

Section I.8 gives Congress the power to "fix the standard of weights and measures," right alongside the power to "coin money, [and] regulate the value thereof." While I think it would be agreed that this wording gives Congress the power to decimalize the measurement of length by reducing the "U.S. foot" to 10 inches and by increasing the "U.S. mile" to 10,000 of these reduced "feet," surely it would be understood that all deeds of land transfer entered into before this change refer to "old feet" and "old miles," and that any attempt to apply "new feet" and "new miles" to pre-conversion agreements would not be warranted by this wording.

By way of conclusion, I would like to point out that the legal tender issue raised anew by Professor Timberlake in his article is particularly timely today, in light of the ongoing savings and loan crisis. We are assured that the S&L deposits formerly guaranteed by the now defunct Federal Savings and Loan Insurance Corporation are backed by the full faith and credit of the United States. Indeed, the Federal Reserve can print however many legal tender paper dollars as are required to cover any past and future losses the insolvent S&Ls might manage to incur. What the S&L deposits are ultimately backed by, therefore, is really the full faith and credit of the *Bureau of Engraving and Printing.*

Although there is no limit to the number of legal tender dollars the Fed can print, monetary theory tells us that there *is* a limit to their purchasing power. Although the government can unquestionably guarantee that depositors will get their dollars back it cannot guarantee that depositors will be able to *buy* with those dollars. If I may quote a recent paper of mine,

> Calling upon the Fed to make up for the past excesses of thrifts and banks would lead to a substantial one-time inflation. But counting on the Fed to write a blank check for all unconstrained future excesses could easily lead to a German-style hyperinflation.
>
> It is conventional to say that the Fed's implicit backing of the *FDIC* and *FSLIC* means that federally insured deposits are as safe as the dollar. It should be cause for great public concern that this translates to mean that the dollar is only as safe as our federally insured depository institutions.[8]

Notes

1. See Shaw, 1895/1967, chart facing p. 179.

2. In 1834 the mint price of gold was actually set to $20.69 . . . (a mint ratio of 16.002:1). This was adjusted in 1837 to $20.67 . . . (15.988:1), where it remained until 1933. The prior mint ratio had been exactly 15:1.

3. Even if the market ratio had been exactly 16:1 at the time of passage—as it had almost been just the year before—changing the ratio *ex post facto* would still have constituted an immediate partial expropriation of the existing rights of creditors, in terms of the more subtle option value implicit in the contract. The 1872 Court was wrong, however, to claim that this was a six percent expropriation, since debtors were fully entitled to use the silver option. Six percent is merely an upper bound on the value of the expropriation.

4. Ironically, the change in the mint ratio was intended to be a "hard money" measure: The pre-1834 *de facto* silver standard was a field day for bank notes, and in particular those of the despised Bank of the United States, since making payments in excess of $1000 in silver specie could easily induce a hernia. Circulating gold coins were seen as a hard money alternative to large denomination bank notes.

5. Restoring a full-bodied silver currency in a country as large as the U.S. would have raised the world price of silver, but it is beyond the scope of the present comment to predict by how much.

6. Paradoxically, the government did not default on at least the interest on its pre-existent or wartime bonds, but paid this in gold. It did default on $33 million of demand notes it had issued late in 1861 (Studentski and Krooss, pp. 142–3), as well as on its contractual obligations to pre-legal-tender enlistees. Since each legal tender act only authorized a specific quantity of legal tender notes, it could be argued that each subsequent issue was a new *ex post facto* expropriation of the obligation of private debt contracted in terms of the prior notes, and a new default on the government's own obligations to troops and other legal tender creditors.

7. Brough (p. 132) states that to the framers, "bills of credit" and "paper money" were synonymous, and that in their experience, this "represented what is known to us as non-convertible legal-tender paper."

8. McCulloch (1987), p. 248.

References

Breckinridge, S.P. *Legal Tender.* New York: Greenwood Press, 1969 [Originally Chicago: University of Chicago Press, 1903].

Brough, William. *The Natural Law of Money.* New York: Greenwood Press, 1969 [Originally New York: G.P. Putnam's Sons, 1896].

McCulloch, J. Huston. "The Ohio S&L Crisis in Retrospect: Implications for the Current Federal Deposit Insurance Crisis," *23rd Annual Confer-*

ence on Bank Structure and Competition. Federal Reserve Bank of Chicago, 1987.

Schaeffer, Claude F.A. *Le Palais Royal d'Ugarit,* vol. II. Paris: Imprimérie Nationale, 1957.

Shaw, W.A. *The History of Currency, 1252 to 1896.* New York: Augustus M. Kelley, 1967 [Originally London: Wilsons & Milne, 1896].

Studenski, Paul, and Herman E. Kroos. *Financial History of the United States.* New York: McGraw-Hill, 1952.

Constitutional and Ideological Influences on State Action: The Case of the First Bank of the United States

by Gregory B. Christainsen

The author would like to thank Jeffrey Rogers Hummel for leads to reference material.

> *While we rightly value a free marketplace in ideas, and while the production of sound ideas is necessary for the construction and sustenance of constitution of liberty, it is unfortunately the case that ideas, moreso than money, are not reliably guided by an invisible hand.*

Introduction

The Founding Fathers did not give the U.S. government the legal authority to issue *fiat* money, but, through the Federal Reserve, *fiat* money is issued.[1] They did not give the U.S. government the legal authority to charter corporations, but corporations have been chartered.[2]

Irrespective of the merits of *fiat* money and the chartering of corporations, such government actions raise questions about the role of constitutions in a politico-economic system. Do they offer only "parchment barriers" to State action that are of no practical consequence? If constitutions are more than parchment, what constraints do they really place on State power, especially in the area of money? If constitutionalism is not effective in limiting state power, is there anything that *is* effective besides the political mood of the time?

This paper will examine such questions with reference to the first Bank of the United States. The first Bank is of particular interest because strong arguments can be made that it should have been declared unconstitutional, and yet there was President George Washington signing its charter less than two-and-a-half years after the Constitution was ratified.

The paper will begin by briefly reviewing the nature of the first Bank, the part of the Constitution that was at issue when it was established, the conduct of the Bank, and the Supreme Court decision that legitimized its existence. The paper will then discuss the dynamics of the growth of government, focusing on the role of the State in monetary affairs and the influence of ideological factors in initiating and expanding this role. This discussion will, in turn, point to difficulties in analyzing the market in ideas, especially during *non-crisis* episodes such as the period just before the establishment of the first Bank.

The First Bank: A Retrospective

Chartered in 1791, the first Bank of the United States was an organization with the characteristics of both a private corporation and a public agency. It was a private corporation insofar as individual citizens owned 80 percent of its shares. It accepted deposits, made loans, and issued notes like an ordinary bank. Its obligations were binding and enforceable against the corporate organization, not the U.S. government. Its notes were not legal tender for any private debt nor for any debt of the U.S. government. Moreover, the bank's directors were personally liable for excessive debts incurred by the bank itself.

But the bank was "public" insofar as the U.S. government owned 20 percent of the shares. It was made the primary depository for funds of the federal government. Finally, its notes were made receivable in payment of federal taxes.

The Bank was the brainchild of Alexander Hamilton. Hamilton was, of course, one of the authors of *The Federalist*, which had sought to persuade the U.S. public to support the ratification of the Constitution. At the time the Constitution was being debated and ratified, anti-federalist sentiment was very strong. There was a concern that the proposed Constitution ceded too many powers to the national government.

To be sure, the Constitutional Convention saw the explicit refusal to empower the federal government in a variety of areas, including the granting of charters of incorporation, but the anti-federalists feared that, among other things, the proposed Constitution contained loose language that could be used to rationalize an expansion of centralized authority. In *The Federalist*, Hamilton and James Madison sought in particular to assuage fears about the "necessary and proper" clause of Article I. This clause said that Congress had the power to make all laws deemed "essential" for carrying out its enumerated powers. And since Congress was explicitly granted authority to do things such as "regulate commerce among the several states" and "provide for the general welfare," a loose construction of the necessary and proper clause could give Congress the authority to undertake myriad activities not spelled out in the Constitution.

To mollify the anti-federalists, Madison emphasized his view, expressed in *The Federalist* No. 45, that the powers of the federal government were to be "few and defined,"[3] and he went so far as to claim that the general welfare clause was inserted into the Constitution by accident: "inattention to the phraseology occasioned doubtless by its identity with the harmless character attached to it in the Instrument [the Articles of Confederation] from which it was borrowed."[4] In *The Federalist* No. 33 Hamilton denied that clauses like the necessary and proper clause opened the way for the emergence of omnipotent authority: "it may be affirmed with perfect confidence that the constitutional operation of the intended government would be precisely the same if these clauses were entirely obliterated as if they were repeated in every article."[5]

How then does one reconcile the Hamilton of *The Federalist* No. 33 with the Hamilton who proposed the creation of the first Bank? It cannot be done. Hamilton was, in fact, not a firm supporter of the Constitution. He wanted a strong central government all along, but knew that anti-federalist sentiment would easily defeat an explicit proposal along those lines.[6] He thus defined the Constitution as the best political compromise available at that time and then set out to subvert it after it was ratified. He was duplicitous. Madison, on the other hand, argued that the chartering of the first Bank was unconstitutional, as did Thomas Jefferson.

Unconstitutional or not, the first Bank is generally agreed to have conducted its affairs in a conservative and prudent manner.[7] The Bank certainly did not have the power to engage in open-market operations like a modern central bank, but it had the capacity to exert considerable influence over the money supply. The United States had only four other (state-chartered) commercial banks at the time of the first Bank's inception, and only the first Bank had a national charter. Within five years, however, the number of state-chartered banks had increased to 22. The first Bank's conservative practices with respect to note-issue, combined with its privileged position, encouraged the circulation of paper and the general expansion of the banking system beyond a specie base. This multiplier effect on the money supply in turn caused wholesale prices to increase by an average of about 72 percent from 1791–1796.[8]

The Bank could also influence the money supply by making loans directly to state banks or by varying the speed with which it cleared notes of state banks that had been presented to the first Bank for redemption. By the time the first Bank's charter came up for renewal (1811), this capacity to influence the money supply and thus the trade cycle was being openly touted as a consideration that bolstered the case for rechartering.[9]

The battle over rechartering was hard-fought, just as the struggle over the original bill had been. The first Bank survived two terms of a Jefferson presidency, largely due to the efforts of Jefferson's Treasury Secretary, Albert Gallatin, who thought the Bank convenient for the management of government finances.[10] By 1811, Gallatin was still Treasury Secretary, and got then-President James Madison also to side with the bank! Rechartering was strongly endorsed by most of the state banks as well. In the end, however, the Republicans in Congress were able to defeat Madison and the Federalists by a single vote in both chambers. The first Bank had to be dismantled.

But only five years later, a second Bank of the United States was chartered, and it was a challenge to its legitimacy by the state of Maryland that finally provoked the Supreme Court to rule on the constitutionality of federal charters of incorporation. The opinion by Chief Justice John Marshall in *McCulloch v. Maryland* (1819) surely ranks as one of the most important in the history of the United States.

In the debate over the establishment of the first Bank, Jefferson and Madison argued that the Constitution permits the U.S. government only those activities necessary to carry out its enumerated powers. Said Jefferson, ". . . the Constitution allows only the means which are *'necessary'* not those which are merely 'convenient' . . ."[11] Marshall did not concur, arguing that the necessary and proper clause could be interpreted more loosely: "Can we adopt that construction . . . which would impute to the farmers of that instrument, when granting these powers for the public good, the intentions of impeding their exercise by withholding a choice of means?"[12]

Marshall did not, in the part of his opinion just exerpted, consider the arguments of *The Federalist,* nor did he refer to the proceedings of the Constitutional Convention, in which a motion by Madison (!) to empower the U.S. government to grant charters of incorporation was rejected. Of course, Marshall was, like Hamilton, a well-known nationalist.

Marshall's effusive biographer, Albert Beveridge, later wrote that Marshall "thus rewrote the fundamental law of the nation" and that the country would be greatly benefitted by a liberal construction of the Constitution.[13] Such a construction was used in *Julliard v. Greenman* (1884), in which the Supreme Court ruled that a liberal view of Congress's borrowing authority, supported by the necessary and proper clause, justified the issuance of legal-tender notes, *i.e., fiat* money.

The Growth of Government Control: Ideological Dynamics

Government control over money, culminating in discretionary issues of fiat currency, is but one, albeit a crucial, aspect of the growth of state power. If the growth of state power is to be curbed, it is essential that the reasons for this growth be better understood. In recent years great strides have been made in this regard most notably by Robert Higgs in his book, *Crisis and Leviathan.*[14] In the present paper, Higgs's analysis of crisis periods in expanding State power is supplemented by a consideration of non-crisis episodes, like that of the first Bank, and a consideration of anthropological factors affecting the rise and fall of ideologies.

The analysis deliberately relegates special interests to a secondary role in the process of government growth. While special interests are certainly important insofar as they can benefit from, and are thereby encouraged to support, State power, it is argued that ideological factors are primary. That is, some collection of respectable beliefs is needed to rationalize self-seeking interest-group activity on behalf of the growth of the State, or else a group's concerns will be more widely dismissed as naked greed. Likewise, a *change* in ideology is needed to delegitimize such groups and break their hold on power.

Finally, precisely what constitutes a group's self-interest—as perceived by either those inside or outside the group—depends on some set of beliefs, *i.e.*, an ideology:

> Though men be much governed by interest, yet even interest itself, and all human affairs, are entirely governed by *opinion.*[15]

The central argument of Higgs's book is that State power ratchets upward as a result of ideological changes during crisis periods such as wars or depressions. Prior to the crisis period, some citizens may put forth an ideology advocating the expansion of government into new areas, and certain interest groups may embrace the ideas either for their own sake or as a rationalization for a narrower self-interest. But the ideas may be those of only a minority. As a result of the crisis, however, there is a tendency to turn toward a central authority, *i.e.*, government, to solve problems. A change in the dominant ideology occurs, and the previously unpopular idea becomes legitimized and enacted. Once the idea gets enacted, a *growing* number of interest groups come to benefit from it. An "Iron Triangle" of private interests, politicians, and bureaucrats becomes entrenched.

Meanwhile, the ordinary citizen gets used to the expansion of government control and comes to accept it. After awhile people may even have difficulty comprehending how the country ever got along without the new government powers.

One additional step is necessary to complete the ideological shift and to ratchet upward the size of government: At some point the expansion of State power must be ratified by the Supreme Court. Ratification is not an early feat, for the Constitution's historical meaning can be quite useful to those who wish to halt the growth of government; it can serve as an ideological rallying point in gaining the support of citizens who are normally apolitical or who might otherwise "free ride" while others attempt to thwart those of a more statist persuasion.

Some of the early New Deal measures such as the National Industrial Recovery Act were thus stricken down by the Court. If, however, the Court is already statist enough, or if the time is one of severe crisis, the ideological forces that can be mobilized by appealing to Constitutional parchment may not be strong enough to contain all centralist urges.

Thus, the crisis of the Great Depression was the key step in a long-run process whereby Social Security, previously rejected as "inappropriate for the federal government," eventually became a "sacred cow." And it was the crisis of the Civil War that led to the issuance and legitimization of *fiat* money in the form of the so-called greenbacks.

What makes the establishment of the first Bank noteworthy is that it was not a "crisis" measure. To be sure, Hamilton saw certain matters—debt administration, a national industrial policy—in which he thought such a bank could be helpful, but there was no acute feeling, as there was during the Civil War or the Depression, that the survival of the nation was an issue.

There are, therefore, more subtle mechanisms at work in the growth of government besides those of crises. Public choice theory can help to articulate the nature of these mechanisms, but it must again be combined with an analysis of ideological factors.

The public choice aspect of the analysis can help to account for the fact that something is being done, *e.g.,* the establishment of the first Bank, that runs counter not only to the "original intent" of the Constitution, but runs counter to ideological currents in the general population, *e.g.,* anti-federalism. The analysis involves the fact that the citizenry has general ideological dispositions, but is perhaps "rationally ignorant" about specific issues. That is, the likelihood of any single individual's vote deciding an election, let alone public policy on a specific issue, is minuscule, so it may not be rational for individual citizens to keep abreast of political controversies. Only if it possesses an ideological fervor that is strong enough to offset the countervailing incentives to set back and free ride will the general citizenry become mobilized. Other issues may be more important in the next election. Alternatively, the citizenry may be totally apathetic.

It is, however, *always* in the interest of certain pressure groups to keep abreast of issues and to try to influence the political process. And if the ideology prevailing within certain elites (politicians, interest groups, intellectuals) differs from that of the general populace, it may be possible to push measures through that would otherwise fail. The final steps in this process consist of, respectively, Supreme Court justices with lifetime tenure who share the elite ideology, and ratchet effect. The justices may, for example, rationalize violations of the Constitution's "original intent" by positing the Constitution as "a living document" that must respond to "the fundamental aspirations of the times." If the elite ideology is victorious in the Supreme Court, popular and political opposition may gradually subside, and people may eventually come to view as "natural" an activity that might have previously been viewed as indefensible. This is the ratchet aspect, which also involves the emergence of the "Iron Triangle" mentioned earlier.

In the case of the first Bank, it must be said again that the Constitutional Convention explicitly rejected the federal government's having a chartering power, and that not only Madison, but Hamilton espoused positions in *The Federalist* that were incompatible with its establishment. Moreover, anti-federalist sentiment was widespread among the general public. But the idea of a national bank had been discussed for quite some time, most notably by Alexander Hamilton and Robert Morris, and federalist and more-thoroughgoing centralist philosophies were more popular among elites than the general public. Thus, while a narrow self-interest was partly involved, it should be noted that the legislation establishing the first Bank passed both houses of Congress by 2–1 votes. Those votes were heavily influenced by a nationalist ideology which existed among the elite group of people, especially among representatives and senators from the North and East.

When the issue finally reached the Supreme Court, John Marshall, a nationalist, happened to be there and helped to legitimize not only the chartering of national banks, but a loose interpretation of the necessary and proper clause that persists in constitutional law to the present day.

Of course, strong ideological counteroffensives against State action can occasionally score victories, and so it was with the campaigns to terminate both the first and second Banks. From a long-run perspective, however, those victories do not look as significant as they did at the time. Time marches on. A crisis, the Civil War, eventually occurred. *Fiat* money was issued and legitimized, in part by citing Marshall's decision in *McCulloch v. Maryland* as a precedent. The National Bank Acts were passed. The failure of government control over money and banking in turn sparked other crises, most notably the Great Depression, which led to still more State control. A ratchet is indeed a good metaphor to use in depicting the process.

The Anthropology of Socialist Ideology

It remains to be explained why there is so often a turning to central authority in crisis situations, and why certain elites are especially prone to turn to a central authority to solve problems even in non-crisis situations.

One can make intriguing arguments that the tendencies have a genetic basis. Hundreds of thousands of years ago in primitive hunting banks, it appears that certain genetically preselected males, referred to as alpha males, were a necessary condition for the survival of the band's members. The alpha males were innately inclined to be leaders, and others were inclined to follow them—not so much because of coercive threats from the alphas, but in a more consensual arrangement.

The economics of the band were such that, in such a primitive environment, the objectives of the group's members were agreed-to and well-defined. They were focused on food and other essentials. There was not so much of a Hayekian knowledge problem as faces today's decision-makers working within an international division of labor. Hayek's emphasis on the importance of knowledge of "circumstances of time and place" was, of course, crucial as the members of the group spread out in search of provisions, but the order of the group was far less complex than the "extended order" (as Hayek calls it) in which we live today. In the primitive environment, then, the best way for the group to economize on the transactions costs involved in its endeavors may well have been to exist as a single firm under "Japanese-style" consensual (or "clan") management.[16] The output of this firm could then be shared among its members. According to Hayek:

> The common pursuit of a perceived physical common object under the direction of the alpha male was as much a condition of its continued existence as the assignment of different shares in the prey to the different members according to their importance for the survival of the band.[17]

One might then argue that, despite tremendous changes over millennia, the genetic factor is still in us, with certain humans (today's alphas) wanting to be authorities and others (the flock) all too ready to surrender to them ("the sanction of the victim"). The impulses manifest themselves particularly strongly during crisis periods because people feel, perhaps unconsciously, their survival to be in question, and that was the basis for the existence of the genetic factor in the first place.

It has been argued in the anthropology literature, however, that the genetic theory may be mistaken. According to this literature, there was a point in the genetic evolution of man when the alpha factor diminished. On this view the phenomenon to be explained over the last few tens of thousands of years is, in fact, cultural rather than genetic, but the rationale for the observed cultural phenomenon is similar to that for the earlier genetic phenomenon. Both have their basis in an evolutionary process in which human survival is felt to be at issue.[18]

A related point is that a continued harping on the role of genetics vs. culture is a secondary matter, and that genetic and cultural factors interact in complex ways without our always being able to discern precisely which factors were responsible for a particular phenomenon.[19] A still-common belief is that "genetic" means "something we can't do anything about" and that "cultural" means "alterable by acts of will." But many genetically-determined eyesight problems can be corrected by eyeglasses, whereas many culturally-determined traits are transmitted to people unconsciously at an early age and may be deeply rooted in society (as disillusioned communists discovered).

This last point is very important in the case of money. As will be argued later, a shift in the ideological consensus in the direction of free banking and less government must involve more than rational arguments. An entrenched *culture* is involved in addition to any genetic factors.

A cultural view on the emergence of State control goes something like this: Rebelliousness notwithstanding, during infancy most children learn to have a certain respect for coercive authority. Historically, various groups nevertheless existed without government. When hostilities occurred as groups encountered one another, however, the market in military services was often a natural monopoly. In other words, it was efficient to vest an authority with coercive powers within a hierarchy as conquest or defense was carried out. As Hume theorized, government—whose essence is a legitimized dominance over a society's coercive power—thus arose out of war.[20]

The authority may then remain as a monarchical form of government even after war has receded. It does this by winning the obedience of the masses through a mixture of force and consent, a consent which arose during the preceding conflict as the authority established himself, and whose longevity depends on the authority's subsequent performance.

Hume theorized on the other hand that a *devolution* of authority could well occur, *e.g.,* from a monarchical to a republican form of government,[21] if an authority so misbehaved as to engender an ideological shift away from the very institution he embodied. In other words, *some* incidents or "crises" can lead to a loss of authoritarian power. This kind of process, it turns out, is probably the key to any hoped-for change from central banking to free banking.

Following such a view, the collapse of well-armed, highly-authoritarian governments in Eastern Europe in 1989 was quite understandable, but, as explained below, those whose disenchantment with Western welfare states is such that they would prefer a libertarian State or even a stateless society will probably have to be more patient. One reason why they will have to be more patient is the well-known phenomenon of cognitive dissonance. This phenomenon implies that brute argumentation by a minority of activists is not likely to be sufficient to overturn a dominant ideology. It may not be sufficient because one of the functions of an ideology is to economize on information costs in such a way as to filter out uncomfortable data presented to the mind and preserve in the individual a sense of security and self-esteem. Thus, evidence to challenge a strongly-held point of view may quite literally not be heard.

For example, I reject out of hand any stories I hear involving references to ghosts even though I have not carefully analyzed all of the allegedly pro-ghost evidence. My anti-ghost ideology lowers my knowledge costs by allowing me to casually dismiss these "threatening" data. Hume argued that such economizing exists for even our most fundamental attitudes—the belief in the existence of matter, the belief in the uniformity of natural laws such as the law of gravity, etc.—and that these attitudes have as their ultimate basis their survival value. More than a century before the appearance of Darwin's *Origin of Species*, Hume wrote that man could not endure if he endlessly played the role of the skeptic who suspends judgment on all matters where there is room for doubt:

> [The skeptic] must acknowledge, if he will acknowledge anything, that . . . were his principles universally and steadily to prevail—[a]ll

... would ... cease ... and men remain in a total lethargy, til ... nature, unsatisfied, put an end to their miserable existence.[22]

As regards the dangers of skepticism for survival, there is, however, an important difference between a skepticism that says, "I doubt the existence of gravity on Thursday mornings," and a skepticism that says, "I doubt the value of free markets." Errors regarding fundamental features of the physical world such as gravitational pull may impinge directly on the survival chances of an individual, whereas errors on matters of political economy may have potential consequences that are more collective in nature. That is, a skepticism about the value of free markets is not as likely to do serious harm to an individual as a skepticism about the dangers of jumping out of a window. Any harm done by depreciating free markets may occur only as a result of *many* people doing so, leading to the decline of a whole society. The individual critic of free markets, perhaps a tenured professor or an unelected judge, may or may not suffer. He may even be garlanded for his "progressive" views. Add in cognitive dissonance, and one can see how errors on matters of political ideology, as opposed to errors about mundane aspects of the physical world, can endure for an extended period.

The establishment and sustenance of an ideology conducive to a free and prosperous society is thus akin to an enormous public-good problem.[23] Only when the dominant rival ideology has been thoroughly demolished by events so as to shake the confidence and status of large numbers of stalwart believers is a freedom-enhancing alternative likely to gain influence. A welfare-statist ideology, for all its defects, cannot be said to have been so demolished. Its demolition might require, *e.g.,* the continued economic decline of Sweden relative to other developed countries, and at least some of Sweden's stalwart defenders will have to admit that the country's super-welfare-statist institutional structure is to blame for its decline.

Another relevant feature of the mind that serves to economize on information costs is its tendency to transfer a disposition acquired to deal with one set of problems to the challenge posed by a somewhat similar, but not identical, set of problems. Only later experience can reveal whether the scientific hypothesis implicit in the transfer—*i.e.,* that the problem-similarities justified the transfer—was borne out.[24] Economizing on information costs is involved in the fact that, by definition, the later experience did not exist at the time the organism *had* to respond to a particular stimulus. For example, when I first traveled to the Orient I did not know for sure if I should shake hands upon meeting people. There were information costs. I initially just transferred a hand-shaking disposition developed in the United States, but soon discovered that in the Orient I should shake hands in some situations, but bow in others.

Human beings have likewise developed a disposition, perhaps rightly, to turn to a central authority in certain situations perceived as survival-threatening, and this disposition has often been transferred to other situations perceived, perhaps wrongly, as crises, or even to situations in which almost everyone agrees there is no crisis but simply "a problem."

Similarly, human beings have learned how to consciously manipulate objects in their environment—*e.g.,* tools for eating or for building shelter—in order to overcome individual survival problems, and this capacity may be (wrongly) transferred to the attempt to deal with "social" problems. People may again think that a conscious arrangement of the elements involved is required for there to be a desirable order, and they may not appreciate the crucial distinction between an individual's planning of his activities and socialistic planning.

Two other sources of socialist ideology are worth mentioning at this point. One source, discussed by Hayek,[25] was the rise of large corporations as a major force in market economics. This rise took place from about the midpoint of the nineteenth century until well past the midpoint of the twentieth century. In such organizations, as in government, resources are allocated primarily by administrative orders, and employees who do not deal with external market conditions may not understand or appreciate the workings of a price system based on private property. They then tend to view all resource allocation issues as questions of administration. And centralized administration of a whole economy constitutes socialism. The phenomenon can thereby be viewed as a subset of the disposition-transfer problem; the disposition to allocate resources within the firm by administrative orders is transferred to society as a whole. This particular source of socialist ideology has probably waned, however, as smaller, high-technology and service firms have become increasingly important.

The other source of socialist ideology worth mentioning here has been the death in a reverential belief in a deity among certain groups. Human, or at least cultural, survival probably requires that people have a sense of meaningfulness as they lead their lives. In primitive societies, the struggle for survival itself does not allow much opportunity to question the significance of one's existence. Even in a non-primitive society the presence of a close-knit community may generate reciprocal expectations among people and sense of purpose. In a society that is both affluent and mobile, however, a belief in a God or God-like figure and perhaps an afterlife may be necessary to lend meaning to one's efforts and to rationalize life's inevitable setbacks. Absent poverty, absent strong community ties, and absent a belief in deity, why should I care much about what I do? I'm just a speck in the universe who is likely to depart from the scene less than 50 years from now. Of course, if history is building toward earthly salvation for man, and if I can participate significantly in history then maybe my life has meaning after all. Socialism, at least in the past, has offered this redemptive quality to intellectuals and others who have been alienated from their societies.[26] Capitalism has never had such a mythic appeal among as many people. It will be interesting to see if overt religions experience a revival among educated people as the messianic quality of socialism continues to fade. Perhaps a messianic environmentalism will suffice.

The foregoing discussion still does not explain why some people, most notably members of certain elites, have been more likely to develop a centralist, statist ideology than others. Professors at major universities, for example, vote overwhelmingly for politicians from the Democratic Party. A socialist or social democrat might like to think that such tendencies have simply reflected the activities of bright people who have self-consciously arrived at certain insights, but what follows is an alternative view: people who specialize in the production and transmission of ideas—intellectuals, literati, the media, government officials—are likely to have a comparative advantage in understanding and articulating explicit chains of deductive reasoning pertaining to relatively abstract subjects. Such people are likely to respect individuals and institutions to the degree that they are perceived to conform to this rationalist proclivity. Relatively inarticulate people who blindly, albeit sincerely, adhere to traditional norms of conduct may be generally less well thought of, and institutions whose basis is difficult to articulate may come under attack.

By contrast, institutions with a well-understood and clearly-articulated rationale, a rationale whose general worthiness no one challenges, may hold the upper hand. Thus, the existence of a central bank such as the Federal Reserve, staffed with well-educated people and charged with the mission of "stabilization" and "fighting inflation" (as if inflation were a disease that had just *somehow* sprung up) may have broad intellectual support even though the bank's actual performance may be quite questionable. Suggestions for "reforming" the Federal Reserve will be viewed as "constructive" while proposals to eliminate it will be viewed as reckless and irresponsible. Proposals to have the bank consciously try to enhance "stability" are likely to be especially appealing to those who put a premium on security, such as professors or government officials who have deliberately bypassed other benefits in order to pursue careers that offer the prospect of tenure.

An opponent of the Federal Reserve who is nevertheless committed to rationalist ideals thus has the formidable job of articulating the case for alternative institutions that might conceivably *end up* producing greater economic stability, but whose most obvious objective is to maximize profits. This tax is enormously difficult, as supporters of free banking have discovered. The task requires expertise in standard economic theory, the workings of the banking industry, monetary history, the pros and cons of Keynesian arguments, the social role of transferable property rights, and even as recent discussions have shown, a sophisticated understanding of game theory.[27] A fundamental part of the task is to demonstrate the importance of *inarticulate* knowledge (*e.g.,* informal knowledge of consumer preferences and of idiosyncratic locations for businesses) and to demonstrate why this knowledge is more likely to be uncovered and used under decentralized, free market arrangements than under central government control.[28] And this argumentation must be conveyed to human beings afflicted with cognitive dissonance. The fact that intellectuals such as professors and judges often depend on government for salaries, grants, and prestige only exacerbates the situation.

A belief that purely intellectual discussion can overturn an ideology such as central banking itself amounts to an ideology for which there is scant intellectual support. A more plausible view is that defenders of free banking can, by force of rational argument, make limited inroads in academia and banking institutions, but that a triumph of free banking would have to await a crisis that somehow completely discredited any kind of nationalized banking authority. Ill-behaved autocrats thus paved the way of democratic republics, and horrific behavior by central banks is the best hope for free banking. A hyperinflation or a depression universally-recognized as attributable to monetary mismanagement might do the job, but such happenings are not on the immediate horizon, at least in the countries where the dominant central banking ideology has its stalwart defenders.

Summary

We have thus seen that several factors may contribute to the socialist ideology that is at the heart of the idea of central banking. The most important of these would seem to be: (1) a propensity to bow to an authority during many kinds of episodes perceived as crises; and, more relevant to the case of the first Bank, (2) what we have termed the disposition-transfer problem. Ideas and ideologies based on (1) and/ or (2) may be mistaken, but reforming them may be extremely difficult given cognitive dissonance, which is in general necessary for human survival, and something akin to a public-good problem in getting people to respect a philosophy of liberty.[29] The difficulties are compounded by the fact that members of certain elites are self-selected for espousing a form of rationalism whereby institutions and customs are not viewed favorably unless they possess features which bear an identifiable and seemingly-logical relationship to objectives in a way that can be clearly (and consciously) articulated.

Conclusion

The expansion of State control over money has been ratified by what can be called political judging, and as one of contemporary America's greatest legal scholars has written, political judging is systemic.[30] The potential for political judging was built into the original constitutional structure, whose outlines were the product of ideological struggle and compromise. The *de facto* constitutional structure then shifted over time as ideological struggle continued, court decisions had to be made, and an overtly statist ideology triumphed. The potential for political judging was realized.

Not only is political judging systemic; the underlying ideological factors are also systemic in that their development is influenced by events in (somewhat) understandable ways. These events were, for their part, influenced by previous ideological struggle.

On one level, the formation, propagation, and institutionalization of ideologies can be viewed as acts of free will. On another level, however, the path of ideological development has been to some degree predetermined in that members of certain elites are self-selected for having a proclivity for rational thought, and this proclivity interacts with events (systematically) to shape elite attitudes toward public policy matters. Only shattering events that discredit a misapplied rationalism may be capable of shattering a dominant elite ideology. As shown by the case of Eastern Europe, the general public can sometimes be relied on to help counter ruling elites, but especially in noncrisis times, most of the general public may be rationally disinterested in taking action.

So it was that Alexander Hamilton, a handsome and brilliant lawyer, though perhaps not a genetically preselected alpha male, carried the day as a nationalist elite overrode anti-federalist sentiment and rational arguments by Jefferson and Madison on behalf of constitutional parchment. The result the first Bank, was the first step toward the creation of the Federal Reserve. A bullet from Aaron Burr finally shattered Hamilton, but not his ideology—or for that matter, John Marshall.

And so it may be that today's supporters of free banking must not only make rational arguments, but, at the same time, see the silver lining in any future financial problems that await us. While such problems may lead to still more State control—as in an all-European central bank, or the reregulation of American banking—they at the same time offer the best hope of shattering the mindset of central banking's stalwart supporters and breaking once-and-for-all the historical ratchet of a statist approach to monetary affairs.

Notes

1. Gregory B. Christainsen, *"Fiat* Money and the Constitution: A Historical Review," in Thomas D. Willet (ed.), *Political Business Cycles* (Durham, NC: Duke University Press, 1988), pp. 242–434.

2. Bernard H. Siegan, *The Supreme Court's Constitution* (New Brunswick, NJ: Transaction Books, 1987), chap. 1.

3. Alexander Hamilton, John Jay, and James Madison, *The Federalist* (Washington, DC: Robert B. Luce, Inc., 1976), p. 303.

4. Max Farrand (ed.), *Records of the Federal Convention*, vol. 3 (New Haven: Yale University Press, 1973), p. 486.

5. Hamilton, Jay, and Madison, *op. cit.*, pp. 198–199.

6. Henry Cabot Lodge, *Alexander Hamilton* (Boston: Houghton, Mifflin and Company, 1886), p. 64.

84   CONSTITUTIONAL AND IDEOLOGICAL INFLUENCES

7. For more detailed treatments of the first Bank's conduct and the constitutional controversy, see the following: John Thom Holdsworth, *The First Bank of the United States* (Washington, DC: National Monetary Commission, 1910); Henry Mark Holzer, *Government's Money Monopoly* (New York: Books in Focus, 1981), chaps. 4–6; Benjamin J. Klebaner, *Commercial Banking in the United States: A History* (Hinsdale, IL: Dryden Press, 1974); John Jay Knox, *A History of Banking in the United States* (New York: Bradford Rhodes, 1900); Burton Alva Konkle, *Thomas Willing and the First American Financial System* (Philadelphia: University of Pennsylvania Press, 1937); John R. Nelson, Jr., *Liberty and Property: Political Economy and Policy Making in the New Nation, 1789–1812* (Baltimore: Johns Hopkins University Press, 1978); Richard H. Timberlake, *The Origins of Central Banking in the United States* (Cambridge: Harvard University Press, 1978), chap. 1; and James O. Wettereau, "New Light on the First Bank of the United States," *Pennsylvania Magazine of History and Biography* 61 (July 1937: 263–85).

8. U.S. Bureau of the Census, *Historical Statistics of the United States, Colonial Times to 1970* (Washington, DC: U.S. Government Printing Office, 1975), p. .202.

9. Timberlake, *op. cit.*, p. 10

10. *Ibid.*, pp. 10–11. Under Gallatin, the government did, however, sell off its shares in the bank.

11. James Truslow Adams (ed.), *Jeffersonian Principles and Hamiltonian Principles* (Boston: Little, Brown and Company, 1928), p. 25.

12. 17 U.S. (4 Wheat) 408 (1819).

13. Siegan, *op. cit.*, p. 15.

14. Robert Higgs, *Crisis and Leviathan: Critical Episodes in the Growth of American Government* (New York: Oxford University Press, 1987).

15. David Hume, "Whether the British Government Inclines More to Absolute Monarchy, or to a Republic," 1741. Published in D. Hume, *Essays: Moral, Political and Literary*, Eugene F. Miller, ed. (Indianapolis: Liberty Classics, 1985), p. 51.

16. For thorough discussions of the factors influencing the boundaries and management of firms, see Oliver E. Williamson, *Markets and Hierarchies* (New York: Free Press, 1975) and *The Economic Institutions of Capitalism* (New York: Free Press, 1985).

17. F.A. Hayek, *New Studies in Philosophy, Politics, Economics, and the History of Ideas* (Chicago: University of Chicago Press, 1978), p. 59.

18. For more detailed treatments, see the following: J. Desmond Clark, "Early Human Occupation of African Savanna Environments," in D.A. Harris (ed.), *Human Ecology in Savanna Environments* (New York: Academic Press, 1980), pp. 41–71; W.H. Durham, "Overview: Optimal Foraging Analysis in Human Ecology," in B. Winterhalder and E.A. Smith (eds.), *Hunter-Gartherer Foraging Strategies: Ethnographic and Archaeological Analyses*

(Chicago: University of Chicago Press, 1981), pp. 218–231; G.L. Isaac, "The Food-Sharing Behavior of Protohuman Hominids," *Scientific American* 238 (4): 90–108; G.L. Isaac, "The Archaeological Evidence for the Activities of Early Hominids," in C.J. Jolly (ed.), *Early Hominids of Africa* (New York: St. Martin's Press, 1978), pp. 219–254; J.R. Krebs, "Optimal Foraging: Decision Rules for Predators," in J.R. Krebs and N.B. Davies (eds.), *Behavioral Ecology* (Oxford: Basil Blackwell, 1978), J.R. Krebs, "Foraging Strategies and Their Social Significance," in P. Marler and J.G. Vandenbergh (eds.), *Handbook of Behavioral Neurobiology* Volume 3: *Social Behavior and Communication* (New York: Plenum Press, 1989), pp. 225–270; and Jeffrey A. Kurland and Stephen J. Beckerman, "Optimal foraging and Hominid Evolution: Labor and Reciprocity," *American Anthropologist* 87 (March 1985): 73–93.

19. Hayek, *op. cit.*, chap. 20.

20. David Hume, "Of the Origin of Government," 1777. Published in D. Hume, *op. cit.*, pp. 39–40.

21. David Hume, *A Treatise of Human Nature*, L.A. Selby-Bigge ed. Second edition revised by P.H. Nidditch (Oxford: Oxford University Press, 1978), p. 540. (Volumes I and II originally published in 1739. Volume 3 originally published in 1740.)

22. David Hume, *An Enquiry Concerning Human Understanding* (LaSalle, IL: Open Court, 1966), pp. 178–179. (Originally published in 1748).

23. The problem is actually more difficult than a public-good problem. The standard public-good of neoclassical economic theory involves a situation in which an individual genuinely values something—*i.e.*, he can at least be said to have a latent demand curve for the good—but realizes that if others will pay for the item, he may be able to free-ride and still receive benefits. He thus withholds his latent demand. In the market for ideas, on the other hand, individuals who fail to respect a philosophy of liberty may not be deliberately free-riding on the efforts of others. These individuals may simply not understand or appreciate a philosophy of liberty. They are therefore not withholding a latent demand. There is no demand there to withhold.

24. See F.A. Hayek, *The Sensory Order: An Inquiry into the Foundations of Theoretical Psychology* (Chicago: University of Chicago Press, 1952).

25. F.A. Hayek, *Knowledge, Evolution and Society* (London: Adam Smith Institute, 1983). p. 40.

26. See Paul Hollander, *Political Pilgrims* (New York: Oxford University Press, 1981), chap. 9.

27. Lawrence H. White and George A. Selgin, "The Evolution of a Free Banking System," *Economic Inquiry* 25 (Summer 1987), pp. 446–447.

28. See Don Lavoie, *National Economic Planning: What is Left?* (Cambridge, MA: Ballinger Publishing Company, 1985), chap. 3. See also his "Appendix: Tacit Knowledge and the Revolution in the Philosophy of Science" in the same book.

29. Supra note 23.

30. Robert H. Bork, *The Tempting of America: The Political Seduction of the Law* (New York: Free Press, 1990), p. 7.

Comment

by Jeffrey Rogers Hummel

Christainsen has written the kind of challenging and encompassing paper upon which commenting is difficult, especially commenting succinctly. He ranges freely from economics to anthropology, bringing in such seemingly arcane concepts as "cognitive dissonance" and "alpha males;" he seeks universals behind such disparate events as the establishment of the first Bank of the United States in 1791 and the collapse of the Iron Curtain in 1990; and all this while he tackles such age-old conundrums as heredity versus environment or the origin of the State. Nearly every topic he touches merits many commentaries longer than his original paper.

Although what I take to be Christainsen's unifying motif—understanding the mechanism of social and political change—intrigues me greatly, I will have to restrain myself. My comments will focus more narrowly upon both the first U.S. Bank and the U.S. Constitution. They are merely a few random but concrete ramblings inspired as I perused the paper.

Let me begin with the United States Bank. Christainsen studiously avoids calling it a central bank. He instead describes it as "an organization with the characteristics of both a private corporation and a public agency." This approach averts some tough questions, questions that some might view as purely semantic. But it obscures Christainsen's *economic* objections to the national bank (in contrast to his *constitutional* objections). Does the first U.S. Bank truly constitute government intervention into the market, as Christainsen implies?

Recall that the bank received its charter before any of the states had enacted general incorporation laws. Thus, all corporations during this period, whether chartered by the state or national governments, had "characteristics of both a private corporation and a public agency." Viewed from this perspective, Congress's economic misdeed may not have been that it chartered an institution that competed with state banks. Rather, its misdeed may have been to charter only a single institution of this sort. Indeed, unlike state-chartered banks, the first and later the second Banks of the United States could engage in interstate branch banking. Imagine how differently American monetary history might have turned out if Congress had moved toward general incorporation at this time, rather than waiting until the Civil War, when the country had become addicted to unit banking.

I am not introducing this counterfactual speculation to defend either the first or second U.S. Banks. I share Christainsen's economic opposition to the national bank, but only because I believe the institution qualifies as a central bank. Whether one agrees, of course, depends on how one defines the term "central bank." A common definition includes only agencies that enjoy a monopoly on issuing bank notes. This definition is so restricted, however, that it even excludes the early Federal Reserve. After all, not until 1935 were the last national bank notes retired.

An alternative definition is a bank that has received some exclusive government privilege, granted to no other bank. Historically, a monopoly on note issue has become the most frequent central bank privilege, but not the only one. Exclusive privileges enjoyed by the first Bank included a Congressional pledge not to charter any competing institutions, the consequent monopoly on interstate branch banking, government subsidization of its capital, the acceptance of its notes by the national government, particularly as payment for taxes, and its utilization as the primary depository for government funds.

Privileges can differ in number, nature, and significance: and they create a wide spectrum of central banks, varying between primarily private institutions with a few government powers, such as the first Bank of the United States, to primarily government powers, such as the first Bank of the United States, to primarily government institutions with vestigal private features, such as the Federal Reserve System. This definition permits us to discern not only the gross differences between the first Bank and the Federal Reserve but also subtle differences between the first Bank and the second Bank.

Although often treated as identical except for size, the first Bank was marginally more private and less public than the second. The national government could own up to one-fifth of the equity of both institutions, but only the second Bank had any designated directors chosen directly by the President (with Senate approval), whereas the President had discretionary authority to sell the government's stock in the first Bank. Only the second Bank paid the government a bonus, of $1.5 million, for its charter. And the government appears to have used state-chartered banks as alternative depositories more extensively under the first Bank, which was not explicitly designated a government depository in its charter, than under the second, which was. Congress also had some supervisory authority over the second Bank, most notably to examine records, whereas it had none over the first. Unsurprisingly, the second Bank was more politicized, from the appointment of William Jones, as undistinguished but loyal Republican politician, as its first President through President Andrew Jackson's famous war against it. Moreover, the management of the second Bank appears to have been less prudent and more erratic than that of the first.[1]

A recognition of the first Bank's character as a central bank may have current policy implications. Milton Friedman and many others have criticized the Federal Reserve's political independence, yet this remains its primary private feature. Perhaps the lesson of the first and second Banks is that the Fed would have greater incentives to exercise monetary restraint if it was more private, rather than less. We do know that the worst inflations in United States history, those of the American Revolution and the Civil War, both in the Confederacy and Union, occurred through the direct issue of *fiat* money without central banking at all. In other words, political control over the money stock was supreme, unattenuated by any private features. This conclusion is also consistent with a few studies that compare the inflation rates of various nations with the degree of political independence of their central banks.[2]

One last point before I leave central banking. While admitting that the first Bank could "exert considerable influence over the money supply," Christainsen observes that "[t]he bank certainly did not have the power to engage in open-market operations" (p. 4). As I interpret the concept, an "open-market operation" occurs when a central bank exchanges its own liabilities for financial instruments on the open market, as opposed to its direct transactions with the government, commercial banks, and other depositories. Open-market transactions can involve the purchase or sale of either a private or a government financial instrument. For instance, the Fed has engaged in open-market operations with both the government's Treasury bills and private bankers' acceptances.

If we grant that the first Bank was a central bank, then open-market operations, by this definition, become its primary transactions. Most of the time it competed with other banks on the open market. Only when the U.S. Bank loaned its notes or deposits directly to state-chartered banks was it doing something else.

Christainsen might object that the first Bank's dealings with the general public and the government were not true open-market operations because its liabilities were not high-powered money. But even should we confine the concept of open-market operations to those central bank liabilities that can become bank reserves, this objection is still problematic. We have already pointed out that the first Bank's notes could be employed to pay national taxes. The monetary significance of this privilege can be gauged by the fact that it was the way the Confederacy put its bills of credit into circulation during the Civil War. Unlike the Union, the Confederate government never made its paper money legal tender for private debts.

The first Bank predated the era of legally mandated reserve requirements, and I know of no investigation of to what extent, if any, state banks and their customers willingly accepted the notes of the United States Bank as reserves. We do know, however, that the period of the first Bank was one in which the official U.S. mint ratio had undervalued gold with respect to silver. Insofar as gold coins could not circulate at a premium above their face value (and they legally could not do so for taxes), the mint ratio brought into operation Gresham's Law and encouraged the circulation of silver over gold. But silver was suitable for small transactions, and so the mint ratio may also have stimulated the circulation of U.S. Bank notes over gold for large transactions.

In fact, forty years later, Senator Thomas Hart "Bullion" Benton of Missouri claimed that Secretary of the Treasury Alexander Hamilton had deliberately established the 1792 mint ratio at different than the market ratio in order to achieve that very result. He had little direct evidence, I hasten to add. Somewhat more plausibly, Benton further maintained that it was the Bank's political influence that killed the many Congressional bills introduced subsequently to correct the mint ratio.[3]

My second thread of comments relates to Christainsen's reflections upon the politics of the national bank. He is intrigued by the bank's receiving its charter during a non-crisis period of American history. The work of Robert Higgs argues that crises as war and depression cause most increases in the size and reach of modern governments. Consequently, the first Bank appears an anomaly.

But can we really say that the early administration of President George Washington was free of crisis? If we do, the Bank of the United States becomes only one small measure in a gigantic surge in State power. The recent ratification of the Constitution had just established for the first time within the United States an independent executive and a central taxing authority. The Federalists, who controlled the new government, imposed a mildly protectionist tariff, tonnage duties that discriminated in favor of American merchants, and a variety of internal taxes. Alexander Hamilton's Treasury Department sprang out of nowhere to become the government's largest, employing 2,000 customs officials, revenue agents, and postmasters, who swarmed across the country, impressing upon the population the central government's grandeur.

The Washington Administration also used trouble with the Indians in the Northwest territory to justify a new army of four thousand regulars. Two militia acts etched the principle of universal military obligation into national statute. Any doubts about the national government's newly acquired prerogatives were dramatically dispelled in 1794, when it smashed the Whiskey Tax Rebellion in western Pennsylvania. For this demonstration, Washington drafted from four state militias no less than 12,950 men—more than he had usually commanded throughout the entire Revolution.

Just to add monetary icing to the Statist cake, Congress, in addition to chartering a bank, also established a permanent government mint. It seems that more than the first Bank cries out for an explanation. Of course, that explanation might be that there *was* a crisis after all. Contemporaries certainly thought so, and not just in the mythical sense, taught in every school book: that is, that the United States was going through a "critical period" between the American Revolution and the Constitutional Convention.

The Federalist regime actually represented the ultimate triumph of the nationalists, a political coalition that had emerged during the Revolutionary War.[4] Hoping to create a strong and effective central government, the nationalists had first gained uncontested control of the Continental Congress at the time of the Yorktown campaign in 1781. Congress appointed Robert Morris, a wealthy Philadelphia merchant, superintendent of the newly created Department of Finance, and from this post he became a virtual financial dictator.

The essential elements of Morris's ambitious program were: (1) concentration of the national government's power within independent executive departments headed by single administrators; (2) reorganization of the standing army along more centralized and hierarchical lines; (3) establishment of a central bank, patterned after the Bank of England; (4) establishment of a government monopoly mint; (5) restoration of public credit by honoring and consolidating Congress's outstanding debt into a perpetually financed liability; (6) assumption by Congress of state war debts; (7) the securing of Congressional power to collect an assortment of taxes—a tariff, a land tax, a poll tax, and a liquor excise.

Morris managed to push through a surprising number of these elements as temporary war measures. For instance, the Bank of North America received a constitutionally dubious charter and opened its doors. The linchpin of Morris's financial system, however, was the power of taxation. An amendment to the Articles of Confederation granting Congress the power to impose an import duty looked in 1782 as if it would receive the required unanimous approval of the states. But because the war was winding down, several states began to have second thoughts. Morris and the nationalists made a last-ditch effort in March of 1783 to coerce the states with the Continental Army. A military coup loomed on the horizon. But when the Newburgh conspiracy aborted, Morris's entire program unraveled.

Morris's failure eventually compelled the nationalists to make an end run around the Articles of Confederation. The centralization of power that they had failed to achieve at war's end, even with the threat of military coup, they finally consummated in 1789, through the Philadelphia convention's political coup. The drive for a more energetic constitution was further assisted by the lingering fiscal crisis left over from the war. Without the power to tax, the Continental Congress had defaulted on its staggering Revolutionary War debt in 1784. Once the Constitution took effect, almost one-half of the new government's expenditures went for interest on this $55 million obligation and on the $20 million worth of state debts that Hamilton had persuaded Congress to assume.

Not only was there a war-engendered fiscal crisis at the national level prior to the Constitution's adoption but at the state level as well. Before Congress assumed the state debts, these obligations created a tax burden undreamed of before the war. This burden, for instance, along with Massachusett's inequitable tax system, touched off Shay's Rebellion in 1786.

According to the nationalist rendition, Shay's Rebellion was an egalitarian assault on the property rights of creditors. The rebels allegedly wanted to escape their private debts through court moratoriums and inflationary doses of paper money. This rendition has some factual basis, but not much. Objecting to extravagant state expenditures and heavy court fees, the rebels actually closed down the courts in order to halt the confiscation of property for unpaid taxes. As in the Revolution before and the Whiskey Rebellion after, they were carrying on the eighteenth century tradition of direct resistance to taxation.[5]

Loyal Massachusetts militia broke this revolt within six months, but it alarmed America's governing classes. Prior to the outbreak, only Virginia, Pennsylvania, and New Jersey had chosen delegates to the Philadelphia convention. Subsequently, every state except Rhode Island sent delegates, and the Continental Congress even endorsed the extra-legal proceedings.

If it seems far-fetched to attribute the Federalist ascendancy to a war that had officially ended six years prior to the Constitutional Convention and eight years prior to the first Bank's establishment, consider the case of France. Allied with the colonists in the conflict against Britain, France was also strained and exhausted from heavy military expenditures. Most historians assign the resulting French fiscal crisis significant weight in provoking that nation's revolution in 1789, the same year as the Philadelphia convention.

Christainsen might wish to draw a sharp distinction between the first Bank and the remainder of the Hamiltonian program. The Constitution *explicitly* authorized tariffs, internal taxes, and other measures—but not a national bank. Which just brings me to my third thread of comments. Christainsen takes as self-evident that a nationally chartered bank, or corporation of any sort, was unconstitutional. But if we examine the framers' original intent, not as lawyers preparing a brief but as historians sensitive to context, a different picture emerges.

Sanford Levinson of the University of Texas Law School has recently emphasized the Constitution's role as the sacred text of America's civic religion.[6] In that role it early became a document to limit government's power. I have already pointed out, however, that the actual Philadelphia convention was dominated by nationalists, who were disgruntled with existing constraints upon central authority. They wanted to establish a consolidated government, under which the states would be subordinate, like countries and local governments within the states.

The final document eventually turned into the hybrid product of a disparate coalition. The nationalist dream of a central government with plenary power slowly eroded away. Some of this erosion occurred just as constitutional myth has it, through the compromises worked out within the convention hall itself. But as Herbert Storing and other scholars have suggested, most occurred outside the convention, through a subtle process of re-interpretation, when the nationalists were compelled to defend their completed handiwork before the general public.[7]

The Articles of Confederation had left the states completely sovereign. When the delegates left Philadelphia, they were confident that the new Constitution in contrast would make the central government completely sovereign. The document's "necessary and proper" clause, "general welfare" clause, "supremacy" clause, and all-encompassing preamble were not sloppy accidents; they implied substantial discretionary powers. The novel idea of dividing sovereignty between the national and state governments had not yet occurred to anyone.

Only after opposition stiffened did the Constitution's supporters, seizing for themselves the misleading label of "Federalists," deny vigorously but disingenuously that the Constitution would subordinate the states. Instead, it would create a delicate balance of powers between the national and state governments, each sovereign within its own realm. In other words, the much-touted federalism of the U.S. governmental system was in no way an intended consequence of the Philadelphia Convention. It was an unintended and insincere concession that the Anti-Federalists wrenched from the Federalists during the ratification struggle.[8]

This Federalist equivocation on the powers granted the national government spilled over into the most controversial issue of the ratification debate: the Constitution's omission of a bill of rights. The Federalists based their response to this Anti-Federalist objection upon a claim that the Constitution provided a government possessing only specifically enumerated powers. As a result, argued Hamilton in *The Federalist* No. 84, a bill of rights would be positively harmful. "They would contain various exceptions to powers which are not granted," and imply that the national government could do anything not specifically prohibited.[9]

The trouble with this argument was that it contradicted a second Federalist argument based on the explicit words of the Constitution. In the very same *Federalist* paper, Hamilton pointed out that the Constitution already contained a truncated bill of rights scattered throughout its clauses. There was a prohibition against *ex post facto* laws and bills of attainder, a ban on religious tests for holding office, guarantees to habeas corpus and jury trials in criminal cases, etc. If a bill of rights was positively dangerous, asked one Anti-Federalist at the Pennsylvania ratifying convention, "how happens it that in [three] instances . . . the danger has been incurred?"[10] This blatant Federalist contradiction cast justified suspicion upon their underlying claim that the Constitution created a government of delegated, rather than plenary, powers.

The promise of the Bill of Rights mollified enough Anti-Federalists to allow the Constitution barely to squeak through. But the first U.S. Bank, along with internal taxes and all the other Federalist measures, aroused a new opposition. The details of the Republicans' decade-long campaign against the Federalists need not concern us. What is important is that it culminated in Thomas Jefferson's election as President in 1800, and the victorious party dismantled much of the Federalist State.

In short, the Anti-Federalists lost on the ratification question, but they won on the question of how the Constitution would operate in practice. The Constitution had not ushered in a consolidated national system of government as the Federalists had intended, but a truly federal system, which is what the Anti-Federalists had wanted. To oversimplify only slightly, the Federalists got their Constitution, but the Anti-Federalists determined how it would be interpreted.

When Chief Justice John Marshall upheld the constitutionality of the Bank of the United States in *McCulloch v. Maryland,* his decision was precisely what many framers had desired. True, the Constitution failed to grant explicit authority to charter corporations, despite James Madison's proposal to that effect at the Philadelphia convention. But evidence suggests that the delegates' rejection of Madison's proposal (done hastily during the Convention's fiscal days) was more deliberate vagueness designed to ease ratification then a clearcut decision to deny Congress power. Jefferson claimed he was told in 1798 that one pro-bank delegate, Gouverneur Morris, had dissuaded Richard Morris, also a delegate, from proposing that the Constitution sanction a national bank, because such a provision would arouse potential opponents.[11]

(There would have been no reason for Marshall to refer to Madison's proposal about corporations in any event. The Philadelphia Convention's proceedings were held behind closed doors, and the delegates had agreed to maintain this secrecy for twenty-five years. Marshall, although at the Virginia convention that ratified the Constitution, had not himself been present in Philadelphia. The convention's official journal was not published until 1819, the same year as *McCulloch v. Maryland,* and it was only a record of motions voted upon. Madison's fuller account did not appear until after his death in 1836, seventeen years subsequent to Marshall's decision.)

When Jefferson opposed the first Bank's initial chartering as unconstitutional on the other hand, he was building upon the concessions that the Anti-Federalist had already won to formulate a constitutional theory of strict construction that was quite a variance with most framers' intentions. Yet Jefferson's theory remained politically viable in spite of Marshall's decision. Even with respect to the bank itself, strict construction partially motivated President Andrew Jackson's resounding veto of the second Bank recharter in 1832 and was thereafter the prevailing national policy until the Civil War.

Like Jefferson, I have no objections to appeals to the Constitution in our efforts at reducing the State. We should strategically employ whatever arguments lend us constitutional legitimacy. Indeed, that is a pragmatic necessity so long as the Constitution remains sacred to Americans. Nevertheless, we must not confuse ourselves about the historicity of our scriptual invocations.

In the final analysis, Christainsen and I reach the same conclusion about the United States Constitution but though different routes. We both recognize that it is a weak bastion against government encroachment without sound ideological reinforcement. But where he sees a document originally designed to limit State power, I see one designed to enhance it. Where he calls attention to the inability of the Constitution to prevent the bank's charter, I would call attention to the ability of the Jeffersonians to turn the Constitution against its Federalist authors. The ideological anomalies requiring historical explanation are not the constitutional failures to constrain government, but the successes.

Notes

1. For a summary of the charter differences, see John Thom Holdsworth and Davis R. Dewey. *The First and Second Banks of the United States,* 1910, Washington: Government Printing Office, pp. 164–75. This volume contains the text of the two charters, pp. 126–32, 267–81.

2. Milton Friedman, "Should There Be an Independent Monetary Authority?" in Leland B. Yeager, ed., *In Search of a Monetary Constitution,* 1962, pp. 219–243, Cambridge: Harvard University Press, Friedman, "Monetary Policy for the 1980s," in John H. Moore, ed., 1984, *To Promote Prosperity: U.S. Domestic Policy in the Mid-1980s,* Stanford: Hoover Institution Press, pp. 43–5; King Banaian, Leroy O. Laney, John McArthur, and Thomas D. Willett, "Subordinating the Fed to Political Authorities Will Not Control Inflationary Tendencies,:" in Willett, ed., 1988, *Political Business Cycles: The Political Economy of Money, Inflation, and Unemployment,* Durham: Duke University Press, pp. 490–505; Banaian, *et al.,* 1983, "Central Bank Independence: An International Comparison," Federal Reserve Bank of Dallas, *Economic Review,* 1–13. Alberto Alesina, "Politics and Business Cycles in Industrial Democracies." *Economic Policy: A European Forum* No. 8 (April 1989), pp. 57–98.

3. Thomas Hart Benton, 1854-6, *Thirty Years' View: Or a History of the Working of the American Government for Thirty Years, From 1820 to 1850,* 2 vol., New York: D. Appleton, pp. 441–4. Arthur J. Rolnick and Warren E. Weber, Feb. 1986, pp. 185–99, "Gresham's Law or Gresham's Fallacy?" *Journal of Political Economy,* 94, shows that both our theoretical and empirical understanding of Gresham's Law during this period requires some modification. I still have some reservations, however, about the extent to which quantity of gold the U.S. government minted, under a regime of free coinage, is a good proxy for the quantity of gold circulating as a medium of exchange. Their case would be still stronger if the U.S. mint had been charging seigniorage. The best historical discussion of the intricacies of U.S. bimetallism remains David

A. Martin's "Bimetallism in the United States Before 1850" *Journal of Political Economy* 76. May/June 1968, pp. 428–42.

4. Good treatments of the nationalist movement include E. James Ferguson, 1961, *The Power of the Purse: A History of American Public Finance, 1776–1790,* Chapel Hill: University of North Carolina Press; Merrill Jensen, *The Making of the American Constitution,* 1958, Princeton: D. Van Nostrand; Merrill Jensen, 1950, *The New Nation: A History of the United States During the Confederation,* New York; Gordon S. Wood, *The Creation of the American Republic,* 1969, Chapel Hill: University of North Carolina Press; and Richard H. Kohn, 1975, *Eagle and Sword: The Federalists and the Creation of the Military Establishment in America, 1783–1802,* New York: Free Press.

5. Forrest and Ellen Shapiro McDonald, 1988, "On the Late Disturbances in Massachusetts," in *Requiem: Variations on Eighteenth-Century Themes,* Lawrence: University Press of Kansas, pp. 59–83. See also Jensen, *The New Nation,* pp. 302–312; David P. Szatmary, 1980, *Shay's Rebellion: The Making of an Agrarian Insurrection,* Amherst; Robert L. Taylor, 1954, *Western Massachusetts in the Revolution,* Providence; Marian L. Starkey, *A Little Rebellion,* 1955, New York; and George R. Minot, 1788, *History of the Insurrection in Massachusetts in the Year 1786 and the Rebellion Consequent Thereon,* Worcester, MA.

6. Sanford Levinson, 1988, *Constitutional Faith* Princeton: Princeton University Press. See also Michael Kammen, 1986, *A Machine That Would Go of Itself: The Constitution in American Culture,* New York: Alfred A. Knopf.

7. Herbert J. Storing, 1981, *What the Anti-Federalists Were For,* Chicago: University of Chicago Press. My view of federalism and the Constitution has also been heavily influenced by William Winslow Crosskey (with William Jeffrey, Jr., on v. 3), 1953–1980, *Politics and the Constitution in the History of the United States,* 3 vol., Chicago: University of Chicago Press.

8. See Storing, p. 79, n. 6, for why "Anti-Federalist" is the best way to render the name of the Constitution's opponents. Christainsen's "antifederalist" obscures the fact that they were the true advocates of federalism, while "Antifederalist" and "anti-Federalist" have other less serious drawbacks.

9. *The Federalist,* Editor, Jacob E. Cooke. Middletown, Conn. Wesleyan University Press 1961, p. 579.

10. Bernard Schwartz, ed., 1971, *The Bill of Rights: A Documentary History,* New York: Chelsea House, v. 2, p. 652.

11. Jefferson's *Anas,* 1957, as paraphrased in Bray Hammond, *Banks and Politics in America: From the Revolution to the Civil War,* Princeton: Princeton University Press, pp. 104–5.

Free Banking, Denominational Restrictions, and Liability Insurance

by Eugene N. White*

In the past half dozen years, banking in the United States before the Civil War has become the object of considerable scholarly interest. Most studies have focused on the "Free Banking Era," a period when there were easy entry and multiple banks of issue. This recent scholarship concludes that "free banking" was safe and efficient with the policy implication that today's corset of banking regulations can be abandoned without disastrous consequences.

These findings represent a remarkable change in the economics profession's view of the Free Banking Era. In the 1950's and 1960's, Hammond and Redlich saw little virtue in free banking.[1] They believed that the evidence showed the need for regulation and a strong central bank. Their influential judgments held sway until the mid-1970's when Rockoff applied the methods of the new economic history to the Free Banking era. In contrast to Hammond and Redlich, Rockoff showed the free banking was not inherently unstable and worked reasonably well. The primary cause of the collapse of some states' free banking systems was not rapacious bankers but poorly designed regulations.[2]

Leading the 1980's wave of scholarship and completing the swing of the pendulum, Rolnick and Weber re-examined the Free Banking era. They pointed out that the economists' opposition to applying *laissez-faire* to banking was based on their understanding of history, not any explicit theoretical argument. Equating the Free Banking era with "unfettered banking," Rolnick and Weber offered their revised interpretation of this period as evidence of a successful

*I am indebted to Howard Bodenhorn, Michael Bordo, William Lang, Hugh Rockoff, and Peter Rappoport for comments and criticism.

unregulated banking regime.[3] They and their followers viewed free banking's problems as simply the consequence of mis-specifying the bond security for banknotes.[4]

While free banking was, at least, a moderate success; it was not a reasonable proxy for unregulated banking. Rockoff tried to refashion the debate by asking what are the institutional requirements for a successful free banking system. But advocates of unregulated banking continue to equate free banking with unfettered banking.[5]

Admirers of the Free Banking era can point to the fact that free banks survived and functioned quite well in the absence of one of today's most vexing government interventions—deposit insurance. Nevertheless, policy makers of the period were concerned that the market was not adequately monitoring banks, leaving the public exposed to what they viewed as excessive risk from holding banknotes. Consequently, banking authorities imposed a variety of regulations on "free" and "unfree" banks to protect the public. In this paper, I will show how regulations designed to protect noteholders were a key feature of virtually all antebellum systems, including free banking.

Regulations were imposed in an attempt to guarantee that bank customers would be able to convert their banknotes into specie. Redemption of banknotes was uncertain because banking is a special case of the principal-agent problem.[6] The principals, the customers, deposited specie with a bank for the transactions services provided by the convenience of banknotes. The agent, the banker, provided these services because part of the specie could be employed in loans and discounts. The multiple principals held banknotes in this fractional reserve system when they believed that the bank would remain solvent and sufficiently liquid to ensure prompt redemption. As in all principle-agent problems, it was difficult for the customers to observe whether the bankers' investments would enable him to meet any immediate demand for redemption.

The concern of a banker for maintaining his reputation is the control mechanism that many admirers of free banking believe guarantee prompt redemption. Yet, monitoring must be effective to ensure that banks will strive to build their reputation. Monitoring may be diminished because, with multiple principals, it is a public good with the attendant free rider problem.[7] The circulation of notes from hand to hand at a distance from the issuer makes matters worse. As Milton Friedman noted, bank contracts to pay are difficult to enforce because individuals hold contracts that are removed "in space and acquaintance, and a long period may elapse between the issue of a promise and the demand for its fulfillment. In fraud as in other activities, opportunities for profit are not likely to go unexploited."[8]

This problem was not unsuperable, and markets for returning banknotes to their issuing institutions developed during the antebellum period. The efficiency of these markets improved over time as the railroad and telegraph sped information and the latest copies of banknotes reported to the public and quickened the return of notes to banks.[9] These technological developments reduced the monitoring problem by lowering costs, first in the cities and then gradually in the countryside, but they did not eliminate it. State governments responded by imposing various regulations in attempts to guarantee banknotes.

Legal minimum denominations on banknotes were the first device employed. This type of regulation attempted to limit the number of principles by excluding the general public who would not monitor banks as carefully as the relatively few members for the business community.[10] These regulations proved difficult to maintain, and beginning in 1829 several states experimented with funds to insure banknotes. These insurance schemes replaced monitoring by the principals with a mixture of regulations designed to limit the activities of the bankers, government supervision, and mutual self-monitoring by the banks induced by co-insurance.

The success of these insurance funds was mixed, reducing their appeal. Thus, in the late 1830's states began to pass free banking statutes that guaranteed banknotes by the deposit of government securities. In theory, this regime offered the public security, by limiting the agents' activities and precisely specifying the backing of banknotes. Viewed within the context of the banking system's development over the whole antebellum period, free banking was not free of regulation. Its principal regulation was, in fact, devised as an alternative to deposit insurance and denominations restrictions. The regulations that recent scholars have regarded as minimal were, in fact the product of an evolving regulatory policy that attempted to solve an important principal-agent problem in banking.

Denominational Restrictions: European Origins

One important common regulation that scholars of the antebellum period have overlooked is the minimum legal denomination on banknotes. Its purpose was to exclude all but businessmen and the well-to-do from using currency. The origins of this regulation can be traced back to eighteenth century Great Britain. To understand the rationale behind this regulation, it is necessary to first take a close look at its development across the Atlantic. In Scotland of the early 1760's, many small banks started up, issuing notes in very low denominations.[11] This "small note mania" was attacked by contemporary experts. The most notable critic was Adam Smith, who observed that:

> Where the issue of banknotes for such small sums is allowed and commonly practiced many mean people are both enabled and encouraged to become bankers. A person whose promissory note for five pounds or even twenty shillings, would be rejected by everybody will get it to be received without scruple when it is issued for so small a sum as a sixpence. But the frequent bankruptcies to which such beggarly bankers must be liable, may occasion a very considerable inconvenience and sometimes even a great calamity to many people who had received their notes in payment.[12]

The Scottish mania led Smith to conclude that *laissez-faire* in banking should be tempered by two restrictions: (1) Banks should be prohibited from "issuing and circulating bank notes .... for less than a certain sum." and (2) Redemption of banknotes in specie should be immediate and unconditional.[13]

Smith's views were widely shared, and in 1765 Parliament banned the issue of notes with an option clause and notes of denominations smaller than ƒ1 in Scotland.[14] Applying the same logic to England, Parliament voted in 1775 to prohibit English banks from issuing notes under ƒ1. Two years later it raised the limited to ƒ5.[15] Minimum denomination restrictions became a key feature of banking regulation in the British Isles. Like Scotland, Ireland imposed a ƒ1 minimum on the notes its banks issued, and banking interests in both countries had to fight efforts in Parliament to raise the minimum to ƒ5.[16]

The most authoritative argument against the issue of small notes was spelled out by Henry Thornton. It captures the essence of the principal-agent problem:

> Country bank notes, and especially the smaller ones, circulate, in a great measure, among people out of trade, and pass occasionally

into the hands of persons of the lower class; a great proportion, therefore, of the holders of them, have few means of judging of the comparative credit of the several issuers, and are commonly almost as ready to take the paper of any one house calling itself a bank as that of another. A certain degree of currency being thus given to inferior paper, even the man who doubts the ultimate solvency of the issuer is disposed to take it, for the time during which he intends to detain it is very short, and his responsibility will cease almost as soon as he shall have parted with it. Moreover, the amount of each note is so small, that the risk seems, also, on that account, insignificant. The notes of the greater and of the smaller country banks, thus obtaining in ordinary times, a nearly similar currency, they naturally fall at a season of alarm into almost equal discredit. If any one bank fails, a general run upon the neighboring ones is apt to take place.[17]

A legal minimum denomination on banknotes was a drastic measure to solve the principal-agent problem. By setting ƒ5 as the minimum denomination in England and Wales and ƒ1 in Scotland and Ireland, Parliament ensured that banknotes would not serve the vast majority of the population as currency. In late eighteenth century London, skilled workers, such as bricklayers and carpenters, earned 3 to 4 shillings per day.[18] The estimated annual earnings in 1781 for farm laborers were ƒ21, for cotton spinners, ƒ42, and for solicitors and barristers, ƒ243.[19] This type of protective legislation thus barred a large fraction of the population from using banknotes.

Focusing on these costs, Cowen and Kroszner have argued that the denomination restrictions had a different purpose—to limit competition in banking to the benefit of existing banks.[20] While this was undoubtedly a consequence of the regulations, this was not the initial intent; and certainly the British economists who favored such regulations were not great friends of rent-seeking behavior. Lawrence White attributed the failure of the Bank of England to issue a ƒ5 note before 1793 to simply overlooking an opportunity for profit.[21] White arrived at this interpretation because he believed that the drive of bankers to maintain their reputation left no principal-agent problem.

Denominational Restrictions in America

In the early years of the Republic, the design of the state banking systems was strongly influenced by the highly-regarded Scottish system and the writings of economists like Smith and Say.[22] American legislators were apparently impressed by the argument for high minimum denominations and these became a standard feature of many states' regulations.[23] The charter of the Bank of the United States prohibited the issue of any notes below $5 dollars, and many states followed suit.

Thomas Jefferson agreed on the need to prohibit the issue of small notes. While no friend of government banks, Jefferson was willing to permit banknotes to be used by merchants but he was adamantly against the general use of banknotes by the public. In 1814, Jefferson advised the Virginia legislature to force banks to eliminate their $5 and $10 notes, leaving in circulation no note below $50 to ensure that:

> . . . bills of such size as would be called for only in transactions between merchant and merchant, and ensure a metallic circulation for those of the mass of citizens.[24]

This was an extreme position, and the $5 limit generally prevailed.

Massachusetts prohibited all notes under $5 in 1799, although the rest of New England appears to have tolerated low denomination notes.[25] Among the mid-Atlantic states, New York had no prohibitions, while New Jersey attempted in 1812 to establish a limit of $4 but rescinded it the following year. States in the South were more likely to set a $5 minimum. In the charters it granted, Maryland established a $5 minimum denomination on notes, and placed no limit on the issue of banknotes. The only constraint was that the total liabilities of the bank could not exceed two times the paid-in capital, but his limit was far above banks' typical liability-to-capital ratio.[26] Virginia adopted a $5 rule beginning with the charter of the Bank of Alexandria in 1792. In 1812–1813, South Carolina passed legislation that prohibited all banks from issuing notes under $5, except the Bank of the State of South Carolina, which had the privilege of issuing $1 banknotes.[27]

Although the minimum denomination adopted by most states was, perhaps, not as high as in Britain, this regulation still kept banknotes from being used as daily currency by the common man. In the early nineteenth century, unskilled workers' daily wages in the Philadelphia area and the Erie Canal were one dollar or under and those of skilled workers were under two dollars.[28]

These regulations were binding as witnessed by the inflow of small banknotes from other states. The federal system that permitted states to set their own regulations make it more difficult to maintain denominational minimums compared to the centralized states of

Europe. Massachusetts found its $5 minimum challenged by the circulation of other states' notes, and in 1802 prohibited the circulation of notes under $5 from other states.[29] The high cost imposed on the public by the forced use of coin led the Massachusetts legislature to allow its own banks to issue notes or $1, $2 and $3 up to five percent of capital in 1805.[30] The low denomination notes issued by the District of Columbia created problems for Maryland and Virginia, which tried to prohibit "foreign" banknotes.

The financial crisis and suspension of payments in 1814 forced many states to suspend or repeal their regulations on banknote denominations. Virginia, a state with a strict $5 limit, responded to the suspension and the demand for small notes by passing a law that allowed the issue of notes as low as $1 until six months after the war.[31] In 1815, New Jersey allowed its banks to issue notes below $1. Massachusetts increased the volume of small notes that any bank could issue to 25 percent of capital, which was probably not a binding constraint.[32]

Once the war was over and convertibility was restored, there was a new campaign to eliminate low denomination notes. This was a formidable task as one estimate placed the total banknote issue under $5 at $7 million and $5 notes at $10 million.[33] Pennsylvania, Maryland, and Virginia passed laws that prohibited the circulation of notes for less than $5.[34] Notes under $1 were forbidden in Ohio in 1819, in Florida in 1828 and in Georgia in 1830.

These denominational limitations helped to keep banking restricted to merchants and the well-to-do. The typical early nineteenth century American bank was consequently a closely controlled enterprise. Even in a region like New England where the number of banks was growing rapidly, individual banks were dominated by a few merchants.[35] Stock ownership was concentrated in the hands of several families and a large fraction of the loans were given to people who would be considered to be insiders today. However, far from representing an abuse, this pattern represented one solution to a bank's various principal-agent problems. Not only were the number of banknote holders limited, reducing the free rider monitoring problem, but the monitoring of customers' loans was made easier. When the largest customers jointly own the bank, there were incentives for cooperation and mutual surveillance.

The drive to remove all notes from circulation gathered steam when the Jacksonian democrats included it in their economic agenda. In the 1820's, they tried to pass a federal stamp tax on banknotes and to prohibit the Treasury from accepting small notes, but these efforts failed.[36] When they began to acquire majorities in the state legislatures, they imposed new regulations. By 1832, the $5 minimum denomination was adopted by Kentucky, Tennessee, Mississippi, Louisiana, Illinois, Indiana, and Missouri. Although the Jacksonian Democrats are better known for their desire to abolish banks, raising the minimum denomination to $5, $10, or $20 was usually considered a reasonable alternative. The anti-bank stance seems to have grown when they realized the difficulties involved in policing the denominational restrictions.

Under Jackson, the federal government put pressure on the states and their banks to cease issuing low denomination notes. In 1836, the Treasury announced that it would discontinue the use of any bank as a fiscal agent that issued notes for under $5.[37] After March 1837, public deposit banks were forbidden to issue notes under $10 and a $5 minimum was imposed on the District of Columbia banks after April 1839.[38] In 1833 Georgia and Alabama added penalties to their laws banning $5 banknotes, while North Carolina set a $4 minimum. Indiana forbade its State Bank from issuing notes for under $5 in 1834. In the Midwest, Illinois and Indiana Democrats successfully engineered legislation to prohibit the issue of any denomination less than $5 in setting up their state banks, but they failed in Ohio and Michigan.[39] In 1835, Connecticut, Maine, and New York prohibited notes of less than $5. Some states, like Missouri in 1836, took even more radical measures and banned notes under $20.[40]

The suspension of specie payments in 1837 and 1839 derailed the Jacksonian's campaign, and many states repealed or temporarily suspended regulations governing small notes to alleviate shortages of coin. In Virginia banks were granted permission to issue $1 and $2 notes provided their total loans and discounts were kept at their level of January 1, 1838. When resumption began again this privilege was again withdrawn.[41] Yet, after the suspensions, other state legislatures found it difficult to eliminate low denomination banknotes. By 1840, small notes were in general circulation in all states except the South. In this period many states permitted the issue of small notes up to a fixed proportion of paid-in capital. This modification of the rule reflects their wariness of the principal-agent problem and their unwillingness to allow banks a free choice in banknote denominations.[42] The great difficulty of restricting the circulation of neighboring states' notes and the suspension of payments in 1814, 1837, and 1839 led some states to consider other forms of regulation to protect holders of banknotes.

Insurance of Bank Liabilities

When Northern states began to abandon denominational restrictions in the 1830's, six—New York, Vermont, Michigan, Indiana, Ohio, and Iowa—attempted to protect banknote holders with insurance. No insurance fund was established in the South where denominational restrictions were apparently still effective. The idea of insurance did not take off as poor design plagued these systems; only three of the systems can be considered successes.

New York was the first state to institute an insurance plan with the Safety Fund Banking System in 1829. In the years immediately preceding the adoption of the Safety Fund, public satisfaction with the banking system was at an ebb. The legislature was constantly besieged by requests for new charters, offering money and favors. In 1827, the legislature issued a revised banking statue to regularize the regulations governing all banks. Payment of dividends, the volume of loans, and the conduct of directors were all limited. Annual reports were required and the issue of banknotes for less than $1 was prohibited. In 1829, most old bank charters were up for renewal and there were 37 applications for new charters. As a remedy for the lack of security for note holders, Joshua Forman introduced an insurance plan. Arguing that the banks who had the exclusive privilege of issuing notes should commonly be answerable for it, he offered a plan to enroll all banks into an association where each should be liable for the obligations of the others by insurance assessments.[43]

All banks were required to join when they renewed their charters, and by 1840 more than 90 percent of bank liabilities were covered. Failing banks' notes and deposits were to be redeemed in full. The funds for protecting notes and deposits were obtained from annual assessments of one-half percent of a bank's capital until their payments totalled three percent of capital. If the fund fell short, special assessments were ordered to a maximum of one-half of capital per year.[44]

In debate, Forman's plan came under attack. The arguments deployed against it show that the opponents felt that it would not solve the principal-agent problem. One representative pointed out that the safety fund would relax "public scrutiny and watchfulness which now serve to restrain or detect malconduct."[45] A number in the Assembly also felt that it would be impossible for the state to monitor the banks and prevent fraud. The city banks were alarmed by the law as they issued fewer banknotes as a fraction of capital compared to the country banks, which they believed were taking greater risks.

These critics correctly perceived some of the New York Safety Fund's defects. The large number of bank failures from 1837 to 1841 exhausted the fund, and it was legally unable to raise enough through special assessments.[46] Poor design produced moral hazard, which was not controlled by regular examinations, and many of the failures were the product of fraud or mismanagement. Stung by large losses, coverage by the fund was limited to only banknotes in 1842. The system was further weakened when in 1838 New York adopted a parallel free banking system, permitting banks to escape additional assessments by switching systems when their charters expired. Hence, by 1860, only two percent of bank liabilities were covered by the Safety Fund.

Vermont copied New York and established a Safety Fund in 1831, adopting most of its characteristics. In addition to the mistakes imported from New York, Vermont made insurance voluntary in 1840. This change in the law permitted even more adverse selection by allowing strong banks rapid exit from the system. The system was forced to shut down a year after a single bank failure in 1857.[47] On the eve of the 1837 panic, Michigan organized a safety fund in 1836 with voluntary membership. Without any accumulated funds it did not weather the depression and folded in 1842.

Unlike these systems, Indiana's plan, adopted in 1834, gave broad powers to regulators to close banks and set a capital-to-asset ratio. Banks in this system were separately owned branches of the State Bank of Indiana. The board of the State Bank, the regulator, was appointed by the member banks who had strong incentives to monitor other members' behavior, as stockholders had double liability and any bank guilty of fraud had unlimited liability. The combination of tough regulation and co-insurance produced a system where no banks failed.[48] However, as opponents of the system pointed out, the banknote security was achieved at a high cost by inducing considerable collusion.

Ohio began insuring banknotes in 1845. Like Indiana it gave regulators broad powers to examine and intervene, imposing high capital requirements and a ten percent reserve fund on notes. In the years before the Civil War, there was one large bank failure in 1857; however, regulators prevented a liquidity crisis by quickly transferring its liabilities and liquidating its assets. Iowa imitated Ohio's successful fund in 1858 with its own system, where there were not failures prior to the Civil War.[49]

These insurance funds did not appear very attractive to other states. The successful funds required strict regulations that allowed banks to collude, leading to charges of monopoly banking. In the other systems, weak regulation produced moral hazard and adverse selection, leading them to fail. In light of the problems of denominational restrictions and insurance, free banking seemed an attractive alternative as it did not induce elements of monopoly and gave an apparently secure guarantee for banknotes.

Free Banking

Although Michigan was the first state in 1837 to adopt free banking, the Michigan legislature simply appropriated a bill that was germinating in the New York legislature.[50] It is thus appropriate to first take a close look at events in this important banking state. The New York free banking law of 1838 was adopted because of a growing opposition to all monopolies granted by the legislature. The Safety Fund system was regarded by many of its opponents as a state-granted monopoly.

As early as 1825 a report to the Senate recommended the restraining laws prohibiting non-chartered banks be repealed. The report argued that private banks would provide more credit to the public and would be successfully monitored by the market.[51] While it made a strong claim for free enterprise in banking, the report noted that if the character of the bankers was not enough security for the public, the legislature might require bonds and mortgages to secure the issue of banknotes.

Interest in free banking grew in the prosperous early 1830's when many new banks were chartered. The total number of banks had risen from 51 in 1830 to a peak of 90 in 1836, and notes in circulation had risen from $12.0 to $22.1 million. Small banks seem to have been prominent in this expansion.[52] When market conditions began to tighten, some banks found redemption difficult. In response, the legislature passed a law forbidding the circulation of banknotes under $5; but this was extremely unpopular, became an issue in the governor's race, and was eliminated in 1837.[53] While most of the debate on banking was friendly in principle to the Safety Fund, there was strong opposition to "monopoly" in banking. As the economic crisis deepened after 1837 and the Safety Fund failed to live up to its promise, supporters of a general law of free banking gained strength. When the free banking law was passed in 1838 the Safety Fund was left untouched.

The New York law allowed any individual or association of individuals to form a limited liability bank with a minimum capital stock of $100,000. It required a specie reserve of 12½ percent against notes which were to be secured by the deposit of United States or New York bonds and mortgages on land in the state.

While New York let denominational restrictions and the Safety Fund wither when it adopted free banking, these various forms of banknote protection co-existed in some states. Virginia's law left the established chartered banks with their $5 limit undisturbed. Secured by state bonds, the free bank's notes were not subject to denominational restrictions. Although entry was not completely free, thirteen new banks soon opened. The older banks responded by adding more branches and competition increased the number of banking offices from 33 in 1851 to 58 in 1855.[54]

In Maryland, another state that strictly adhered to the $5 rule for banknotes, the public complained of a shortage of coin. Some banks responded by issuing lower denomination notes, and banknotes from other states began to circulate. The legislature responded by imposing more stringent penalties on small denominations in 1852, in spite of considerable popular protest. The state Senate considered a law creating a bond-secured note issue, but the state retained its chartered banking system and resisted the adoption of a free banking law.[55]

After Louisiana was hit hard by the Panic of 1837 and subsequent depression, a new banking law was adopted in 1842 in an attempt to give noteholders and depositors an iron-clad guarantee. No limit was set on note issue, but banknotes had to be secured by one-third specie and two-thirds 90 day paper. Funds from deposits were to be invested in short-term loans, and only capital was to be put at risk in longer-term investments. In 1852, the demand for more credit and more banks produced the Louisiana free banking act. This act permitted free entry, imposed a $5 minimum denomination, required banknotes to be backed by U.S. and state bonds, and retained the 1842 reserve requirements.[56]

Banking debates in the Midwest clearly show how denominational restrictions and bond security were seen as alternative solutions to the principal-agent problem. Although Democrats were more anti-monopoly, often favoring legal minimum denominations or free banking.[57] Many Whigs picked up the idea of free banking under general incorporation laws with notes backed by bonds. The Whig position was one of moderate liberalism. John Niles, a Whig proponent of free banking in Indiana, argued that "the business of issuing paper to circulate as money is of a widely different character [from other enterprises] and must be governed by stringent rules."[58] Monopoly, in the form of the Safety Fund system, was too high a price for security, and he recommended a bond collateral to protect noteholders.

What, in effect, the Democrats and Whigs did was compete for the votes of the common man. The anti-bank Democrats offered protection by prohibiting either banks or high denominations while the Whigs offered bond-secured banknotes. This division was, for example, clear at Ohio's Constitutional Convention, where 80 percent of the Democrats voted to prohibit chartering banks of any kind. Another alternative that Ohio Democrats were willing to accept was free entry into banking and a prohibition on notes smaller than the most valuable coin issued by the federal government.[59] The weakness in this Democratic proposal was that unexpected international specie outflows could produce coin shortages. By comparison, free banking acts generally did not stipulate denominational restrictions, thus avoiding occasional but painful shortages in low denomination media of exchange.

By 1852 Ohio, Indiana, Illinois, and Wisconsin passed free banking laws. In each case the bill was backed by a coalition of Whigs and Democrats. Once free banking laws were passed in the Old Northwest, the hard money Democrats continued to oppose them, offering, like the Democratic governor of Indiana, additional legislation to control the banks, and in particular limitations on denominations of $5 or $10.[60]

In Michigan, where the first free banking system had collapsed, out-of-state banknotes were the primary form of currency. The Democratic governor warned that experience showed that even bond-secured currency was not entirely safe. The solution he thought was a $5 minimum, and he recommended it to all states, as it would check:

> over bank issues, expansions and contractions in the money market... and the raging and dangerous spirit of speculation so common to the people of our country, would be guarded against.[61]

This sentiment was shared by the new Republican governor who in 1855 vetoes a new free banking bill. He explained that he could not accept the bill because he was concerned about banks' prompt redemption of notes and the absence of any prohibition of small notes. However, when a free banking bill passed the legislature in 1857, it contained no provisions to limit denominations. When submitted to the public in a referendum, it passed by a wide margin.

In the Panic of 1857, the free banking system of the Old Northwest managed with moderate losses. The general reaction was not to abolish but reform the free banking systems, ensuring that the required bonds provided adequate security for banknotes. Free banking was not a perfect system because of the inherent problem in writing the rules for the bonds deposited by banks to guarantee their banknotes. As Rockoff has pointed out, the banking authorities were faced with a difficult decision in setting the "legal price" of these bonds.[62] If the market price exceeded the legal price by a relatively small amount, banks found it profitable to issue banknotes and sound banking systems, such as those found in New York, Louisiana, and Ohio, appeared. When the market price of the required bonds was far above the legal price, it became unprofitable to issue banknotes; and few banks opened, as in Massachusetts. If the market price fell far enough below the legal price, "wildcat" banking could arise with banks rapidly increasing their note issue to turn a quick profit before failing. Several disasters of this nature occurred during the period in Michigan, Illinois, Wisconsin, Indiana, Minnesota, and New Jersey.[63]

Although it can only be done crudely, it is interesting to examine the fortunes of free and "unfree" banking systems. In New York, the losses of Safety Fund banks and free banks can be compared. This is only a very rough comparison as noteholders of failed Safety Fund banks often suffered because there was no prompt redemption. These costs cannot easily be imputed, but after selling off assets of failed banks, the Safety Fund paid out $2.8 million for 16 bank failures between 1829 and 1866.[64] In contrast, 34 of New York's free banks failed but their total losses were only slightly over $600,000.[65] Failure rates and other measures do not suggest that free banking enjoyed any large advantage over chartered banking. James Kahn has shown that the mean life expectancies were greater for non-free banks.[66] One key aspect which is often overlooked is the convergence over time between the chartered banking and free banking systems. In a number of states, the question of free entry was not so important as charters were readily granted. Very early in the nineteenth century, the banking industry had become quite competitive in Pennsylvania.[67] This is certainly the case in Maryland and Massachusetts.[68] These states had *de facto* free entry but did not force banks to secure their banknotes with bonds. This development emphasizes that in many states the purpose of the bond provisions of free banking laws was to provide protection to the noteholders.

Conclusion

While the Free Banking Era is often treated today as an example of how well an unregulated banking system can operate, this interpretation fails to recognize the role of a bond-secured currency. Over the course of the antebellum period, Americans struggled with the design of state banking systems, attempting to find a solution to the principle-agent problem inherent in fractional reserve banking. They experimented with denominational restrictions, insurance, and bond-secured banknotes. When well-designed, these regulations could produce a certain degree of protection at varying costs. While none of these experiments is ideal, they are worthy of study because they illuminate the problems faced by all banking regimes.

Notes

1. Hammond, Bray, *Banks and Politics in America: From the Revolution to the Civil War* (Princeton, 1957), chapters 18 and 19. Fritz Redlich, *The Molding of American Banking* (New York, 1968), Part I, chapter 8.

2. Rockoff, Hugh, *The Free Banking Era: A Re-Examination* (New York, 1975) and "The Free Banking Era: A Re-Examination," *Journal of Money, Credit and Banking* (May 1974).

3. Rolnick, Arthur J. and Warren E. Weber, "New Evidence on the Free Banking Era," *American Economic Review* (December 1983), p. 1081.

4. Rolnick, Arthur J. and Warren E. Weber, "The Causes of Free Bank Failures: A Detailed Examination," *Journal of Monetary Economics* (November 1984), pp. 267–291 and Andrew J. Economopoulos, "Illinois Free Banking Experience," *Journal of Money, Credit and Banking* (May 1988), pp. 249–64.

5. Rockoff, Hugh, "Institutional Requirements for Stable Free Banking," *Cato Journal* (Fall 1986), pp. 617–634. One example of this confusion of free banking with unregulated banking is George A. Selgin, *The Theory of Free Banking* (Totowa, 1988). Similarly, Cowen and Kroszner argue that Scottish free banking was not a good proxy for unregulated banking. Tyler Cowen and Randall Kroszner, "Scottish Banking before 1845: A Model for Laissez-Faire?" *Journal of Money Credit and Banking* (May 1989), pp. 206–20.

6. The following exposition is analogous to the principle-agent problem for corporate control described by the Greenwald and J.E. Stiglitz, "Information, Finance and Markets: The Architecture of Allocative Mechanisms," (mimeo, September 1989).

7. Stiglitz, Joseph E., "Credit Markets and the Control of Capital," *Journal of Money, Credit and Banking* (May 1985), pp. 144–5.

8. Friedman, Milton, *A Program for Monetary Stability* (New York, 1959), p. 6.

9. Gorton, Gary, "Free Banking, Wildcat Banking and the Market for Bank Notes," (October 1989).

10. Stiglitz discusses the concentration of equity ownership as a means to solve the free rider problem in corporate control. Stiglitz (1985), p. 144.

11. Checkland, Sidney G., *Scottish Banking, A History 1695–1973* (Glasgow, 1975), pp. 104–6, 118–21.

12. Smith, Adam, *The Wealth of Nations* (New York: Modern Library, 1937 [1776]), p. 307.

13. Smith (1776), p. 313. The demand for unconditional payment, a stiff requirement, bears on the issue of banking runs and the need for a central bank. Adherence to this rule would have prevented the suspension of payments that banks used in nineteenth century America where there was no lender of last resort to control panics.

14. The legal minimum denomination was a binding constraint on banks. Five shilling notes alone had accounted for 17 percent of chartered bank notes and a larger share of the smaller unchartered banks. Munn, Charles W., *The Scottish Provincial Banking Companies, 1747–1864* (Edinburgh, 1981), p. 21.

15. White, Lawrence H., *Free Banking in Britain: Theory, experience, and debate, 1800–1845* (Cambridge, 1984), p. 39.

16. Ollerenshaw, Philip, *Banking in nineteenth-century Ireland: The Belfast banks, 1825–1914* (Manchester, 1987), pp. 22–7.

17. Thornton, Henry, *An Enquiry into the Nature and Effects of the Paper Credit of Great Britain* (Fairfield [1802], 1978), pp. 179-80.

18. Schwarz, L.D., "The Standard of Living in the Long-Run, 1700-1860," *The Economic History Review* (February 1985), pp. 36-9.

19. Lindert, Peter H. and Jeffrey G. Williamson, "English Workers' Living Standards during the Industrial Revolution: A New Look," *Economic History Review* (February 1983), p. 4.

20. Cowen and Tyler, (1989), pp. 224-5.

21. Lawrence White (1984), pp. 38-9.

22. Bryan, Alfred C., *History of State Banking in Maryland* (Baltimore, 1899), pp. 14-16. George T. Starnes, *Sixty Years of Branch Banking in Virginia* (New York, 1931), pp. 27-8.

23. Dewey, Davis R., *State Banking Before the Civil War* (Washington, D.C.: National Monetary Commission, 1919), p. 64.

24. Jefferson, Thomas, "Letter to John Adams," *The Writings of Thomas Jefferson* (Washington, D.C., 1907, Vol. XIV, p. 78.

25. Dewey (1910), p. 64. There was an exception for the Nantucket bank.

26. Bryan, (1899), pp. 30-5.

27. Dewey (1910), pp. 64-68. The case of South Carolina clearly shows the mixed motives of some of this legislation conferring privileges as well as attempting to protect the public.

28. U.S. Department of Commerce, *Historical Statistics of the United States* (Washington, D.C., 1975), Vol. I, pp. 163-4.

29. Dewey (1910), p. 64.

30. The limit was raised to 15 percent of capital in 1809, reduced to ten percent in 1812. Dewey (1910), pp. 64-5.

31. Starnes (1931), p. 50.

32. In 1835, the Massachusetts bank's capital was $30 million, and their total note issue $9.4 million, just somewhat over 25 percent. Lamoreaux (1986), p. 654.

33. Dewey (1910), p. 68.

34. In Maryland, the banks collaborated to eliminate notes under $5 from circulation in 1820. The next year the state formally prohibited banknotes under $5. Bryan (1899), p. 71-2.

35. Lamoreaux, Naomi R., "Banks, Kinship, and Economic Development: The New England Case," *Journal of Economic History* (September 1986), pp. 647-68.

36. Martin, David A., "Metallism, Small Notes and Jackson's War with the B.U.S.," *Exploration in Economic History* (Spring 1974), pp. 234 and 242.

37. Martin (1971), pp. 268-9.

38. Martin (1971), p. 243.

39. Shade, William G., *Bank or No Banks: The Money Issue in Western Politics, 1832-1865* (Detroit, 1972), p. 39.

40. Dewey (1910), pp. 68-71.

41. Before the banks could act, the demand for small notes was so great that a premium arose on Maryland small notes in Virginia. Starnes (1931), pp. 92–7.

42. Pennsylvania attempted to police its $5 rule but it was eventually repealed in 1861 when the state legislature permitted the issue of lower denomination notes up to 20 percent of paid-in capital. New York formally repealed its dead letter $5 rule in 1855. Dewey (1910), pp. 71–3.

43. Chaddock, Robert E., *The Safety Fund Banking System in New York, 1829–1866* (Washington, D.C., 1910), pp. 252–62.

44. Calomiris, Charles W., "Deposit Insurance: Lessons from the Record," *Federal Reserve Bank of Chicago, Economic Perspectives* (May/June 1989), p. 12.

45. Quoted in Chaddock (1910), p. 265.

46. Calomiris (1989), p. 12–3. Only in 1866 was the fund finally able to pay all outstanding claims.

47. Calomiris (1989), pp. 14–5.

48. Calomiris (1989), pp. 15–6.

49. Calomiris (1989), pp. 16–7.

50. The idea of a bond-secured currency was not entirely new. Before the Act of 1765 was passed, there were calls in Scotland for banks to deposit securities to back the notes they issued. Checkland, (1975), p. 254.

51. Chaddock, (1910), p. 371.

52. The average circulation for a bank with $100,000 was $160,000, but banks with capital exceeding $300,000 circulation rarely exceeded capital. Chaddock (1910), pp. 276–7 and 296.

53. Chaddock (1910), p. 278.

54. Starnes (1931), pp. 103–5 and Table 5.

55. Bryan (1899), pp. 116–23.

56. Caldwell, Stephen A., *A Banking History of Louisiana* (Baton Rouge, 1935), pp. 53–84.

57. Shade (1972), p. 111–19.

58. Quoted in Shade (1972), p. 132.

59. Shade (1972), pp. 137–9.

60. Shade (1972), pp. 171–8.

61. Quoted in Shade (1972), p. 191.

62. Rockoff (1974), pp. 148–9.

63. Economopoulos (1988) offers a good example of how in Illinois even a careful crafted free banking law could produce a banking collapse when bond prices dropped unexpectedly.

64. This figure was obtained using data provided by Chaddock (1910), pp. 332 and 359–366.

65. This is the estimate of Rolnick and Weber (1983), p. 1085.

66. Kahn, James A., "Another Look at Free Banking in the United States," *American Economic Review* (September 1985), pp. 881–5.

67. Schwartz, Anna J., "The Beginning of Competitive Banking in Philadelphia, 1782–1809," *Journal of Political Economy* (October 1947), pp. 417–31.

68. Sylla found that charters were routinely granted in Massachusetts after 1820. Richard Sylla, "Early American Banking: The Significance of the Corporate Form," *Business and Economic History* (1985), p. 108.

Comment

by James A. Dorn

Fraud and artifice constituted a large chapter in the history of our
early banking; and when they were lacking, gross ignorance all too
frequently took their place.

—Henry E. Miller[1]

In describing the process of monetary and banking reform,
William Niskanen (1989, p. 468) has used the analogy that "the
Niagara River is about as smooth five miles below the falls as above
the falls, but the transition is a bitch." This analogy seems especially
appropriate to describe money and banking in the antebellum era—a
period that has been called "an era of monetary chaos," in which
economic growth took place "in spite of the monetary system, not
primarily because of it" (Haines in 1966, p. 128).

During the antebellum era, there was constant experimentation
with alternative banking regimes for the supply of inside money
within an overarching commodity—reserve system for the provision
of outside or high-powered money. In the process of reform, there
was genuine concern for protecting noteholders from banks defaulting on their contractual agreements to redeem notes in specie. But
regulations were also motivated by self-interested bankers and legislators who saw opportunities for gain by implementing anti-competitive measures. Furthermore, widespread ignorance of sound
principles of money and banking in the pre-Civil War era meant that
the development of banking would necessarily occur slowly, by trial
and error, as individuals acquired the relevant knowledge.

A broader understanding had to be acquired of the difference
between alternative banking principles, especially the difference
between ultimate security and immediate redemption as methods to
safeguard noteholders. Bankers and the public also had to gain an

understanding of the importance of deposits as a form of currency and the unique ability of banks to create or destroy deposits—and, hence, expand or contract the quantity of circulating media—by their credit policy. Most significantly, there was a need to understand the role of self-interest in banking and the appropriate institutional framework to steer competitive forces toward stable banking, as well as the recognition of the difference between a single bank and the system as a whole.

A study of the history of alternative banking regimes in the ante-bellum era—state chartered banks, New York safety-fund banks, free banks, the Suffolk system, as well as the national banking system—can enhance our understanding of the impact of institutional change on the behavior of banks. In his paper, Eugene White examines a part of this history, namely, the development of state banking regulations in the form of limits on small-note denominations, bank liability insurance, and the bond collateral requirement under free banking. He views the history of these regulations as an evolutionary process driven by a desire on the part of regulatory authorities to protect note-holders and to resolve the principal-agent problem inherent in a fractional reserve banking system.

The basic problem, as he sees it, is that the principals (note-holders) face positive monitoring costs in policing their agents (banks) to ensure specie payment. Taking a public interest view of banking regulation, White provides a careful analysis of the effectiveness of limits on small-note denominations, insurance schemes, and bond collateral requirements in lowering monitoring costs and increasing noteholder confidence. In taking a public interest view of regulation, however, he loses sight of other aspects of the regulatory process. And by omitting the *laissez-faire* Suffolk banking system from his study, he fails to properly recognize the importance of immediate convertibility (as opposed to ultimate security) as a mechanism for disciplining bankers and resolving the principal-agent problem.

It also would have been useful to flesh out the idea—often over-looked in the antebellum era—that, ultimately, safe and sound bank-ing requires stable money.[2] By focusing on regulations presumably designed to protect noteholders, White ignores the role of bank deposits as part of the circulating media, and the importance of controlling both notes and deposits to achieve stable money. In this respect, more could have been said of early attempts at establishing reserve requirements as a method of making currency "as good as gold."

Nevertheless, White's attempt to use the principle-agent framework and the public interest perspective to understand antebellum banking regulations are fruitful exercises, as they force one to think more clearly about the regulatory process and its effect on safe and sound banking.

A Public Interest View of Bank Regulations

White argues that states introduced denominational limits on banknotes, insurance funds, and bond security requirements for free-bank notes primarily to protect noteholders. In particular, he emphasizes that so-called free banking was not unregulated banking; it was, instead, part of the evolution of banking regulations supposedly designed to lower monitoring costs and to protect the public against bank runs.

In White's view, the antebellum regulations were motivated by a public interest theory of regulation rather than by a desire on the part of bankers and legislators to promote their own self-interest. It is White's opinion, therefore, that "banking authorities imposed a variety of regulations on 'free' and 'unfree' banks *to protect the public*" (emphasis added). As such, he disagrees with Cowen and Krozner's explanation of banking regulations, namely, as devices to limit competition and to protect existing banks' market shares. He also implicitly disagrees with Lawrence H. White's reasoning that under *laissez-faire* banking there is no principal-agent problem, because private bankers have an incentive to maintain their bank's reputation.

The purpose of White's paper, then, is to "show how regulations designed to protect noteholders were a key feature of virtually all antebellum systems." He contends that "regulations were imposed in an attempt to guarantee that banks' customers would be able to convert their banknotes into specie." And he further argues that in antebellum America noteholders faced high monitoring costs and a free-rider problem: "monitoring may be diminished because with multiple principles, it is a public good with the attendant free-rider problem." Although banknote reporters, improved transportation, and better communications helped reduce the monitoring problem, they did not eliminate it. Accepting the monitoring problem as a given, White sees state governments responding "by imposing various regulations in attempts to guarantee banknotes." He then proceeds to examine restrictions on banknote denominations, liability insurance, and bond security requirements as devices to resolve the monitoring problem and to provide a sound paper currency.

Legal Minimum Denominations on Banknotes

White traces U.S. state banking regulations against small-note denominations to European banking practices and to the writings of Adam Smith and Henry Thornton—both of whom thought it sound banking practice to prohibit the issue of small-denomination notes as a way to protect the public As White observes, "American legislators were apparently impressed by the argument for high minimum denominations and these became a standard feature of many state regulations.

Although not as stringent as regulations in Great Britain, U.S. restrictions on small-note denominations helped eliminate small notes from circulation. And with fewer noteholders, the public-goods problem associated with the monitoring problem diminished, or so argues White. Nevertheless, White thinks that restricting small banknotes from circulation was "a drastic measure to solve the principal-agent problem," because it prevented the widespread use of paper currency as a transactions medium.

Even though White believes restrictions on small-note denominations reflected a public interest theory of regulation, he also tells us that (1) the federal system operated to circumvent state restrictions on note denomination because out-of-state notes would tend to circulate in those states banning small-denomination banknotes; and (2) the suspension of specie payments (convertibility) in 1814, 1837, and 1839 led many states to abandon minimum denomination requirements. In other words, there was a market demand by the public for small banknotes, and the note restrictions did not pass the market test. This fact implies, contrary to White's public interest hypothesis, that the driving force behind legislation to place minimum denomination requirements on banknotes was the self-interest of city bankers and merchants, not the desire by small traders to overcome the free-rider problem.

The demise of restrictions on small notes was also hastened by writers such as Richard Hildreth and H.C. Carey who favored a *laissez-faire* approach to money and banking. They questioned Adam

Smith's argument that small-note denominations were socially harmful, and especially attacked the argument that abolishing low-denomination notes was desireable because it would save specie—a kind of
mercantilistic argument.³

Hildreth, in *his Banks, Banking, and Paper Currencies* (1840),
stated that allowing small notes to circulate would not have adverse
effects on monetary stability or cause bank runs; and he disagreed
with the notion that accumulating specie in banks' vaults was socially
beneficial. Runs are produced when *depositors*, not small noteholders,
lose confidence in the banking system. Moreover, large noteholders,
will redeem their notes *before* small noteholders. Replacing small
notes with specie would not improve banking stability; bankers must
first obtain the metal and in doing so must necessarily contract their
earning assets. In the process, the decrease in full-bodied money in
circulation would have the same adverse effect as a reduction in paper
currency.⁴

Carey takes a cost-benefit approach to the question of the social
value of small-note restriction. He succinctly argues that "one-dollar
notes will not be used unless the benefit derived from them exceed
the cost of furnishing them, and if it does so, their use is beneficial to
the whole community" (Carey 1838, p. 117).⁵

The unpopularity of restrictions on small-note denomination is
recognized throughout White's paper. And in this discussion of the
antebellum history of small-note circulation, F.A. Walker ([1878])
1968, p. 482) contends that "in the United States notes of $1 and $2
have at all times formed an important element of the issues, and in
sections notes for fractions of a dollar have been issued" (emphasis
added).⁶ Finally, White tells us that "by 1840, small notes were in
general circulation" except in the Southern states (p. 15). Rather than
supporting a public interest theory of regulation, I believe this
evidence is more consistent with a public choice explanation.

Insurance Schemes

Beginning with the New York Safety Fund in 1829, several states
introduced insurance schemes to increase the confidence of noteholders and to minimize the risk of bank runs. White, therefore, views
liability insurance as an alternative to restrictions on banknote
denominations as a means to solve the principal-agent problem.
Opponents of the Safety Fund, however, argued that bank liability

insurance created a moral hazard problem, making noteholders and depositors less vigilant in their choice of banks. If so, banks would have incentive to overissue, and noteholders' ability to redeem their notes would be jeopardized during a panic. The Safety Fund system might be able to handle defaults by single banks, but would not be able to survive a system-wide failure.[7]

A large number of banks did fail in the 1837–41 period—because of overall monetary instability—and, as expected, the Safety Fund was unable to provide adequate protection. Consequently, White tells us that beginning in 1842, member banks only insured notes, not deposits.

The flawed design of the New York Safety Fund and the advent of free banking helped to bring about the demise of this insurance scheme. In contrast, White indicates that the insurance scheme instituted in Indiana was on a sounder basis; there were no bank failures but the insurance requirements provided an opportunity for banks to collude.

Like the minimum note denomination requirement, the Safety Fund did nothing to ensure convertibility or to adopt sound banking principles and to maintain stable money. Although the Safety Fund could prevent runs on single banks, it could do nothing to prevent system-wide runs, which stemmed from monetary disequilibrium (*i.e.,* from erratic changes in outside money or from financial panics that led to a drain of specie and a credit crunch).[8] Consequently, although the Safety Fund was an improvement, it did not rid the banking system of the principal-agent problem for noteholders.

The public interest argument for the Safety Fund can also be questioned. Opponents of the Fund, for example, claimed that the Fund was a scheme to favor country banks—where note circulation was more important than bank deposits—at the expense of large deposit banks in New York City. The scheme was also seen as a way to favor unsound banks at the expense of sound banks. Finally, the Safety Fund did nothing to limit the number of banks, which would also be a way to minimize the principal-agent problem.[9]

The Bond Collateral Requirement and Free Banking

White sees the bond collateral requirement as the third stage in the evolution of a regulatory mechanism to deal with the principal-agent problem in securing banknotes. Again, he assumes that this particular regulation was driven by the desire to protect noteholders; it was done in the public interest. But there are other explanations of the emergence of free banking that do not necessarily correspond either to the need to solve the monitoring problem or to satisfy the public interest.

The introduction of free banking in New York in 1838 had been preceded by an increasing distrust of government, especially its right to confer monopoly privilege through the grant of state bank charters. This climate paved the way for a *laissez-faire* attitude toward banking. As Fritz Redlich (1968, p. 202) stated: "In the 1840's the idea of Free Banking won minds all over the United States. . . . Free Banking represented so perfectly the underlying spirit of the period that everybody seemed to have been just waiting for the formula."

Free banking also gained popularity because there was a growing demand for credit, and any law that relaxed entry restrictions into banking was bound to gain widespread support. In this regard, White notes that even as early as 1825, free banking was being discussed in favorable terms. He calls to mind a report of the U.S. Senate, stating that "private banks would provide more credit to the public and would be successfully monitored by the market."

White also mentions that the opening of free banks in New York provided an exit from the Safety Fund's assessments. Thus, instead of rechartering under the Safety Fund system, banks had an incentive to join the new free banking system.

In sum, the *laissez-faire* climate, the desire for more credit (and banknotes), and the incentive to avoid assessments under the Safety Fund all point to the difficulty of relying on the need to resolve the monitoring problem as the *primary* explanation for the emergence of free banking.

The public interest rationale for free banking and its bond security requirement can also be questioned. The public interest argument, as interpreted by White, is that by helping to ensure convertibility, the bond collateral requirement would lower monitoring costs and serve the noteholders' interests. Legislators appear here as working in the interest of noteholders to assure that bankers fulfill their contractual obligations.

The problem with the public interest explanations is that the bond collateral requirement also created a ready market for government debt. As one commentator expressed it, the New York free banking law would have a tendency to "raise up a clamorous horde of advocates for a perpetual State loan and national debt, to supply the demand for public stocks."[10] And as Bray Hammond (1957, p. 596) pointed out:

> The free-banking law was a step backward from the Safety Fund, not forward. But it was a great thing politically. It was all things to all men. It promised more business opportunities, more banks, more money, and protection for the public. It also established a new market for bonds at a time when enthusiasm for public improvements was producing a flood tide of bond issues.

White makes one final attempt to justify a public interest view of free banking. He notes that some states granted banks charters on relatively easy terms—having, in effect, *"de facto* free entry"—but had no bond collateral requirement. He then argues that "this development emphasizes that in many states the purpose of the bond provisions of free banking laws was to provide protection to the noteholders."

There appears to be a *non sequitur* in White's line of reasoning. The fact that no bond collateral requirement existed in states having *de facto* free entry does not necessarily mean that the collateral requirement was introduced in free-banking states primarily to protect noteholders (*i.e.,* to protect the "public interest"). As we have seen, *political* motives played a key role in the incorporation of the bond security requirement into the free banking system.

More to the point, it does not follow that noteholders were less at risk in free-banking states than in states with *de facto* free entry and no bond security requirement. Indeed, as the Suffolk banking system showed, bond security was inferior to the promise of immediate redemption as a way of resolving the principal-agent problem and protecting noteholders from default. Under free banking, convertibility was roundabout and by no means assured. Under the Suffolk system, on the other hand, timely redemption was used to discipline note issue and made the Suffolk system one of the safest and soundest banking systems in the antebellum period.[11]

In this vein, Hammond (1957, p. 556) argues:

> The operations of the Suffolk Bank showed *laisser faire* at its best. With no privileges or sanctions whatever from the government, private enterprise developed in the Suffolk an efficient regulation of bank credit that was quite as much in the public interest as government regulation could be. A New Yorker wrote in 1858 that

his state, "even with aid of statutes and 'revised statutes,'" had a
system "far inferior to that created by the voluntary Suffolk Bank
system."

Hammond goes on to argue that the "greater success [of the Suffolk
system] was owing to the greater earnestness with which note
redemption was pursued in Boston, and this greater interest seems to
have been but one reflection of the conservatism that prevailed
there."

Public Choice and Public Ignorance

The theory of public choice and rent seeking has pointed to the
self-interest of government officials and the attempt of private
parties to benefit from government's power to regulate economic
activity as the driving forces behind regulation. Of course, regulatory
measures will be advertised as being "in the public interest." But, in
fact, the regulatory process often leads to anticompetitive results that
impair the market's ability to bring about socially beneficial outcomes. This has certainly been true of banking regulation.

Throughout the twentieth century, banks have been regulated
with "good intentions," but the common result has been unintended
adverse consequences for the spontaneous market order. By blocking
open-market competition, the experimentation and discovery process
that characterize free markets have been frustrated. Banking regulation during the antebellum era also appears to have been promoted
under the guise of public interest. However, because the underlying
regulatory process was driven by rent seeking, the actual results often
differed from the results desired by consumers (i.e., the socially beneficial results).

For example, limits on small-note denominations, when
enforced, deprived individuals of a convenient means of payment for
everyday transactions. This restriction, in effect, prevented the free
choice of currency and, as Carey noted, conferred net losses on
society.

The New York Safety Fund legislation, while well-intended, had
internal flaws and resulted in anticompetitive behavior and created a
moral hazard problem. This regulation was inferior to the laissez-faire
Suffolk banking system, in which insurance was absent but banknotes
were readily convertible into specie. As Hammond (1957, p. 562) puts
it: The Suffolk system "aimed at profits, but what it achieved was the

public good. The Safety Fund sought the public good but under impossible conditions and achieved bankruptcy."

The bond collateral requirement under free banking was intended to create a safe and sound banking system, but provided an artificial market for government debt and imparted a perverse elasticity to paper currency. It also did nothing to control the growth of demand deposits.[12] (Of course, the free banking system did expand banking services and operated quite satisfactorily in New York and other states.[13])

Public Ignorance and the Search for Stable Money and Banking

In the antebellum era, there was considerable ignorance about the principles of money and banking. There was confusion, for example, between ultimate security and immediate redemption as alternative banking practices, and the implications of each for safe and sound banking. There was also a lack of understanding of the role of banks in creating circulating media in the form of demand deposits, and not enough attention paid to the difference between inside money and outside money.

With regard to the public's ignorance of sound principles of money and banking prior to the Civil War, Miller ([1927] 1972, p. 152) writes:

> To a certain extent the old fallacy, so much in evidence during the colonial period, of confusing ultimate security with immediate redeemability, or, at least, of tending to give little attention to the latter, persisted well into the nineteenth century. Bond-secured issue, safety fund, limitation of circulation to a certain proportion to capital, received far more emphasis than specie reserve; and in some measure, at least, the cause seems to have been failure adequately to perceive the significance of reserves.

White, in his focus on banking regulations that incorporate the principle of ultimate security, misses the opportunity to examine the principle of immediate redeemability, especially as it operated in the Suffolk banking system.[14]

But even the Suffolk system could not withstand overall monetary disturbances originating from outside the banking system. For example, Hammond (1957, p. 563) relates that "the Suffolk, to be sure, availed no more than the Safety Fund to prevent general suspension in 1837." And, in their study of alternative banking regimes, Bordo and Schwartz (1989, p. 8) state: "The Suffolk system was no bulwark against instability in the monetary system."

The intimate relation between monetary stability and banking stability was not well understood in antebellum America. The key idea is, as expressed by Bordo and Schwartz (1989, pp. 33–34): "Price level stability . . . is a prerequisite for safe and sound banking. . . . If the outlook for future price level stability is doubtful, the success of a self-regulated banking system is also doubtful."

Despite public ignorance, banking reform did occur, and it should be emphasized that progress was made in the move toward safer and sounder banking. People do learn from their mistakes, if given the proper incentives. What White reminds us of is that institutional change in banking is a learning process, and those changes that reduce monitoring costs are most likely to persist. This message was conveyed to F.A. Walker over a century ago:

> While the New York system [of free banking] can not be accepted as based on sound principles of money, or even of banking policy, it proved, at the time, so great a check upon the wild and reckless paper-money banking that had prevailed almost universally throughout the country, and it had so clear an effect in educating the public mind to more correct views of the banking functions and of the responsibilities attaching to note-issues, that it should be spoken of with respect by the historian of American money (Walker (1878) 1968, p. 505).

Conclusion

When regulations work contrary to the market, the market will tend to circumvent them in some fashion. This was certainly the case in antebellum America. When small notes were driven out of circulation by state law in a particular state, the notes of other (nonregulated) states filled the gap. And when individuals found it costly to monitor banks to determine the credibility of the redemption agreement, they printed bank recorders and discouraged redemption.[15]

Ultimately, the public interest will be best served by allowing self-interest to operate within a private market system. The difficulty is to discover the best set of institutions to direct self-interest toward the public good.

White presents a partial picture of the banking institutions and regulations that existed in the antebellum period. To get a fuller picture, it is necessary to add a public choice perspective and to consider the role of self-regulation as it existed in the Suffolk system.

White's contribution is to remind us of the complex events that occurred in trying to design a safe and sound banking system. By viewing the regulatory process from a public interest perspective and by operating within the principal-agent framework, White forces one to think more clearly about the nature of the antebellum banking regulations that he so carefully analyzes.

Notes

1. *Banking Theories in the United States Before 1860* ([1927] 1972, pp. 7–8).
2. See, for example, Bordo and Schwartz (1989).
3. For a summary of the key arguments used by Smith and others in favor of banning low-denomination banknotes, see Miller (([1927] 1972, pp. 142–44). See also Timberlake (1974) for a general discussion of the controversies surrounding the issuance of small notes.
4. Hildreth's arguments against restricting small notes are presented in Miller ([1927] 1972, p. 145).
5. Quoted in Miller ([1927] 1972, p. 145).
6. See also Raguet (1840, pp. 137–40) for discussion of the history of small-note issues; in Miller ([1927] 1972, p. 481). Timberlake (1981) presents substantial evidence of the significance of fractional currency and small notes throughout the twentieth century.
7. For a discussion of the Safety Fund banking system, see Hammond (1957, pp. 556–63) and Miller ([1927] 1972, p. 150–51).
8. See, for example, Miller ([1927] 1972, p. 151).
9. See Miller ([1927] 1972, p. 150–51) and Hammond (1957, p. 558).
10. Quoted in "Free Banking," *Democratic Review* (1839, p. 445); in Miller ([1927] 1972, p. 149)
11. For a discussion of the Suffolk Bank, see Hammond (1957, pp. 549–56) and Palasek (1988).
12. According to Hedges (1938, p. 25):

The note currency under the free banking system came to have a sort of perverse elasticity, fluctuations in its volume occurring in response to variations in the market for bonds rather than in response to the needs of trade. . . .

In addition to the inelastic note currency which it initiated, the free banking law had another serious defect. It made no provision for specie reserves to insure current redemption of either notes or deposits.

On the same topic, Hammond (1957, pp. 595–96) writes:

Rigidly limiting the issue of notes to the amount of bonds pledged to secure them seemed at the time to be a safeguard against inflation as well as a guaranty of individual note issues. But as such it amounted to nothing. It merely put a movable limit on the amount of notes each bank could issue—for the more bonds it bought, the more notes it could put out and the more bonds it could buy—and it put no limit on the number of banks. On the contrary, it multiplied them. And most important of all, it did absolutely nothing about deposit liabilities, which were a far more dangerous medium of inflation.

Moreover, even as a guaranty and when they were "good," as the bonds accepted in New York usually were, their market value in a period when banks were in trouble was apt to be low and to be driven still lower by their sale in large amounts at the hands of bank supervisors seeking funds for the redemption of defaulted issues. Knowledge that the fund existed might make the public suppose itself secure, and to that degree make it secure, but the pledged bonds otherwise could do nothing to prevent suspension and little to mitigate it.

See also Selgin (1988, pp. 13–14).

13. See, for example, Rockoff (1974), and Rolnick and Weber (1982, 1983).

14. Palasek (1988) considers the operation of these two principles in her comparison of the New York free-banking system and the Suffolk system. She finds the Suffolk system superior and closer to a true *laissez-faire* banking system than the so-called free-banking system as it existed in New York and other states.

15. Commenting on the social pressure that operated to discourage redemption, Bullock (1900, p. 83) wrote:

Nothing was more common than a state of public opinion which condemned every attempt to obtain specie from the banks. To ask one of these institutions to fulfill the promise printed on the face of its bills was a disgraceful act, which indicated a lack of public spirit, or was proof positive of a desire to start a "run." In Ohio, Indiana, and Missouri, between 1855 and 1859, certain persons who presented notes for redemption were threatened with lynching or a coat of tar and feathers [quoted in Nussbaum 1950, p. 578].

See also F.A. Walker ([1878] 1968, pp. 481–83) for further evidence of the social stigma attached to those who sought to redeem their notes for specie.

132   COMMENT

References

Bordo, Michael D., and Anna J. "The Performance and Stability of Banking Systems Under 'Self-Regulation': Theory and Evidence." Paper presented at the Joint Universities Conference on "Regulating Commercial Banks: Australian Experiences in Perspective," Canberra, Australia, 1–2 August 1989.

Bullock, Charles J. *Essays on the Monetary History of the United States.* New York: Macmillan, 1900.

Carey, Henry C. *The Credit System in France, Great Britain, and the United States.* Philadelphia, 1838.

"Free Banking." *Democratic Review* 5 (1839).

Haines, Walter W. *Money, Prices, and Policy.* 2d ed. New York: McGraw-Hill, 1966.

Hammond, Bray. *Banks and Politics in America: From the Revolution to the Civil War.* Princeton, N.J.: Princeton University Press, 1957.

Hedges, Joseph E. *Commercial Banking and the Stock Market Before 1863.* The Johns Hopkins University Studies in Historical and Political Science, Series LVI, No. 1. Baltimore, Md.: The Johns Hopkins Press, 1938.

Hildreth, Richard. *Banks, Banking, and Paper Currencies.* Boston, 1840.

Miller, Harry E. *Banking Theories in the United States Before 1860.* Reprint. Clifton, N.J.: Augustus M. Kelley, 1972.

Niskanen, William A. "Rethinking the Case for Central Banking." *Cato Journal* 9 (Fall 1989): 467–69.

Nussbaum, Arthur. *Money in the Law.* Brooklyn, N.Y.: The Foundation Press, 1950.

Palasek, Karen Y. "Institutional Constraints and Instability in New York and New England: Free Banking and Monetary Crises, 1811–1863." Ph.D. dissertation, George Mason University, 1988.

Raquet, Condy. *A Treatise on Currency and Banking.* 2d ed. Philadelphia, 1840.

Redlich, Condy. *A Treatise on Currency and Banking.* 2nd ed. 1951. Reprint. New York: Johnson Reprint Corp., 1968.

Rockoff, Hugh. "The Free Banking Era: A Reexamination." *Journal of Money, Credit, and Banking* 6 (May 1974): 141–67.

Rolnick, Arthur J., and Warren E. Weber, "New Evidence on the Free Banking Era." *American Economic Review* 73 (December 1983): 1080–91.

Selgin, George A. *A Theory of Free Banking: Money Supply under Competitive Note Issue.* Totowa, N.J.: Rowman & Littlefield, 1988.

Timberlake, Richard H., Jr. "Denominational Factors in Nineteenth-Century Currency Experience." *Journal of Economic History* 34 (December 1974): 835–50.

Timberlake, Richard H., Jr. "The Significance of Unaccounted Currencies." *Journal of Economic History* 41 (December 1981): 853–66.

Walker, Francis Amasa. *Money.* 1878. Reprint.. New York: Augustus M. Kelley, 1968.

Southern Banking During the Civil War: A Confederate Tool and Union Target

by Gary M. Pecquet

The Civil War drastically altered the money and banking system of the United States. Before the war, banks operated under state control and direction. Southern states used such powers to mold their banks into a wartime monetary regime with most of the features of a central bank. The Confederacy used that banking system to facilitate the monetary expansion needed to finance the war. Southern banks subsequently became a target of the Union war effort. The North embarked upon policy commitments designed to discredit the Confederacy's financial commitments and thereby repudiate its currency. The National Banking Act adopted by the North in 1863 promised an end to the era of state banking—undermining the legitimacy of the Confederate monetary system. Northern battlefield victories eventually doomed Confederate monetary finance.

The "tug of war" over Southern banking produced the National Banking system which survived the conflict. The new system effectively served Northern war objectives. It provided revenue for the U.S. Treasury and repudiated the Confederate currency at the same time. The National Banking system was not designed to efficiently satisfy the post-war, peace-time currency demand of the country, however. Indeed, the trend towards centralized banking should be considered as a product of the war itself.[1]

State Banking Before the Civil War

Prior to the Civil War, banks were considered to be quasi-public institutions, rather than strictly private, profit-seeking entities.[2] It was believed that noteholders needed special protections against unsound banking practices. To this end, two states (Texas and Arkansas) outlawed banking institutions altogether. Other states, including North and South Carolina, chartered specific institutions to operate as banks on a case by case basis. Several other states (Alabama, Florida, Georgia, Louisiana, Tennessee, and Virginia) adopted a uniform set of regulations, called "Free Banking Laws," under which any potential entrant into the banking industry must operate.

Banking assets consisted chiefly of specie, inter-bank notes and deposits, business loans, government bonds, and real estate. Banking liabilities included bank notes (the primary component of money supply), deposits and the equity claims of capital. During ordinary times, both notes and deposits could be redeemed in specie upon demand. State laws usually placed heavy penalties upon bankers who did not redeem their notes in gold. According to the Free Banking Laws then in vogue, the failure to redeem even one note meant that the state could close the bank, sell the bank's securities held as collateral, and even reimburse the noteholders (Rolnick and Weber, 1988, 47–48). Chartered banking established equally effective protections for noteholders. The 1860 charter of the Bank of North Carolina did not require the immediate liquidation of the bank upon specie suspension; but it called upon the state to collect a four percent tax on all unredeemed notes and held the bank liable to pay their noteholders, twelve percent upon the face value of the notes per diem! (Holder, 1937, 367–376). Other common noteholder protection clauses generally found in antebellum banking laws gave noteholders (not depositors) the first lien on banking assets, placed limits upon the number of notes which could be issued, and held bankers personally liable for the losses of the bank upon the value equivalent of their investment (Rolnick and Weber, 1983, 1982–1983).

Despite the strong wording in those antebellum banking laws, the state legislatures remained lords over their respective banking system. State governments could rewrite, revoke, and suspend the provisions protecting noteholders. At the eve of the Civil War, the condition of banks varied widely throughout the South. The Georgia banks suspended specie payments during the 1857 crash and were still off the gold standard when war began (Savannah Banks, 1865). Florida was just beginning to reestablish banking in 1860 when war broke out (Dovel, 1955). Louisiana operated under a constitutional provision that explicitly prohibited the legislature from removing the penalties for specie suspension or authorizing banks to suspend specie payments in any way. Because of that constitutional provision, Louisiana experienced the 1857 panic and even endured several months of the Civil War without suspending specie (Bragg, 1941, 67–72 and Morgan, 1985, 43).

Secession and Specie Suspension

In the fall of 1860, the election of President Lincoln began the political crisis that led to the secession of several states. These states did not organize the Confederacy until February 1861. In March, Lincoln assumed the Presidency of the Union, and war broke out at Ft. Sumter in the following month. During these critical months, Southern state legislatures began to enact the measures that would convert the banking system away from specie convertible bank notes and paved the way toward the issue of Confederate money needed to finance the war.

The first step down the road to a Confederate monetary system involved the suspension of specie payments on bank notes and deposits. State legislatures authorized the suspension of specie payments by the weaker banks unable to sustain the withdrawal of gold by noteholders and depositors in the time of political uncertainty (Schwab, 1901, 124–131). State politicians, however, exerted influence upon the stronger banks to suspend specie payments also (Schweikart, 1985). Most Southern states went off the gold standard in this manner before the Confederacy was organized (Godfrey, 1978, 69–71). By securing the "voluntary" consent of banks to suspend specie payments, Southern banks depended upon the good graces of the state legislatures to remain in operation. In return for suspending the bankers' legal obligations to noteholders, state legislatures throughout the South required banks to advance the government emergency war loans (Bass, 1942, 217; Boyd, 1915, 198; Bryan, 1953, 58–59 and Schweikart, 1985). This provided the seceding states with the start-up money needed to make hasty war preparations.

The suspension of specie payments naturally severed the connection between gold and bank-note prices. By the end of 1860, the suspended bank notes from North Carolina and Tennessee traded at five to ten percent discounts below the U.S. gold dollar (*Mobile Price-Current*, December 15, 1860). But the suspension of specie payments also effectively prevented the $25 million in gold held in bank vaults from entering circulation. The bank gold could be held hostage by the state legislatures which could threaten to enforce the antebellum banking liabilities against uncooperative banks.[3] Most of the early loans advanced to the state governments were paid in the form of bank notes and deposits.[4] Very little gold actually left the banking system after suspension (Godfrey, 64).[5] It remained in bank vaults under the watchful eye of state authorities while the credit advanced to the states represented an increase in claims against the bank gold. By September 1861 the increased claims against banking assets and battlefield uncertainties increased the discount on suspended Southern bank notes to 12–15 percent below the gold dollar (Thian, 1880, 328–330).

Confederate Currency and Southern Banking

The organization of the Confederate government and the issue of Confederate bonds and currency marked the next phase in the establishment of the Confederate monetary regime. The Provisional Confederate Congress met in February 1861 and promptly re-enacted the customs and duties enforced under the old United States law at the time of secession. After war broke out in April, the Union naval blockage promptly reduced these revenues to a trickle. The Confederate Treasury Secretary, C.G. Memminger, had to find new revenue reserves.

How did Memminger accomplish this conversion to a monetary system designed to facilitate war finance? Let us first remark what the Confederacy did not do. The Confederate Congress never seized control over the Southern banks by statutory compulsion. The Confederate treasury notes never became the legal tender of the land.[6] Individuals could contract in any currency they chose. They could deal in gold or even U.S. greenbacks until an 1864 statute prohibited the latter (Todd, 1954, 117).

Instead, the Southern banking system was converted into a Confederate monetary regime with the full cooperation of the state legislatures. The Southern states remained masters over their own banking systems, and the Confederate monetary regime did not represent a break from antebellum "monetary constitution" which maintained banking under the domain of "states rights."

Secretary Memminger secured the permission of state governments to adopt three measures designed to make Confederate treasury notes acceptable as currency. First, the state legislatures rewrote their tax codes.[7] Before the war, taxes had to be paid in gold or in the notes of "specie paying banks of the state." During 1861, the tax codes were rewritten making tax collections payable with the "Treasury notes of this state or the Confederate States of America" in addition to "hard currency." Of course, the people preferred to pay their taxes in the discounted paper currencies rather than gold when the tax receivers accepted both currencies on an equivalent dollar basis.

Second, state legislatures required their suspended banks to accept Confederate and state treasury notes on deposit. Banks now obligated to the state legislatures for permission to suspend specie could be required to meet these conditions—or else be closed down (Schweikart, 1985). Georgia bankers would later complain, "A distinction was made between banks and every other corporation and individual of this state. The latter were allowed to refuse payment of their debts in any but specie currency, or compromise on such terms as to suit themselves, whilst banks were required under heavy penalties to themselves and their officers to receive both state and Confederate notes in payment of all the monetary securities which they possessed" (Savannah Banks, 1865).

The Louisiana and Mobile banks were to last to suspend specie and accept Confederate notes on deposit. On September 11, 1861, Secretary Memminger appealed to the officers of the New Orleans banks and the Governor of Louisiana. He argued that the value of treasury notes depended upon their acceptance as money. President Davis and the entire cabinet backed Secretary Memminger, and the Louisiana Governor appealed to the New Orleans banks to suspend specie despite the prohibition of specie suspension clearly delineated under the state constitution. By November, all but one of the New Orleans banks reluctantly suspended specie and began to accept Confederate notes on deposit. The Mobile banks followed shortly thereafter (Bragg, 1941, 70–71; and Morgan, 1985, 25).

The third plank in the Confederate monetary order required banks to accept Confederate treasury notes in the adjustment of all bank balances between themselves. As South Carolina Governor Pickens (1862, 8–10) remarked, "To this extent, [the Confederate notes] are thus made equivalent to gold and silver, and of course it gives them almost exclusive circulation." Governor Pickens called upon the legislature to carefully monitor the banks and determine if any banks have pursued a course deemed "not patriotic or proper," and if so, the benefits of the specie suspension act could be denied as far as those institutions were concerned."[8]

The Southern banks were thus conscripted into the service of the Confederate war effort as surely as any drafted soldier. That transformation was accomplished entirely within the antebellum laws that permitted state legislatures to suspend specie, except in the case of Louisiana. When the Confederate currency began to be widely used in September 1861, the Confederate notes exchanged at only a few cents below the gold dollar while the suspended bank notes traded at 10–15 percent discounts (Thian, 1889, 328–330).

The establishment of Confederate money as banking reserves actually supported bank-note values by giving them a legally recognized conversion value. In the Richmond currency markets the bank notes traded about par with the Confederate dollar until the end of 1862 (Richmond Newspapers). The Confederate currency "backed" the Southern bank notes. What supported the value of the Confederate currency?

The Confederate Monetary and Financial System

The recent rational expectations literature embraced by Neil Wallace (1981) and Thomas Sargent (1982) argues that the value of money depends upon the expectations of future fiscal policy in addition to debt that is outstanding. In particular, it depends upon the government's willingness and capacity to resume specie parity in the future (see, for example, the monetary historical research by Calomiris, 1988a and 1988b; Smith, 1985a; and 1985ab). The legitimacy of the Confederate Banking System rested upon antebellum state banking law. A Confederate victory, or even a compromise peace settlement resulting in the *status quo ante,* would have re-opened the ports and resumed the customs collections. Those victory and non-defeat expectations "backed" the Confederate debt. Only an unconditional surrender to a Union committed to a new monetary system would have repudiated the Confederate government and its obligations entirely.

The Confederate debt consisted of the non-interest bearing treasury notes, which became the medium of exchange, numerous classes of bonds, and call certificates. The bonds initially bore 8 percent interest coupons payable semi-annually in specie. The Treasury did not have sufficient amounts of coin to honor the specie pledges and paid the interest in depreciated Confederate currency instead. No attempt was made to compensate the bondholders for this loss. The "call certificates" were an unusual obligation, which initially paid 6 percent interest, but the rate was gradually reduced to 4 percent by the end of the war. The 6 percent call certificates could be purchased in $500 denominations and "called" or reconverted into cash at par. That asset was provided at a perfectly elastic supply, or nearly so, at the stated rate of interest. The unique redemption feature implies that the Confederate dollar price of the call certificates would never have fallen below par (Davis and Pecquet, 1990, 135).

Call certificates and Confederate bonds were close substitutes. Consequently, the Confederate dollar price of these bonds did not fall until the final months of the war. In fact, the nominal interest rates in Confederate securities actually fell during most of the war despite rampant inflation and military defeats. When these assets are converted into their gold dollar market values and future interest payments are assumed to be made in specie, then the real Confederate interest rates were high, volatile, and reflected war events (Davis and Pecquet, 1990).

Bank deposits in seven Southern states grew from $69 million in April 1862, to $10 million by January 1863, to $168 million by the beginning of 1864 (Godfrey, 1978, 118–119). Southern banks were required to receive Confederate notes on deposit. They had no choice in the matter, but there was practically no private loan demand during the war (Godfrey, 1978, 82–83). Apparently, few people started new commercial enterprises during the war and even fewer wanted to borrow depreciated Confederate notes. The banks had little choice but to purchase Confederate securities. Between April 1862, and January 1863, Southern banks purchased $40 million additional Confederate bonds, called investment bonds (Godfrey, 1978, 118–119). Other banks simply chose to acquire interest bearing cash and call certificates.[9] Southern banks were wedded to the Confederate dollar whichever choice they made.

The Southern banking system performed most of the service of a central bank in time of war. The banks accepted the currency printed by the treasury of deposit. The banks used these cash deposits to provide a ready market for Confederate bond sales. The vast quantities of gold in bank vaults were kept out of circulation facilitating the widespread acceptance of Confederate money and providing potential reserves to redeem the many bank deposits and notes whenever a peace treaty might have been signed and specie payments resumed.[10]

As the war proceeded, millions and millions of Confederate notes, bonds, and call certificates were issued. That expansion increased the claims against the future taxing capacity of the Confederate government and the bankheld specie. Consequently, all Confederate obligations tended to depreciate against the gold dollar. Table 1 below documents the Confederate dollar price of one U.S. gold dollar at various stages in the war in the Richmond auction markets.

Table 1
The Price of One Gold Dollar in Confederate Money During the Civil War

	1861	1862	1863	1864	1865
January	____	$1.25	$ 3.00	$20.00 to 20.50	$45 to 60
February	____	1.25	4.00	22.50 to 25.00	45 to 65
March	____	1.30	5.00	23.00 to 24.50	70 to 60
April	____	1.40	5.50	22.00 to 23.00	60.00
May	$1.10	1.40	5.50	18.00 to 21.00	
June	1.10	1.50	7 to 8	17.00 to 19.00	
July	1.10	1.50	9.00	20.00 to 23.00	
August	1.10	1.50	12 to 13	22.50 to 25.00	
September	1.10	2.50	12 to 13	22.50 to 27.50	
October	1.15	2.50	14.00	26.00 to 27.00	
November	1.15	3.00	15 to 17	27.50 to 33.50	
December	1.20	3.00	18 to 20	34.00 to 49.00	

Sources: (Todd, 1954, 198)

The Confederacy printed $250 million in non-interest bearing treasury notes and a sum of $455 million in all forms of cash and call certificates before the end of 1862 (Godfrey, 43). The Southern banks, outside of Louisiana and Tennessee, owed $50 million in bank notes by the beginning of 1862 and issued very few for the duration of the war. (Banks obtained more than enough Confederate currency from deposits). Despite the relative increase in the Confederate currency during 1862, the bank notes continued to be linked to the Confederate dollar by state law. On the Richmond markets bank notes exchanged between .98–1.00 in the C.S.A. money.

Banking Under Union Occupation

By the beginning of 1862, Southern banks were an integral part of the Confederate monetary regime and the Confederate monetary system became a strategic target of the Union war effort. The rich banking center in New Orleans fell to Union naval forces during April 1862 (only a few months after these same banks had agreed to suspend specie and support the Confederacy). The Confederates shipped most of the New Orleans bank specie out of the city before the arrival of Union occupation troops. Other bank assets remained in New Orleans. Confederate treasury notes and bank notes composed the preinvasion money supply. What would happen to the money supply under Union occupation?

General Benjamin "Beast" Butler promptly prohibited the exchange of Confederate notes or any securities—rendering them useless in New Orleans. General Butler permitted the circulation of the local bank notes which became the primary medium of exchange (Doyle, 1959). The suspended bank notes traded at widely different values depending upon their expected conversion value following the war when the bank's specie could be restored (see Table 2 below). Under U.S. law, the New Orleans banks were liable to redeem their outstanding notes in "greenback" dollars. The "greenback" was a paper currency issued by the North to finance the war. This currency could not be converted to gold either—but it commanded a much higher market price than the Confederate dollar. The bankers were

Table 2
Bank Note Prices in Occupied New Orleans

Bank Note	Greenback Price
Bank of Louisiana	$ .59 – .62
Crescent City Bank	.75 – .80
Merchants Bank	.38 – .40
Canal Bank Notes	1.02 – 1.04
Citizens Bank Notes	1.03 – 1.04

The Southern Bank never suspended specie payments and continued to redeem its notes in gold coin despite public pressure by the Confederates and Union occupation.

Source: *Banker's Magazine*, 14, new series, no. 1, (July, 1864) 72–73.

made liable for the emergency war loans they had advanced to Louisiana, and they were legally obligated to redeem these claims in a more precious currency! (Caldwell, 1935, 91–96).

Most of the New Orleans bank notes traded below the greenback dollar. A few such bank notes, however, were actually worth *more* than the greenback dollar. The Louisiana constitution did not recognize specie suspension for any reason whatsoever. A bank note premium above the greenback dollar indicated that at least some people believed that the antebellum liability rules might be endorsed following the war. The New Orleans currency market gave the following quotations for May 27, 1864. One gold dollar was worth about $1.78 in greenback currency at the time. The sole New Orleans bank which resisted pressure to suspend specie for the Confederates still continued to operate on a gold basis for two years after the Union occupation.

The upper coast of North Carolina also fell to Union forces in the spring of 1862. This region contained branches of two North Carolina chartered banks. During Union occupation, these branches corresponded with their parent banks in Confederate territory, transferred funds, and continued operation. Confederate notes deposited on account were quickly shipped to the Confederate-held portion of the state "for safekeeping," while the branches in the occupied regions conducted most of their business in bank notes and deposits denominated in Confederate dollars.[11]

Individuals residing within the Confederacy learned of General Butler's repudiation of Confederate money. When Charleston, South Carolina became threatened by a similar naval invasion during the summer of 1862, some of the local citizens refused to accept Confederate currency preferring bank notes instead. South Carolina bank notes began to trade at 10 percent premiums above the Confederate dollar. An eyewitness remarked regarding the appreciations of banknotes' prices, "One explanation I have heard is that in New Orleans the notes of state banks were allowed to circulate while Confederate notes were not" (Thian, 1880, 567).

Bank notes were supported by Confederate currency as a direct consequence of state law, and state law presided over the antebellum monetary system. No temporary occupation policies established on the field of battle could overturn the monetary constitution. Even in the event of a Northern victory, a peace treaty returning the South to the Union before 1863 would have probably upheld the state authority over the banking system. What remained of the Confederate government could have negotiated terms for a partial redemption of the currency. The adoption of the National Currency Act by the United States Congress in February 1863, would alter this monetary constitution by committing the Union to a post-war banking system directly subject to the federal government. The act would and did repudiate the Confederate currency.[12]

The Emancipation Proclamation and the National Currency Act

During the initial stages of the war, President Lincoln and the Republican Congress made no post-war policy commitments. The only stated wartime objective was to "preserve the Union." On slavery Lincoln declared, "I have no purpose, directly or indirectly, to interfere with the institution of slavery in the states where it exists" (Randall, 1953, 478–480). Meanwhile, bills introducing banking reforms went nowhere in Congress. It was an important element of Lincoln's war strategy not to alienate the border states by announcing any sweeping policy reforms.

By the fall of 1862, the border states had been occupied and secured by Union troops, and it became prudent to consider postwar policy commitments. The Emancipation Proclamation, for example, would turn the war into a referendum on slavery by declaring all slaves residing in Confederate-held territory to be once and forever free. This executive action clearly violated the antebellum Constitution of the U.S., but Lincoln believed that such an action became legitimate under the scope of presidential war powers. In other words, wartime emergencies provided "windows of opportunity" for Constitutional reform.

On a cost-benefit analysis, the Emancipation Proclamation served the Union war effort very well (Trefousse, 1975, 1–36). It eliminated the possibility of European intervention on behalf of the South by turning the Confederacy into a pro-slavery pariah.[13] It provided a new source of Union conscripts at a time when northern whites threatened draft riots. It was also hoped that the Proclamation might disrupt the Confederate economy by inducing mass defections among slaves. On the negative side, the emancipation of slaves was unpopular in the North. The Republicans lost Congressional seats in the

November 1862 elections. The Proclamation made a compromise peace treaty between North and South virtually impossible. The Confederate government could not renounce slavery as part of a peace compromise. After the Emancipation Proclamation became official on January 1, 1863, Lincoln could not legally unfree the slaves either. The prospects of a return to the status quo ante became nil (Franklin, 1963, 136–143 and Randall, 502, 672).[14]

The Proclamation completely altered the character of the war. It derailed peace movements in both the North and South by eliminating the prospects of compromise—but it increased the ante. Northern victory now required the complete military conquest of the Confederate government.

On the heels of the Emancipation Proclamation, the National Currency Bill was reintroduced in Congress January 8, 1863. This time it received the endorsement of President Lincoln as a much needed financial measure. Even so, the bill faced a couple of close calls. It passed in the Senate in a 23–21 vote after a key Senator switched his vote in favor of the bill following a last minute appeal.[15] A tie vote would have killed the bill because the vice president opposed the measure. After another close vote, 78–64, in the House, Lincoln signed the National Currency Act into law February 20, 1863 (Helderman, 1931, 133–141; and Knox, 1969, 96).

The National Currency Act promised to end the era of state control over banking by establishing a new system of nationally chartered banks. The national banks were to issue a uniform currency, keep 25 percent reserves in the form of legal tender (greenbacks), buy the U.S. war debt, and were forbidden to pay out any kind of note at a discount. (*Statutes at Large of the 37th Congress*, 655–682). The final provision was intended to demonetize the depreciated state bank notes in the North and support the greenback currency. Subsequent revisions of the act actually levied taxes upon outstanding state bank notes.

A controversial provision of the National Currency Act placed a strict limit at $300 million upon the number of national bank notes to be issued. Since the quantity of greenback was also strictly limited under other legislation, (see Mitchell, 1903, 119), the National Currency Act deliberately produced a scarcity of paper money. Henry C. Carey, a contemporary economist, condemned the act "monopolistic" because of the restriction on the note issue (Helderman,

146–147). But it was precisely because of the restriction on note issue that the National Currency Act could establish a seigniorage for the issue of new national bank notes. The chief legislative purpose of the act was to assist the North in financing the war. The national banks were forbidden to invest in corporate stocks and real estate and required to purchase U.S bonds as collateral for the circulation notes. In that manner, the banks and the U.S. treasury "shared the privilege of circulation" as William Graham Sumner (1896, 143) once remarked.

But there are numerous potential sources for government revenue. Why did President Lincoln select this peculiar and indirect method to raise federal war funds? The answer is that note limitation did not provide for a uniform increase of the new national currency. The rebellious Southern states would obviously be left out of their *pro-rata* shares of the seigniorage. Moreover, the National Currency Act renounced state control over the banking system and thereby attacked the legitimacy of the Confederate monetary regime which had been legally established with state legislative approval. In the aftermath of a Union victory, Confederate currency and securities of all sorts would now become worthless. The outstanding Southern bank notes would remain private obligations of the bankers to be redeemed according to the antebellum liability rules and the dictates of occupying authorities. In other words, the occupation policies of General Butler became the official wartime policy commitments in Washington.

The Emancipation Proclamation committed President Lincoln to the unconditional surrender of the Confederate government by eliminating the prospects of a compromise return to the status quo ante, and the new National Banking system in effect "bet" on the outcome of the war. The bankers holding the U.S. war debt would now realize a capital gain if the Confederacy were defeated and its currency repudiated. A potential currency vacuum in the "conquered provinces" would increase the demand for U.S. greenback dollars and consequently the real value of the bank held war debt. Thus, Lincoln not only raised war revenue with the National Currency Act he created powerful political allies in financial circles at the same time. The real losers in this transfer of wealth consisted of those holding Confederate securities and that group had no representation in Washington. It is not often that a belligerent can shift the incidence of its own financial measures to its enemy, but the National Currency

Act actually accomplished this result. Every subsequent Union battlefield victory translated into a capital gain for Northern bond-holders (Roll, 1972, 480) and a capital loss for those holding Confederate currency and securities (Davis and Pecquet, 1990).

The Collapse of Confederate War Finance

According to the rational expectations hypothesis, markets adjust instantaneously to changes in monetary and fiscal policy commitments. The impact of the Emancipation Proclamation and National Currency Act upon the Southern currency seems to support the hypothesis. Two days before the introduction of the National Currency bill into the U.S. Congress, the Richmond markets recorded a 20–30 percent premium on Southern bank notes (*Richmond Daily Whig*).[16] The Confederate dollar price of Southern bank notes became established at $1.50–1.75 following the adoption of the National Currency Act by the North, and the two currencies behaved independently for the duration of the war (see Table 3).

Table 3
The Prices of Southern Bank Notes in Confederate Dollars

Dates	Type of Bank Note	Price
Dec. 1861–1862	All Bank Notes	$ .98 – 1.00
Jan. 1863	NC Banks	1.25 – 1.30
	SC Banks	1.30 – 1.35
	VA Banks	1.25 – 1.30
Feb. 1863	NC Banks	1.35
	SC Banks	1.40
	VA Banks	1.35
March 1863	GA Banks	1.50 – 1.75
	NC Banks	1.50 – 1.75
	SC Banks	1.50 – 1.75
	VA Banks	1.50 – 1.75
April 1863	All Bank Notes	1.60 – 1.75
May 1863	All Bank Notes	1.60 – 1.75
June 1863	All Bank Notes	1.75 – 1.85
July 1863	All Bank Notes	2.25 – 2.30
Aug. 1863	No Data Available	
Sept. 1863	All Bank Notes	3.00
Oct. 1863	All Bank Notes	3.00

Table 3 (cont'd)
The Prices of Southern Bank Notes in Confederate Dollars

Dates	Type of Bank Note	Price
Nov. 1863	All Bank Notes	3.00
Dec. 1863	All Bank Notes	3.00 – 3.50
Jan. 1864	AL Banks	3.15
	GA Banks	2.90
	NC Banks	2.90
	SC Banks	2.90
	VA Banks	2.90
Feb. 1864	All Bank Notes	3.00 – 3.50
March 1864	Va Banks	3.00 – 4.00
April 1864	GA Banks	2.00 – 2.50
	NC Banks	3.00 – 3.50
	SC Banks	2.00 – 2.50
May 1864	GA Banks	3.00 – 3.50
	NC Banks	3.00 – 3.50
	SC Banks	2.50
	VA Banks	2.50
June 1864	GA Banks	2.50
	NC Banks	2.50 – 3.00
	SC Banks	1.50
	VA Banks	2.00
July 1864	GA Banks	2.50
	NC Banks	3.50
	SC Banks	1.50
	VA Banks	1.50
Aug. 1864	GA Banks	2.50
	NC Banks	3.00
	SC Banks	1.50
	VA Banks	1.50
Sept. 1864	GA Banks	2.50
	NC Banks	3.00 – 4.00
	SC Banks	2.00 – 2.25
	VA Banks	2.00 – 2.25
Oct. 1864	GA Banks	2.50 – 4.00
	NC Banks	3.00 – 4.50
	SC Banks	2.50 – 3.00
	VA Banks	2.50 – 3.00
Nov. 1864	GA Banks	3.00
	NC Banks	4.50
	SC Banks	2.75
	VA Banks	2.75

Table 3 (cont'd)
The Prices of Southern Bank Notes in Confederate Dollars

Dates	Type of Bank Note	Price
Dec. 1864	GA Banks	2.75 – 3.00
	NC Banks	5.00 – 6.00
	SC Banks	2.50 – 3.50
	VA Banks	2.50 – 3.50
Jan. 1865	GA Banks	3.00
	NC Banks	6.00 – 7.00
	SC Banks	3.00
	VA Banks	2.65 – 3.00
Feb. 1865	GA Banks	3.00
	NC Banks	5.00 – 7.00
	SC Banks	2.00
	VA Banks	3.00

Source: Newspaper Market Reports in Richmond, Virginia for several city newspapers. The data for the summer of 1864 came from Wilmington, N.C.

The premium on Southern bank notes arose from the announced policies outside of the Confederacy which promised to repudiate Confederate money, but reimburse noteholders from the liquidation of Southern banking assets. After two decisive Confederate defeats at Vicksburg and Gettysburg during July 1863, the bank notes exchanged for about three Confederate dollars. The eventual Southern defeat was anticipated on the currency markets. After 1863, Southern banking assets suffered from heavy taxes and battlefield pillage and plunder (Schweikart, 1987, 305–306). The erosion of banking assets prevented further increases in Southern bank note prices.

A 200 percent premium on the $50 million of outstanding bank notes displaced the purchasing power of $100 million in Confederate Treasury notes. The value of other non-confederate monetary assets, such as gold held by the public, also appreciated due to the anticipated Union victory. The clearest indication of the crowding out of Confederate currency can be seen in the money–price relationship. John Munro Godfrey (123) provides the best estimates of the Confederate money supply to date. Although his estimates contain certain inaccuracies and do not constitute the final word on the monetary estimation in the Confederacy,[17] Godfrey's estimates do provide some evidence of the crowding out effect (see Table 4). Before 1863, the money supply increased faster than prices and after that date Southern prices outpaced monetary growth rates.

Table 4
Changes in the Confederate Money Supply and Prices, 1861–65

Date	Money Supply (Jan. 1861 = 1.0)	Prices (Jan.–Apr. 1861 = 1.0)
1861		
Jan.	1.0	1.0
Apr.	1.0	1.0
July	1.1	1.1
Oct.	1.6	1.4
1862		
Jan.	2.9	1.9
Apr.	4.4	2.8
July	6.2	3.8
Oct.	8.7	5.3
1863		
Jan.	11.7	7.6
Apr.	12.9	11.8
July	14.5	13.3
Oct.	17.3	18.8
1864		
Jan.	20.5	28.0
Feb.	22.3	29.5
Apr.	14.5	44.7
July	15.3	40.9
Oct.	16.4	40.0
1865		
Jan.	18.3	58.2

Sources: Money supply, Table 6.3: and prices, Lerner, "Money, Prices and Wages in the Confederacy, 1861–65," *Journal of Political Economy*, Vol. 63 (February 1955), p. 24.

From Godfrey, John M., *Monetary Expansion in the Confederacy* (New York: Arno Press, 1978).

The depreciation of Confederate currency and securities impeded the ability of the Confederate printing presses to command resources. The Confederate Congress responded to the erosion of purchasing power by enacting a series of direct taxes during the final years of the war. Beginning in 1863, the Confederacy imposed an 8 percent *ad valorem* tax on all agricultural products, and it was made retroactive to cover the production during 1862. The Congress levied another 8 percent tax on all kinds of money. The sale of most goods was subjected to a 10 percent profits tax. A graduated income tax with rates ranging from 2 percent to 15 percent fell on all non-salaried income. The Confederate Congress added new taxes during the following year (Todd, 1954, 142–152).

Inflation soared despite the adoption of numerous taxes. By the end of 1863, the Confederate dollar traded for only five cents in gold (see Table 1). In December 1863 Secretary Memminger recommended an extensive currency reform measure that would have immediately converted the outstanding currency into bonds and provided that only future currency issues would remain receivable for taxes (Capers, 1893, 343–347 and Yearnes, 1960, 203–208). His intention was to enhance the value of the new currency and increase the purchase power of the Confederate printing presses.

The Confederate Congress had a mind of its own, however. Public choice theory (Buchanan and Tullock, 1962) demonstrates that the best laid plans of mice and statesmen often go astray when confronted by the "mathematics of politics." By the beginning of 1864, the Confederate Congress contained senators and representatives from a number of states which were wholly or partly occupied by the North. A swift, total repudiation of the outstanding currency would have imposed a relatively greater burden upon the states within the Confederate lines where most of the currency circulated. Numerous currency bills introduced into the Confederate Congress (Yearns, 203–208) pitted the representatives from the eastern seaboard and Alabama, which favored mild currency repudiation, against those congressmen from the occupied states who favored more drastic currency repudiation measures. In the end, the Confederate Currency Reform Act of February 17, 1864, proved to be a terrible compromise which discredited the government's financial obligations without assisting the treasury (Pecquet, 1987).

The Confederate Currency Reform Act divided the outstanding non-interest bearing Treasury notes into four classes according to denomination. Most of the currency would be convertible into a new issue of treasury notes at a rate of three old dollars to two new ones. The exchange would begin on April 1, 1864, except for the region west of the Mississippi, where the exchange was scheduled to occur in July. Five-dollar bills were allowed to retain their face value until July 1 and October 1 west of the Mississippi. Hundred-dollar bills were subject to a special 10 percent per month tax if they were not exchanged for 4 percent bonds, and small denominations below five dollars would never depreciate at all! None of these provisions touched the state-issued treasury notes and bank notes that were creatures of state legislatures and consequently immune (Pecquet, 223).

Although the law placed a $200 million limit on the issue of new currency, the fact that the old currency could be converted into new tax receivable issue of Confederate money defeated the purpose of Secretary Memminger's original proposal. Memminger wanted to enhance the purchasing power of the Treasury by repudiating the old notes or making them convertible into non-tax-receivable bonds (Caper, 343–347). The actual Currency Reform Act did not do this. It created unnecessary confusion in Southern markets (Pecquet, 225–234). Moreover, much of the new issue of currency had to be used to exchange for the old currency. Instead of purchasing much needed war resources, many Treasury notes were used to make currency conversion (Godfrey, 35). The Currency Reform Act immobilized the Treasury's ability to make necessary war expenditures.

Numerous difficulties interfered with Confederate war finance during the final stages of the war. The Union occupation of the Mississippi river valley made it extremely difficult to ship the new Confederate currency to the armies of the Trans-Mississippi west (Pecquet, 235–239). When the city of Richmond became threatened, the Confederate printing presses had to be relocated in Columbia, S.C. (Todd, 87–89). That interruption deprived the Treasury of funds during the critical summer months of 1864. Moreover, the Currency Reform Act imposed a statutory limit on the issue of new currency. The Confederate Congress authorized the issue of additional Treasury notes to pay arrears due to the army, but President Jefferson Davis vetoed the measure in order to preserve the fiscal integrity of the government (Yearns, 211). Meanwhile the desertion from the armies soared. In October 1864 President Davis admitted that two-thirds of the troops were absent from their ranks. General Robert E. Lee attributed the high rates of desertion to inadequate supplies of food and clothing (Reid and White, 1985, 70–72).[18]

A contrast between the National Currency Act and the Confederate Currency Reform Act of 1864 indicates just how badly outmatched the Confederacy was in the War Between the Monetary Regimes. The South fought a defensive war; the North sought to dominate. The South constructed a monetary regime based upon the legitimacy of the antebellum state banking system. The North strategically attacked that legitimacy by committing to a new monetary system. The North exported its financial burdens and monetary system upon the South. The South lost control over its own monetary system as it lost on the battlefield. The desperate South began to repudiate its own currency in order to protect its ability to purchase goods with future monetary issues. The South did not dare to repudiate bank notes and state-issued currency because its legitimacy depended upon states' rights. Moreover, the South even lacked the leadership to repudiate its own currency properly; the actual Currency Reform Act achieved the opposite of the stated objective, and the Confederate armies went undersupplied and often unpaid.

As the war continued, matters got increasingly worse for the Confederate treasury. The Confederate taxes continued to erode Southern banking assets. Larry Schweikart (1987, 305–306) estimated that due to the effects of "taxflation" only 36 percent of an average bank's total assets (excluding Confederate securities) remained by the end of 1864. Scorched earth policies by the Union armies also destroyed many assets owned by farmers and railroads who were indebted to banks.[19] With the purchasing power of the Confederate dollar down to two cents in gold and most of the capital assets consumed by taxes and wartime destruction, the Confederacy had no where to turn.

During March 1865, less than a month before Appomattox, the Confederate Congress enacted a forced specie loan measure, which authorized the treasury to "borrow" up to $30 million in specie from banks and other corporations (Todd, 81). Since that amount exceeded the probable quantity of gold in the entire South, the act amounted to a license to rob banks![20] Professor Jonathan Hughes recently summarized, "In the South the financial rout was probably worse than the military debacle. Lee negotiated for an army at Appomattox. The same cannot be said for Confederate finances." (Hughes, 1990, 251).

The end of the war left the Southern monetary system in ruins. Confederate money and securities became worthless and the Southern bank notes traded at much depreciated values. The specie dollar price of the bank notes issued by seventy banks throughout Georgia, South Carolina, North Carolina, and Virginia stood at $.167. The bank notes from states hit less severely by the conflict did only slightly better. Similar un-weighted average specie dollar prices for bank notes issued in Alabama, Louisiana, and Tennessee ranged at $.325, $.470 and $.326 respectively (*Banker's Magazine,* October, 1865, 347–348).

Since bank notes were the senior obligation for banks, the specie discounts indicate that virtually every Southern bank was technically insolvent after the war. Most Southern banks eventually underwent bankruptcy proceedings, although the process actually took a number of years. The formal bankruptcy proceedings of the Bank of North Carolina began in 1868 (Holder, 1931, 394–406). The Planter's Bank of Savannah, Georgia underwent bankruptcy during 1870. Its note-holders received twenty cents on the dollar (Planters Bank of Georgia *Papers*). Not many Southern banks survived for more than a few years. The only bank in South Carolina to do so obtained a private loan, purchased many of its own notes at $.20 on the dollar, and rechartered as a National Bank (Bridwell and Rogers, 1984, 27–30).

The liquidation of Southern banks and bank notes contributed to the monetary vacuum upon which the 1863 National Currency Act had anticipated. By 1870, only 3.5% of all the National Banks operated in the eleven former Confederate states (*Report of the Comptroller of the Currency,* 1918, 289–325). The North subjected the losers of the Civil War to the new monetary regime: one that imposed a dearth of currency upon the defeated in order to sustain wartime policy commitments made during the heat of battle.

The Legacy of the Union Policy Commitments

The National Currency Act served the Union war effort very admirably. It raised revenue. It solidified the political support needed to prosecute the war, and it attacked the purchasing power of the Confederate printing presses all at the same time! The new National Banking System was never designed to satisfy the post-war, peace-time needs of the U.S. economy particularly well. The $300 million dollar restriction upon the issue of National Bank notes erected an entry barrier into the banking business (Sylla, 1969). The inadequacy of currency issues undoubtedly imposed hardships upon conducting business. People had to rely upon coin, illegal currencies (Timberlake, 1981), and checking accounts instead of cash (Dowd, 1989, 142–143}. Kevin Dowd (144) also believes that the note restriction made the U.S. banking system particularly prone to panics.

Those shortcomings composed only part of the excess burden arising from the Northern war financial commitments.

The monetary instability which highlighted the post-war years (Friedman and Schwartz, 1963) should be interpreted as a product of the political uncertainty arising from the Union wartime policy commitments made during the heat of battle. The National Currency Act placed money and banking policy under federal control. Would the re-admission of the South reverse the National Currency Act and abort the commitments made to the holders of U.S. warbonds? The Emancipation Proclamation freed the slaves. How could this commitment be enforced on unwilling Southerners? The former Confederate states were subjected to occupation and political domination during the "Reconstruction Era," which lasted until 1876.

Historically, the Emancipation Proclamation and National Currency Act supported each other. Emancipation provided the rationale to extend the franchise to blacks. It also extended the dominance of the Republican party in Washington for many years. The National Currency Act established the National Banking system and a whole class of Northern bond holders with a direct economic interest in appreciating the currency and maintaining the Republican Party in power until the war debt could be repaid on a gold basis. It is not surprising that the Fourteenth Amendment, which extended citizenship to the former slaves, also guaranteed the Northern war debt and explicitly repudiated the Confederate obligations. The former Confederate states were required to ratify this amendment as a condition to rejoin the Union.

The wartime policy commitments made by President Lincoln and the Republican Congress provide a helpful context from which to examine the monetary history during the post-war years 1865–1879. The political controversies between the "hard money" advocates, who wanted to return to the gold standard, and the "easy money" interests, who favored the issue of more greenbacks, can be interpreted as a continuance of the war itself. The "hard money" advocates came primarily from the northeast. The appreciation of the greenback dollar meant a capital gain to the National Banks holding the war debt. The Southerners, deprived of the seigniorage, became supporters of the "greenback movement." Before the war, most southerners had been "hard money" advocates. Their conversion to easy money can be understood as an opposition to the wartime policy tax imposed upon them.

In 1874 the Democrats won control over Congress by opposing specie resumption and favoring the issue of more greenbacks. The lame duck Republican Congress enacted the Specie Resumption Act, anyhow. The Act placed the federal government on a course scheduled to redeem the greenbacks in gold upon demand by 1879. Republican Presidents prevented Congress from reversing that course by the threat of the veto.[21] The greenback dollar gradually appreciated until the United States Treasury could resume specie payments in 1879. The rate of return on the banking capital tied up the issuing of notes remained very high during the postwar period. Phillip Cagan (1963, 22–23) calculated the annual return to be 31% during 1879 alone.

The resumption of specie payments by the United State Treasury finally pegged the value of the greenbacks and the war debt to the gold dollar. At last, the North won the financial Civil War fourteen years after the shooting stopped.[22]

Notes

*The author gratefully acknowledges the helpful suggestions and comments made by William Hutchinson and Larry Schweikart on earlier versions of this paper. Any errors and omissions remain the sole responsibility of the author.

1. Larry Schweikart (1987, 267–313) describes the impact of the war upon the Southern banks. Both sides usurped and destroyed banking assets.

2. Christopher G. Memminger, who later became the Confederate Secretary of the Treasury, argued in the 1830's that banks were public institutions designed for the convenience of the people. They were not entitled to speculate by taking advantage of special circumstances to advance the interest of stockholders to the detriment of the public. This is why Memminger and many others favored banking regulations to protect noteholders and depositors etc. (Capers, 1893, 130–131). It was also the attitude which made banks a prime target during wartime emergencies. Perhaps, if the infant free banking system had become well established and the regulatory safeguards could eventually have been removed, Civil War finance might have taken a much different form.

3. Those implicit threats were very effective. In South Carolina, for example, the State legislature levied a $1,800,000 loan in December 1861. An Exhibit B (no. 1) of a report by the State Department of Treasury and Finance

indicated that only two banks refused to advance their share of the loan. Subsequently, Exhibit B (no. 3 displays those banks purchasing the loan by March 1,, 1862 (Chief of the Department of Treasury and Finance, 1862; 9, 11). In Georgia one of the Savannah banks was reluctant to loan the state $50,000 at 6 percent interest, but following a threatening letter from the Governor the Bank agreed to advance the money at 7 percent (Bryan, 58).

4. Typical was the Planters' Bank of Savannah, Georgia which advanced the state a $50,000 loan in January 1862 in exchange for 8 percent state bonds. It merely credited the amount to the state on its books. It made no specie shipments. One month later, the bank advanced the state another $100,000 by shipping Confederate notes to the state treasury (Planters' Bank of the State of Georgia *Papers*).

5. See also the official *Bank Statements* (1862) compiled by the Treasury Department of the State of North Carolina.

6. Confederate Treasury Secretary Memminger opposed making the Confederate treasury note legal tender because he believed that it was unnecessary. Confederate money circulated anyhow. He feared that a legal tender act would unnecessarily arouse public doubts and suspicions about the currency (Schwab, 1901, 90).

7. The tax codes were re-written by every Confederate state during 1861 or early 1862.

8. The states carefully monitored and scrutinized their banks. Laws regulating the expenditure of bank specie were sometimes enacted. The South Carolina legislature extended specie suspension in December 1863 upon the condition that banks could not pay out any gold or silver as dividends or for any purpose except to the state or Confederate government (*Statutes at Large: Acts of 1863*, 164).

9. The Farmer's Exchange Bank of South Carolina, for example, held 81 percent of all its cash holdings in the form of interest bearing treasury notes and "call certificates" (Godfrey, 92).

10. Antebellum banks themselves were probably sounder than their reputation. When the state Constitution protected them from legislative intervention, the Southern Bank of New Orleans proved that operations on a specie basis could continue even in wartime (Bragg, 71).

11. See the following records:

(1) *Bank of Cape Fear, Washington, North Carolina, Letter Book,* 1860–1870 (Duke University, Durham, N.C.).

(2) *Bank of Cape Fear, Washington, North Carolina Ledge Book,* 1857–1868.

(3) *Bank of North Carolina Windsor Branch Cashier's Book* (University of North Carolina, Chapel Hill)

12. As a comparison, even the holders of Nazi warbonds and German currency were reimbursed with postwar currency in ratios of 100:1 for bonds and 10:1 for currency in 1945 (Hughes, 1990, 251).

13. Historian J.G. Randall (503) believes that the odds of a European recognition of the Confederacy went probably to zero as a consequence of Lincoln's Proclamation. The institution of slavery faced universal hostility among Europeans.

14. The critics of the Lincoln Administration fully recognized that the Proclamation changed the nature of the war. Orestes A. Brownson, Clement L. Valladingham, William C. Fowler, Samuel S. Cox and others complained that the Proclamation had now made it impossible for a hasty compromise settlement. According to historian John Hope Franklin (1963) Lincoln had become the captive of the Abolitionists.

Democrats denounced the Proclamation because they feared that it would "protect that war indefinitely" (Randall, 502). Some Southerners did not seek a separate peace with the North during the bitter last years of the conflict. In North Carolina the "Peace Society" promoted a reconstruction and a united nation "on the basis of the old constitution." This notion was very popular (Randall, 672). After the Proclamation, President Lincoln held out for the restoration of the Union and the abandonment of slavery" (Randall, 615). It would have meant political suicide within his own party for Lincoln to do otherwise. Compromise became impossible after January 1, 1863.

15. Senator John Sherman (Ohio) made an impassioned speech in behalf of the National Currency bill on February 10, 1863. He gave many arguments in support of the bill including the sound financing it promised and the effect that a national currency would have in promoting "national unity." He ranked "preserving our national existence [sic?]. . ." as important reasons to support the bill no matter what one may think "on the disputed matter of the condition of the African race in this country." A text of this speech can be found in Kroose and Samuelson, 1969, 1355–1380. As a result of his speech and another appeal made by the Treasury Secretary Chase, a key vote was changed on the Senate floor. The bill passed the Senate by 23–21 votes on February 12, 1863 instead of being killed with a tie vote (Knox, 1969, 96).

16. The newspaper blamed the premium on Baltimore Banks in the North who had begun purchasing Southern bank notes at a discount below the greenback dollar (above the Confederate dollar). Could this have indicated "insider information?"

17. The South contained a wide diversity of monies and near monies including interest and non-interest bearing treasury notes, large denominations of call certificates convertible into cash on demand, state-issued treasury notes, bank notes, and bank deposits before the popularity of checking. Godfrey's (1978) estimates are more complete than the often cited data from

Lerner (1955), but both monetary estimates need further adjustments (see Pecquet 1987).

18. For a general discussion of the problems of pay and morale in the Confederate armies see Scheiber (1969).

19. The comptroller of the state of Georgia estimated that banking capital in his state fell from $71 million to $45 following General Sherman's devastating march through Georgia in 1864 (Bryan, 1953, 64).

20. When Richmond fell, the Confederacy removed $326,000 in gold from the banks in that city. During the chaotic collapse of the Confederate government, $200,000 of this gold was lost to "freebooters." The Southern armies also burned several banking buildings to deny them to federal troops (*Banker's Magazine* June, 1865, 1003 and July, 1865, 85).

21. Even as late as 1876, European speculators hoped for a Democratic victory at the polls because they hoped that the United States might assume payments on the Confederate war bonds they held. Prices for these bonds rose during the Hayes-Tilden election dispute in which a special commission had to be established to award the electoral votes from several disputed states (Schwab, 38). A compromise settlement awarded the Presidency to the Republican in exchange for an end to Reconstruction. Three years later, the federal government resumed specie payments.

22. Since the Emancipation Proclamation and the National Currency Act were part of the same package, the transfer of wealth from the South to the Northern creditors might be viewed as a necessary price to end slavery. As an economist, it does not disturb me when people are paid to provide public goods. The National Banking Act did saddle the nation with an inferior monetary system for many years to come. No one should pretend that the National Banking system served monetary requirements any better than did state banking, however. Perhaps the best alternative is state banking with strict Constitutional safeguards against specie suspension as shown by the Louisiana experience.

References

Bass, J. Horace, 1942, "Civil War Finance in Georgia," *The Georgia Historical Quarterly*, 26, (September–December) 213–224.

Boyd, William K., 1915, "Fiscal and Economic Conditions in North Carolina During the Civil War," *North Carolina Booklet*, 14, 195–219.

Bragg, Jefferson Davis, 1941, *Louisiana in the Confederacy* (Baton Rouge: L.S.U. Press).

Bridwell, Ronald and George Rogers, 1984, *The South Carolina National Bank* (The South Carolina National Bank, Columbia, S.C.).

Bryan, T. Conn, 1953, *Confederate Georgia* (Athens, Georgia: University of Georgia Press).

Buchanan, James M. and Gordon Tullock, 1962, *The Calculus of Consent* (Ann Arbor, MI, University of Michigan Press).

Cagan, Philip, 1963, "The First Fifty Years of the National Banking System—An Historical Analysis," in D. Carsen, *Banking and Monetary Studies* (Chicago: Dow Jones Irwin).

Caldwell, Stephen A., 1935, *A Banking History of Louisiana* (Baton Rouge: L.S.U. Press).

Calomiris, Charles, 1988a, "Institutional Failure, Monetary Scarcity and the Depreciation of the Continental," *Journal of Economic History*, 48 (March) 47–68.

Capers, Henry D., 1893, *The Life and Times of C.G. Memminger,* (Richmond: Everett Waddey Co., Publishing).

Davis, George and Gary Pecquet, 1990, "Interest Rates in the Civil War South," *Journal of Economic History*, 50, (March) 133–148.

Dovel, J.E., 1955, *History of Banking in Florida* (Orlando, FL., Florida Bankers Association).

Dowd, Kevin, 1989, *The State and the Monetary System* (New York: St. Martin's Press).

Doyle, Elizabeth J., 1959, "Greenbacks, Car Tickets, and the Pot of Gold," *Civil War History*, 5, no. 4, (December) 345–362.

Franklin, John Hope, 1963, *The Emancipation Proclamation* (Garden City, New York: Doubleday Press).

Friedman, Milton and Anna Schwartz, 1963, *A Monetary History of the United States: 1867–1960* (Princeton, N.J., Princeton University Press).

Godfrey, John M., 1978, *Monetary Expansion in the Confederacy* (New York: Arno Press).

Helderman, Leonard C., 1931, *National and State Banks: A Study of Their Origins* (Boston and New York: Houghton Mifflin Co.).

Holder, Branston Beeson, 1937, *The Three Banks of the State of North Carolina 1801–1872* (Ph.D. Thesis, Chapel Hill, North Carolina: University of North Carolina).

Hughes, Jonathan, 1990, *American Economic History* (3rd Edition) (Glenville, Illinois).

Knox, John J., 1900, *A History of Banking in the United States* (New York: Bradford and Rhodes and Company). Reprinted 1969 (New York: Augustus M. Kelley Publishers).

Krooss, Herman and Paul Samuelson, 1969, *A History of Banking in the United States*, Volume 2, (New York, Augustus M. Kelley Publishers).

Lerner, Eugene, 1955, "Money, Prices, and Wages in the Confederacy, 1861–1865," *Journal of Political Economy*, 65 (February) 20–40.

Mitchell, Wesley Clair, 1903, *A History of the Greenbacks* (Chicago: The University of Chicago Press).

Pecquet, Gary M., 1987, "Money in the Trans-Mississippi Confederacy and the Confederate Currency Reform Act of 1864," *Explorations in Economic History*, 24, (April) 218–243.

Randall, J.G., 1953, *The Civil War and Reconstruction* (Boston: D.C. Heath and Co.).

Reid, Brian and John White, 1985, "A Mob of Stragglers and Cowards: Desertion from the Union and Confederate Armies, 1861–1865," *Journal of Strategic Studies*, 8, No. 1 (March) 64–77.

Roll, Richard, 1972, "Interest Rates and Price Expectation During the Civil War," *Journal of Economic History*, 32, (June) 476–498.

Rolnick, Arthur and Warren Weber, 1983, "New Evidence on the Free Banking Era," *American Economic Review*, 73, no. 5, (December) 1080–1091.

Rolnick, Arthur J. and Warren E. Weber, 1988, "Explaining the Demand for Free Bank Notes," *Journal of Monetary Economics*, 21, 47–71.

Sargent, Thomas, 1982, "The Ends of Four Big Inflations," in Robert Hall (ed.) *Inflation Cases and Effects*, 41–97, (Chicago: Chicago University Press).

Scheiber, Harry N., 1969, "The Pay of Confederate Troops and Problems of Demoralization: A Case of Administrative Failure," *Civil War History*, 15, No. 3 (September) 226–236.

Schwab, John C., 1901, *The Confederate States of America, 1861–1865: A Financial and Industrial History of the Civil War* (New York/London: Schribner and Son).

Schweikart, Larry, 1985, "Secession and Southern Banks," *Civil War History*, 31 (June) 111–125.

Schweikart, Larry, 1987, *Banking in the American South from the Age of Jackson to Reconstruction* (Baton Rouge: L.S.U. Press).

Smith, Bruce, 1985a, "American Colonial Monetary Regimes: The Failure of the Quantity Theory of Money and Some Evidence in Favor of an Alternative View," *Canadian Journal of Economics*, 18, (August) 531–65.

Smith, Bruce, 1985b, "Some Colonial Evidence on Two Theories of Money: Maryland and the Carolinas," *Journal of Political Economy*, 93, (December) 869–884.

Sumner, William Graham, 1896, *A Banking History of the United States* (New York: *The Journal of Commerce and Commercial Bulletin*). Reprinted in 1971 (New York: Kelley Publishers).

Sylla, Richard, 1969, "Federal Policy, Banking Market Structure and Capital Mobilization in the United States 1863–1913," *Journal of Economic History* (December).

Thian, Raphael P. (compiler), 1880, *Correspondence with the Treasury Department of the Confederate States of America: Appendix Part IV 1861–1862* Washington, D.C.).

Timberlake, Richard, 1981, "The Significance of Unaccounted Currencies," *Journal of Economic History,* 41, pp 853–866.

Todd, Richard C., 1954, *Confederate Finance* (Athens, Georgia: University of Georgia Press).

Trefousse, Hans L., 1975, *Lincoln's Decision for Emancipation* (Philadelphia, New York, and Toronto: J.B. Lippincott Company).

Wallace, Neil, 1981, "A Miller-Modigliani: Theorem for Open Market Operations," *American Economic Review,* 71, 267–274.

Yearns, Wilfred B., 1969, *The Confederate Congress* (Athens, Georgia: University of Georgia Press).

References (Other Printed Sources)

Chief of the Department of Treasury and Finance, 1862, *Report of the Chief of the Department of Treasury and Finance to His Excellency Governor Pickens* (Columbia, South Carolina: R.W. Gibbes, printer to the convention, South Carolina Library, University of S.C., Columbia, S.C.).

Pickens, Governor F.W., 1862, "Message No. 1 of His Excellency F.W. Pickens to the Regular Session of November 1862" (Columbia, South Carolina: State of S.C. Press, South Carolina Library University of S.C., Columbia, S.C.).

Report of the Comptroller of the Currency, 1918.

Savannah Banks, 1865, "To the Honorable the Members of [sic.] of the Senate and House of Representatives of the State of Georgia in General Assembly Convened" (Atlanta, Georgia: A Petition signed by the representatives of eight banks from that city).

Treasury Department of North Carolina, 1862, *Bank Statements,* December 17 (Printed by the state, University of N.C. Library, Chapel Hill, N.C.).

United States Congress, *Statutes at Large of the Thirty-Seventh Congress.*

References: Newspapers and Periodicals

The Banker's Magazine and Statistical Register.

Mobile—Prices current (untitled and found in Duke University Archives).

Richmond Daily Whig (Richmond, Virginia).

Richmond Enquirer (Richmond, Virginia).

Washington Journal (Wilmington, N.C.).

References: Manuscript Sources

Bank of Cape Fear, Washington, N.C. Letter Book, 1860–1870 (Duke University, Durham, North Carolina).

Bank of Cape Fear, Washington, N.C. State of the Bank, 1857–1868 (Duke University, Durham, North Carolina).

Bank of North Carolina, Windsor Branch Ledgers Journal (University of North Carolina, Chapel Hill, N.C.).

Planter's Bank of the State of Georgia Papers (University of North Carolina, Chapel Hill, North Carolina).

Comment

by Tyler Cowen

Pecquet's paper consists of two distinct, although nicely interwoven parts. First, he provides an excellent survey of Confederate monetary and financial policy. Although writers such as Todd, Schweikart, and Morgan have covered similar ground, Pecquet's own contributions contain what is best in these other writers. Pecquet's work is a strong attempt to analyze Confederate monetary policy by synthesizing modern monetary theory, public choice economics, statistical techniques, and historical knowledge.

Second, Pecquet's paper deals more specifically with the economic warfare that the Union successfully conducted against the Confederacy. Confederate war finance basically collapsed as a result of clever Union policies designed to undermine the credibility of Confederate financial commitments to its creditors.

I found interesting insights in both parts of Pecquet's paper. Pecquet's analysis of Confederate wartime fiscal and monetary policies raises the question of whether *fiat* currency actually helps a government fight wars. The possibility of wartime seigniorage has traditionally been one of the most influential factors in generating support for central banking and government money. But when closely examined, this argument is doubtful.

A number of replies to the wartime seigniorage argument can be made. First, wartime seigniorage does not necessarily increase a government's ability to fight a war. The presence of *fiat* money will decrease a government's credibility and thus weaken the economy. If market participants know they cannot depend upon a sound currency, economic activity will suffer, and so will the war effort. The presence of a seigniorage tax may thus actually cause overall government revenue to decline. Although Pecquet does not explicitly make this argument in general form, much of his evidence can be read as critical of the wartime seigniorage argument along precisely these grounds. *Fiat* money did not do the Confederacy any favors.

Government control of money and banking institutions, however, did help the Union win the war. This brings us to the second reply to the wartime seigniorage argument. Wartime seigniorage may be bad because it increases a government's ability to fight aggressive wars. Advocates of the wartime seigniorage argument nearly always invoke the picture of an innocent, helpless nation, beseiged by nasty aggressors. But the nasty aggressors themselves are using wartime seigniorage. If a government gives us the perogative of wartime seigniorage, this government is less likely to start an aggressive war. The benefits of obtaining a more civil government may outweigh any possible wartime seigniorage benefits enjoyed during defensive wars.

Again, Pecquet's paper can be read as supporting this argument. Without access to wartime seigniorage, the Union might have thought twice about conducting the war against the Confederacy. Even if war could not have been avoided, perhaps the Union would have been forced to moderate its aggressive efforts.

Do the two arguments against wartime seigniorage contradict each other? The first asserts that the presence of wartime seigniorage makes it harder to finance a war effort, while the second asserts that wartime seigniorage should be restricted to make wars more difficult. The answer depends upon the distribution of seigniorage costs and benefits across winning and losing nations.[1]

Although market-oriented nations would clearly be better off if all countries renounced wartime seigniorage, is it optimal for a single peace-loving country to unilaterally abandon wartime seigniorage? We must consider not only the costs and benefits for a country once a war comes. Renouncing wartime seigniorage will make a peace-loving country less likely to evolve into a country that fights aggressive wars.

I now turn to the second part of Pecquet's paper, the discussion of Union economic warfare. His analysis here is a welcome relief from the common assumption of benevolent policymakers attempting to further social welfare.

Today, a considerable literature exists on international cooperation between benevolent policymakers who wish to further macroeconomic stability. The attempt to coordinate policies usually achieves a superior outcome, at least if the policymakers know the true macroeconomic model. This approach to international relations, however, would not command wide assent if generally applied to studies of imperialism, military spending, espionage, and research and development. So why should we consider it the benchmark case for macroeconomic policy? Pecquet's analysis recognizes that international economic relations, especially during wartime, are characterized by self-interest and double-dealing.

The plausibility of non-cooperative macroeconomic policy across nations is heightened by the relationship between economic power and military might. Countries that avoid recessions and grow rapidly may prove to be stronger military opponents.[2] For this reason, countries may not wish to engage in economic cooperation.

We should not evaluate the importance of a theory of macroeconomic conflict strictly with reference to today's world. In 1990, the world's greatest economic powers (America, Japan, and Western Europe) also have reasonably friendly relations with each other. This has rarely been the case throughout history. Scenarios involving economic conflict have been far more common. It remains to be seen whether the world will revert back to a more mercantilist conception of international relations.

A more general theory of international economic conflict would be useful.[3] Pecquet's story about economic warfare against the Confederacy is but one example of a more general phenomenon. Examples of hostile macroeconomic relations between different nations or regions are common. Many have argued that the French demand for reparations following World War I was motivated by a desire to destroy the German macroeconomy and prevent Germany from achieveing great power status. Similarly, the French run on gold near the collapse of the Bretton Woods system may have been motivated by a desire to cripple American world hegemony. More blatantly, Nazi Germany attempted to ruin the British economy during World War II by introducing counterfeit British pounds.

A more subtle example of economic warfare can be found in the current relationships between the two Germanies, as reunification approaches. The choice of currency conversion rate between East and West marks has been the subject of much dispute. This is hardly a cooperative game, since a favorable conversion rate gives the East Germans seigniorage at the expense of West Germany. Conversion at an unfavorable rate would likely lead to a flood of refugees (must they now be called migrants?), further straining the West Germans welfare system. In other words, the East Germans are basically saying to the West Germans: give us some seigniorage or we will attack your country. The institution of a one-to-one exchange rate illustrates the power of such a threat.

Most international economic orders are constructed to place their architects in a relatively favorable economic and political position. The Bretton Woods system allowed the United States to inflate and reap seigniorage at the expense of other nations. The nineteenth century gold standard allowed the Bank of England to set the macroeconomic pace for much of the rest of the world.

A theory of international economic conflict could consider various different game-theoretic maneuvres. Decreasing the stability of bootstrap equilibrium, for instance, is one way that a country can sabotage the macroeconomy of an enemy. *Fiat* currencies or claims to *fiat* currencies (e.g., government bonds) are valued only because their holders expect that this value will persist through the future. If an enemy threatens not to respect this value should they win, *fiat* currency will lose some value now, and issuing government bonds will become more difficult. Seigniorage profits are more difficult to earn on a currency that has already lost much value, because velocity is more sensitive to inflationary expectations. Furthermore, the interest rate on government borrowing will contain a higher risk premium. For both reasons, war finance will become less efficient. This scenario corresponds to Pecquet's analysis of the North's policy in the Civil War.

Enemies and rivals may also exert macroeconomic influence by attempting to create financial crises. Circulation of rumors about the stability of the banking system is a possible destabilizing act. The enemy or rival may itself organize a run, á la de Gaulle, if the country's currency is convertible into gold or some other commodity.

Counterintuitive results are also possible. For instance, the presence of an enemy may enable a better macroeconomic policy than would otherwise be possible (I am not suggesting that these benefits outweigh the costs of conflict and warfare). A country could inflate during wartime, for instance, without necessarily destroying the credibility of its central bank as an inflation-fighter. The presence of a wartime enemy may also help a government credibility to precommit to a policy. Attempts to be frugal or streamline the bureaucracy may have more impact when the survival of the country is at stake.

The presence of a war may also blunt the influence of certain special interest groups and enable public interest legislation to be passed. The income tax withholding system (introduced during World War II) is sometimes cited as an example here, although I am not convinced that this was a positive development.

Wars or the threat of war may also discipline politicians into implementing superior economic policies. In the absence of potential for conflict, politicians may shirk and pursue their own objectives with economic policy, rather than strengthening the economy. When the threat of conflict approaches, however, the costs of political shirking increase. Politicians commanding weak economies can be bullied, humiliated, and even conquered by opposing countries. The incentive to build up national economic and military power increases. In my piece cited above, I argue that such incentives were an important factor behind the historical development of capitalism. The growth and strengthening of militarism, however, was clearly a negative side to this development.

These observations, as well as Pecquet's work, might fit into a more general theory of international economic conflict. In the meantime, Pecquet is to be commended for his careful synthesis of economic history and public choice theory.

Notes

1. A cross-sectional statistical study of wartime seigniorage would prove interesting. For instance, did the Nazis or Great Britain benefit more from inflationary war finance?

2. Countervailing factors may prevail, however. Countries in recessions may be stronger threats because their citizens have less to lose through military adventures. Or they may acquire a Spartan sense of self-discipline that proves useful during wartime.

3. I have attempted the beginnings of such a theory in my "Economic Effects of a Conflict-Prone World Order," *Public Choice* (1990) 64: 121–134.

National Bank Notes as a Quasi-High Powered Money

by George A. Selgin
Lawrence H. White*

The "inelasticity" of national banking currency (1863–1913) has been a common theme in both primary and secondary literature (*e.g.*, Conant, 1896; Noyes, 1910; Smith, 1936; Timberlake, 1978; Livingston, 1986). The term "inelasticity" is generally used in this literature to mean "inadequate expandability." It denotes the failure of the currency stock to expand with national income, with seasonal demands for currency (particularly for "crop-moving"), or with extraordinary currency demands during financial panics.[1] The recognized source of inadequate expandability was the National Banking Acts' requirement that federal government bonds be purchased and deposited in advance as par-valued collateral for the issue of bank notes. The Gold Standard Act of 1900, the Aldrich-Vreeland Act of 1908, and the Federal Reserve Act of 1913 all sought to address this problem by allowing increases in the stock of currency without additional bond collateral.

A distinct "inelasticity" problem, considered equally important at the time, has attracted surprisingly little attention since. The stock of currency failed not only to expand when demand for currency grew, but also to contract when demand subsided. The fundamental reason was that national bank notes had little "homing power," that is, were unlikely to be returned quickly to their issuers for redemption. Once issued, the notes became a semi-permanent part of the currency stock, or a quasi-high-powered money. This phenomenon presents a puzzle. National bank notes were liabilities to their issuers, just as low-powered checkable deposits were, and did not serve to meet banks' legal reserve requirements. Yet the notes circulated interchangeably with legal tender (greenbacks and gold), were seldom redeemed, and thus formed part of the base supporting broader monetary aggregates (Friedman and Schwartz, 1963, pp. 50, 781–2).

Reform-minded experts (*e.g.*, Walker, 1863; Laughlin, 1894 and 1898; Sprague, 1904) found this *downward* inelasticity of national bank currency was at least as worrisome as its upward inelasticity. An excess stock of notes would not be rapidly corrected.[2] Legislated limits on aggregate note issue before 1875, and the bidding up of collateral bond prices in later years, in fact prevented secular overexpansion. But the experts feared that measures to provide for upward elasticity by eliminating these constraints would prove inflationary and hence abortive unless the problem of downward inelasticity was solved at the same time. They also noted the problem of season and cyclical excess stocks of notes during periods of slack demand. These contributed to the pronounced seasonal and cyclical fluctuations in interest rates characteristic of the National banking regime (Miron, 1986; Mankiw, Miron, and Weil, 1987).

Why Bank Notes Are Not High-Powered Under Free Banking

In a "free banking" system with legally unregulated note issue and a commodity standard, bank notes are a low-powered money, more or less like checks in our current banking system (White, 1984; Selgin, 1988). Each bank faces a determinate demand to hold its brand of notes. Absent an increase in that demand, the bank cannot increase its note-issue without holding additional outside money reserves, because it can expect to face adverse clearings.

Active redemption. A bank in a free banking system receiving a rival issuer's note promptly returns it for redemption in reserve money. The recipient does not reissue the rival's note because there is profit in increasing the circulation of its own notes. It does not retain the note because reserve money dominates it as an asset: Both are non-interest-bearing, while reserve money carries less default risk and is useful for meeting a wider variety of redemption demands. Banks clear and settle with one another frequently in order to enjoy promptly the reserves received in positive clearings and to limit the potential size of adverse clearings (Selgin and White, 1987).

Just as active check clearing restricts a bank's ability to expand profitably its loans and deposits, given its initial reserves, active note redemption restricts its ability to add profitably to its note circulation.

Unwanted notes will be either redeemed over the counter or (more commonly) deposited into rival banks which will return the notes for redemption through the clearing system. In either case the issuer loses an equal quantity of reserves. Active note redemption thus confronts the individual bank with marginal liquidity costs that rise more steeply the swifter and surer is redemption. Once the expanding bank's reserves fall below the profit-maximizing prudential level, it will stop expanding its balance sheet.

Less obviously, active note redemption also keeps the aggregate quantity of notes within limits set by the public's asset-holding preferences. A given quantity of high-powered reserves, in a given state of redemption technology, will support only a certain volume of gross redemptions of notes (and checks). The system therefore has a unique equilibrium volume of notes and deposits.[3]

If banks in a plural note-issue system were to reissue rather than to actively redeem one another's notes, notes would become a quasi-high powered money. No longer would interbank settlements confront an over-issuing bank with adverse clearings, and an under-issuing bank with positive clearings. Divergences from the equilibrium stock of notes would not be corrected as rapidly. Only the longer-run check of outflows or inflows of reserves (for a small economy on an international commodity standard) would remain to move the banking system as a whole toward monetary equilibrium.[4] Short-run stability is accordingly reduced when banks lack the motive, ability, or opportunity to redeem one another's notes.[5]

Note-brand discrimination. Redemption effectively checks an aggregate excess supply of bank notes only when the system specifically redeems the notes of the bank(s) causing the excess. This requires that note holders discriminate among brands of notes, preferring to hold the various brands in definite quantities. Equilibrium market shares in the bank note industry cannot be indeterminate (White, 1984, pp. 14, 89–98; Selgin, 1988, pp. 42–7).

With perfect note-brand discrimination, an aggregate over-issue brings reserve losses to a small bank equal to its contribution to the over-issue. In contrast, were excess notes redeemed without regard to brand, the bank would experience reserve losses equal only to its fraction of the total circulation times the excess. The remaining burden of redeeming excess notes would be borne by other banks. A "common pool" problem would exist, the marginal liquidity costs of its over-issue being largely external to the individual bank. Each bank would face inadequate incentives to limit its issues.

Four rationales for note-brand discrimination can be identified: (1) An issuer may have a locational advantage. (2) Notes may differ in the perceived solidity of their issuers. (3) Some other quality may differ across brands, so that different brands cater to the preferences of different subsets of the population. These three rationales appeal to some sort of product differentiation among brands of notes.

A distinct rationale for note-brand discrimination is (4) a filtering process that may be termed "incidental discrimination." Consider a retailer who acquires currency in the normal course of a business day. His currency balances at the end of the day are unlikely to match those he wishes to hold at the beginning of the next day, either in total quantity or in the mix of denominations. To deposit excess currency on some days and draw out extra currency on others, and to change denominations, he goes to the bank at which he keeps an account. If his bank takes in notes of all brands, but pays out only its own, then the currency deposit and denominational swaps incidentally involve a brand-replacement process. The outcome is as if the retailer deliberately discriminated in favor of his bank's notes. Absent other kinds of discrimination, this process makes banks' equilibrium shares of the note market conform to their shares of the deposit market. The clearing process will then effectively check an over-issue.[6] With the national banking regime in mind, however, it is important to observe that incidental discrimination occurs only when an issuing bank generally pushes its own notes instead of paying out notes issued by other banks.

Historical Examples of Active Note Redemption

Examples of active note redemption may be found in the relatively unregulated banking systems of Scotland before 1844, Canada before 1914, and New England and New York State prior to 1861.

Scotland. British advocates of free banking frequently praised the Scottish note-exchange system in the decades prior to the Bank Charter Act of 1844 (Checkland, 1975, pp. 437; White, 1984, pp. 87–93). Notes circulated at par throughout the country. In testimony before a Parliamentary Select Committee (British Sessional Papers, 1826, p. 48), the Scottish banker Alexander Blair described how the system promptly curtailed over-issues:

> I conceive it impossible there should be an over-issue of
> notes under the system of exchanges which exists at present. The
> whole of the banks of Scotland exchange their notes twice in a
> week; those exchanges at the branches are settled by orders on
> Edinburgh; those orders are brought into the Exchange in
> Edinburgh, and they are all settled and paid twice a week by drafts
> on London at ten days' date; therefore any notes which have been
> issued over and above what the circulation of the country neces-
> sarily would absorb, are immediately returned on the banker so
> issuing them, and he is obliged to give his bill on London, which is
> paid with real funds there.

Blair concluded that each bank cautiously avoided "undue issue of
notes" because "such a proceeding would operate to its disadvantage
and to its loss, and against the check of the exchanges."

The result was an effective restraint against an excess supply of
any bank's notes. Four decades later Robert Somers (1873, p. 161)
estimated that the average note circulated only 10–11 days before
being redeemed.

Canada. The importance of active redemption as a check on
over-issue was similarly affirmed in Canadian experience (Root, 1894;
Johnson, 1910). The Canadian banker B.F. Walker (quoted in
Cornwell, 1869, pp. 24–5) remarked that, in light of the note-
exchange system,

> no bank dares to issue notes without reference to its power to
> redeem. . . . The presentation for redemption of every note not
> required for purposes of trade, is assured by the fact that every
> bank seeks, by the activity of its own business, to keep out its own
> notes and, therefore, sends back daily for redemption the notes of
> all other banks. . . . It is because of this daily actual redemption that
> we have never had any serious inflation of our currency.

In the 1890's the average Canadian bank note was redeemed an estimated twelve times a year (Laughlin, 1898, p. 330).

Universal par redemption came relatively late to Canada's geo-
graphically dispersed banking system. Before 1890, a member of the
public might find a note discounted even by branch offices of the bank
that had issued it. Only the head office had to redeem at par. Discounts varied with the interlocal balance of trade between issuing and
redemption points. Discounts on rival banks' notes reflected the
receiving bank's redemption costs (Breckenridge, 1910, p. 132). A few
banks, however, redeemed their notes at par throughout the country.
Legislation passed in 1890 required all banks to offer par redemption

in officially appointed cities in each of the seven provinces, accelerating the spread of par redemption which the founding of clearinghouses in Halifax (1887) and Montreal (1889) had already begun to encourage. The Canadian authorities considered a plan requiring all bank offices to accept all notes without discount. Had it not been withdrawn in response to bankers' objections, the plan would have imposed redemption costs on the accepting banks rather than the original issuers. As we shall see, the United States did introduce such a policy, and it discouraged active note redemption.

The United States. Several effective note redemption systems operated in the United States before the Civil War. The best known was the Suffolk system in New England, which operated from the 1820's until 1858, when it was superceded by the Bank for Mutual Redemption and the New England Assorting House (Trivoli, 1979). The Suffolk, a Boston bank, agreed to redeem notes of country banks that kept a reserve at the Suffolk. Discounts on country bank notes eventually vanished. By 1858, annual redemptions through the Suffolk reached $400 million, with a note stock of only $38 million. The average New England bank note (see Table 1 and Chart 1) was thus being redeemed more than 10 times a year (U.S. Congress, 1897–98, p. 452).[7]

The Suffolk system made it difficult for any bank to circulate more notes than the public wished to hold. A Connecticut bank cashier recalled that this bank could not expand its circulation beyond a definite amount "without the notes coming home without delay." Every effort by the bank to push out more notes "was met by the unconscious resistance of the public, which refused to take and hold the notes for which it had no use." The public deposited excess notes at par with rival banks, speeding the notes back to their issuers (American Bankers Association, 1878, pp. 47–8). We shall see that Connecticut bankers faced much different conditions during the national banking era.

In the 1850's an arrangement similar to the Suffolk system, and partly inspired by it, took shape in New York City. The New York Assorting House initially accepted New York country banks' notes at a discount of one-quarter of one percent. Competition with country banks' redemption agents eventually pushed the discount rate for most New York State bank notes to one-eighth of one percent.

Table 1

obs	NOTES	REDEM	REDEM/Yr.
1834	14841.00	76000.00	5.120949
1835	18241.00	96000.00	5.262869
1836	22480.00	127000.0	5.649466
1837	21168.00	105000.0	4.960318
1838	17808.00	77000.00	4.323899
1839	19136.00	107000.0	5.591555
1840	16571.00	94000.00	5.672561
1841	18443.00	109000.0	5.910101
1842	15734.00	106000.0	6.737003
1843	16324.00	104000.0	6.370987
1844	22933.00	126000.0	5.494266
1845	25618.00	138000.0	5.386838
1846	26870.00	142000.0	5.284704
1847	30660.00	165000.0	5.381605
1848	26349.00	178000.0	6.755475
1849	28840.00	199000.0	6.900139
1850	31718.00	221000.0	6.967652
1851	30536.00	243000.0	7.957820
1852	41273.00	245000.0	5.936084
1853	53046.00	288000.0	5.429250
1854	53442.00	231000.0	4.322443
1855	47742.00	341000.0	7.142558
1856	53990.00	397000.0	7.353214
1857	43095.00	376000.0	8.724910
1858	37968.00	400000.0	10.53519

New England Bank Notes Outstanding and Redemptions by the Suffolk Bank, 1834–1858 (in Thousands of Dollars).
Source: L. Carroll Root, "New England Bank Currency." *Sound Currency* 2(13) (June 1895), pp. 253–84.

Other parts of the United States relied on less centralized means for note redemption. The West had seventy different note-redemption agencies by 1850, along with hundreds of private brokers, functioning "like separate and peculiar absorbants" to gather and return notes that had been "casually carried out of their proper sphere of action" (Spahr, 1926, p. 78).

By the outbreak of the Civil War, banks thus had few opportunities to issue notes without redeeming them for long periods. After the passage of the National Banking Acts of 1863 and 1864, circumstances changed dramatically. State banks stopped issuing notes, and active note redemption became rare.

Chart 1
Note redemptions by the Suffolk System.

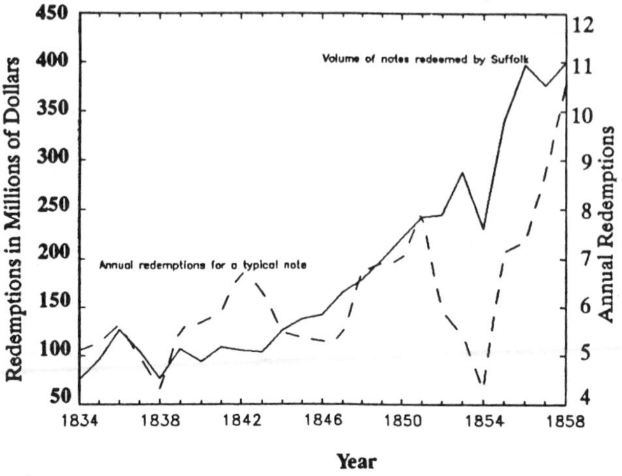

Source: Root (1895)

Note Redemption Under National Banking

Before 1874. The original National Banking Acts appear superficially to encourage active note redemption. The express purpose of the Act of February 25, 1863 was "to provide a national currency . . . and to provide for the circulation *and redemption* thereof" (emphasis added). Secretary of the Treasury Salmon Chase agreed to support the Act only if it included provisions for routine note redemption to check inflation (U.S. Treasury, 1861, p. 18; Million, 1894, p. 254). National banks had most of the usual reasons to compete for shares of the circulation. Because national bank notes bore the issuer's name and location, and after 1874 its charter number in red ink, they could in principle be sorted and returned for redemption.[8]

The law of 1863 specified that national banks had to redeem their notes in lawful money at their counters on demand. The revised law of June 3, 1864 additionally compelled par redemption at one of sixteen designated redemption cities. Though received by the federal government, national bank notes were neither legal tender for payments to individuals, nor (unlike greenbacks before 1879 or gold and greenbacks afterward) countable as lawful bank reserves. The law thus appeared to reinforce banks' usual motives for actively redeeming rivals' notes.

National banks nonetheless rarely treated one another's notes as they treated checks. Though banks in some large cities occasionally sorted local notes from the mass of "foreign" notes received daily, and returned the local notes for redemption, national banks generally retained and re-issued the notes of other banks. *Hunt's Merchants Magazine* (September 1864, p. 248) reported a case in which two New Haven, Connecticut national banks had issued approximately $300,000. Half a year later they had not yet been asked to redeem a single dollar. Andrew J. Frame, President of the Waukesha National Bank of Wisconsin, stated (American Banker's Association *Proceedings*, 1907, p. 137) that his bank "never sent in a dollar of fit national bank notes for redemption":

> We simply pay our national bank notes over the counter, retaining legal reserve money, and can see no earthly reason why we should lose time and pay express charges, even to Milwaukee, to have a note redeemed that is good beyond question. The United States Treasurer's report . . . shows conclusively the great bulk of the national banks have done likewise.

Francis Bowen (1866, p. 773) commented that a national bank could "pay out its bill on the morning after it receives them from the Comptroller, with a comfortable assurance of not seeing more than a stray one or two of them again for a twelve-month." Instead of returning to their source, national bank notes became "part of the permanent money stock."

In the first decade of the national banking system, 1864–1874, notes were sent to the Treasury only when worn beyond use. As far as we know, these returns were virtually the only redemptions. Though $315 million of notes were in circulation, less than $18 million had been returned for replacement with fresh notes during the first five years (see Table 2). Even at their peak in 1873 such returns were only about 10 percent of the outstanding stock of notes. At that rate, the typical note would circulate 10 years before being redeemed, more than long enough to have worn out. (Today's one-dollar bills wear out in less than two years.) The deteriorated condition of national bank notes, an obvious symptom of low homing power, was much deplored at the time. A writer for the *Banker's Magazine* (cited in James, 1938, pp. 399–400) declared that "the state of the currency is not too strongly described by the word *filthy*. There is a serious risk in counting any large number of small bills in the ordinary way of wetting the fingers at the lips; and the effluvium arising from a closed box of currency would justify the interference of the Board of Health."

Table 2
National bank notes returned to the Treasury for destruction
under the Act of June 3, 1864 (by fiscal year).

Prior to October 31, 1865	$ 175,490
Nov. 1, 1865–Oct. 31, 1866	1,050,382
Nov. 1, 1866–Oct. 31, 1867	3,401,423
Nov. 1, 1867–Oct. 31, 1868	4,602,825
Nov. 1, 1868–Oct. 31, 1869	8,603,729
Nov. 1, 1869–Oct. 31, 1870	14,305,689
Nov. 1, 1870–Oct. 31, 1871	24,344,047
Nov. 1, 1871–Oct. 31, 1872	30,211,720
Nov. 1, 1872–Oct. 31, 1873	36,433,171
Nov. 1, 1873–Oct. 31, 1874	49,939,741

Source: *Comptroller of the Currency, 1874*, p. xiv; *Bolles*, 1885, p. 346

1874 and after. Under pressure to relieve northeastern city banks of their accumulations of excess notes, Congress in 1874 established the National Bank Redemption Agency under Treasury Department auspices in Washington, D.C. National bank notes still fit for use could now be redeemed through the Treasury as well as at the issuers' counters. Each national bank was required to contribute legal tender equal to five percent of its outstanding circulation to a redemption fund at the Treasury. Banks sending in notes were paid out of the fund, and the issuing bank then replenished its share. Significantly, the costs of note redemption, including sorting and transportation costs, were assessed against issuing banks in proportion to the quantity of their notes received, redeemed, and returned by the Treasury.

As soon as it opened the new Agency received a flood of notes, both fit and worn, for redemption. For the first time national banks experienced significant note-redemption demands. During the fiscal year ending October 31, 1876, over $209 million of national bank notes were shipped to Washington, more than half of the outstanding circulation. A year later the flow peaked at 75 percent of the stock. At that rate a typical note was redeemed once every 16 months.

The Redemption Agency nonetheless fell well short of the Scottish, Suffolk, or Canadian systems in comprehensiveness. Even the 16-month average period of circulation of 1877 far exceeded the two-week to one-month averages of the other systems. Redemptions processed in 1877, almost $214 million, were well below the annual redemptions of the Suffolk Bank decades earlier (see Chart 1). Laughlin (1898, p. 339) estimated that in 1890, when approximately $200 million of national notes were in circulation, national banks received about $4 million of one another's notes daily. Had they redeemed all of them, they would have shipped close to $1.3 billion to the Treasury, making the average circulation period about eight weeks, close to those of the other systems. The actual Redemption Agency volume in 1890 was $36 million, implying redemption less than once every five years. If Laughlin's estimate is roughly correct, national banks in 1890 redeemed fewer than three percent of the notes they received.

The improvement in note redemption was tenuous as well as incomplete. Regretting the unexpected burden of its redemption duties, the Treasury sought to reduce it. Secretary of the Treasury John Sherman (who as a Senator in 1864 had praised the long circulation period of national bank notes for economizing on the use of paper) announced in September 1878 that, effective October 1, parties transmitting notes to Washington for redemption would have to pay their own express charges (*Bankers' Magazine,* November 1878, pp. 326–7). The Treasury had previously assessed these charges against note issuers. The new regulation, together with the prohibition against discounting other national banks' notes, meant that national banks would once again suffer losses in redeeming notes.

Sherman's decision caused redemptions to plummet from nearly $243 million in fiscal 1877 to less than $62 million in fiscal 1880. They fell to a low of less than $60 million in 1881, despite an increase in the stock of national bank notes from $322 million to $346 million (see Table 2 and Chart 2). As might be expected, most of the decline in redemptions came in shipments of fit notes, which fell from $151 million to $6.7 million.

On December 1, 1879, Sherman's order was modified to permit transportation costs for unfit notes to be paid by the issuing banks from the five percent fund. This brought about a partial recovery in redemptions of worn notes. The Treasurer (U.S. Treasury, 1880, p. 330)

Table 3
Redemptions of National Bank Notes at the Treasury
1874–1915 (by fiscal year)

Category	1875	1876	1877	1878
Circulation Outstanding	$354,238,291	$344,483,798	$321,828,139	$320,625,04?
Returned	155,520,880	209,038,855	242,885,375	213,151,458
Present	43.90	60.68	75.47	66.48
Redeemed Fit	26,166,291	102,478,700	151,070,300	152,437,300
Redeemed Unfit	115,109,445	78,643,155	62,518,600	51,585,400
Total Redeemed	141,275,736	181,121,855	213,588,900	204,022,700
Total Retired	10,912,666	24,324,687	25,050,755	12,009,875
Dollar Cost/1000	2.2326	2.0735	1.66572	1.5630

Category	1879	1880	1881	1882
Circulation Outstanding	$324,244,285	$339,530,923	$346,314,471	$359,736,05(
Returned	157,656,645	61,585,676	59,650,259	76,089,327
Present	48.62	18.13	17.22	21.15
Redeemed Fit	112,411,800	24,980,500	6,763,600	3,801,500
Redeemed Unfit	40,204,700	29,861,700	40,080,700	53,838,500
Total Redeemed	152,616,500	54,842,200	46,844,300	57,640,000
Total Retired	8,056,701	6,401,916	12,344,799	16,808,606
Dollar Cost/1000	1.58	2.6209	2.6942	1.80416

Category	1883	1884	1885	1886
Circulation Outstanding	$359,868,524	$347,746,363	$327,022,283	$314,815,97(
Returned	102,699,677	126,152,572	150,209,129	130,296,607
Present	28.53	26.27	45.93	41.38
Redeemed Fit	15,572,100	26,255,500	45,634,800	46,701,100
Redeemed Unfit	59,875,000	72,260,700	72,669,700	54,532,935
Total Redeemed	75,447,100	98,516,200	118,304,500	101,234,035
Total Retired	23,552,279	26,857,689	28,462,225	29,557,588
Dollar Cost/1000	1.55639	1.31978	1.257	1.3091

Table 3 (cont'd)
Redemptions of National Bank Notes at the Treasury
1874–1915 (by fiscal year)

Category	1887	1888	1889	1890
Circulation Outstanding	$293,792,052	$265,622,692	$230,648,247	$196,248,499
Returned	87,689,687	99,152,364	88,932,059	70,256,947
Present	29.85	37.32	38.55	35.80
Redeemed Fit	20,786,640	17,453,780	17,084,590	12,590,880
Redeemed Unfit	30,506,030	25,843,765	27,443,340	23,275,005
Total Redeemed	51,292,670	43,297,545	44,527,930	35,865,885
Total Retired	37,368,289	50,163,957	46,386,122	33,633,889
Dollar Cost/1000	1.58644	1.52297	1.4549	1.5616

Category	1891	1892	1893	1894
Circulation Outstanding	$175,911,373	$172,113,311	$174,755,355	$205,322,804
Returned	67,460,619	69,625,046	75,845,225	105,330,844
Present	38.54	40.45	43.40	51.30
Redeemed Fit	12,543,220	16,676,700	24,166,150	39,893,840
Redeemed Unfit	27,494,445	36,282,335	43,394,418	50,944,080
Total Redeemed	40,037,665	52,959,035	67,560,568	90,837,920
Total Retired	25,329,027	96,232,721	9,037,651	10,929,536
Dollar Cost/1000	1.52757	1.96339	1.35518	1.06599

Category	1895	1896	1897	1898
Circulation Outstanding	$207,860,409	$217,133,390	$232,888,449	$228,170,874
Returned	86,709,133	108,260,978	113,573,776	97,111,687
Present	41.71	49.85	48.76	42.56
Redeemed Fit	35,055,620	46,946,190	37,659,960	27,124,260
Redeemed Unfit	40,094,540	43,866,375	69,014,688	54,858,156
Total Redeemed	75,150,160	90,812,565	106,674,648	81,982,416
Total Retired	13,068,369	11,233,150	11,092,355	15,990,460
Dollar Cost/1000	1.15	1.125	1.0701	1.29646

Table 3 (cont'd)
Redemptions of National Bank Notes at the Treasury
1874–1915 (by fiscal year)

Category	1899	1900	1901	1902
Circulation Outstanding	$239,287,673	$260,293,746	$339,884,257	$358,173,941
Returned	90,838,301	96,982,608	147,486,578	171,869,258
Present	37.96	37.25	43.39	47.98
Redeemed Fit	23,472,650	25,620,660	57,668,715	57,303,520
Redeemed Unfit	50,530,828	49,006,445	71,432,232	89,646,745
Total Redeemed	74,003,978	74,627,105	129,100,947	146,950,265
Total Retired	16,649,275	17,909,793	18,626,437	20,085,275
Dollar Cost/1000	1.39611	1.33558	0.9956	0.92444

Category	1903	1904	1905	1906
Circulation Outstanding	$383,173,195	$428,886,482	$468,285,475	$538,065,425
Returned	196,429,621	262,141,930	308,298,760	296,292,885
Present	51.26	61.12	65.84	55.07
Redeemed Fit	62,563,430	92,025,555	106,286,870	88,930,700
Redeemed Unfit	104,604,266	136,444,405	174,417,383	184,561,828
Total Redeemed	167,167,696	228,469,960	280,704,253	273,492,528
Total Retired	26,272,086	30,936,971	25,857,368	24,724,135
Dollar Cost/1000	0.9026	0.8471	0.8099	0.84528

Category	1907	1908	1909	1910
Circulation Outstanding	$589,445,599	$662,473,554	$680,666,307	$707,919,327
Returned	240,314,681	349,634,341	461,522,202	502,498,994
Present	40.07	52.78	67.80	70.98
Redeemed Fit	43,140,205	62,194,650	89,629,100	118,015,100
Redeemed Unfit	168,940,465	196,449,108	321,445,552	343,545,283
Total Redeemed	212,080,670	258,643,758	411,074,652	461,560,383
Total Retired	25,454,255	39,535,156	89,562,083	32,288,770
Dollar Cost/1000	0.98615	0.90366	0.79762	0.88066

Table 3 (cont'd)
Redemptions of National Bank Notes at the Treasury
1874–1915 (by fiscal year)

Category	1911	1912	1913	1914
Circulation Outstanding	$724,911,069	$739,940,744	$750,906,777	$755,598,359
Returned	551,531,596	649,954,710	675,889,000	706,756,602
Present	76.08	87.84	90.01	93.54
Redeemed Fit	107,017,870	198,550,800	218,884,750	226,402,100
Redeemed Unfit	398,279,110	417,932,800	426,431,860	462,276,515
Total Redeemed	505,296,980	616,483,600	645,316,610	688,678,615
Total Retired	34,976,840	28,527,711	24,089,035	26,852,200
Dollar Cost/1000	0.81977	0.78233	0.77293	0.74312

Category	1915
Circulation Outstanding	$943,887,520
Returned	782,633,567
Present	82.92
Redeemed Fit	130,389,450
Redeemed Unfit	330,110,347
Total Redeemed	460,499,797
Total Retired	304,426,225
Dollar Cost/1000	0.65147

Source: *Annual Report of the Treasurer of the United States,* various dates.

Chart 2
Redemptions of national bank notes at the Treasury, 1874–1908
(by calendar year)

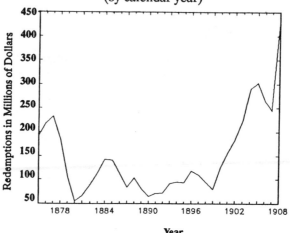

Year

Source: *Annual Report of the Treasurer,* various dates

explained that "the labor and annoyance of assorting the notes unfit for circulation from the currency coming into the banks' hands, and of holding them until an amount accumulates sufficient to be forwarded to the Treasurer, seems to deter many banks from returning them for redemption." Fearing further physical deterioration of the currency, the Treasury revoked Sherman's 1878 order entirely on January 13, 1881. This restored the 1874–1878 arrangements, except that assorting expenses were now charged to banks according to the value rather than the number of their notes redeemed (U.S. Treasury, 1882, p. 377).

Redemption of fit notes continued to decline, reaching a low of $3.8 million in 1882, even an aggregate circulation reached its nineteenth-century peak of over $359 million. Redemptions of fit notes rebounded somewhat thereafter, but the ratio of redemptions to currency outstanding curiously did not return to pre-1878 levels until after 1907. The reason may have been the reduced profitability of note issue after 1881, which enhanced interior banks' incentives to hold scarce notes as vault cash rather than ship them to their city correspondents.

What Made National Bank Notes a Quasi-High-Powered Money?

Two results of national banking regulation account for the banks' practice of re-issuing rather than redeeming other banks' notes. First, the motives for note-brand discrimination by members of the public were small by comparison with a free banking system. Secondly, banks themselves had less incentive to redeem one anothers' notes.

Lack of note-brand discrimination. In a free banking system, as discussed above, individuals deliberately discriminate among note brands for three reasons: (1) to avoid the high transactions costs from using un-current and non-local notes where branch banking is incomplete; (2) to avoid holding unfamiliar or untrusted brands of notes; and (3) to satisfy individual tastes. Less preferred notes, received in the course of trade, are redeemed over the counter, or sold to note brokers or deposited with banks who then redeem them.

The revised Act of 1864 eliminated the transaction-cost motive for note-brand discrimination by requiring all national banks to receive one another's notes as par "for any debt or liability." Merchants no longer had to discount out-of-town notes. All national bank notes could be deposited or traded at par anywhere. The uniform bond-collateral provisions of national banking law eliminated the information-cost motive by making all bank notes equally free from default risk. As marginal brand-monitoring costs fell to zero, individuals became willing to hold an unlimited variety of note brands. According to Cleveland (1905, p. 83), a note holder "inquired as to the credit of the bank through which the note was issued, but relied entirely on his claim against the security held in trust by the Treasurer."[9] National bank notes were considered as safe as greenbacks. The notes' uniformity in all other aspects eliminated other quality distinctions (the third motive) as well.

Having became indifferent among various brands of bank notes, and between bank notes and greenbacks, the public ceased altogether, according to economist Francis Bowen (1866, p. 773), to heed "the rather indistinct announcement on the face of the note, which refers the responsibility and profits of its issue to some obscure village." In consequence the notes had "no local habitation, only a local name, which might just as well be erased. New Hampshire bills circulate as well as any in Texas: Texas bills do well enough in New

Hampshire." Brand preferences of the public ceased to provide an impetus for note redemption.

Lack of active interbank note redemption. Incidental discrimination remained possible. This requires, however, that each bank push only its own notes while drawing in and redeeming notes of other banks. The national banking laws attenuated the incentives of banks to do so, in at least two ways:

(1) Banks lost the motive of trying to increase the circulation of their own notes. State banks withdrew from issuing their own notes as a result of the prohibitive tax imposed in 1865. Until 1875, the law placed a ceiling on aggregate national bank circulation. Later the low yield on collateral bonds, relative to alternative assets, made bankers indifferent to whether other banks' notes were circulating instead of their own (White, 1989).[10] Indeed, many called for improved facilities for retiring their outstanding notes so that they could realize a profit on the collateral bonds.

(2) Banks lost the motive of redeeming rivals' notes in order to safeguard their own reserves. Given the lack of profitability in pushing notes, there was no reason to worry that other banks would try to accumulate and present for redemption such a substantial quantity of one issuer's notes as to embarrass that issuer. For another bank to collect many of one issuer's notes would furthermore have been exceedingly difficult: The par-acceptance rule allowed notes to circulate diffusely across the country, and branching restrictions limited the scope for collecting points. In the absence of any chance of "note duelling," or for significant over-the-counter redemption by the public, a Nash equilibrium without active redemption prevailed.

One motive for note redemption did remain: Notes could not be counted as lawful reserves.[11] The structure of reserve requirements, however, made this motive effective only in the central reserve city of New York. Country banks were permitted to keep most of their lawful reserves as deposits with reserve city correspondents, who in turn could keep reserves as deposits with central reserve city correspondents. Country and reserve city banks could exchange notes for lawful reserves by depositing them with their correspondents, who after 1864 had to receive the notes at par. Interbank depositing of notes was more profitable than redemption for legal tender. Both the notes and the burden of redeeming them were passed on to the banks of New

York City, creating the glut of notes that prompted the reform of 1874.

Correspondent banks in New York City, and likewise Eastern banks that in certain years apparently could have profitably expanded their issues, did not actively redeem notes before 1874 because sorting and transporting costs were too high. Sorting costs vary directly with the number of different brands and denominations to be sorted.[12] Transportation costs also increase with the number of brands of notes, assuming that each brand must be shipped to a different redemption point. Transportation costs are lower if there are multiple redemption points for some note brands, and both costs are lower, owing to economies of scale, if all notes can be sent to a small number of central assorting houses for sorting and exchange. Redemption costs were extraordinarily high under national banking because branching restrictions supported a very large number of widely dispersed banks of issue. There were more than 1,600 note-issuing national banks in 1867, and many more in subsequent years, with no centralized redemption facility before 1874.

The puzzling low redemption rate even after 1874, when the National Bank Redemption Agency opened, was probably due in part, as already mentioned, to the lack of profit to a national bank in pushing its own notes. It was also due to interior banks' inability to accumulate notes rapidly enough to meet the $1,000 minimum remittance accepted by the Redemption Agency without undue loss of interest. Most interior banks continued to ship notes to their correspondents, extending the notes' periods of circulation (compare Bell, 1912, pp. 45–7). More than half of the notes received by the Treasury were sent by the New York banks, with shipments from Philadelphia and Boston next in size.

Restriction against discounting notes. High costs of sorting and transportation alone need not have prevented interbank note redemption. As in Canada before 1890, banks might have charged discounts sufficient to cover the costs of redeeming rival banks' notes. The Comptroller of the Currency estimated in 1873 that a discount of one-eighth to one-quarter of one percent would have been adequate to ensure prompt redemption of most country notes by banks in New York City (Knox, 1903, p. 115). Higher discounts might have been required at first, but experience elsewhere suggests that the discounts would have fallen to zero as the banks developed more efficient note-exchange procedures in their efforts to extend the boundaries of par circulation for their notes. Note discounts prompted the formation of the Suffolk system, the New York Assorting House, and the organized note exchanges of Scotland and Canada.

The 1864 Act, requiring national banks to accept one another's notes at par, precluded discounting. It thereby removed any incentive for the public to use note brokers, while simultaneously preventing the banks themselves from profitably brokering notes. It inadvertently blocked the issue elsewhere. As Francis Bowen (1866, p. 771) remarked, the authorities made "a bungling attempt to copy the Suffolk and New York Clearinghouse systems or rather their results," by insisting on mandatory par acceptance.[13] They failed to see that active redemption had historically been the mother and not the daughter of par redemption. Bowen (p. 773) observed that "the machinery is provided in the law for redemption of any bank bill . . . . But then it is in nobody's interest to put this machinery to use." The same legal restrictions that made the national currency uniform also prevented it from being actively redeemed, and thus made it a quasi-high-powered money.

Restriction against immediate re-issue. A final cause of downward inelasticity in the short run was a required six-month lag between a bank's contracting its note circulation and subsequently expanding it. This lag, enforced between 1882 and 1900, discouraged the retirement of notes returned to their issuer for redemption, because a note-retiring bank would disqualify itself from satisfying increased customer demands for notes in the near future. The bond collateral requirement made it costly for a national bank to retain its own notes in its till, as banks in unregulated systems did during seasonal periods of low note demand. These restrictions, together with the low homing power of notes, encouraged banks to place returned notes back into circulation immediately.

Consequence of Quasi-High-Powered Status for Notes

Feared potential for over-issue. The quasi-high-powered status of national bank notes meant that their issuers lacked what was normally the most powerful incentive to limit the quantities of their note liabilities to the quantities demanded at the existing price level. An individual ban typically did not have to fear any marginal loss of liquidity from expanding its circulation. At the aggregate level an increase in the stock of national bank notes would, either by serving as bank till money or by pushing greenbacks out of circulation and into legal reserves, allow a multiple expansion of the loans and deposits of the banking system as a whole, just as if an equal amount of greenbacks had been issued (Cleveland, 1905, pp. 165–6; Bell, 1912, p. 42; Friedman and Schwartz, 1963, pp. 50, 781–2). By itself, a plurality of issuers of a homogeneous high-powered money is clearly inconsistent with monetary stability (Klein, 1974).

Banking experts sharply criticized the weak homing power of national bank notes. Dunbar (1904 [1897], p. 241) found it "singularly at variance with the principle of having a wholesome restraint upon the operations of each bank by itself, which governs our treatment of other demand liabilities." Sprague (1904, pp. 527–8) assailed the "inelasticity on the side of contraction" which "removes from the banks individually and as a whole some of the consequences of their operations for which they should be immediately responsible." Such authorities naturally feared that removal of the bond collateral restrictions would allow notes to be over-issued unless provisions for active redemption were simultaneously made. Dodsworth (1895, p. 199) worried that his own

> proposed enlargement of the freedom of issue might easily run into an excessive supply of circulation and an illegitimate expansion of bank credits. That possibility is so obvious that a measure which failed to provide protection against such a result would be radically defective, and, after brief trial, would bring upon itself the condemnation of the conservative sentiment of the country. The only safe means of preventing such a failure is to provide arrangements which would allow the utmost facilities of dispatch and economy for forwarding the notes for redemption.

We discuss in detail elsewhere the impact of such worries on the course of monetary reform (Selgin and White, 1990).

The quasi-high-powered status of national bank notes also gave grounds for the complaint that national banks enjoyed a "double profit" on their circulation. The banks allegedly earned interest first on the bonds deposited as note collateral, and then again on the loans made with the notes (Dunbar, 1904 [1897], p. 241). Such complaints may simply have reflected discomfort with the leveraging of bank capital through fractional reserve banking. Yet in one respect a national bank *was* less constrained in expanding its assets than a bank in a free banking system. Because it faced little threat of adverse note clearings, a national bank with one dollar of excess lawful reserves could potentially expand its assets and liabilities by several dollars, whereas a bank in a normal competitive system could expand by only one dollar.[14] Of course, the opportunity costs of acquiring and holding collateral bonds did limit note expansion. But national banks could expand their note issues until their competition for collateral drove the price of eligible bonds high enough to exhaust any excess profit.[15] The same compulsory bond-collateral system that had loosened constraints on issue by erasing note-brand discrimination now discouraged issue by raising the costs of acquiring needed collateral.

    Cyclical instability. According to several knowledgeable contemporary observers (*e.g.,* Meade, 1898, pp. 217–21; Knox, 1903, pp. 104–5, 115), the treatment of national bank notes as quasi-high-powered money contributed to cyclical monetary instability. Rather than being redeemed locally, notes in excess supply in the interior traveled *via* payments or *via* interbank deposits to the Northeast and ultimately to New York City. New York banks, finding an accumulation of country notes in their vaults, were hard-pressed to convert them into useful assets. Before 1874 they sometimes resorted to selling notes at a discount for greenbacks (Friedman and Schwartz, 1963, p. 21 n. 8), or to lending country notes at zero interest to borrowers who were expected to repay their loans in greenbacks (*Commercial and Financial Chronicle,* 22 January 1870, pp. 102–3).

    Much of this lending took the form of call loans for stock market speculation. In the late summer and fall, as interior banks drew cash from their correspondents to meet the seasonal demand for currency associated with the fall harvest, the currency movement would reserve itself. The drain of cash into the interior confronted the Northeast with credit stringency, and sometimes with a currency shortage, as reserve losses forced banks to contract their loans.

    After 1874 New York banks could redeem unwanted notes and receive immediate payment from the subtreasury for them, but the issuers were not called upon to replenish the redemption fund immediately (Cagan and Schwartz, 1990). The reform therefore did not discourage the seasonal shipments of currency to the City. The sluggishness of the note redemption process, together with the lack of note brand discrimination, left issuers still individually unconstrained by seasonal variations in note-holding demand.

Chart 3
Redemptions, excess reserves, and call loan rates of New York banks, 1890–1908

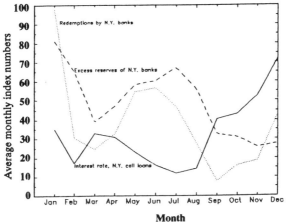

Month

Source: Commercial and Financial Chronicle, various dates

The redemptions gave the New York banks excess reserves rather than excess country notes to lend at call (and did not immediately reduce the excess reserves of country banks), allowing the seasonal pattern in interest rates to persist. Between 1890 and 1908, increases in excess reserves of New York banks, which largely followed interbank shipments of excess currency to New York, were associated with decreases in interest rates on call loans and 60–90 day paper in the New York money market (see chart 3).[16] Thus the high-powered status of national bank notes offers at least a partial explanation for the marked seasonality of interest rates between 1890 and 1910, a feature of the pre-Fed monetary regime emphasized by Allen (1986), Miron (1986), and Mankiw, Miron, and Weil (1987).

Figure 1 offers a simple general-equilibrium analysis of these co-movements based on the well-known graphical device of Patinkin (1965, p. 259). Curves MM, BB, and CC represent combinations of the price Level P and loan interest rate r consistent with equilibrium in the money bond (loan), and commodity markets respectively. In the fall, the MM curve shifts leftward with an increase in the public's demand for currency balances and the associated decline (given the national banking restrictions) in excess bank reserves. At the same time the BB curve shifts leftward with an increase in loan demand (an

**Figure 1: Seasonal Movement in Interest Rate
under the National Currency System**

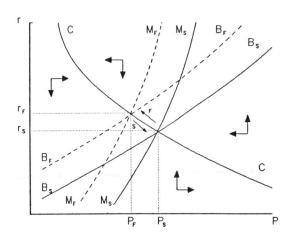

excess supply of bonds corresponds to the excess demand for money
at the initial levels of P and r, abstracting for simplicity from shifts in
the CC curve). In the spring the demand for currency decreases, shifting the curves in the opposite direction.

   Had there been regular active redemption of national bank
notes, interior banks would not have exported credit expansion and
contraction to the Northeast. Excess country notes would have been
intercepted by rival banks, redeemed, and removed from circulation
before leaving the interior. Notes that did make their way to the
Northeast would likewise have been returned to their issuers promptly for redemption instead of swelling the quantity of high-powered
money in the system as a whole. The original issuing banks would not
have found it profitable to reissue the notes until such time as the
demand to hold their currency rose. The seasonal movements of
funds to and from the Northeast would consequently have been far
less pronounced. A periodic excess of high-powered money would
have been nipped in the bud, rather than spilling over into the bond
market and causing a temporary drop in interest rates.

   This argument suggests that interest rates should be less seasonal in a country with a seasonally elastic stock of bank notes. The contrast between variations in the United States currency stock and
interest rates, and corresponding figures from Canada, is therefore

instructive. Seasonality in the demand for currency was common to both agricultural countries. The actual circulation of bank notes showed substantial seasonal variation in Canada during the period 1890–1908, when there was virtually no seasonal variation in the United States (see Chart 4). During the same period, consistent with our argument, interest rates on Montreal call loans showed much less seasonal variation than New York or Boston rates (Rich, 1988, pp. 49–50, 178). The seasonal pattern in New York call loan interest rates was in fact roughly similar to the seasonal pattern in the circulation of Canadian bank notes (see Chart 5). The greater interest-rate instability of the United States reflected in part the inelasticity of the national currency stock.

Chart 4
U.S. national bank note circulation and Canadian
bank note circulation, monthly figures, 1890–1909

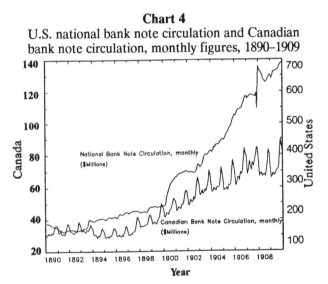

Source: Curtis (1931), Annual Report *of the Comptroller of the Currency, various dates.*

Chart 5
Seasonal movements in Canadian bank note circulation
and New York loan rates, 1890–1908

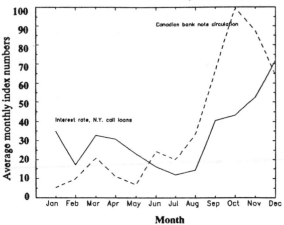

Source: *Curtis (1931)*, Commercial and Financial Chronicle, *various dates.*

Faced with the troublesome "inelasticity" of quasi-high-powered bank note currency, reformers had a choice. They could replace national bank notes with an alternative high-powered currency subject to centralized and presumably more rational quantity control. This was the road taken toward the Federal Reserve System. Alternatively, reform could undo the notes' quasi-high-powered status by dismantling the legal barriers to active redemption. Important efforts were made to achieve more active note redemption, both privately through banking industry cooperation and publicly through deregulatory legislation (Selgin and White, 1990). The movement ultimately failed to achieve its legislative aims because of political obstacles to deregulation, particularly to branch banking.

References

Allen, Andrew T. 1986, "Private Sector Response to Stabilization Policy: A Case Study," *Explorations in Economic History* 23 (July): 253–68.

American Bankers Association, 1878, *Proceedings.*

Baltensperger, Ernst. 1980. "Alternative Approaches to the Theory of the Banking Firm," *Journal of Monetary Economics* 6 (January): 1–37.

Bell, Spurgeon. 1912, "Profit on National Bank Notes," *American Economic Review* 2 (March): 38–60.

Bolles, Albert S. 1885, *The Financial History of the United States from 1861 to 1885.* New York: D. Appleton.

Bowen, Francis. 1866, "The National Banking System," *Bankers Magazine* (April): 769–85.

Breckinridge, R.M. 1910, *The History of Banking in Canada.* Washington: Government Printing Office.

British Seasonal Papers. 1826, *Report from the Select Committee Appointed to Inquire into the State of the Circulation of Promissory Notes under the Value of £5 in Scotland and Ireland.* V1.3, Parliamentary Paper no. 402.

Cagan, Phillip. 1963, "The First Fifty Years of the National Banking System—An Historical Appraisal," in Deane Carson, ed., *Banking and Monetary Studies.* Homewood, IL: Richard D. Irwin.

Cagan, Phillip, and Schwartz, Anna J. 1990, "The National Bank Note Puzzle Reinterpreted." Unpublished MS, Columbia University and NBER.

Cannon, James Graham. 1910, *Clearing Houses.* Washington: Government Printing Office.

Champ, Bruce A. 1990, "The Underissuance of National Banknotes During the Period 1875-1913." Unpublished MS, University of Western Ontario.

Cleveland, Frederick A. 1908, *The Bank and the Treasury.* New York: Longmans, Green, and Co.

Commercial and Financial Chronicle. Various dates, New York.

Comptroller of the Currency. Various dates, *Annual Report.*

Cornwell, William C. 1869, *The Currency and the Banking Law of the Dominion of Canada Considered with Reference to Currency Reform in the United States.*

Dodsworth, W. 1895, "Our Paper Currency—As It Is and As It Should Be," In *Sound Currency 1895: A Compendium.* New York: Reform Club Sound Currency Committee.

Dunbar, Charles Francis. 1905. *Economic Essays.* New York: Macmillan.

Friedman, Milton, and Anna Jacobson Schwartz. 1963, *A Monetary History of the United States, 1867-1890.* Princeton: Princeton University Press.

Gilbart, James William. 1834, *The History and Principles of Banking.* London: Longmans.

Goodhart, C.A.E. "Profit on National Bank Notes, 1900-1913," *Journal of Political Economy* 73 (October): 516–22.

Holladay, James. 1934, "The Currency of Canada," *American Economic Review* 24 (June): 266–78.

James, F. Cyril. 1938, *The Growth of Chicago Banks.* 2 vols. New York: Harper & Brothers.

James, John. 1976. "The Conundrum of the Low Issue of National Bank Notes," *Journal of Political Economy* 84 (April): 359–67.

Johnson, Joseph French. 1910, *The Canadian Banking System*. Washington: Government Printing Office.

Klein, Benjamin. 1974, "The Competitive Supply of Money," *Journal of Money, Credit, and Banking* 5 (November): 423–53.

Knox, John Jay. 1903, *A History of Banking in the United States*. New York: Bradford, Rhodes, and Co.

Laughlin, J. Laurence. 1898, *Report of the Monetary Commission of the Indianapolis Convention*. Chicago: University of Chicago Press.

Mankiw, N. Gregory, Jeffrey A. Miron, and David N. Weil. 1987, "The Adjustment of Expectations to a Change in Regime: A Study of the Founding of the Federal Reserve," *American Economic Review* 77 (June): 358–74.

Meade, Edward S. 1898, "The Deposit-Reserve System of the National Bank Law," *Journal of Political Economy* 2 (March): 209–24.

Million, John Wilson. 1894, "The Debate on the National Bank Act of 1863," *Journal of Political Economy* 2 (March): 251–80.

Miron, Jeffrey A. 1986, "Financial Panics, the Seasonality of the Nominal Interest Rate, and the Founding of the Fed," *American Economic Review* 76 (March): 125–40.

Mullineaux, Donald J. 1987, "Competitive Monies and the Suffolk Bank System: A Contractual Perspective," *Southern Economic Journal* (April): 884–97.

Mullineaux, Donald J. 1988, "Competitive Monies and the Suffolk Bank System: Reply," *Southern Economic Journal* (July): 220–23.

Patinkin, Don. 1965, *Money, Interest, and Prices*, second ed. New York: Harper and Row.

Phillips, Chester Arthur. 1920, *Bank Credit*. New York: Macmillan.

Rich, Georg. 1988, *The Cross of Gold: Money and the Canadian Business Cycle, 1867–1913*. Ottawa: Carleton University Press.

Root, L. Carroll. 1895, "New England Bank Currency." *Sound Currency* 2 (January): 253–84.

Scott, William A. 1908, "Rates on the New York Money Market, 1896–1906," *Journal of Political Economy* 12 (May): 273–98.

Selgin, George A. 1988, *The Theory of Free Banking*. Totowa, NJ: Rowman and Littlefield.

Selgin, George A. 1990, "Free Banking and Monetary Stabilization," unpublished MS, University of Georgia.

Selgin, George A., and Lawrence H. White. 1987, "The Evolution of a Free Banking System," *Economic Inquiry* 25 (July): 439–57.

Selgin, George A., and Lawrence H. White. 1988, "Competitive Monies and the Suffolk Bank System: Comment," *Southern Economic Journal* (July): 215–19.

Selgin, George A., and Lawrence H. White. 1990, "Monetary Reform and the Redemption of National Bank Notes, 1863-1908," unpublished MS, University of Georgia.

Smith, Vera C. 1936, *The Rationale of Central Banking.* London: P.S. King.

Spahr, Walter Earl. 1926, *The Clearing and Collection of Checks.* New York: Bankers Publishing Company.

Sprague, O.M.W. 1904, "The Distribution of Money Between the Banks and the People since 1893," *Quarterly Journal of Economics* 18 (August): 513-28.

Sylla, Richard E. 1975, *The American Capital Market, 1846-1914.* New York: Arno Press.

Timberlake, Richard H. 1978, *The Origins of Central Banking in the United States.* Cambridge: Harvard University Press.

Trivoli, George. 1979, *The Suffolk Bank: A Study of a Free-Enterprise Clearing System.* London: Adam Smith Institute.

United States Congress. 1897-1898, Committee on Banking and Currency, *Hearings and Arguments 1896-98.* Washington: Government Printing Office.

United States Treasury. 1861, *Annual Report* (Finance).

White, Lawrence H. 1984, *Free Banking in Britain.* Cambridge: Cambridge University Press.

White, Lawrence H. 1898, "The Growing Scarcity of Banknotes in the United States, 1865-1913," unpublished MS, University of Georgia.

Notes

*The authors thank the Institute for Humane Studies and the George Edward Durell Foundation, for research support. Helpful comments were received from Peter Selgin, Kurt Schuler, and seminar participants at I.H.S. and at the University of Georgia. Jim Michaels provided exceptionally able research assistance.

1. Thus "inelasticity" should *not* be interpreted here as $(dn/dx)(x/n) > -1$.

2. Banking theory (Baltensperger, 1980) normally relies on rising marginal liquidity costs—the increasing probability of reserve depletion through adverse clearings—to explain the limits to the expansion of inside money.

3. The reserve optimization model underlying these arguments is presented by Baltensperger (1980), White (1984, ch. 1), and Selgin (1988, chs. 3-6). Even if all banks expand their issues in unison, so that none suffers net adverse clearings, the resulting increase in gross clearings will raise the variance of clearings and thereby raise each bank's profit-maximizing prudential reserve. The banking system's aggregate demand for reserves then exceeds available reserves, and the expansion will not be sustained.

4. We are not denying that international arbitrage would constrain domestic prices and interest rates within limits, but rather that international

gold flows would *instantly* correct any excess supply or demand for currency. We are indebted to John James for raising this issue.

5. Market forces promote the emergence of active note redemption in a free banking system once there are several banks of issue. Bilateral note exchange and redemption in turn lead to multilateral clearing and elimination of discounts on domestic notes (par acceptance) (Selgin and White, 1987; Selgin, 1988, ch. 2).

6. The conformity of note market shares to deposit shares under incidental discrimination is a conjecture at this point. The process has yet to be formally modeled. If incidental discrimination is sufficient to determine note market shares, Harry Johnson's (1969) hypothesis that the stability of a competitive monetary system requires Chamberlinian product differentiation becomes a hypothesis about the necessary conditions for stable deposit market shares.

7. An 1843 Massachusetts law forbade banks from paying out notes other than their own, further ensuring active note redemption. The law appears merely to have compelled what was already standard practice for most banks. For further discussion of the contractual structure of the Suffolk system see Mullineaux (1987; 1988) and Selgin and White (1988).

8. On the back of national bank notes appeared the coat of arms of the state in which the issuing bank was chartered. From 1902 to 1924 geographical code letters were added to further aid sorting and redemption: N for New England, E for East, S for South, M for Midwest, W for West, and P for Pacific.

9. There is an obvious parallel here to the way in which deposit insurance today leads to non-discrimination among brands of deposit, also with regrettable consequences.

10. A similar phenomenon was seen in Canada after 1903. The standard practice had been for banks to redeem one another's notes actively. After 1903 a legal restriction limiting note-issue to the amount of paid-in capital began to bind some banks. Those banks began "to treat the notes of other banks very much as if they were [their] own," re-issuing rather than redeeming them (Johnson 1910, p. 65).

11. There was initially some confusion over whether the 1864 provision for par acceptance entitled banks to use their own notes in final settlement of clearing balances. Their use for settlement at some of the smaller clearinghouses provoked Comptroller of the Currency Freeman Clark to issue a sternly worded circular threatening the sale of securities of any bank that "failed to redeem its notes in lawful money when presented by a bank the same as if presented by an individual" (*Commercial and Financial Chronicle*, 14 October 1865, p. 482; also Comptroller of the Currency, 1865, p. 12). Despite Clark's threat, some smaller clearinghouses, including Buffalo and St. Paul, continued to use national bank notes for settlement (Cannon, 1910, p. 38).

12. At least we assume that this is so when notes are sorted by hand. With electronic sorting, as used for checks, the costs imposed by one more brand might be negligible.

13. A misguided attempt to mimic the Suffolk and New York Clearinghouse systems can also be seen in the provisions of national banking law allowing country banks to count deposits at city banks as legal reserves. Such interbank deposits arose under the earlier systems as a means for providing active redemption of country notes that found their way to the city. Under national banking they were not used for redemption of stray notes, but in fact could be augmented by interbank shipment of notes (compare Sylla, 1975, pp. 90–91).

14. This "rule of excess reserves" was enunciated by C.A. Phillips (1920, pp. 33–34). For a recent discussion see Selgin (1987, ch. 3).

15. Phillip Cagan (1963) and others (Goodhart, 1965; James, 1976; White, 1989; Cagan and Schwartz, 1990; Champ, 1990) have wondered or tried to explain why national banks failed to exhaust what Cagan identifies as opportunities for excess profits from note issue, especially during the 1890's. In a work in progress we examine whether improvements in note redemption, raising marginal liquidity costs, can help resolve this puzzle.

16. Other determinants of New York banks' excess reserves were, in order of significance: (1) movements of gold and greenbacks between banks and the public; (2) movements between the banks and the New York subtreasury; and (3) international gold flows (Scott, 1908, pp. 286–92). From 1902–1907 Treasury Secretary Shaw actively intervened in the New York market by shifting funds from the subtreasury to the banks in the fall, and back in the spring, in an effort to reduce the seasonal fluctuations in bank reserves and loan rates (Timberlake, 1978, ch. 12; Allen, 1986).

Comment

by Richard Sylla

As one who spent a considerable portion of his youth studying the operation of the National Banking System, I welcome the thoughtful and careful attention given to some of its features by George Selgin and Larry White.

In the turn-of-the-century era, the main complaint of those who sought to change or reform the system was its "inelastic" stock of currency. The emphasis of the complaint, as Selgin and White note, was that the stock of currency failed to expand as the demand for currency grew. Currency demand varied seasonally, cyclically, secularly, and, of course, it soared during bank runs and panics.

The flip side of concern about the inelasticity of currency expansion is concern about the inelasticity of currency contraction. This aspect of inelasticity is the one Selgin and White emphasize, as did some turn-of-the-century writers. Since national bank notes were not actively redeemed, the stock of notes did not contract when currency demand declined. As a result of this failure of the quantity of bank notes to adjust to demand, Selgin and White argue, the burden of adjustment was placed on interest rates. Interest rates had wide seasonal swings, as shown in their Chart 3. Moreover, there was an inflationary potential in the failure of bank notes to contract when demand for them fell. Unlike the seasonal swings of interest rates, this potential was not realized in the late nineteenth century because, at first, a ceiling on the total allowable issue and, later, adverse regulatory and market incentives for note issue prevented over-expansion. If those conditions had changed, some feared that an inflationary potential of downward inelasticity of note issues might have been realized.

These actual and potential problems of downward inelasticity resulted from national bank notes being regarded by the public and the banks as high-powered money instead of as liabilities of individual banks. National bank notes were so regarded because they were backed by U.S. government bonds. They were, in effect, liabilities of the U.S. government rather than of the banks that issued them. Knowing this, the public had no interest in redeeming notes, and because of the public's attitudes, the banks could easily pay out any national bank notes or hold them as liquid (but not, for national banks, legal) reserves. Therefore, the banks, like the public, had no incentive to redeem notes of other national banks that came into their possession. Without active redemption—which is the standard Selgin and White hold up in order to judge the National Banking System—currency contraction was inelastic, leading to interest rate swings and, potentially, inflation.

At the end of their paper, Selgin and White note that reform of the National Banking System to solve the problem of inelasticity could have taken two alternative roads. One was a central bank that would have its own high-powered currency that it could expand and contract as demand varied. This—in the form of the Federal Reserve System—was the road taken. Studies cited by Selgin and White show that the Fed actually did smooth out the seasonal variation in interest rates, although it hardly seems to have reduced the inflationary potential of excess high-powered money. The road not taken—I suspect it is the road Selgin and White think should have been taken—was to "undo the notes' quasi-high-powered status by dismantling the legal barriers to active redemption" (p. 190).

It seems to me that active redemption could have been achieved only by removing the U.S. government bond backing of national currency. In that event, bank notes would have been backed by the variegated assets of individual banks, as was the case before the Civil War under the state banking systems. There would be as many brands of notes as there were banks issuing notes. But one of the objectives of the National Banking System—the initial law of 1863 that enacted it was entitled the National Currency Act—was to create a *uniform* national currency. This objective was achieved: the public regarded the several forms of paper currency as equivalent and interchangeable under the National Banking System, and also as interchangeable with gold and silver money after resumption in 1879. To achieve active note redemption would have involved undoing one of the successes of the National Banking System. The trend of modern monetary history, moreover, seems to be in the direction of uniform currencies, so I doubt that the road not taken in 1914 was then a viable alternative.

Turning to another issue, I note that Selgin and White cite the passages from Friedman and Schwartz in which they explain why they (Friedman and Schwartz) treated national bank notes as high-powered money. Selgin and White do not cite the passages in Friedman and Schwartz (*Monetary History*, pp. 168–69) that deal with the inelasticity problem. In those passages Friedman and Schwartz talk about two senses of inelasticity, one "clearly valid," the other "highly dubious." The valid sense of inelasticity, according to Friedman and Schwartz, was the absence of interconvertibility between deposits and currency, which was the problem of banking panics that led to suspensions of convertibility of deposits into currency. A lender of last resort or some other method of increasing currency in response to panic demands was the solution to this "valid" problem of inelasticity. Such a solution would prevent panic demands for currency from leading to a large contraction of the stock of money.

The dubious sense of inelasticity, according to Friedman and Schwartz, was the notion that the money stock should conform to the "needs of trade," expanding as business expanded and contracting as business contracted. This is the real bills doctrine, which Friedman and Schwartz, following Lloyd Mints and other writers all the way back to Henry Thornton, regard as fallacious. Nonetheless, this seems to be the sense of inelasticity that Selgin and White adopt in their paper. They argue that active note redemption would prevent excessive creation of bank notes and deposits. I would like to ask them if this means that the real bills doctrine is correct rather than fallacious, and that Friedman and Schwartz, Mints, Thornton, *et. al*, were wrong to worry about a money stock that expanded and contracted in accordance with the "needs of trade."

Selgin and White argue that the inelasticity of national bank notes—their non-conformity to the needs of business—caused seasonal and cyclical fluctuations to short-term interest rates. They present no evidence on cyclical fluctuations, but they do show in their charts that excess reserves of New York banks were negatively correlated with call money rates. Since national bank legal reserves could not include national bank notes, it seems to me that the purported connection of inelastic, high-powered national bank notes with sea-

sonal interest rate movements is rather tenuous. I would add that
national bank notes during the 1890 to 1908 period shown in Selgin
and White's charts were only about 11 to 22 percent of high-powered
money, so it is difficult for me to believe that seasonal fluctuations of
national bank reserves (which—again—did *not* include national bank
notes) could have been determined in any significant way by the inelastic properties of national bank note issue.

Let us suppose, however, that Selgin and White are correct, and
that the inelasticity of national bank note issue was reasonable for
wide seasonal fluctuations in short-term interest rates. Was that
necessarily bad? In the U.S., the currency stock (and possibly the
money stock) was relatively stable seasonally while market interest
rates varied a lot. In Canada, where notes were actively redeemed,
the currency stock expanded and contracted seasonally (Selgin and
White, chart 5), while short-term interest rates were more stable than
in the U.S. It is not self-evident that fluctuating quantities of currency
are to be preferred to fluctuating price (interest rates). The Canadian
system and, later, the Federal Reserve System in the U.S. may have
reduced seasonal variations in short-term interest rates compared to
their seasonal variation under the National Banking System. I assume
seasonal variations in interest rates were anticipated under the
National Banking System, but even if they were not, were Canada and
the post-1914 U.S. a lot better off because their seasonals in interest
rates were damped compared to the seasonals under National Banking System?

I have a special interest in the answer to this question. In a
recent paper, I and two colleagues found that the volatility of stock
and bond market returns in the U.S. during the era of the National
Banking System was considerably less than it has been in the Federal
Reserve era, even though short-term interest rates have been less
volatile in the Fed era (see Jack W. Wilson, Richard Sylla, and Charles
P. Jones, "Financial Market Panics and Volatility in the Long
Run,1830–1988," in Eugene N. White, ed., *Crashes and Panics: The
Lessons from History,* Homewood, IL: Dow Jones/Irwin, 1990). Is it
possible that a stable, even "inelastic," monetary regime could promote stability of long-term asset returns even as it fostered swings of
short-term interest rates? Is it possible that an "elastic," "needs of
trade" monetary regime, in stabilizing short-term interest rates,
actually fosters more instability of long-term financial asset returns?

If the mark of a good paper is that it stimulates at least as many questions as it answers, then I think that George Selgin and Larry White have written a paper that is very good indeed.

A Tale of Two Dollars: Current Competition and the Return to Gold, 1865-1879

by Robert L. Greenfield and Hugh Rockoff[1]

Economic historians tend to focus on the public-policy measure that achieves dramatic results, whether intended or unintended, good or bad. Sometimes, however, the policy measure that achieves less-than-dramatic results has its own lesson to teach.

The writings of Hayek (1978) and Klein (1974) have led econo-mists to wonder whether room exists for monetary units besides the established national unit. Could a foreign or privately-issued unit gain currency? Would competition promote monetary stability? U.S. monetary history may shed some light on these questions; for midway through the Greenback Era, the U.S. government itself attempted to launch an alternative monetary unit. This tale of two dollars begins with the Civil War inflation.

Civil War Inflation

Congress, in 1846, enacted legislation that required the federal government, in conducting financial transactions, to use specie. The Treasury thus became independent of the banking system, and Salmon P. Chase, Lincoln's first Secretary of the Treasury, fully intended to preserve the Independent Treasury. Chase insisted that the government's creditors remit loans in one piece and fully in spe-cie. Consequently, in late 1861, when the government placed a large loan, the banking system experienced substantial reserve drains. The removal of Confederate officials from the British ship Trent—the Trent Affair—briefly raised the specter of another war with Britain, and the pressure on the banks grew. On December 31, 1861, the banks suspended convertibility. The government quickly followed suit, suspending payments on the $50 million issue of demand notes authorized by the act of July 17, 1861.

Suspension would probably have come anyway, even had Chase's loan policy been different and even had the U.S. not crossed swords with Britain. The monetary expansion that came later would have required suspension (Friedman and Schwartz 1963, p. 69, n. 64). In the public's mind, however, Chase's loan policy and the newsworthy Trent Affair became the causes of suspension.

Even after the British crisis had passed, the federal government's finances remained desperate. On February 12, 1862, Congress authorized an additional $10 million in "old" demand notes. The act of February 25, 1862, the first (and what was to have been the last) Legal Tender Act, brought the inconvertible-note total to $150 million (Barrett 1931, p. 33). The act of March 3, 1862, and the act of June 20, 1864, together added another $300 million, bringing the authorized issue to $450 million. Some of the $449 million actually issued circulated hand to hand; banks used the rest as their reserve asset.

Chase himself had considered the greenbacks an inflationary threat and therefore had only grudgingly concurred in their issuance (Shuckers 1874, p. 239). He saw in a system of national banking associations, which he had much preferred all along, a way of getting the greenbacks out of circulation, while in a noninflationary way achieving his goal of a uniform national currency. The National Currency Act (known later, in amended form, as the National Bank Act) of 1863 offered banks a federal charter and, along with the charter, the authority to issue national bank notes. National bank notes came from the newly-established Office of the Comptroller of the Currency. To obtain these notes, engraved with his bank's name, the banker deposited U.S. Treasury bonds as collateral. The Comptroller then issued notes totaling up to 90 percent of the bonds' value, par or market, whichever stood lower. In effect, then, the national bank note was a government monetary liability, and most studies (e.g., Friedman and Schwartz 1963; Cagan 1965) consider it, along with the greenback, a high-powered money.

Before the end of the Civil War, monetary expansion would more than double the general price level. The public paid particular attention to the premium on gold. In July, 1864, the price of gold reached $2.85 for the quantity of gold that, in 1861, had defined one dollar (Mitchell 1908, pp. 31–42).

Toward Resumption

As an objective of post-war monetary policy, specie resumption did not command unanimity. "Why go back to gold?" parties who favored sticking with the wartime inconvertible paper money argued. The country already had a national currency. Besides, resumption at the 1861 parity would deflate prices, punishing debtors. Resumption at gold's postwar price—devaluation—crossed some congressional minds but never contended for adoption as national policy (Timberlake 1978, p. 116). "Resumption" meant resumption at the 1861 price of gold.

The resumptionists themselves divided into factions. One faction favored immediate resumption at the 1861 parity, even though in December 1865, the price of gold stood half again as high as in 1861 and the wholesale price level even higher. Salmon Chase, by this time Chief Justice of the United States Supreme Court, in a letter to newspaper publisher Horace Greeley, put it plainly: "The way to resumption is to resume" (Shuckers 1874, p. 410).

Another resumptionist faction sought a set schedule to govern the monetary contraction required to roll prices back to their prewar level. Once the premium on gold had disappeared, gold payments would resume at the prewar parity. Hugh McCulloch, Andrew Johnson's Secretary of the Treasury, took the first step down this road by severely contracting the money supply. Although on December 18, 1865, it had given McCulloch its blessing, as business slowed, Congress began to doubt the advisability of unconstrained contraction. An act of April 12, 1866, therefore limited McCulloch to a $10 million contraction over the succeeding six months and a $4 million per month contraction thereafter.

After the country got a good taste of contraction, however, sentiment mounted in favor of "growing up to the currency." Economic growth and the demands it would place on the existing money supply would eventually push prices down to the point where, at the 1861 price of gold, foreign-trade flows would balance.

Growth-produced deflation soon became the accepted policy; and an act of February, 1868, forbade further contraction of the currency. The wording of the Resumption Act of 1875, however, left McCulloch's successors at the Treasury latitude to undertake some contraction of their own (Timberlake 1978, p. 118). Together, contraction and growth-produced deflation led finally to conditions permitting smooth specie resumption at the prewar parity. Resumption occurred on January 1, 1879, the date specified by the act of 1875.

The California Dollar

Devaluation or a decision not to resume at all would have excluded California from the *monetary* union; throughout the war, California had for its unit of account clung to the standard weight of gold. In California, the greenback fell to a substantial discount. In July 1864, for example, a one-dollar United States note sold in California for as little as $.35 gold (Wright 1916, p. 87). In California, the inconvertible greenback never gained currency as a medium of exchange and, until resumption, had a flexible nominal price (though a price constrained by the possibility of arbitrage, as, for example, by buying bills on London, selling them, and using the proceeds to buy bills on New York). "California handled such currency as it handled other forms of merchandise" (Wright 1916 [1980], p. 87).

The United States notes fared badly in California despite their having legal-tender status. Newspapers sometimes served public notice that a certain named person had, at its face value, forced the depreciated government currency upon his creditors, a practice disparaged as "greenbacking." To avoid being victimized, California sometimes wrote contracts calling specifically for payment in gold. The California legislature responded with the Specific Contract Act of 1863, upheld by the California Supreme Court and, later, by the United States Supreme Court. The act sanctioned contracts written explicitly in terms of the gold dollar (Moses 1893, p. 20).

In the East, the notes and deposits of national and state banks, circulated because they were convertible into the dominant domestic currency, the greenback. To Californians, however, greenbacks were not domestic currency; they were foreign exchange, bought and sold at the prevailing market price.

California's (and other western states') adherence to gold split the country into two distinct currency areas. A flexible rate of exchange between the greenback and the California (i.e., gold) dollar served as the monetary link between the country's two sections.

Legal Restrictions on Gold-Convertible Money

Even in the East, however, gold did not entirely disappear from financial use. Customs duties had to be paid in gold. The Public Credit

Act of 1869, furthermore, reiterated the government's intention to make interest payments and repay principal in gold. Many railroads, too, issued bonds that promised interest and principal payable in gold. The U.S. Treasury actually issued gold certificates. The act of March 3, 1863, which authorized the Treasury to issue the gold certificates, permitted a fiduciary issue as large as 20 percent. But from late 1865, when the certificates first appeared, through 1878, when issuance ceased, the Treasury never took advantage of the fiduciary-issue provision; the certificates were fully-covered (Friedman and Schwartz 1963, p. 25, n. 11).

That these certificates did not find their way into general circulation might suggest that some legal restriction hampered their use; and, in fact, although the smallest denomination Treasury gold certificate was twenty dollars, most issues began at 100 dollars (Friedberg and Friedberg 1968, pp. 94–95). Banks, however, could issue gold-denominated money in virtually any form the public wanted.

Even before resumption, some national banks, especially in New York, with its active foreign trade, offered deposits denominated in gold. On October 3, 1872, gold deposits stood at $6,171,000 and, on September 3, 1873, at $12,102,000 (Friedman and Schwartz 1963, p. 28–9, n. 17).

Nor did any legal restrictions block issuance of gold-denominated banknotes. A July 12, 1870, amendment to the National Currency Act provided for the organization of national gold banks. Like ordinary national banks, national gold banks were to issue notes secured by U.S. government bonds. Like ordinary national bank notes, national gold bank notes were to come from the Comptroller of the Currency, who as long as the bonds were at par or better, would deliver gold notes in an amount equalling 80 percent (instead of the usual 90 percent) of the deposited bonds' par value. Congress levied a 25 percent reserve-requirement ratio on the national gold banks. But whereas the ordinary reserve-city national bank could satisfy its 25 percent reserve requirement by holding greenbacks, the national gold bank had to hold gold (or silver) coin.

The very first national gold bank, the Kidder National Gold Bank, organized in Boston, with a charter dated August, 1870. Its president, Henry P. Kidder, and cashier, Oliver W. Peabody, were the major figures of the Boston investment house Kidder, Peabody & Co.[2] The Kidder National Gold Bank never succeeded in keeping in circulation any part of the $120,000 in gold notes that the Comptroller had delivered. Before November, 1872, when it went into voluntary liquidation, however, the Kidder Bank apparently did a limited business in deposits (Dillistin 1950, p. 139).

Only in California did national gold notes actually circulate. California's national banks—as many as nine coexisted before the rest of the country, on January 1, 1879, resumed general specie payments—made their distinctiveness clear. They took names such as "The First National Gold Bank of San Francisco" and "The National Gold Bank of D.O. Mills & Co." Table 1 shows the extent to which their notes, which became known as "yellowbacks" or "goldbacks" (Cross 1946, p. 274), and deposits gained acceptance. (Estimates place the Pacific coast's 1862-1879 monetary gold stock at about $25,000,000 (Comptroller of the Currency, *Annual Report*, 1903, p. 99).

The Resumption Act of 1875 took effect on January 1, 1879. On February 14, 1880, Congress passed an act that provided for the voluntary conversion of national gold banks into ordinary national banks. With time, the gold banks would delete "Gold" from their names and have the Comptroller recharter them as ordinary national banks. The First National Gold Bank of San Francisco, California's first national bank, for example, eventually became The First National Bank of San Francisco. It remained in business as The Crocker First National Bank of San Francisco until 1986, when it became part of Wells Fargo, N.A.

Table 1
California Gold Banks, 1871-1879[3]

Year	Number	Note Circulation (in thousands)	Deposits (in thousands)
1871	1	$ 277	$ 199
1872	3	1,366	3,144
1873	5	1,988	3,193
1874	6	2,108	5,406
1875	9	2,172	3,654
1876	9	1,414	2,499
1877	9	1,399	2,985
1878	9	1,437	3,403
1879	8	1,451	2,870

Source: (*Armstrong and Denny 1916* [1980], p. 148)

Why Gold Banks?

Why did the Treasury want to launch the yellowback? The answer, in part, reflects the Treasury's recognizing California's resistance to inconvertible paper money and seeking to bolster the market for government bonds by giving Californians a paper money that they could live with but a paper money that would require a deposit of government bonds as collateral. Congressional debate and executive documents, however, show that the government hoped that the gold note would gain some currency in the East as well.

John Sherman of Ohio, who chaired the U.S. Senate's finance committee, introduced the currency bill. Usually, monetary historians remember the currency bill for its enlarging and reallocating the authorized issue of ordinary national bank notes (Timberlake 1978, pp. 94–100). Sherman, however, took his bill's gold-bank provision quite seriously. "We have assurances," Sherman said, "that banks will be organized under this system at once on the Pacific coast, thus unlocking . . . a portion of gold that must necessarily be used now for the ordinary channels of circulation. In the city of New York there is now a commerce going on of over six hundred million dollars, all of which is carried on the gold basis and so great is the necessity for paper money to represent this gold business that they actually deposit $50,000,000 of gold coin in the Treasury of the United States, and receive gold notes without interest, merely to facilitate the ordinary transaction of . . . this business.

"So in the cities of Charleston and New Orleans, where cotton is measured by the gold standard, they can very readily use these coin notes. . . . These banks . . . will furnish to the people a sure currency based on coin, payable in coin, having all the requisites that is possible to have to provide the best national currency" (*Congressional Globe*, 41:2, p. 700).

Comptroller of the Currency Hiland R. Hilburd, in his 1870 annual report, echoed Sherman's introduction. "Under the provisions . . . of the act approved July 12, 1870, authorizing the establishment of national gold banks for the issue of circulating notes redeemable in specie," Comptroller Hilburd wrote, "but one bank has yet been established, the Kidder Bank of Boston, Massachusetts. . . . Information has been received that several other institutions of this character are in process of organization, or in contemplation, two or three of which are in California. It was not anticipated that specie-paying

214

banks would be established to any considerable extent, at present,"
Hilburd went on to say, "in those sections of the country where a
paper currency, based upon the legal tender issues of the Government, already prevails; although it was, and still is, supposed that one
or more gold banks might be established and successfully conducted
in each of those cities on the Atlantic seaboard where a considerable
foreign trade is carried on, and in which a certain amount of business
is necessarily transacted upon a specie basis."

Senator Sherman's introduction and Comptroller Hilburd's
report thus suggest that in 1870 the government thought that the
gold-based currency would hasten resumption. The emergence of the
gold banks, by economizing on gold, would cut into the premium on
gold. The Treasury therefore could more easily lay in its own stock of
gold, needed when the time to resume came. "If all the business of
this kind that is carried on in the cities of Boston, New York, Philadelphia, and Baltimore could be concentrated in one or two banking
institutions of this kind," Hilburd concluded, "its extent would
undoubtedly warrant the employment of a very respectable amount
for its exclusive accommodation" (Comptroller of the Currency,
Annual Report, 1870, pp. VII, VIII).

In his November 10, 1871 report, however, the Comptroller's
optimism with regard to the gold banks' prospects, both in California
and elsewhere, seems more guarded. "Since my last report," he
wrote, "but one bank has been established on a gold basis—the First
National Gold Bank of San Francisco. . . . It is presumed that the success of this institution is not so flattering as to induce the organization
of others of a similar character, though, in view of the obstacles and
the opposition it meets, it holds its own and is gradually winning its
way into public confidence."

The Comptroller then took unfavorable notice of the west
coast's attachment to gold. "The tenacity with which the Pacific States
adhere to a gold currency is quite notable," he says. "Whether it is
equally praiseworthy is another thing. It is not clear that those states
derive any substantial benefit from the course they have pursued, and
it is beginning to be manifest that the United States are not all benefitted by it. The substitution of a paper currency in California and
other gold-producing states for their present hard money would probably set free for the use of the Government and the whole country
some thirty or forty millions of gold. . . ." (*Annual Report,* 1871, p. VII).

A full year and one-half elapsed before the Comptroller had call to issue another gold-bank charter. The second and all successive gold banks organized in California; none organized in the East.

Supply or Demand?

To explain the absence of eastern gold banks, we might look first to supply and the costs of issuing gold notes rather than ordinary national bank notes. Originally, the notes that reserve-city national banks issued bore a 25 percent reserve requirement. In 1874, however, the Treasury established the redemption-fund system. A national bank had to maintain with the Treasury a greenback deposit no smaller than five percent of the bank's note circulation. Although the Treasury used the deposit to clear the bank's notes, the redemption-fund deposit counted as reserves against the bank's deposit liabilities. In effect, then, after 1874, ordinary national bank notes carried no reserves requirements (Cagan 1965, p. 87n). National gold bank notes, however, continued to carry their original 25 percent reserve requirement.

Gold banks suffered in another way, too. On depositing a $100 face-value bond, a gold bank could issue but $80 in notes, whereas an ordinary national bank could issue $90.

Two pieces of indirect evidence cast doubt on this supply-side explanation of the gold banks' eastern absence. The first is the behavior of California's note-to-deposit ratio after resumption.

Figure 1
California National Banks: Banknote-to-Deposit Ratio

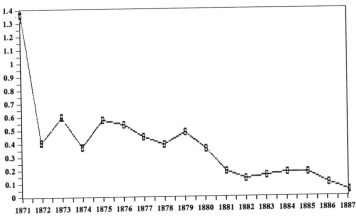

After 1879, the resumption year, ordinary national banks could issue convertible notes and on conditions more liberal than those pertaining to the national gold notes. California's note-to-deposit ratio, however, shown in Figure 1, exhibits no reversal of its downward trend.

Second, although being rechartered as ordinary national banks under the act of February 4, 1880, would have relieved their notes of reserve requirements and also provided an additional $10 to issue per $100 bond deposited, the California gold banks did not rush to be rechartered. In fact, not until 1884 did the national gold notes disappear, and numismatic evidence exists to suggest that national gold notes were issued as late as April, 1883, nearly four years after the notes of ordinary national banks had become convertible into gold (Philpott 1934, p. 718).

On the demand side, the gold-based currency's weakness in the East might appear attributable to the public's expectations concerning resumption. By the early 1870s, deflation of the greenback price level had established itself as policy (Timberlake 1978, p. 118). The public expected the greenback dollar to appreciate. Speculators thus had a one-way option.

But speculating that the greenback would appreciate did not require holding greenbacks themselves; any greenback-denominated asset would do. Besides, to judge by California's continued inability to spawn an ordinary national bank, the greenback, into which an ordinary national bank would have kept its own notes convertible, made no noticeable gains in California. And we have no reason to suppose that Californians, most of whom refused the greenback, were any less inclined to speculate than anyone else. Something other than the anticipated appreciation of the greenback dollar, therefore, must have accounted for the national gold note's eastern demand-side weakness.

In the East, the gold note lacked demand because something other than the established unit of account denominated the gold note. When a dominant medium of exchange exists, such as the greenback (or nowadays the Federal Reserve note), its unit defines the unit of account. To be taken seriously, an issuer of any other medium of exchange will have to denominate his medium of exchange in units of the dominant medium of exchange.

In California, no medium of exchange had acquired the dominance that elsewhere had been acquired by the greenback. No particular medium of exchange *defined* California's unit of account. Instead, the standard weight of gold served as a kind of independently-defined unit of account. Various media of exchange, the national gold note among them (but gold coins, too, some privately minted), hitched onto the independently-defined unit. If the national gold banks had suspended convertibility and thereby severed the note's connection with the unit of account, the national gold note would have disappeared, because Californians did not consider that (or any other) *particular* medium of exchange their unit of account.

Conclusion

Just as the greenback had failed to catch on in the West, so the national gold rate failed to catch on in the East. Where it lacked a connection to the established unit of account, neither the greenback nor the gold note could become a general medium of exchange. Nowadays, a medium of exchange denominated in something other than the Federal Reserve note would likely meet the same fate. The public seems very strongly to prefer having a single, definite unit of account.

Notes

1. Fairleigh Dickinson University, Madison, and Rutgers University, New Brunswick, respectively.

2. The rapidity with which the Kidder Bank got underway raises the question whether the Kidder group helped promote the gold-bank legislation. The Kidder-Peabody papers, however, make no mention of the Kidder National Gold bank. Nor does the most complete history of Kidder-Peabody & Co. (Carosso 1979) include a reference to the bank. In a companion piece, "Yellowbacks, Greenbacks, and Gold: Currency Competition in the American 1870's," we give a more detailed account of the Kidder Bank.

3. The "Report of the Condition of the National Banks at The Close of Business on Friday, October 1, 1875," included in the *Annual Report of the Comptroller of the Currency* for 1875, the year of peak yellowback circulation, refers to nine national gold banks. The gold banks, each with its October 1, 1875 gold note circulation, were: First National Gold Bank, Oakland ($80,000); Union National Gold Bank, Oakland ($31,570); First National Bank, Petaluma ($156,740); National Gold Bank of D.O. Mills & Co., Sacramento ($220,000); First National Gold Bank, San Francisco ($605,575); National Gold Bank and Trust Company, San Francisco ($399,582); Farmer's National Gold Bank, San Jose ($239,940); First National Gold Bank, Santa Barbara ($79,940); and, First National Gold Bank, Stockton ($358,710).

References

Armstrong, Leroy and J.O. Denny. 1916. *Financial California: An Historical Review of the Origins and Progress of Banking in the State.* Reprinted, Arno Publishing Co.: New York, 1980.

Barrett, Don C. *The Greenbacks and Resumption of Specie Payments, 1862–1879.* Harvard University Press: Cambridge, 1931.

Cagan, Phillip. *Determinants and Effects of Changes in the Quantity of Money 1875–1960.* National Bureau of Economic Research, Princeton, NJ: Princeton University Press, 1965.

Cagan, Phillip, 1963. "The First Fifty Years of the National Banking System—An Historical Appraisal," in Deane Carson, ed., *Banking and Monetary Studies,* Comptroller of the Currency. Homewood, Illinois: Richard D. Irwin, Inc., pp. 15–42.

Carosso, Vincent P. *More Than a Century of Investment Banking: The Kidder, Peabody & Co. Story,* New York: McGraw Hill, 1979.

Comptroller of the Currency. *Annual Report.*

Congressional Globe.

Cross, Irving, 1946. "Californians and Hard Money," *California Folklore Quarterly,* January, pp. 270–277.

Cross, Irving. 1927. *Financing an Empire: Banking in California,* 4 vols. San Francisco: The S.J. Clarke Publishing Co.

Dillistin, William H. 1950. "National Gold Banks and Bank Notes," *The Numismatist,* March, pp. 133–139.

Friedberg, Robert, and Jack Friedberg. 1968. *Paper Money of the United States,* Sixth Edition, New York: The Coin and Currency Institute, Inc.

Friedman, Milton and Anna J. Schwartz. 1963. *A Monetary History of the United States,* National Bureau of Economic Research, Princeton, NJ: Princeton University Press.

Hayek, F.A. 1978. *Denationalization of Money: The Argument Refined,* Hobart Paper Series, London: Institute of Economic Affairs.

Kidder, Peabody & Co. Papers. Special Collections, Baker Library, Harvard University.

Kindahl, James. 1961. "Economic Factors in Specie Resumption: The United States, 1865–1879," *Journal of Political Economy,* 69, 31–48.

Klein, Benjamin. 1974. "The Competitive Supply of Money," *Journal of Money, Credit, and Banking,* pp. 423–453.

Lester, Richard A. 1939. "Retention of the Gold Standard in California and Oregon During the Greenback Inflation," in his *Monetary Experiments: Early American and Scandanavian,* Princeton, NJ: Princeton University Press.

Mitchell, Wesley C. 1903. *A History of the Greenbacks,* Chicago: University of Chicago Press.

Moses, Bernard. 1903. "Legal Tender Notes in California," *Quarterly Journal of Economics,* pp. 1–25.

Philpot, W.R., Jr. 1934. "National Gold Bank Notes, *The Numismatist,* November, pp. 717–719.

Shuckers, Jacob W. 1874. *The Life and Public Services of Salmon P. Chase,* New York: D. Appleton and Company.

Timberlake, Richard C., Jr. 1978. *The Origins of Central Banking in the United States,* Cambridge, MA: Harvard University Press.

Wright, Benjamin C. 1916. *Banking in California, 1849–1910,* San Francisco: H.S. Crocker Co. Reprinted by Arno Press: New York, 1980.

Comment

A Tale of Two Dollars: Currency Competition and the Return to Gold, 1865–1879
by Joseph T. Salerno

The stated purpose of the paper by Robert L. Greenfield and High Rockoff is to attempt to derive a lesson for public policy from a less-than-dramatic monetary experiment which was initiated in the United States in 1870. While I believe that Greenfield and Rockoff have identified a potentially fruitful experiment, I have questions about their interpretation of the factual background of the experiment and the conclusions they draw from it. Most significantly, I question their main thesis that the national gold banks authorized by the amendment to the National Currency Act of July 12, 1870 represented an attempt by the U.S. government to "launch an alternative monetary unit." Despite my reservation on this crucial point, however, I do consider the period during which the experiment occurred to hold valuable lessons concerning the possibilities and the institutional preconditions of currency competition.

Before we are able to determine whether national gold bank notes or "yellowbacks," as they were called, can be classified as an independent alternative to existing monies in the United States, we must be clear about what those monies were. From the breakdown of bimetallism in 1853 until the U.S. Treasury and state bank suspensions of specie payment on December 30, 1861, the gold dollar, legally defined as 23.22 grains of pure gold, effectively served as the uniform medium of exchange for the entire United States (Paul and Lehrman 1982, 63–66).

In the states east of the Rocky Mountains, these dollars circulated in the form of gold coins as well as of state bank notes and deposits redeemable in gold coin upon demand. In the Pacific states, the medium of exchange was embodied almost exclusively in gold coin. In California and Oregon, for example, banks of issue were expressly prohibited by the state constitutions and they were only a few banks of deposits. Also in circulation were the U.S. Treasury notes redeemable in gold and fractional silver coins (Lester [1939] 1970, 163; Mitchell 1903, 141–42).

After the first Legal Tender Act of February 25, 1862, United States notes or "greenbacks" swiftly became the "domestic currency," that is, the medium of exchange used in everyday transactions, of the Eastern states. Although gold coins disappeared from circulation as a result of the operation of Gresham's Law, gold continued as a parallel currency in the East, because of its use in foreign trade. In fact, in order to accommodate foreign exchange dealers, New York national banks among others offered demand deposits denominated in and payable in gold dollars as an alternative to greenback-denominated deposits (Friedman and Schwartz 1963, 28–29 fn. 17; Mitchell 1903, 142). In addition, the federal government continued to pay interest on a large portion of its debts in gold and to require import duties to be paid in gold (Mitchell 1903, 142). There is evidence that uncoined gold was used as the medium of exchange in large domestic transactions (Anderson [1917] 1936, 148–49).

The extensive employment of the gold dollar as an alternative currency in the East naturally led to its use alongside the greenback dollar as a unit of pricing and of economic calculation. Thus Benjamin M. Anderson ([1917] 1936, 422) concludes that, during the greenback era, "People *thought* in both standards."

Circumstances differed considerably west of the Rockies during this era. By all accounts residents of the Pacific states made little or no use of greenbacks in exchanges or in cash balances (Moses 1892; Mitchell 1903, 142; Lester [1939] 1970, 164–65). Merchants refused to accept the greenback dollar at par in current transactions and deposit banks in California and Oregon refused to accept greenback deposits under any circumstances. Instead, people clung tenaciously to the gold dollar as their domestic currency. Thus gold continued to be used for everyday purchases of consumer goods and wage payments, and as the stipulated means of repayment in credit transactions.

There was, however, a foreign-exchange demand for greenbacks on the part of those importing goods from the East. Technically, therefore, a regime of parallel currencies also existed in the Pacific states, with greenback dollars exchanging for gold dollars at a market-determined exchange rate. It is doubtful, however, that, outside of a narrow circle of currency speculators, money brokers, and those directly involved in trade with the Eastern states, economic calculation took place in terms of both dollars to the same extent that it did in the East.

My account of the facts is substantially in agreement with the account given by Greenfield and Rockoff. However, Greenfield and Rockoff draw an important inference from these facts which appears to me to be questionable although it is the main prop upon which much of their argument rests. The questionable inference is embodied in the author's statement that "No particular medium of exchange *defined* California's unit of account. Instead, the standard weight of gold served as a kind of independently-defined unit of account" (Greenfield and Rockoff 1990, 16). This is a startling conclusion given the facts as the authors present them, because, as we saw above, they clearly recognize that, in the Pacific states, the gold dollar was not only the standard pricing unit, but, in the form of gold coin, was physically present as the purchase-good in almost every domestic exchange. Indeed, there was an estimated $25 million of gold and silver coin in circulation on the Pacific Coast during the greenback era (Lester [1939] 1970, 162). Moreover, there was no bank note circulation and, with very few banks of deposit, presumably little use of checks.

Of course, the authors do not intend to deny that gold coin was used almost exclusively as the medium of exchange in California. Their point is that no particular *brand* of gold dollar had achieved dominance in circulation in California, where the issuance of exchange media denominated in the gold dollar was undertaken by a number of competing institutions, including private mints. Moreover, none of these institutions was responsible for originating the standard weight of gold as the unit of account. This contrasted with the situation in the East, where the greenback dollar, which was solely the creation of the U.S. Treasury, dominated as medium of exchange and defined the accounting unit. Hence the authors' conclusion that, in California, media of exchange were denominated in, but did not define, the gold dollar, which therefore existed as an "independently-defined unit of account."

While plausible, Greenfield and Rockoff's argument is based on an apparent confusion, which could have been avoided had they addressed the issue of the evolution of the gold and greenback dollars. Contrary to what the authors seem to imply, a thing does not attain the position of a general medium of exchange by virtue of its brand name but by virtue of its qualities as a specific commodity.

Without going into great depth, the theory of the evolution of money as formulated by Carl Menger ([1950] 1981, 257–85) and later refined by Ludwig von Mises ([1952] 1971, 30–37, 108–24) and Murray Rothbard (1974); tells us that the general medium of exchange originates on the market as the most saleable commodity in the previous state of barter. Money thus initially circulates as a generic and unbranded commodity. The unit of account then naturally emerges as a standard weight unit of the money commodity that is convenient for calculation, for example, pound, ounce, or gram. It is only later with the advent of coinage that the money commodity is branded to certify weight and purity and to distinguish between different issuers and that coins of particular weights come to be designated by distinctive names.

But regardless of the emergence of special currency names and the proliferation or dominance of specific currency brands, the generic money commodity itself retains the position of the general medium of exchange, and the unit of account continues to be rigidly defined as a weight of this commodity. Thus, contrary to Greenfield and Rockoff, in California, the medium of exchange and unit of account were inextricably linked, with the commodity gold in various shapes and forms functioning as the "dominant" medium of exchange and the unit of account "defined" as a "dollar," which was another name for the standard weight of gold.

This analysis also sheds light on the evolution of the greenback dollar. Whether it is a credit money, for which the public from the first entertained reasonable expectations of an eventual resumption of specie redeemability, or whether it was a pure fiat currency, for which such expectations were entirely absent, the greenback dollar could only emerge as a general medium of exchange and accounting unit by virtue of its previous link with gold. Indeed the forerunners of the irredeemable greenbacks were U.S. Treasury notes redeemable on demand in specie, whose issue was authorized by the act of July 17, 1861, and even ". . . these notes were acceptable with reluctance" by banks and the public (Mitchell 1903, 26). It is only after state banks had suspended specie payments on December 31, 1861, in effect forcibly shaking gold loose from its dominant position as a medium of exchange, that the Treasury suspended and the greenback dollar came into being as an independent entity. The passage of the first Legal Tender Act on February 26, 1862, which authorized a fresh issue of the irredeemable notes, cemented the greenback's standing as the dominant medium of exchange east of the Rockies.

The point is that the greenback dollar never could have attained its standing by political fiat alone, independently of a preexisting relationship with market-chosen commodity money. The greenback dollar did not emerge *ex nihilo* as a pure brand name.

Moreover, it is clear that, as a medium of exchange, the generic gold dollar was more dominant on the Pacific Coast than the greenback dollar was in the rest of the Union. The gold dollar was well entrenched as a medium of exchange and unit of account in the East, since it did function as an intermediary in some types of domestic exchanges and was held in business cash balances and as part of the monetary reserves of banks. In contrast, greenbacks in California played almost no role in domestic exchanges and were not held in cash balances by the public. As Greenfield and Rockoff (1990, 15) themselves point out, even Californians who were bullish on the prospects for resumption and inclined to speculate on the long-term appreciation of the greenback did not need to hold greenbacks, since speculative gains could have been secured by acquiring and holding any interest-bearing greenback-denominated asset.

Once we recognize that the generic gold dollar was a medium-of-exchange as well as a unit-of-account dollar in California and in the East, we are able to evaluate Greenfield and Rockoff's main thesis: that the bank notes issued by the national gold banks constituted a new and independent currency.

The national gold bank notes were redeemable upon demand in gold coin and the issuing institution was required to maintain a reserve of gold and silver coin equal to twenty-five percent of the notes in circulation (Dillistin 1950, 133–34). In drafting this legislation, the government intended that the gold notes would displace the full-bodied gold coin circulation of the Pacific Coast and perhaps also would be used in foreign-exchange transactions in the East in place of Treasury gold certificates and gold deposits of New York banks, both of which were effectively if not legally backed by one hundred percent fold reserves (Friedman and Schwartz 1963, 25 fn. 11, 28–29 fn. 17). It was thus the hope of the government that the fractional-reserve yellowbacks would help to facilitate resumption by economizing on the gold in circulation and in the monetary reserves of financial institutions, thereby reducing the premium on gold and permitting the Treasury to lay in the needed stock of gold at a lower cost. However, this hope was never realized, because only ten national gold banks were organized, one in Boston, which never issued any gold notes, and nine in California (Philpott 1934, 717–18; Dillistin 1950, 134–35).

Greenfield and Rockoff's attempt to square the absence of gold note circulation in the East with its development, albeit limited, in California rests on their thesis that the national gold bank note was an independent and self-subsisting medium of exchange. Thus they argue that, in California, which lacked a "dominant" medium of exchange, the gold note was able to easily "hitch onto" the independently-defined unit of account, that is, the standard weight of gold. Conversely, they attribute the failure of gold notes to gain currency in the East to the fact that there the greenback already dominated as the medium of exchange. Somewhat inconsistently, the authors conclude that the inability of the greenback to catch on in the West and of the gold note to catch on in the East was a consequence of the fact that each "lacked a connection to the established unit of account," rather than to the dominant medium of exchange (Greenfield and Rockoff 1990, 16).

In any case, Greenfield and Rockoff conclude that the general lesson to be learned from the national gold bank episode is that for an item to gain acceptance as a medium of exchange, it must be denominated in units of the dominant medium of exchange, where one exists. This implies that, from the standpoint of current U.S. monetary policy, the issue of an alternative medium of exchange denominated in something other than Federal Reserve notes would fail to gain currency among the American public (Greenfield and Rockoff 1990, 17).

The essential problem with Greenfield and Rockoff's explanation of the varying fortunes of the gold note on the opposite sides of the Rocky Mountains is based on what I have argued above is a misinterpretation of the facts. Once it is recognized that the generic gold dollar was both the medium of exchange and the unit of account in California during the greenback era, there ceases to be mystery about why the gold note achieved acceptability. The gold note was accepted in exchange and held in cash balances precisely because it was redeemable in gold coin, the general and exclusive medium of exchange. The gold note therefore was not a newly issued medium of exchange. Given confidence in the issuing institution's ability to maintain convertibility of the gold notes, market forces insured a rigidly uniform purchasing power for gold coins and gold notes of equal denominations. The gold notes therefore substituted to some extent for gold coin in people's cash balances because it represented a more convenient way to hold and pay gold dollars.

Regarding the status of greenbacks in California, it is not quite correct to say, as the authors do, that they did not "catch on." Despite the fact that they were not denominated in units of the dominant medium of exchange (or in the established unit of account), the greenback dollar did emerge as a parallel currency by virtue of the interlocal trade relations existing between California and the Eastern states. As Ludwig von Mises ([1934] 1971, 179–80; Robbins 1971, 22) was the first to note, from the point of view of the theory of exchange-rate determination, there is no difference between two currencies used side by side in the same region and two currencies each of which are considered to be the domestic currency of one region and the foreign exchange of the other.

The same general analysis can be applied to explain the failure of the gold note to catch on in the East. The explanation does not lie, as Greenfield and Rockoff claim, in the fact that gold notes were not denominated in terms of the dominant greenback dollar—after all Treasury gold certificates and gold deposits at national banks also had no link with the greenback dollar and yet each achieved a circulation. Rather, it is probably that the absence of national gold bank notes in the East is due to the fact that, for certain transactions, these notes were considered less convenient than checks drawn on a national bank gold deposit and that, for transactions better served by gold-backed currency, Treasury gold certificates were preferred because they were perceived to have a lower default risk.

Despite the above criticism, I believe that the policy lesson which Greenfield and Rockoff uphold is both true and important. Currency competition can only emerge out of an evolutionary market process and cannot be implemented in one fell swoop by legal fiat or by a private entrepreneurial scheme. Certainly, this is the lesson we learn from the extreme reluctance of the residents of the bankless Pacific states to accept the greenback as their domestic currency, while the greenback gained swift acceptance among the residents of the remaining (loyal) states whose attachment to the gold dollar had long been attenuated by their repeated subjection to depreciated and inconvertible state bank notes.

References

Anderson, Benjamin M., Jr. [1917] 1936. *The Value of Money.* New York: Richard R. Smith.

Dillistin, William H. 1950. "National Gold Banks and Bank Notes." *The Numismatist* (March), pp. 133–39.

Friedman, Milton and Anna Jacobson Schwartz, 1963. *A Monetary History of the United States, 1867–1960.* Princeton: Princeton University Press.

Greenfield, Robert L. and Rockoff, Hugh. 1990. "A Tale of Two Dollars: Currency Competition and the Return to Gold, 1865–79." Unpublished MS.

Lester, Richard A. [1939] 1970. *Monetary Experiments: Early American and Recent Scandinavian.* Devon, Great Britain: David and Charles Reprints.

Menger, Carl. [1950] 1981. *Principles of Economics.* Trans. James Dingwall and Bert F. Hoselitz. New York University Press.

Mises, Ludwig von. [1952] 1971. *The Theory of Money and Credit.* 2nd ed. Irvinton-on-Hudson, N.Y.: The Foundation of Economic Education, Inc.

Mitchell, Wesley Clair. 1903. *A History of the Greenbacks: With Special Reference to the Economic Consequences of Their Issue, 1862–65.* Chicago: The University of Chicago Press.

Moses, Bernard. 1892. "Legal Tender Notes in California." *The Quarterly Journal of Economics* 7 (October): 1–25.

Paul, Ron and Lehrman, Lewis. 1982. *The Case for Gold: A Minority Report of the U.S. Gold Commission.* Washington, D.C.: Cato Institute.

Philpott, W.A., Jr. 1934. "National Gold Bank Notes." *The Numismatist* (November), pp. 717–19.

Robbins, Lord. 1971. *Money, Trade and International Relations.* London: The Macmillan Press Ltd.

Rothbard, Murray N. 1974. *What Has Government Done to Our Money?* 2nd ed. Novato, Cal.: Libertarian Publishers.

The Performance of the Federal Reserve in Pursuing International Monetary Objectives

by Anna J. Schwartz

When the Federal Reserve Act was passed in 1913, the United States was on the gold standard. Section 14 of the Act, dealing with open market operations, authorized the remittance and collection of foreign currency balances with respect to those parts of the current account that the central banking system would have handled. However, parties other than central banks and treasuries at the time dealt with external finance and foreign collections. In addition, Section 14(3) authorized the Federal Reserve Banks to maintain accounts with foreign correspondents. The Act accordingly laid out no specific or general international monetary objectives for the new regional banks.[1]

The Act was no sooner passed than the gold standard condition on which it was based ceased to hold. Before the System began operations, World War I had begun. Very soon the belligerents effectively left the gold standard and a flood of gold started coming to the United States to pay for purchases by the Allies. By the end of the war, the U.S. had imposed the embargo on gold imports.

During the 1920's, the New York Federal Reserve Bank and its governor, Benjamin Strong, played the leading role in the System's relations with other countries. Foremost among his objectives was the re-establishment of a worldwide gold standard. Toward that end, he arranged agreements to extend credit to Poland, Great Britain, Belgium, Italy, and Romania. The agreement with Britain was the most important, involving the largest extension of credit.

Strong's death in 1928 effectively ended this episode of the involvement of the Federal Reserve Bank of New York in foreign monetary developments. Resentment by others in the System of

Strong's personal initiatives in international arrangements led to the enactment of Section 14(g) in 1933, assigning to the Board of Governors "special supervision over all relationships and transactions of any kind entered into by any Federal reserve bank with any foreign bank or bankers, or with any group of foreign banks or bankers . . . ."[2]

In addition to the European countries that pegged their currencies to gold under Strong's influence, other countries followed suit in that continent (Austria, Denmark, Hungary, Latvia, Netherlands, Norway, Sweden), as well as in Asia (Japan) and Latin America (Chile.)

The collapse of the gold-exchange monetary standard to which most countries had returned by 1929 was signaled by Britain's abandonment of gold in September 1931. The world monetary system split in two, one part following Britain to form the sterling area, the other following the United States in the gold bloc. The suspension of the gold standard in the United States on the proclamation of a bank holiday on March 6, 1933, also marked a transfer of power over international monetary objectives from the Federal Reserve to the Treasury and other government agencies in Washington, D.C.

In the period from 1933 to 1961 the chief developments affecting U.S. international monetary relations included: the June 1933 World Monetary Conference, the variable price of gold until January 31, 1934, the U.S. managed gold standard thereafter, the Tripartite Agreement of September 25, 1936, and the establishment of the Bretton Woods monetary system in 1946. The Treasury Department made the principal decisions for the United States in each of these developments.

The Federal Reserve became an active player again in 1962, although clearly subordinate to the Treasury. International monetary objectives undertaken during the following decades related to foreign exchange management. Under the Bretton Woods system, doubts grew about the commitment of the U.S. to buy or sell gold at $35 per ounce in transactions with foreign monetary authorities, as its balance of payments weakened steadily after 1950.

In 1961, the Treasury activated the Exchange Stabilization Fund that was established in 1934 to deal in gold and foreign exchange. In 1962 the Federal Open Market Committee authorized the Federal Reserve Bank of New York to buy or sell foreign currencies on behalf of the FOMC in both spot and forward markets. The Federal Reserve negotiated a network of swap facilities with the central banks of other countries.

The breakdown of the Bretton Woods system in 1971 and the shift to generalized floating exchange rates in early 1973 did not lesson direct official intervention, compared with the pegged parity system, to maintain the open market price of currencies. By the end of the decade the Federal Reserve and the Treasury were intervening in the foreign exchange market virtually on a day-to-day basis. Holdings of foreign currencies by the two authorities began to balloon following the Plaza Agreement of September 1985 and continue to date.

In addition to foreign exchange market intervention, both the Federal Reserve and the Treasury became heavily involved, after the problem surfaced in 1982, in dealing with troubled international debtors and domestic banks with large exposure. In retrospect, not only the banks but also the Federal Reserve had erred, the regulator because it had cast a benevolent eye on the growth of bank lending abroad during the 1970's.[3]

The chief issue in discussing international monetary objectives of the Federal Reserve relates to their compatibility with domestic monetary objectives. In each of the sub-periods, the issue arises: Did international monetary objectives conflict with or support domestic monetary objectives? The opposite question is also pertinent: Did some domestic monetary objectives help or harm other countries?

In the account of international monetary objectives presented here, the Federal Reserve figures in only two of the three sub-periods of its existence. It was shunted aside in the middle sub-period. Its eagerness to re-emerge as a significant player in the third sub-period has public choice implications.

The paper is organized in four sections. Section 1 covers the period from 1914 to 1933, which Benjamin Strong dominated until his death in 1928. How his well-meaning actions in sterilizing gold flows to and from the U.S. and the darker intentions of the Governor of the Bank of France with respect to gold inflows served to undermine the gold exchange standard established during the 1920's is a theme of this section.[4]

Section 2 covers the period from 1933 to 1961, highlighting the role of agencies other than the Federal Reserve—the Treasury, its Exchange Stabilization Fund, the Reconstruction Finance Corporation, its subsidiary the Export-Import Bank, the State Department's

Lend-Lease Administration, the European Recovery Administration—in administering international monetary objectives. Even though the International Monetary Fund after 1945 was supposed to be the manager of foreign exchange policy for its member nations, U.S. agencies remained active.

Section 3 covers the period from 1961 to 1990, when the Federal Reserve, under the guiding influence of the Treasury, became a significant player in foreign exchange markets. A key issue here is whether there is legal authority for the Federal Reserve's currency intervention, and what the monetary consequences have been of its acquisition of a growing portfolio of foreign currencies as well as the cost to taxpayers. Another issue is the legal basis for the Federal Reserve's warehousing of currencies for the Treasury. In this period also the Federal Reserve along with the Treasury attempted to micromanage dealings between domestic creditor banks and debtor countries in resolving international debt delinquency.

Section 4 summarizes the record of the Federal Reserve's international monetary objectives.

J. Benjamin Strong's Initiatives

Benjamin Strong, who was elected governor of the Federal Reserve Bank of New York in October 1914, was the dominant figure in the System until his death fourteen years later. At an early stage in his incumbency, he sought to enlarge his understanding of the operation of central banks of other countries. In this connection he made the first of many trips to Europe in February 1916, and remained abroad until mid-April. At the Bank of France he met the governor and other officers and discussed establishing an account there to handle foreign business of the Reserve Banks and a counterpart account for the Bank of France at the U.S. institutions, without reaching a definite agreement. In London he met Lord Cunliffe, the governor of the Bank of England, and Montagu Norman, then an assistant to the deputy governor, with whom he later formed a close personal and professional friendship.

Strong brought back a memorandum jointly prepared by him and Bank of England representatives with provisions for the Federal Reserve Bank of New York to establish an account with the Bank of England's account to be in the form of earmarked gold—since the Reserve banks could receive deposits only from member banks and the U.S. government—and for the Bank of England to purchase sterling bills for the Federal Reserve Bank of New York on request.[5]

Strong's wish to see the Bank's arrangement with the Bank of England implemented was granted in August 1916, when the Federal Reserve Board approved it, with the proviso that no operations would be undertaken before the end of the war without authorization. The State Department ruled that such an agency did not contravene U.S. neutrality. In February 1917 the Board also approved agency relations between the New York Bank and the Bank of France. Thus Strong laid the groundwork for the role he destined the Federal Reserve System to play—at a time when its international operations were limited—during the 1920's in international financial arrangements.

Wartime changes greatly enhanced the position of the New York Reserve Bank and of Strong as its head. The Bank, located in the central money market, transacted most of the Treasury's foreign exchange dealings, distributed payments to foreign countries and to suppliers of war goods to them.

In July 1919, on behalf of the Bank, Strong sailed to Europe, remaining there until September. He proposed to gather information on European conditions, to discuss operation of the agreement between the Bank and the Bank of England, and to see about the Bank's purchase of gold from the Reichsbank, at the Treasury Department's request, to furnish food to Germany. He expressed an interest in promoting "a better understanding between the managements of the various important central banks of issue," but no concrete results followed.[6]

On a round-the-world trip in 1920 to recover his health that tuberculosis periodically undermined, Strong was impressed by the need to restore monetary stability in countries that had left the gold standard during the war. However, the flow of gold from these countries to the United States in 1921–1922 threatened monetary stability here if expansionary actions were the response. As a solution, Strong sought to vary earning assets of the Federal Reserve in inverse relation to gold holdings—contrary to gold standard rules. He had no awareness of the distortions of the world monetary system this policy would ultimately wreak.[7]

Nothing came of a proposal by Strong in February 1922 for an international stabilization fund giving the Federal Reserve a central role in restoring the international financial system. A failed attempt to restructure the international monetary system was made at the Genoa Conference in April–May 1922 on international economic and financial problems, at which the United States was represented unofficially. The British delegation to the conference presented a set of proposals that would have placed London at the center with non-reserve-center countries authorized to hold their reserves partly in foreign exchange. U.S. opposition, expressed by Strong, centered on the conflict the Genoa proposals created between U.S. domestic monetary stability and the monetary stabilization problems of impoverished countries with governments whose finances were disordered dictating their central banks' policies.[8]

Strong had three objectives: countering business downturns by open market purchases; achieving price stability; and promoting world monetary reconstruction in the postwar period. In cooperation with the existing central banks of Europe and the newly established ones after the war, he saw the possibility of recreating a world in which currencies would again be convertible and international financial relations would revert to their peacetime character.

Strong took the lead in international financial negotiations in the postwar period, individually representing the Federal Reserve System, although always with the knowledge and approval of the other governors and the Federal Reserve Board as well as the Administration. The cooperation between central banks that developed, usually at Strong's initiative, stood in marked contrast to the tension that existed in international political relations.

Strong regarded international reconstruction as a contribution to the welfare of the European countries and of the United States. The restoration of gold standards would halt the flow of gold to this country, reduce inflationary pressures, and eliminate discretionary management of the money supply. At the same time recovery abroad and exchange rate stability would stimulate demand for U.S. exports and promote international lending.

Before reconstruction was possible, Strong believed that the parties had to reach a settlement concerning German reparations and inter-allied war debts. With respect to the latter, he favored a limited moratorium, hoping that it would temper existing bitter feelings. As for reparations, the end of the German hyperinflation in November 1923 and the adoption of the Dawes Plan in September 1924 set the stage for the larger purpose that Strong had in mind. The Plan required a series of annual German payments, stabilization of the German currency in terms of gold, and the flotation of the Dawes loan in the United States and other countries, part of which was to be used to provide gold reserves to the Reichsbank.[9]

In planning international stabilization, a number of principles guided Strong. For one, he knew that it had to be arranged on a country-by-country basis, when initial conditions for success—balanced fiscal budgets, balanced international trade accounts, non-inflationary monetary conditions, a responsible central bank of issue holding adequate gold reserves—were in place.[10]

Under these conditions, a nation was entitled to financial assistance. Central banks would then be prepared to extend foreign credits to the central bank—never the government—of such a nation. The government of a stabilizing country could, however, borrow in capital markets abroad, if necessary, using part of the proceeds to retire its short-term debt in the central banks' portfolio. It would thus reduce its domestic debt and increase its foreign exchange reserves. Both Norman and Strong played pivotal roles in implementing these arrangements, since each in his own capital market could determine whether a foreign loan should be approved and whether the Bank of England and the Federal Reserve would participate in a loan to the central bank that wanted to return to the gold standard.

A second principle that Strong emphasized was his opposition to formal conferences of central bankers on his judgment that many central banks were creatures of their government, their policies dictated by political interests rather than by monetary considerations only. He also declined to be in the position of representing the only institution at such a meeting with lending capacity where the would-be borrowers could outvote him. Finally, he held that since the United States had not joined the League of Nations, it was improper for Federal Reserve officials to attend a conference of world central banks that might adopt a program that public opinion would judge as not in the interest of this country.[11]

The success of the flotation of the Dawes Loan in New York and eight European centers meant that reparations were temporarily not a disturbing factor in international affairs. Economic recovery in Germany followed. Its stabilized currency had a firmer foundation than in the immediate post-hyperinflation period. Capital outflows from the United States in the wake of the 1924 U.S. recession buoyed the European exchanges. Norman and Strong found the time propitious in the spring of 1925 to achieve the next major step in their program of international monetary reconstruction, namely, restoring sterling to its pre-war parity with gold.

Before England returned to the gold standard in April 1925, except for the United States and a few other countries, no gold standard world existed. On England's return, other countries fell in line, so that by early 1926, more than two dozen countries had linked their currencies to gold.

For sterling to be viable at its pre-war parity, Strong and Norman agreed that British prices had to be in line with U.S. prices, interest rates in New York had to be lower than in London, and a settlement had to be reached on British war debts to the United States. Although Strong thought the terms of payment of the debts in early 1923 unwise, he advised Norman to accept them as preferable to continued uncertainty about the outcome. Restoration of the gold standards, however, could not be contemplated so long as the issue of German reparations disturbed foreign exchange markets. Once that question appeared to have been settled, it became possible to address the relations between economic conditions in this country and Britain.

The wartime and postwar rise in prices in Britain had exceeded the rise in the United States. The subsequent fall in prices in Britain was not as great as the U.S. price fall. Of one thing Strong was certain: a price rise here to close the gap, induced either by gold imports or expansionary monetary policy, was not desirable. A domestic policy of price stability was in the best interest of both countries. The question, however, remained of how to achieve the downward adjustment of British prices. In the upshot, Britain returned to gold before the downward adjustment of its price level had been completed. The interest rate differential to shift long-term borrowing from London to New York was, however, achieved.[12]

Having established the conditions for reinforcing the gold standard in Britain, Strong next had on his agenda the provision of credits to the Bank of England and the British government. He proposed a credit of $200 million by the Federal Reserve to the Bank of England that was approved in January 1925. Arranging a credit for the British government by J.P. Morgan delayed the final decision to resume until April 28, 1925. During the two years they were in effect neither the Bank of England nor the British government drew on these credits.

When Strong sailed to Europe in June 1925, Britain had apparently returned to gold successfully. Short-term balances and gold flowed to London, strengthening the sterling exchange rate. On visits to capitals of western European countries that had recently resumed, Strong grew concerned that gold inflows would lead them to ease credit conditions. At the same time news from home suggested that credit conditions needed tightening.[13]

On his return to the United States in mid-September, Strong found rising speculation in the stock market and commodities. An increase in the discount rate at the New York Reserve Bank, taken on January 8, 1926, would compel the Bank of England to raise its rate also, as it did on December 3, 1925, in anticipation of the increase here. The United Kingdom faced the dilemma that domestic conditions required monetary ease whereas maintaining the tie of sterling to gold as its pre-war parity required monetary tightness. The dilemma for Strong was that his response to domestic needs here hampered Norman whom he wanted to help.

While in Europe, Strong had discussed with Belgian officials steps to stabilize its franc, and negotiations for credits from foreign central banks and a loan to the government continued through the rest of 1925 until mid-March 1926, when the stabilization effort collapsed. Strong returned to Europe at the end of April 1926 and resumed the effort to link the Belgian franc to gold. Because he fell ill in September 1926 and had to return home, an associate of Strong's at the New York Bank completed the negotiations on behalf of the Belgian stabilization.[14]

While in Europe in 1926, Strong met with officials in France, Italy, and Poland to discuss steps needed for stabilization of their currencies. The issues that confronted monetary authorities at the time were spawned by the effects on Britain and the United States of inflows of foreign balances into Germany and France. Borrowing abroad accounted for the German inflows. The actions of the Poincaré government in July 1926 to deal with the chronic French budget deficit and the uncertainty about the exchange rate of the franc on stabilization stimulated capital flows to France. The franc was stabilized de facto vis-à-vis the dollar in December 1926 at about four cents. Private purchases of francs soared, based on the belief that the currency would be revalued upwards following the announcement that France had repaid a loan from the Bank of England in a lump sum in April 1927. For the French authorities the source of the inflows was the London and Berlin money markets, and the solution was to raise interest rates in those markets.

Strong knew of the tensions between the French and the Germans and British, and expressed concern that these currents would undermine the gold standard in both German and Britain. Moreover, further tightening to curb stock market speculation might be in order in New York, leading to gold inflows that would further endanger the gold reserves of countries abroad. He concluded that an informal meeting of central bankers would be helpful. At his invitation, Norman, Schacht of the Reichsbank, and Rist of the Bank of France met with him on Long Island from July 1 to 6 at the home of Ogden Mills, Under Secretary of the Treasury. The next day they attended a lunch as guests of the Federal Reserve Board in Washington. Treasury officials also attended.

The conference essentially arranged that New York would ease in order to remove the pressure on London and Berlin to tighten and that central bank demand for gold would be met in New York rather than in London. A rise in Federal Reserve credit partly offset a gold outflow from the United States, as the Bank of France and the Reichsbank shifted their gold purchases from London to New York. By the end of 1927, Strong judged the outcome of the Long Island central bankers' conference a success: recession in the United States reached a trough in November, and European exchange rates strengthened.[15]

Strong left for Europe in December 1927 to continue efforts to stabilize the currencies of Italy, Poland, and Romania. Working with Norman and representatives of the Bank of Italy, he participated in negotiations to stabilize the Italian lira at 5.26 cents, 27 percent of its pre-war gold value. A group of thirteen central banks joined with the Federal Reserve and the Bank of England to grant $75 million in credit to the Bank of Italy. Arrangements were also concluded for credits from investment bankers. On December 22, stabilization became official, but Strong had no illusions that under Mussolini the Bank of Italy would be independent of political influence.[16]

Strong's introduction to the Bank of Poland dated from December 1924. Established as part of a monetary reform in May 1924, when the zloty was valued in gold at 19.3 cents, equal to the 1914 franc, the Bank of Poland sought correspondent relations with the Federal

Reserve Bank of New York. The Federal Reserve Board approved in February 1925. When the Polish balance of payments turned adverse in August, the Bank of Poland obtained $10.5 million credit from the Reserve Bank of New York against a gold deposit in the Bank of England but, despite the loan, the zloty depreciated in exchange markets.

In December 1925, the Polish minister to the United States approached Secretary of the Treasury Mellon about arranging a loan to the government to stabilize the zloty. Mellon advised him to see Strong. The minister was adamant that Poland sought U.S. assistance only, not that of England or the League of Nations, which usually had a role in stabilization agreements. Stalemate followed in 1926, with no agreement on alternative plans and in any event a halt in negotiations following the Pilsudski coup d'éat. In February 1927, while Strong recuperated in Biltmore, North Carolina, different parties interested in the Polish situation visited him, including the private bankers who had floated Polish loans, a successor banking firm, Polish and French representatives—the Bank of France had become interested—and Norman. In the end, the Bank of Poland submitted a stabilization plan to Strong with a request for a central bank credit. Strong orchestrated participation by 14 central banks in the credit. In Norman's view, the central bank credit was based on negotiations of private bankers, rather than the reserve.

The stabilization decree, fixing the zloty at 11.22 cents in a gold exchange standard, was announced on October 13, 1927. The Polish government's borrowing arrangements with private bankers followed. In this stabilization the Bank of England had no leading part, and Strong's efforts to divorce central banks from political rivalries came up short.[17]

The political overtones in the case of the stabilization of the Romanian leu proved even more blatant than in the Polish case. In 1926 the leu was worth less than half a cent, compared to its 1914 parity of 19.3 cents. In December 1927 the government proposed to negotiate a loan with American private bankers and then ask the Bank of France to provide central bank credits without involving the League of Nations. Norman insisted that Romania apply to the League of Nations for assistance and not follow the Polish example. Strong, however, agreed to accept a plan stabilizing the leu presented to him by Bank of France officials in March 1928, but refused to act as

a joint initiator of the plan. He proceeded to obtain approval in principle on 4 April by the Federal Reserve Board for a credit of $10 million
to be granted by the New York Bank to the National Bank of
Romania.[18]

Strong sailed for Europe in May 1928, hoping to reconcile the
hostile governors of the Bank of England and the Bank of France, and
to help protect the gold reserves of the former. Strong's final meeting
with Norman ended in a dispute. Norman could not forgive Strong's
alignment with the Bank of France. Strong, on the other hand,
believed that he was only trying to preserve central bank cooperation.
In Paris for discussions at the Bank of France, Strong made little progress in smoothing relations between its officials and Norman. The
completion of the stabilization of the leu was not achieved until after
Strong's death.[19]

The Federal Reserve System was left without a leader either in
domestic or international monetary policy. The goals of a stable price
level, stable economic conditions, central bank cooperation, and a
revitalized gold standard that Strong had worked for were all sacri-
ficed between 1929 and 1933.

In 1929, when most countries of the Western world had returned
to a monetary standard involving fixed exchange rates between different national currencies, it seemed that Strong had succeeded in
attaining his international monetary objectives. Yet the whole system
went under in the next few years. The gold–exchange standard itself
contributed to its demise. It made the international financial system
vulnerable to disturbances. Central banks that held legal reserves as
bank deposits or sterling-denominated assets in London and a few
other financial centers would withdraw their holdings on a suggestion
of difficulties in the center, and the withdrawals in turn exacerbated
the center's difficulties.

In addition, neither the United States nor France observed gold
standard rules. Both countries amassed gold, together accounting for
59 percent of the world's stock in 1928, and did not permit gold inflows
to expand the money stock and gold outflows to contract it. England
especially and other countries with inadequate gold reserves had to
adopt restrictive monetary policies when the surplus countries
refrained from expansionary policies that would have eased the
domestic economic situation of the deficit countries.

In the case of the Bank of France, even had it sought to expand its money supply in response to gold inflows that continued through 1932, it was limited by the absence of power to conduct open market operations, thus adding to deflationary pressure on the rest of the world. It sterilized gold inflows and in turn experienced deflation.

The role of the United States in exposing deflation by monetary contraction beginning in 1930, the protectionist Smoot-Hawley Tariff of that year, and tax increases in the midst of depression could not have been foreseen by Strong. Despite falling output, shrinking exports, and growing payments deficits, none of the leading countries that Strong had helped return to gold had left the gold standard or depreciated their currencies by the time the U.S. emerged from the depression in 1933. Those countries formed the gold bloc that did not give up gold until several years later, at the cost of continued deflation.

Britain, however, abandoned gold in September 1931 and an informal group of countries pegged their currencies to sterling, reviving their economies when they did so. After Britain left gold, a foreign run on U.S. gold led to further deflation here. Concern about the gold standard led the Federal Reserve to resist monetary expansion until the collapse of the banking system in March 1933.

We can only conjecture how the international money system would have developed after World War I had Strong not been imbued with the passion to reconstruct it in the image of the pre-war gold standard. He was an architect who was aware of the flaws in the gold standard that he promoted, but did not know how to fashion a better one. He achieved domestic economic stability from 1922 to 1928, but did not live to try to avert the domestic and worldwide instability that followed.

The creation of one international monetary institution during the period following Strong's death may be noted: the Bank for International Settlements, founded by the principal central banks in January 1930. The U.S. monetary authorities have not taken up seats on the board of the BIS to which the U.S. subscription entitles them, but the Federal Reserve regularly participates as an observer in the monthly meetings in Basle. The BIS is a club of international central bankers mainly responsible for operations in foreign exchange markets. Negotiations for increases in the lines of swap credits central banks later made available to each other were conducted at BIS meetings. Its role in later events will be noted below.[20]

2. International Monetary Objectives Excluding Federal Reserve Involvement, 1933–1961

The new administration on March 4, 1933, excluded the Federal Reserve from decisions about its international monetary objectives. It rejected policy proposals from the New York banking community as tainted with gold-standard orthodoxy, albeit with no clear notion of what might replace the gold standard. It was also firm in assigning to the Treasury Department responsibility for international monetary decisions, despite the abysmal ignorance in this regard of Secretary of the Treasury Morgenthau. What remained for the Federal Reserve was to preoccupy itself with domestic not international monetary policy.

In March 1933 the administration unequivocally took the country off the gold standard. At the London World Economic Conference in June 1933, with 64 countries attending, Roosevelt unilaterally decried the importance of stabilizing the price of the dollar in terms of other currencies. The conference achieved nothing.

In October the administration initiated a gold-buying program authorizing the Reconstruction Finance Corporation to buy gold from U.S. mines and on world markets, the price to be set in consultation with the Secretary of the Treasury and the President. The major impetus for the gold-buying program was the hope that it would raise commodity prices.

The dollar fluctuated in exchange markets from April 1933 until the Gold Reserve Act of January 1934 fixed the price of gold at $35 an ounce. The Act also gave the government title to all monetary gold held by the Federal Reserve Banks, including gold the public had surrendered.

The substitution of a fixed price for gold meant that the U.S. authorities were committed to buy all that was offered by foreign monetary authorities and domestic producers. For the United States, the purchases meant an increase in the dollar value of other exports relative to dollar value of imports. For gold-producing countries, the purchases meant a higher price for one of their products, hence an expansion in the gold industry relative to other industries and a rise in income. For gold-standard countries, the price fixed for gold in the

United States determined the rate of exchange between their curren-cies and dollars. They either had to adjust their internal price level to that new rate—in the process presumably disposing of some of their reserves as measured in ounces of gold—or to change their own fixed price of gold. For all gold-standard and non-gold-standard producing countries, the gold purchases meant a reshuffling of international trade in response to a decreased U.S. demand for products other than gold, and an increased demand for such products by gold-producing countries; the program meant an increased supply of products from the United States and a decreased supply of products other than gold from gold-purchasing countries. Finally, international trade had to adjust to measures adopted by gold-standard countries to meet loss of their reserves.

Of the gold revolution profit, $2 billion became the capital of a new agency of the Treasury—the Exchange Stabilization Fund. The Secretary of the Treasury was authorized to deal in foreign currencies and make other investments from the Fund.

Another domestic policy had severe repercussions on foreign countries. The Silver Purchase Act of June 1934 directed the Secre-tary of the Treasury to buy silver at home or abroad until the price had risen to $1.29 an ounce or the stock of silver totaled one-quarter of the value of the combined gold and silver stock. Privately owned silver bullion was to be turned over to the government at 50.01 cents an ounce. Appreciation of China's silver currency that began in 1933 and was intensified by the U.S. silver purchase program led to outflows of silver from China and deflation internally. Other countries with silver coinage whose bullion values rose above their face values replaced them with paper currency. The U.S. thus adopted a policy for domes-tic reasons without any understanding of its destabilizing effects on other countries.[21]

The gold bloc countries ultimately failed to maintain their gold parities. The Belgian currency was devalued in March 1935. Italy introduced exchange controls in 1935, as did Poland in April 1936. The devaluation of the franc in September 1936, jointly announced by Paris, London, and Washington signaled a resumption of govern-ment—treasuries and ministries of finance, not central banks—coop-eration after several years of aloofness.

Under the Tripartite Monetary Agreement, the three countries' exchange stabilization funds agreed on the management of exchange rates. Each country would cable the other two each day the price in its own currency at which it would buy and sell gold. The quotations were valid for 24 hours, so no risk of exchange loss would arise during that period. Belgium, Holland, and Switzerland also accepted the agreement. The arrangement was ad hoc. In fact, until 1939 the stabilization funds intervened in exchange rate movements to an extent that they were pegged rather than freely fluctuating.[22]

Intergovernmental arrangements became even more important once World War II broke out. American aid to the Allies provided by the State Department's Lend Lease Administration shrank commercial overseas trade. UNRRA, the Export-Import Bank, and the European Recovery Administration after the war financed import needs of liberated countries. All these agencies engaged in management of foreign exchange.

Looking ahead to postwar needs, in the United States during the war the leading planners were in the State Department and the Treasury Department. It was they, not officials of the Federal Reserve, who outlined proposals for the maintenance of monetary systems and foreign exchange markets and international investment. The organizations based on the planning that were ultimately created were the International Monetary Fund to deal with temporary balance of payment problems, and the World Bank to deal with longer-run problems of reconstruction and development.

In the early postwar years bilateral payment agreements prevailed among trading countries. A multilateral payments arrangement, the European Payments Union, was introduced in 1950 and disbanded in December 1958, when the chief signatories made their currencies convertible. Under the Payments Union, central bank members received and made payments, and granted and received credit, with the BIS as agent, consolidating each member's debt to or claim on the Union into an overall net debt or claim, much as a clearing house operated. With convertibility, central banks were no longer pivotal.

The Bretton Woods system was designed to operate with the United States as the reserve currency country. Other countries pegged their currencies to the dollar. The attitude of the United States initially was paternalistic. Wartime destruction and disruption had left European and Asian countries with limited productive capacity and had swelled the immediate postwar demand for U.S. exports.

To promote economic recovery in the rest of the world, the United States encouraged an outflow of dollars by official U.S. aid, military spending, and private investment. The United States did not protest discriminatory tariff and quota restrictions applied by West European countries.

As Europe and Japan recovered, the U.S. balance of payments turned negative. For the non-reserve currency countries, a weakening of the U.S. balance of payments was acceptable so long as they desired surpluses in their balance of payments to increase their dollar reserves. Once assets denominated in dollars grew in excess of the rest of the world's demand for them, non-reserve currency countries insisted on action by the United States to right its balance of payments.

The successful operation of the Bretton Woods system depended on foreign central banks intervening with their own currencies against the dollar to maintain par values, and the United States standing ready to buy or sell gold at $35 an ounce in transactions with monetary authorities. The U.S. balance of payments accordingly was determined by the exchange parities other countries established. When the reserve currency in the system became overvalued and the non-reserve currencies undervalued, there was no pressure on those countries to revalue their currencies.

A portent of the troubled future of the Bretton Woods system was that in 1960 for the first time U.S. gold reserves declined below the level of its total liquid liabilities to all foreign holders of assets denominated in dollars. A focus of pressure on the U.S. dollar was the London gold market. In March 1960, the price rose above $35 an ounce, as European central banks and private investors bought gold for dollars. The Bank of England sold gold to stabilize the price, but the U.S. Treasury initially was unwilling to restore the Bank's holdings. Hence, when a rise in the price of gold occurred in October, the Bank did not intervene. On October 27, with the price reaching $40, the Treasury agreed to sell gold to the Bank. A year later, an agreement to create a gold pool was reached among the United States and seven European central banks. Each member undertook to supply an agreed portion of net gold sales to stabilize the gold market with the Bank of England acting as an agent for the group.[23]

The growing doubts about the sustainabiity of the U.S. gold commitment set the stage for the activation by the Treasury in 1961 of the

Exchange Stabilization Fund and the re-emergence of a role for the Federal Reserve System in pursuing international monetary objectives.

3. An Active Federal Reserve in International Monetary Affairs

In the period since the Federal Reserve regained a role in international monetary affairs, three sub-periods may be distinguished:

(A) As the Bretton Woods system floundered, 1962–1971, futile efforts were made to obstruct devaluations of currencies of countries with weak balances of payments and revaluations of currencies with strong balances of payments. Towards these ends, exchange market intervention was organized on the basis of a network of swaps—inter-central bank credits. In addition countries imposed a wide range of capital controls. Here the focus is mainly on U.S. intervention and U.S. controls.

(B) The breakdown of Bretton Woods in 1971 and the abortive efforts to reinstate it were followed by a shift to floating exchange rates by the United States, Canada, Japan, Switzerland, and the United Kingdom, with the EEC countries, Sweden and Norway, establishing a joint float. The dispersion of inflation rates among the industrialized countries, and the higher variability of inflation since the late 1960's made a fixed exchange rate system increasingly subject to frequent changes in par values, and hence enforced floating. Intervention even under floating rates was often massive as countries sought to oppose market judgments on currency values. The United States intervened as often and as massively as did other countries. The sub-period has two possible terminal dates, one, October 6, 1979, when the Federal Reserve announced a wide-ranging set of measures to tighten control and halt the acceleration of U.S. inflation, the other, the announcements by the Reagan Administration in 1981 that it would limit U.S. intervention only to instances of serious market disorder.

(C) The final sub-period covers the role of the Federal Reserve (and the Treasury) in dealing with troubled foreign country debts to large U.S. banks, and the enormous increases in foreign currency holdings for foreign exchange market intervention by the two authorities since the Plaza Agreement of September 1985. Earlier interventions had been conducted with swaps.

(A) Deficits in the U.S. balance of payments and declining U.S. gold reserves fueled political decisions in the early 1960's on ways to cope with these developments.

An inter-central bank credit swap network was established along with the start of Treasury and Federal Reserve interventions in foreign exchange markets. The legal basis for Treasury intervention is beyond question—Congress authorized the creation of the Exchange Stabilization Fund to deal in gold, foreign exchange, securities, and other credit instruments for the purpose of stabilizing the exchange value of the dollar. The legal basis for Federal Reserve intervention is, however, questionable. There is no general and positive legislative authorization for the System to operate in foreign currencies. In addition, the legal authority for Federal Reserve so-called warehousing of foreign currencies for the Treasury, an action it first took in November 1963, and more recently in increasing amounts, is doubtful. Warehousing amounts to a direct loan from the Federal Reserve to the Treasury, bypassing Congressional appropriations. Further discussion of these issues will be found at a later point in this section.[24]

In its initial operations on March 13, 1961, acting through the Federal Reserve Bank of New York as its agent, the Exchange Stabilization Fund sold foreign D-Marks to reduce the premium on that currency. On February 13, 1962, the Federal Open Market Committee authorized the Bank to buy or sell foreign currency on its account in both spot and forward markets. For this purpose access to a stock of foreign currencies in addition to the limited amounts held by the Exchange Stabilization Fund was needed. For this reason the Federal Reserve negotiated a network of swap facilities with the central banks of other countries.

The swap provided a specific amount of foreign currency in exchange for an equivalent dollar credit for the foreign central bank, with each party protected against loss due to a change in the par values of the other party's currency. Invested balances of both parties earned the same rate of interest, foreign balances in special U.S. Treasury certificates, Federal Reserve balances in interest-earning deposits abroad. Balances were available for payments to the other party or for foreign exchange market transactions. The swap was a credit line, usually for three-month periods, renewable at maturity. By drawing on the credit, both parties initially raised their gross reserves. The Federal Reserve normally used the proceeds of a swap to absorb foreign official dollar holdings; these transactions, in effect, provided forward cover to foreign official dollar holders, reducing their incentive to convert dollars into gold.

Repayments of short-term swap credits meant a corresponding decline in gross reserves. For the United States this could entail a loss of gold. To deter this eventuality, the Treasury began issuing nonmarketable securities, with maturities of 15 months to two years, denominated in the holder's currency, to fund outstanding swap debt.

The chief currency under pressure, apart from the dollar, was sterling. Persistent or recurring U.K. balance of payments deficits impaired the credibility of sterling's external value. In November 1964 the Federal Reserve Bank of New York mounted a rescue operation, assembling a credit package of $3 billion, of which other central banks provided $2 billion, the Bank and the Export-Import Bank $1 billion, for the Bank of England to use in support of sterling. Nevertheless, the sterling rate sagged, with enormous losses by the Bank of England. In September 1965 the Federal Reserve Bank, other central banks, and for the Bank for International Settlements provided additional short-term credits to the Bank of England, intervening in the foreign exchange market by aggressively buying sterling. Success for a brief period in raising the rate on sterling enabled the Bank of England to recover some of its earlier reserve losses. Trouble again loomed in the summer of 1966. The Federal Reserve expanded its swap lines, providing a major increase to the Bank of England swap facility. By the end of March 1967 the Bank of England was able to liquidate completely $1.3 billion credits borrowed during the summer of 1966 from the Federal Reserve and the Bank for International Settlements group of central banks. The three-year effort to preserve sterling at $2.80 ended in November 1967, when it was devalued to $2.40. In the first year after devaluation, new credits drawn by the Bank of England totaled $3.5 billion.

Sterling, however, was a sideshow. The main act was the dollar's performance. Measures to help improve the U.S. balance of payments included advanced repayment by several countries of long-term debts to the United States. The interest rate ceiling on time deposits held in the United States by foreign official institutions was removed. In 1964, the United States for the first time also drew on its gold tranche in the IMF.[25]

In 1961 the Federal Reserve embarked on "Operation Twist," an effort to hold long-term interest rates down and short-term interest rates up, with the aim of promoting domestic economic expansion and maintaining short-term capital inflows. Since the domestic lenders and borrowers could freely shift between securities of different maturities, no twist of the term structure was achieved, and both short- and long-term capital were equally mobile internationally.[26]

An interest equalization tax, imposed in 1964, to curb capital outflows from the United States, was made retroactive to 1963, when it was first proposed. The tax extended in 1967, the rate rising from one to one and a half percent. The following year the rates on new foreign portfolio investment by U.S. citizens were again raised. In 1968, the "voluntary" controls the United States imposed in 1965 on capital outflows, became mandatory, the President claiming authority under the Trading with the Enemy Act of 1917. Standby authority to impose mandatory controls on foreign lending by banks and other financial institutions was granted the Federal Reserve.

The gold pool functioned until a surge of buying led to the suspension of the arrangement in March 1968. The members of the pool announced that they would no longer supply gold to the London or any other gold market and that they no longer held it necessary to buy gold from the market. Official transactions between central banks were to be conducted at the official price of $35 an ounce, but the gold price for private transactions was to be determined in the market. In March also the statutory gold reserve requirement against Federal Reserve notes was abolished.

One measure the U.S. authorities might have taken was a rise in the dollar price of gold, thus increasing the value of the stock and the flow of reserve assets. If other countries did not follow suit by adopting a proportional increase in the price of gold in their currencies, the United States in this way might have obtained a devaluation of the dollar. Had the price of gold risen, the gold demands of other countries might have been satisfied without the rundown in U.S. reserve assets. Some countries might also have revalued because of the inflationary consequences of their payments surplus, given the gold-based increase in their asset holdings.

The United States, however, opposed a change in the monetary price of gold. Such action would have required an Act of Congress, which would have produced a long and unsettling debate in the two

Houses, during which time the foreign exchange markets would have been disturbed. Moreover, there was no assurance that other countries would not make corresponding changes in their own par value. It was feared that confidence in the stability of the monetary system would be seriously impaired by a change in the official dollar price of gold. Given the fixed dollar price of gold when national price levels were rising, gold became an undervalued asset with a resulting gold shortage.

Since palliatives to improve the balance of payments proved ineffective, deficits had to be financed either by drawing down reserves or seeking external credit or borrowing facilities, while surpluses obviously increased reserve accumulations. Contrary to the expectation of the way the Bretton Woods system would operate, financing of payments imbalances for the most part was arranged through credits governments extended on a bilateral basis and through international borrowing and lending activities of commercial banks. Thus, facilities for international borrowing and lending activities, apart from IMF drawing facilities, became an increasingly important part of the system.

Official dollar reserves of the surplus countries were augmented at times by actions those countries took in the Eurodollar market. Dollars acquired by their central banks and deposited in the Eurodollar market either directly or through the BIS would usually be relent to private borrowers who could resell the dollars to the central banks.

When the Nixon administration took office in January 1969, it distanced Treasury policy planning from the Federal Reserve Bank of New York, and curtailed the role of the Bank's president at BIS meetings. A Republican administration was bent on distinguishing itself from its Democratic predecessors. The Bank believed that propping up the fixed-rate exchange system was a paramount objective and deplored, as did Treasury officials in the ongoing administration, a shift to floating.[27] The new administration in April 1969 relaxed somewhat existing restraints on capital outflows. U.S. officials also held bilateral talks with officials of a number of other countries to explore limited exchange rate flexibility. Germany revalued in 1969, but the general view in Europe was that the United States would escape the discipline of its payments imbalance if it could count on other countries to revalue. In the end the measures the Republican administration adopted were not obviously different from those that a Democratic administration would have chosen.

The pattern of deficits and surpluses in balances of payments persisted and worsened in 1970 and 1971. The U.S. current account surplus dwindled and the U.S. capital account deficit grew dramatically, producing current account surpluses and capital inflows in other countries.

In March 1971, several European countries requested conversion of officially held dollars into gold to enable them to pay for an increase in their IMF quotas. The payout reduced the U.S. gold stock to the lowest level since 1936. Disbelief of market participants in the pegged external values of currencies precipitated turbulence in the foreign exchange market. The persistent outflow of funds from the United States overwhelmed foreign exchange markets in the first few days of May 1971. On May 5, seven European countries closed their foreign exchange markets, and five others on several continents withdrew their support for the dollar and suspended dealings in D-marks, guilders, and Swiss francs. On May 9, both Germany and the Netherlands announced that their currencies would float, since they could not maintain exchange rates within the established margins.

The Bretton Woods system might have been able to survive an end of gold convertibility. It could not survive the inflationary policies of the center country that characterized the period from the mid-1960's on. The onset of steadily rising prices in the United States is generally associated with the financing of the Vietnam war and expanded Federal social programs. Both a rise in the rate of monetary growth and in fiscal deficits may be observed from 1965 to 1960, with two significant attempts to reverse the inflationary process—the 1966 credit crunch and the 1969 decrease in monetary growth supplementing a 1968 tax increase. Non-reserve center countries were unwilling as a group to adopt the inflationary policies that the reserve-center country was pursuing.

(B) The imbalance between U.S. gold reserves and outstanding dollar liabilities and the weakening U.S. balance of payments position occasioned the changes the United States introduced on August 15, 1971 to achieve a dollar devaluation. Chief among them (besides a price and wage freeze, tax increases, and federal spending cuts) was a ten percent import surcharge on fifty percent of total U.S. imports. The convertibility of the dollar into gold was formally suspended, as was the use of the swap network through which dollars could be exchanged with central banks for other currencies. The effect was to oblige other countries to hold dollars or to trade them for a price determined in the market and so revaluing their currencies.

Foreign exchange markets abroad, except for Japan, shut down. The Japanese initial attempt to maintain the pegged rate of the yen compelled them to purchase $4 billion in the two weeks after August 15. The yen was then freed to float upward; other currencies floated when exchange markets were reopened on August 23. France introduced a dual exchange market, with trade and government exchange dealings based on the par value, financial exchange dealings at a floating rate. The goal of the United States and its partners, however, was to restore a repegged system of exchange rates.

After much negotiation, a readjustment of currency parities was arranged at a meeting at the Smithsonian Institution in Washington on December 17–18, 1971. In return the United States agreed to withdraw the import surcharge. The par values of other currencies were revalued, with the proviso that 2.25 percent margins of fluctuations (replacing the former one percent margin) above and below the new so-called central exchange rates were permissible. The Canadian dollar, which had been floating since May 1970, continued to float. The Smithsonian agreement also specified that the official dollar price of gold would henceforth be $38, a formal devaluation of the dollar of 7.9 percent. While the dollar remained inconvertible, the new official dollar price of gold implied a depreciation of the gold-value of the dollar rather than an appreciation of the dollar value of other currencies.[28]

The central rates established at the Smithsonian meeting crumbled during the nine months following the floating of sterling in June 1972, after its brief membership in the EEC snake. Disbelief of market participants in those rates was revealed in the gold and foreign exchange markets. Money growth and inflation rates continued to rise in the United States and both the balance of trade and the balance of payments deficits soared, with a corresponding surge in the dollar holdings of the industrialized European countries and Japan. Capital controls were imposed by the Netherlands and Japan before sterling was floated and Germany followed suit afterwards.

On February 10, 1973 Japan closed its foreign exchange market and suspended support of the dollar. New central values were set in a hurried round of negotiations, although the lira, yen, Canadian dollar, the U.K. and Irish pounds, and the Swiss franc all floated. Again the official dollar price of gold was raised (this time to $42.22), leaving unchanged the gold value of other currencies. The new central rates did not staunch the flow of dollars abroad, and a further crisis erupted in March 1973.

This time the major industrialized countries discontinued pegging their exchange rates to the dollar. The EEC countries in the snake, which had been activated in April 1972, plus Sweden and Norway agreed to a joint float, with Germany revaluing by three percent (in terms of Special Drawing Rights) in relation to the other members. Though a large group of non-industrialized countries pegged to the dollar, the dollar currency area worldwide contracted; another group of countries pegged to the French franc or to the pound.

It was initially assumed that floating was a temporary expedient to be succeeded by a reformed par value system. The United States took the lead in opposing the return to such a system. The U.S. view prevailed. With the suspension of official gold convertibility, and widespread departures from the IMF's par value provisions, negotiations were held to codify, in the form of amendments to the IMF Articles, the international monetary arrangements that had evolved in practice.

The amended IMF Articles, agreed on in early 1976 and implemented in April 1978, provide for the future possibility of a system of stable but adjustable par values; such a decision by the Fund would require an 85 percent affirmative vote by the IMF members, thus giving the United States an effective veto. The provisions in the amended IMF Articles relating to establishment of par values specify that the common denominator of the system shall not be gold or a currency.

The main source of growth of foreign currency reserves since 1973 was in the form of dollars. The demand for reserves increased under floating rates in part because of the willingness of countries to intervene. Little intervention occurred during the four months following the float in February 1973, but the progressive decline in the weighted exchange rate of the dollar in the following five months led to a declaration by the governors of the central banks of the Group of Ten to support the dollar. In July 1973 the Federal Reserve Bank of

New York began to intervene with its own small holdings of foreign currency—$4 million at the end of 1973—or with the much larger total of foreign currency resources available through swap agreements.

Concerted exchange intervention was agreed to by the Federal Reserve, the Bundesbank, and the Swiss National Bank in May 1974, after several months of dollar depreciation. After September, renewed weakness developed through March 1975, as sales of dollars by countries supporting weaker currencies exceeded purchases of dollars by countries resisting the appreciation of their currencies. These operations therefore added to the market supply of dollars, and depressed the dollar's exchange rate.

In 1976, the Federal Reserve bought foreign currencies to support first the Italian lira, then the French franc, and sterling. Intervention was also conducted to moderate appreciations of the D-mark, the Swiss franc, and the yen. Renewed weakness of the dollar in early 1977 was met by large purchases of dollars by the Bank of England and Bank of Italy, undertaken to limit the appreciation of their currencies and to rebuild their reserve positions. During the final quarter of the year, as the dollar dropped sharply, the Federal Reserve increased the scale of intervention. In 1978 the Federal Reserve was joined by the Exchange Stabilization Fund, which negotiated a new swap facility with Bundesbank.

The decline in the weighted average exchange value of the dollar accelerated in 1978. An anti-inflation program announced on October 24 (involving fiscal restraints, voluntary wage and price standards, and a reduction in regulatory actions) did not moderate the dollar's slide on the exchange market. On November 1, the administration and the Federal Reserve took further action. Foreign exchange resources equivalent to $30 billion were mobilized to finance intervention as needed to support the dollar, in cooperation with Germany, Japan, and Switzerland.

The Federal Reserve raised the discount rate from 8.5 to 9.5 percent, and imposed a two percent supplementary reserve requirement on large time deposits. During the last two months of 1978, U.S. exchange market intervention in support of the dollar totaled $6.7 billion, accompanied by significant purchases of dollars by the three cooperating countries. By mid-June 1979, the dollar's value on a trade-weighted basis had risen from its 1978 low by about ten percent, and U.S. authorities had repurchased a greater sum of foreign currencies than had been sold in the last two months of 1978. The dollar then began to weaken, and U.S. intervention sales of foreign currencies, chiefly D-marks, resumed. Gross sales amounted to $9 billion equivalent between mid-June and early October. In addition the Federal Reserve raised the discount rate to 11 percent.

On October 6, 1979, the Federal Reserve announced a wide-ranging set of measures to tighten monetary control (a shift in operating procedures from control of the Federal Funds rate to control of bank reserves; an increase in the discount rate to 12 percent; a marginal reserve requirement on banks' managed liabilities), and the dollar began to appreciate. After April 1980, however, the dollar began to decline, a movement that was reversed in September.

From October 1979 on, the Federal Reserve intervened frequently, operating on both sides of the market. When the dollar was in demand, it acquired foreign currencies in the market and from correspondents to repay earlier debt and to build up balances. It was a buyer from February to March. From late March to early April and beyond, it sold D-marks and lesser amounts of Swiss francs and French francs. By the end of 1980, it was intervening in the foreign exchange markets virtually on a day-to-day basis. It owned $5 billion in foreign currencies at that date.

Shortly after taking office, the Reagan Administration announced its intention to limit U.S. intervention to instances only of serious market disorder, to discontinue the policy of building up currency reserves, and to cut back on short-term swap arrangements with foreign countries. The reason given for the shift in policy was the administration's view that intervention was both costly and ineffectual. Large purchases of dollar-denominated assets by foreign central banks in 1977–78 did not prevent the dollar from depreciating, and their large sales of dollar assets in 1980–81 did not prevent the dollar from appreciating. The way to restore exchange rate stability was by the creation of more stable domestic conditions.[29]

In its preoccupation with intervention and disregard of the importance of stable domestic conditions, the Federal Reserve labored like Sisyphus. The domestic economic condition that dominated this sub-period was the inflation rate. In the belief that the inflation rate was slow in falling in response to recession in 1970 and as a way to staunch the growing balance of payments deficit, the Nixon

Administration sought a quick solution by resorting to direct controls on prices and wages in August 1971. The policy was in effect for the next three years. Initially, wages and prices were frozen for ninety days. Subsequently, mandatory wage and price guidelines were imposed that were gradually relaxed. Monetary growth was expansionary during this period, so when controls were eased in 1973, pent-up excess demand quickly restored the inflation rate to is underlying trend rate.

In 1974-75, contradictionary monetary growth accompanied an extraordinary rise in the real price of energy following the Arab oil embargo of 1973. The supply shock raised the inflation rate well above the trend rate for several quarters. An unprecedented level of unemployment in the post-World War II experience as a result of the recession of 1974-75 led to accelerated money growth and fiscal deficits in 1976-1978. Once the effects of both the removal of price controls and the external energy supply shock had worked their way through economic processes, the inflation rate fell to its trend rate in 1976. In 1977-1978, the inflation rate moved up again. A further assault on the inflation problem in 1979 by means of monetary and fiscal restraint was thwarted by a second rise in the real price of energy. Despite overall monetary restraint in 1980, the consumer price index increased by 13.5 percent, and the trade-weighted exchange rate of the dollar stood at 87 percent of its base value in 1972.

(C) The decision of the Reagan Administration in 1981 to limit U.S. intervention did not deter central banks of other countries from continued active intervention. Through most of the first term of the administration the dollar appreciated, reaching a peak in February 1985 that was 42 percent above its 1980 average. For many economists and corporate officials from the real sector this was a clear case of misalignment that was responsible for the widening deficit in the U.S. merchandise trade balance and a heavy loss of jobs in the traded goods sector.

In January 1985 James A. Baker, III, then White House chief of staff, and Donald Regan, Treasury Secretary, attended the G-5 meeting at which the finance ministers proposed increasing the extent of foreign exchange market intervention. That month also the two officials switched jobs. At the Plaza Hotel on September 22 the finance ministers and central bank governors announced their agreement that "in view of the present and prospective change in fundamentals, some orderly appreciation of the main non-dollar currencies against the dollar is desirable. They stand ready to cooperate more closely to encourage this when to do so would be helpful."

Repeated meetings of the participants reaffirmed the principles of the Plaza Agreement until the Group of Six major industrial countries met at the Louvre Palace on February 22, 1987, when they announced that existing exchange rate ranges were broadly consistent with economic fundamentals and that they would "cooperate closely to foster stability of exchange rates around current levels."

The principles that guide central bank governors and finance ministers in their choice of exchange rates to support have never been explained. It is doubtful that, even if they were seriously committed to stabilizing exchange rates, they could do so by interventions. The notion that these officials can determine better than markets the correct level of exchange rates is an illusion.

Appreciation of the dollar from 1981 to 1985 occurred in response to the market's decision that the after-tax rate of return was higher here, thanks to disinflation and new tax provisions, than elsewhere in the world. Dollar exchange rates depreciated in 1985–1986 as the market reacted to relative monetary growth rates of the industrialized countries. What mattered was that the Federal Reserve expanded the money supply by buying assets, whether domestic or foreign, at a higher rate than authorities elsewhere were expanding their money supplies. The markets have since shown that, as relative monetary growth rates have changed, so have exchange rates.[30]

Differences in monetary growth rates affect expectations about the revival or subsidence of inflation and ultimately of actual inflation rates among countries. These differences in turn produce either exchange rate depreciation or appreciation.

If changes in relative monetary growth rates are sufficient to alter bilateral exchange rates, what role does official intervention play? Whether official intervention affects national money supplies depends on whether or not a central bank sterilizes its sales or purchases of foreign currencies. When the Federal Reserve intervenes to depreciate the exchange value of the dollar, it purchases foreign currencies, and issues dollars to pay for them. Unless it sells off other domestic assets to withdraw the additional reserves it has injected into the domestic monetary system—it sterilizes its purchases—it will have expanded monetary growth. A similar operation occurs when the Federal Reserve intervenes to appreciate the exchange value of the dollar. It then sells foreign currencies and collects dollars in payment. Unless it purchases other domestic assets to match what it has withdrawn from the domestic monetary system—unless it sterilizes its sales—it will have contracted monetary growth. Non-sterilized intervention is monetary policy based on open market operations in foreign rather than domestic assets. It could just as well be conducted as domestic monetary policy and its effects on exchange rates would be identical. Sterilized intervention has no lasting effect and probably no effect at all on exchange rates.

Most Federal Reserve intervention has been sterilized, so its effects on exchange rates are negligible. In recent years, however, the Federal Reserve and the Treasury have accumulated huge amounts of foreign currencies, $45 billion by January 1990, mainly D-marks and yen. If the dollar appreciates against these currencies, taxpayers will experience losses in proportion to the appreciation of the dollar.

Nothing in the Federal Reserve Act of 1913 and as amended authorizes foreign currency operations by the Federal Reserve System. Section 14(e), which empowers the Federal Reserve to maintain accounts with foreign correspondents, served as the legal justification in January 1962 for approval by the Federal Open Market Committee of a program of System foreign currency operations to be conducted by the Federal Reserve Bank of New York.

The approval was based on an opinion of the FOMC's General Counsel, concurred in by the General Counsel of the Treasury and the Attorney General of the United States, that the Federal Reserve Banks under existing law were authorized to conduct such operations. Two governors dissented. One believed that legislation was needed to clarify the System's authority to acquire, hold, and sell foreign currencies. The other also questioned the legality of the proposed operations, and in addition saw no need for two separate agencies to be engaged in buying and selling foreign exchange, since Congress had conferred upon the Treasury's Exchange Stabilization Fund such authority.

Congress has never examined the legal grounds for Federal Reserve intervention nor of Federal Reserve warehousing of foreign currencies for the Treasury. Initially, the Federal Open Market Committee may have relied on the Thomas Amendment (to the 1933 Agricultural Adjustment Act that authorized the Secretary of the

Treasury to sell the Federal Reserve $3 billion in Treasury bills in addition to those it held) as the legal justification for these loans. However, the Thomas Amendment expired in 1981. Since 1977, when the FOMC agreed to a suggestion by the Treasury that the Federal Reserve undertake this operation when resources of the Exchange Stabilization Fund were inadequate, the amount set has risen from an initial $1.5 billion to $10 billion set in September 1989. In December 1978, the Federal Open Market Committee extended warehousing to the Treasury's General Fund as well as the Exchange Stabilization Fund. The Treasury has used these loans from the Federal Reserve, not appropriated by Congress, to acquire foreign currencies.

Apart from its preoccupation with exchange market intervention in the second half of the 1980's, the Federal Reserve's main international monetary concern from 1982 on was the troubled debt of third-world borrowers to which exposure of U.S. banks was significant. In the forefront of agencies fashioning a rescue program for the debtors was the Federal Reserve. Its initial assumption was that the international debt problem had arisen because the industrialized world was experiencing a sharp recession accompanied by a rise in short-term interest rates. These conditions had aggravated the burden of variable rate loans that the banks had extended. So it was not clear whether it was a domestic concern—the solvency of U.S. creditor banks, whose loans were a multiple of their equity—rather than the international ramifications that motivated the Federal Reserve.

The first action the Federal Reserve took was to step up the growth rate of M1, with the aim of reducing interest rates and sparking economic recovery. The main focus of the strategy, however, was on continued lending to the troubled debtors by creditor banks, the IMF, the World Bank, export credit agencies, and the industrialized countries. The Federal Reserve, the Exchange Stabilization Fund, and the Bank for International Settlements agreed to provide emergency bridge loans, until the commercial and IMF lending, each conditional on the other, could be arranged. The banks in addition were expected to restructure debt.

In the event, as the years dragged on with no resolution of the international debt difficulties in sight, it became obvious that the basic problem was the insolvency of the foreign country debtors. They could not service their debts because they had not used their borrowed resources productively. Their problems centered on high inflation rates, large government deficits, overvalued exchange rates, and domestic economic policies that inhibited growth and encouraged capital flight.

When the debt problems erupted, the Federal Reserve and other bank regulators did not urge the banks to reduce dividends and build loan loss reserves. Instead public policy was based on the fiction that the Latin American debt on the books of the bank were assets that had full face value, despite their discounted value in secondary markets. The official strategy was rejected by the banks in 1987 when they acknowledged the likelihood of credit losses on their Latin American loans by increasing their loan loss reserves.[31]

The Treasury has replaced the Federal Reserve as the manager of debt negotiations. Neither authority has devised a strategy that dominates what voluntary bargains between the debtor countries and the creditor banks might have accomplished without intervention by third parties.

4. Summary of the Record of the Federal Reserve's International Monetary Objectives

One question is the relation, if any, between the Federal Reserve's foreign and domestic monetary objectives. In the 1920's, one student argued, international considerations were paramount and domestic economic objectives were unimportant, and in 1930–1933, the opposite ordering prevailed. Another student concluded that foreign considerations were seldom important in the 1920's in determining the domestic policies followed but were sometimes marshalled as support when foreign and domestic considerations happened to coincide. In either case, no one in the System other than Benjamin Strong was as ardently committed to central bank cooperation. What is indisputable is that the action of the Federal Reserve in raising the discount rate in September 1931 put international considerations ahead of domestic policy considerations.[32]

The Federal Reserve was not actively engaged in international monetary policy decisions post-1933 until war broke out. The Treasury was the agency in charge and employed the Federal Reserve Bank of New York merely to execute its policy decisions. During the postwar period before 1960, the Federal Reserve was outside the loop of international policy considerations. If domestic policy dominated the

1923–1929 period, as it surely did the 1948–1960 period, it is noteworthy that these are the two sub-periods in Federal Reserve history with the lowest variability of money, price, and real income growth.[33]

The Federal Reserve's involvement in exchange market intervention during the final decade of the Bretton Woods system and the period since exchange rates floated was a distraction to no purpose from its domestic responsibilities. Had the Federal Reserve continued the record of low variability of money, price, and real growth, the turmoil in the pegged exchange rate system after 1960 might have been avoided. Under floating rates, managing them would not have occupied a high priority had the Federal Reserve preserved the record of low money, price, and real income variability. Less variability in these variables would have made exchange rates less variable.

Rumors circulate of current disagreement between the Federal Reserve and the Treasury on intervention policy. The program of sterilized intervention has no perceptible effect on exchange rates. It has resulted in the unlimited increase in the portfolio of holdings of foreign currencies, with the possibility of large losses on their sale. The Federal Reserve may need to enlist the help of Congress to extricate itself from the decision it made in 1962 to engage in intervention. Just as it needed the help of Congress in 1951 to free itself from the Treasury as the active maker of monetary policy, it may need Congressional hearings now to free it from domination by the Treasury as the maker of intervention policy.

Hearing should afford the Congress an opportunity to sort out the legality of the Federal Reserve's intervention and warehousing operations in the past 28 years. In addition, they should afford the Federal Reserve an opportunity to air the economic issues posed by intervention.[34]

In recent testimony to Congress, Chairman Greenspan reiterated the Federal Reserve's commitment to maximum sustainable growth and zero inflation. If each country pursued a similar policy, a stable international monetary system would result. Banking risk would decline in conditions of price stability, and credit judgments would be less distorted in the absence of inflationary surges and disinflationary plunges. Troubled debtors and problem banks would be fewer.

To seek the common good for all, as emphasis on central bank cooperation and policy coordination proposes, is an invitation to international meetings and high-minded rhetoric. The actuality is often recrimination because differences in national objectives take precedence over professions of commitment to the common good. The example of the tensions among the countries that Strong wanted to assist in the 1920's is an object lesson. The world of national interest is no different today. Rather than promoting a global nirvana, much better to set a goal of price stability for each country to achieve on its own.

Notes

1. See the text of section 14 of the Federal Reserve Act in the 1914 *Annual Report of the Secretary of the Treasury* (1915, 118–119).

2. See the text of section 14(g) in *Digest of Rulings of the Board of Governors of the Federal Reserve System to 1937* (n.d., 472).

3. See Schwartz (1989, 15–16) for this feature of the debt problem.

4. The unmistakable animus a governor of the Bank of France bore Britain and Germany during the stabilization of the franc from 1926 to 1928 colored the actions he determined. See Moreau (1954, *passim*).

5. Chandler (1958, 94–96).

6. Chandler (1958, 140–147). The quotation is from a letter by Strong to the governor of the Netherlands Bank.

7. Chandler (1958, 165–166; 191–199). See also Friedman and Schwartz (1963,, 279–285).

8. Clarke (1967, 33–40).

9. Chandler (1958, 268–277).

10. Chandler (1958, 278–280).

11. Chandler (1958, 280–281).

12. Chandler (1958, 291–322).

13. Chandler (1958, 324–331).

14. Chandler (1958, 332–352).

15. Chandler (1958, 360–376).

16. Chandler (1958, 381–390).

17. Chandler (1958, 390–403).

18. Chandler (1958, 403–415).

19. Chandler (1958, 415–422).

20. Auboin (1955, *passim*).

21. Friedman and Schwartz (1963, 462–476; 483–491). For a different view on China and U.S. silver purchases, see Brandt and Sargent (1989, 31–51).

22. Clark (1977, *passim*); Bloomfield (1950, 158–166).

23. Schwartz (1983, 14–26).

24. Board of Governors of the Federal Reserve System, *49th Annual Report* (1963, 54–63); *50th Annual Report* (1964, 117–118). *1961 Annual Report of the Secretary of the Treasury* (1962, 378–379).

25. Schwartz (1983, 26–32); Solomon (1977, 86–99, 114–124, 176–187).

26. Friedman and Schwartz (1963, 636).

27. See Robert Roosa's debate with Milton Friedman in American Enterprise Institute (1967, 38–39); Coombs (1976, 204–205).

28. Schwartz (1983, 32–43); Solomon (1977, 188–209, 216–234).

29. Council of Economic Advisers, *Annual Report* (1982, 172–173).

30. Council of Economic Advisers, *Annual Report* (1989, 116–117).

31. Schwartz (1989, 1–19).

32. Hardy (1932, 108); Wicker (1966).

33. Friedman and Schwartz (1963, 594).

34. The House Committee on Banking, Finance and Urban Affairs held hearings on foreign exchange market intervention on August 14, 1990. The Under Secretary of the Treasury was a witness. No one from the Federal Reserve appeared.

References

Auboin, Roger. 1955, *The Bank for International Settlements, 1930–1955. Essays in International Finance.* No. 22. Princeton: Princeton University Press.

Bloomfield, Arthur I. 1950, *Capital Imports and the American Balance of Payments, 1934–1939.* Chicago: University of Chicago Press.

Board of Governors of the Federal Reserve System. n.d., *Digest of Rulings From 1914 to October 1, 1937.* Washington, D.C.

Board of Governors of the Federal Reserve System. 1964, *49th Annual Report.* Washington, D.C.

Board of Governors of the Federal Reserve System. 1964, *50th Annual Report.* Washington, D.C.

Brandt, Loren and Thomas J. Sargent. 1989, "Interpreting New Evidence About China and U.S. Silver Purchases." *Journal of Monetary Economics* 23, 31–51.

Chandler, Lester V. 1958, *Benjamin Strong, Central Banker.* Washington, D.C.: Brookings Institution.

Clarke, Stephen V.O. 1967, *Central Bank Cooperation, 1924–31.* Federal Reserve Bank of New York.

Clarke, Stephen V.O. 1973, *The Reconstruction of the International Monetary System: The Attempts of 1922 and 1933. Princeton Studies in International Finance,* No. 33. Princeton: Princeton University Press.

Clarke, Stephen V.O. 1977, *Exchange-Rate Stabilization in the Mid-1930's: Negotiating the Tripartite Agreement.* Princeton: *Princeton Studies in International Finance,* No. 41. Princeton: Princeton University Press.

Coombs, Charles A. 1976, *The Arena of International Finance.* New York: John Wiley.

Council of Economic Advisers. 1982; 1989, *Annual Report.* Washington, D.C.: Government Printing Office.

Friedman, Milton and Anna J. Schwartz. 1963, *A Monetary History of the United States, 1867–1960.* Princeton: Princeton University Press.

Friedman, Milton and Robert V. Roosa. 1967, *The Balance of Payments: Free Versus Fixed Exchange Rates.* Washington, D.C.: American Enterprise Institute.

Hardy, Charles O. 1932, *Credit Policies of the Federal Reserve System,* Washington, D.C.: Brookings Institution.

Moreau, Emile. 1954, *Souvenirs d'un Gouverneur de la Banque de France.* Editions M.-Th. Genin, Paris, Librarie de Médicis.

Schwartz, Anna J. 1983, "The Postwar Institutional Evolution of the International Monetary System," in *The International Transmission of Inflation,* Michael R. Darby *et al.* (eds.) Chicago: University of Chicago Press.

Schwartz, Anna J. 1989, "International Debts: What's Fact and What's Fiction." *Economic Inquiry* 27 (January: 1–19).

Solomon, Robert. 1977, *The International Monetary System, 1945–1976: An Insider's View.* New York: Harper & Row.

U.S. Secretary of the Treasury. 1915, 1962, *Annual Report.* Washington, D.C.: Government Printing Office.

Comment

The Performance of the Federal Reserve in Pursuing International Monetary Objectives

by Charles W. Calomiris

In her informative paper Anna Schwartz describes a rather neglected aspect of U.S. monetary policy history from 1913 to the present—interventions in foreign currency markets. The record of such policy, Schwartz shows, can only be described as dismal. Every identifiable policy objective—from attempts in the 1920's to coordinate the actions of different countries' central banks (and thus maintain the gold standard), to the attempted maintenance of a fixed dollar standard under Bretton Woods—has been a failure. The achievements of current (post-1973) policy are impossible to judge, because its objectives are not clearly defined, and the actions of policymakers are not matters of public record. Schwartz doubts the potential advantages (or even effectiveness) of *ad hoc* intervention, and questions the legality of the Federal Reserve's involvement. Furthermore, she argues that secrecy promotes instability in the exchanges, as agents try to guess what policies the Fed and the Treasury are likely to pursue. Schwartz concludes from the U.S. experience that explicit intervention in exchange markets to maintain fixed exchange rates is not ultimately credible because domestic policy objectives ultimately will undo such arrangements, and that *ad hoc* secret intervention is ineffective and destabilizing. It would be best, she argues for central banks to focus on maintaining steady domestic monetary growth and stable domestic prices, and not let themselves become distracted by foreign exchange objectives.

Schwartz's account is divided into three periods—an early period of attempts by the Fed (especially Benjamin Strong) to maintain the gold standard; a middle period after the collapse of the gold standard in the 1930's, during which the Treasury Department managed policy under a variety of exchange-rate regimes; and a final period of joint Fed-Treasury intervention, dominated by the *ad hoc* interventions of the post-Bretton Woods floating-exchange rate regime.

The first period is one in which individual efforts by powerful central bankers, rather than governments, dominate the scene. Strong takes it upon himself to establish accounts and contacts with other prominent central bankers in other countries, especially England and France. He eschews formal conferences and committees, preferring behind-the-scenes gentleman's agreements. These attempts at coordination, however, were unsuccessful. Central bankers often participated in destabilizing withdrawals from one another's banks during crises, and more generally, refused to play by the "rules of the game" during periods of normalcy. In particular, failures to expand currency supply by countries that experienced reserve inflows contributed to the steady deflation that ultimately brought the entire system down.

The second period begins with the collapse of the gold standard, accompanied by widespread disillusionment with gold, and with central bank policymaking. In the U.S., the management of foreign exchange policy was transferred to the Treasury Department. New policies included: the Treasury gold-buying program, which took the form of the maintenance of a fixed price of gold under the 1934 Gold Reserve Act; the Exchange Stabilization Fund, which authorized *ad hoc* intervention by the Treasury into foreign exchange markets; and later the Tripartite Agreement of 1936 among the governments of Britain, France, and the United States. This agreement established no explicit rules for coordination of policy, except for notification of changes in each country's maintained price of gold. In practice, however, exchange rates were maintained.

Immediately after World War II, bilateral arrangements between countries dominated the scene, except for the multilateral coordination of exchange rates among European countries that lasted from 1950 to 1958. The creation of the International Monetary Fund in 1946 is given short shrift in Schwartz's account, although an analysis of its aspirations and shortcomings fits well with the general message of the paper. The IMF, like many of the arrangements Schwartz analyzes, was founded on hopes and good intentions, but not rules, nor any clear mechanism for creating a world order based on credible rules. Its charter espoused vague goals of international cooperation, expansion of trade, and exchange rate stability, but it did not set any timetable for the achievement of such goals, and in practice the "transitional period" during which countries were permitted to maintain exchange controls and to avoid cooperation was indefinite (see Yeager, 1976, pp. 390–406). Ultimately, the IMF would pursue *ad hoc* policies in the guise of flexible "rules" (*e.g.,* quotas and par values), it would allow permanent inconvertibility of member country currencies, and it would create authority for loans (standby credits) that lay outside its Articles of Agreement.

The only long-lived attempt at postwar exchange rate management came, not from international cooperation through the IMF, but from the leadership of the United States in the dollar-based Bretton Woods system. Under this arrangement countries would peg their currencies to the dollar, while the United States maintained a fixed dollar price of gold for purposes of transactions with other monetary authorities. There was no mechanism for maintaining the real value of the dollar, or reversing the persistent U.S. payments deficits of the 1960's. Rather than correct the fundamental problem of excessive U.S. money growth, central banks attempted to support currencies through swaps and restrictions on capital flows. As the system foundered, the Federal Reserve again came to play a role in exchange rate management through its *ad hoc* interventions in currency markets after the reactivation of the Exchange Stabilization Fund.

Schwartz views the collapse of the Bretton Woods system from 1971 to 1973 as the inevitable result of a failure to coordinate monetary policy over the previous decade and a half, and she questions the goals and effectiveness of continuing interventions of the Treasury and the Fed under floating exchange rates. Since the collapse of fixed exchange rates the authorities have engaged in secret sterilized intervention, with no apparent rules to guide them. Schwartz argues that sterilized intervention is ineffectual because it leaves the money supply unchanged. She also argues that the Fed's involvement in these transactions may be outside its lawful purview. Furthermore, the Fed's involvement in foreign currency markets distracted it and the government from their proper objective—to stabilize domestic prices through stable, credible domestic monetary policy. Such distractions have also included Operation Twist and the interest equalization tax.

Finally, the secrecy of Fed and Treasury policy and the absence of any clear rules that guide it have added unnecessary uncertainty to foreign exchange markets, which has been counterproductive.

Schwartz concludes from her historical analysis that the failures of exchange rate management are an unavoidable feature of *realpolitik*.

> To seek the common good for all, as emphasis on central bank cooperation and policy coordination proposes, is an invitation to international meetings and high-minded rhetoric. The actuality is often recrimination because differences in national objectives take precedence over professions of commitment to the common good. The example of the tensions among the countries that Strong wanted to assist in the 1920's is an object lesson. The world of national interests is no different today. Rather than promoting a global nirvana, much better to set a goal of price stability for each country to achieve on its own.

My main criticisms of Schwartz's paper revolve around this last paragraph of her paper. I find little to argue with in her summary of the failures of the recent past, but I think there are reasons to question the lessons she draws from them for policy today. I see the lessons of the policy failures from the 1920's to the present as somewhat more limited.

First, let me stress areas of agreement relevant for policy. A policy of sterilized intervention indicates a strange belief by policymakers that foreign exchange markets are somehow separate from domestic money markets, and that limited interventions can move exchange rates. Economic theory, however, leads one to expect that absent any changes in fundamentals (including the money supply process) the value of the dollar will not change. Government interventions may affect exchange rates if they signal changes in fundamentals; otherwise they are liable to have little or no effect. The main effects of sterilized intervention, then, are to waste government resources by taking unprofitable and risky open positions in currency markets, and to create confusing signals about possible changes in Fed policy, which serve to destabilize exchange markets.

I also agree with Schwartz that unsustainable attempts to manage exchange rates create more problems than they solve. Periodic collapses of exchange rates, and anticipation of them, are likely to be more disruptive to international capital and commodity transfers than the constant inconvenience of hedging against changes in floating rates. This is especially true if attempts to support exchange rate parities take the form of capital controls, or other distortionary policies (gold buying, interest equalization taxes, etc.). Thus the main lesson I draw from the last seventy years of exchange market intervention is that attempts to manage exchange rates *that are not part of a credible set of rules spelled out in advance* eventually must fail and destabilize the economy in the process of failing. It should come as no surprise that *ad hoc* policies—much less secret ones—that do not establish observable rules for intervention, and fail to provide a mechanism that makes the maintenance of the rules credible, always end up as destabilizing failures.

All of the policy experiments analyzed by Schwartz meet one or both of these criteria for failure. The gentlemen's agreements of the 1920's were entered into in an uncoordinated, non-explicit manner. Furthermore, countries came on to the gold standard sequentially, making policy independently, and setting parities at levels that eventually biased the system to international deflation as more and more countries entered, which made the system costly to maintain. There was no explicit set of rules which any country could be judged to have violated, short of ultimate failure to maintain fixed exchange rates.

The Bretton Woods system did not establish a mechanism for limiting long-run U.S. balance of payments deficits. Short of voluntary discretionary policy by the U.S., therefore, the system was doomed to fail. The post-Bretton Woods years offered the most extreme example of a lack of stated objectives, coordination, or a mechanism to provide credible exchange rate stability in the long run.

Rather than view these as examples of failed attempts to establish rules for international coordination in managing exchange rates, I would describe them as unsurprising failures of *ad hoc* discretionary policy by individual countries to produce long-run exchange rate stability. In setting up the Bretton Woods system, for example, there was some discussion of providing means to restrict domestic independence of monetary and fiscal policy, as Eichengreen (1990) points out.

> U.S. dominance of the negotiations was also responsible for the inadequacies of the adjustment mechanism. Owing to American opposition, no incentives for adjustment by surplus countries, other than the unwieldy and ultimately unworkable scarce currency clause, were incorporated into the agreement. Seeing the U.S. as the prospective surplus country, American officials used their leverage to eliminate provisions that might have forced them to revalue the dollar or pay a tax on their international reserves. . . . It

was American officials who struck from the first unpublished draft
of the White Plan articles providing for international oversight of
domestic monetary and fiscal policies (chapter 13, pp. 13–14).

A revised system that would allow such oversight over the supply of
international reserve currency was again proposed by Robert Triffin
in 1960 (see Yeager, 1976, pp. 620–622), and has been recently cham-
pioned in a different form by Ronald McKinnon (1984).

Would international coordination of a fixed exchange rate system
be desirable, and if so, would it be politically feasible? Schwartz views
credible coordination as impossible, and therefore, undesirable to
attempt. But, as I have argued, she has mainly examined examples
where rules and coordination were lacking, and this evidence does not
speak to the issue of the potential credibility of rules. There is no discussion of the possible advantages of such coordination in Schwartz's
paper—an unsurprising omission, given her pessimism about establishing credible rules. In what follows, I briefly set out some arguments for the feasibility and desirability of international coordination
of fixed exchange rates.

The question of the feasibility (or credibility) of rules ultimately
comes down to the question of whether individual countries will find
it in their interest to abide by rules that they help establish for the
common good. Recent work by Bordo and Kydland (1989) and
Calomiris (1989) argues that governments have found ways of resolving potential problems of time inconsistency historically. These
authors draw on the pre-World War I experience to show how state-
contingent rules for maintaining the gold standard and repaying government debt obligations were made credible through a variety of
devices. These devices generally took the form of setting up incentive
structures for governments to abide by the rules they created. The
simplest form of such incentives, first espoused by Alexander
Hamilton, was the fixed cost of reversing legislated policy. Additional
incentives came from state-contingent penalties and benefits in debt
markets (especially foreign debt markets) that depended on whether
a government abided by the rules.

As Bordo-Kydland and Calomiris point out, sometimes rules
were relaxed for finite periods during which it made sense to suspend
convertibility or the protection of certain classes of government creditors; but the state-contingent nature of these rules was understood,
and penalties for "justifiable" suspensions were slight. Examples of

such temporary relaxations abound. For example, in Britain the Peel Act of 1844—which required 100 percent gold reserves for Bank of England currency—was sometimes suspended during financial crises. Rather than view this as a failure, Lord Overstone (the prominent "Currency-school" architect of the Act) argued that flexibility was necessary, and in no way threatened credibility. Helms (1939) writes of Overstone's views:

> Overstone contended that in spite of the fact that the restrictive provision of the Act was suspended in 1847 the principle of the Act remained intact. "The principle of the Act is to regulate and control all those actions upon the bullion which arise from legitimate causes, and are capable of being controlled by measures which rest upon principle...." The letter of relaxation was ... accompanied by a protective provision. It was specifically stipulated that the rate of interest charged by the bank must not be less than 8 percent. Overstone asserted that the absence of such a safeguard would have made relaxation a dangerous measure ... Lord Overstone contended that in case there was extreme pressure and it was, therefore, necessary to relax the restrictive feature of the Act, attention should be given to the state of the exchanges before such step was taken. The period of foreign drain should be over and the exchanges decidedly favorable before a letter of relaxation was issued.... There was a great deal of agitation to provide for relaxation by law, but Overstone contended that recourse should be made difficult, but not entirely impossible (pp. 96–97).

Clearly, Overstone had in mind a state-contingent rule that would be credible because of the difficulty of relaxation, and the penalties (high interest rates) occasioned by its use. Furthermore, he made clear that the maintenance of the gold standard should take precedence over short-run domestic policy.

Eichengreen (1990) analyzes the success of fixed exchange rates under the classical gold standard, and their failure under the interwar and post-World War II periods. He argues for the central importance of coordination among trading partners, in addition to fiscal credibility of individual countries. Coordination reduced the cost of maintaining fixed rates, and thus increased their viability.

> For the commitment to the gold standard to be fully credible, the authorities had to have the capacity as well as the desire to defend it. Here international cooperation was the key. The Bank of England stood ready to let gold go when it was needed in the United States. The Bank of France stood ready to lend specie to the Bank of England or purchase sterling bills when the British

gold parity was endangered. The Reichbank and the Russian Government came to the aid of the Bank of England in periods of exceptional stringency. On other occasions the favor was returned .... Thus, the resources upon which any one country could draw when its gold parity came under attack far exceeded the reserves of its central bank.... What rendered the commitment to the existing parities credible was that the commitment was international, not merely national. That international commitment was activated through international cooperation (chapter 2, p. 17).

Eichengreen points to several institutional features of the classical gold standard that made cooperation feasible, including few political and military conflicts among nations, the coordinating role of the Bank of England (which acted as a central clearinghouse for capital and gold transfers), and the elasticity of British capital flows. The willingness of other countries to follow the lead of Britain was partly a consequence of the central role of sterling in the exchange rate system. Given credible coordination among governments and central banks, private capital flows reinforced official actions and were stabilizing. In contrast, during the interwar and post-World War II periods, in the absence of coordination among authorities, fears of devaluation prompted destabilizing capital flows.

One might argue that the Peel Act and the classical gold standard were shown to be infeasible because they ultimately fell by the wayside. But their eventual demise does not argue against their feasibility *for long periods of time.* No domestic rule or international system can withstand the tests of millennia, nor need it be viewed as credible enough to warrant implementation. At any reasonable rate of discount a rule that is credible for, say, 10 years or more is worth implementing if it can be shown to be sufficiently desirable in the interim.

What then are the presumed benefits of targeting exchange rates? McKinnon (1979, 1984) has stressed the advantages to international commerce that flow from predictable international prices. Another argument for the desirability of fixed exchange rate rules also can be traced to the policies of Overstone and the Currency school. He saw credible fixed exchange rate rules as a means for disciplining domestic monetary policy to ensure long-run price stability and rapid balance of payments adjustment.

The modern monetarist view of the advantages of rules over discretion is the legacy of Overstone and his Currency school. But, unlike Schwartz, Overstone saw fixed exchange rates along with credible rules to preserve them as the preferred means for achieving this objective. Indeed, the main motivation for the Peel Act was to prevent discretionary sterilization of international reserve flows, which might prolong necessary domestic adjustment, and possibly threaten the long-run maintenance of the gold standard. Thus along with reducing short-run international price volatility, the main argument for fixed exchange rates is the long-run discipline they impose on monetary authorities.

In large part, then, the conflict between the Schwartz and Overstone policy prescriptions reflects different presumed relationships between foreign currency stabilization objectives and domestic stability. Schwartz sees foreign exchange management as a distraction from domestic money-supply management, or possibly even worse-a vehicle for protecting irresponsible policies by pressuring foreign powers to enter into *ad hoc* arrangements that disguise the true nature of domestic policy. In sharp contrast, Overstone sees exchange rate commitments as a disciplinary force on monetary policy, which facilitates domestic price stability and rapid macroeconomic adjustment to balance of payments disturbances. Yeager (1976) restates the case for viewing fixed exchange rate regimes as promoting rules over discretion domestically:

> A floating exchange rate is no panacea. Monetary independence and insulation mean freedom for prudence and recklessness alike. Freedom from unhealthy external constraints means freedom from healthy ones also. If these constraints are *needed*, then, by assumption, so are fixed exchange rates. . . . If a country cannot or will not maintain internal balance for itself, and if it needs the anti-inflationary rates, then, by assumption, exchange rate flexibility is inflationary in a permissive sense. . . . The "discipline" argument for fixed exchange rates, and especially for the gold standard, appeals to people who mistrust their own governments (p. 643).

For example, it might be argued that Italy has gained discipline by agreeing to align its exchange rate with the German mark. This arrangement works because both countries are responsible for intervening accordingly to clearly specified rules, because membership in the European Monetary System (EMS) is valuable, and because failure to comply with the rules of membership may lead to ejection from the coalition. It is also worth noting that the precursor to the EMS, the European Payments Union (EPU) of 1950–1958 was similarly successful in maintaining stable exchange rates, partly because it included mutual oversight over domestic policies (see Yeager, 1976, pp. 411–422).

To summarize, the disagreement between the Schwartz and Overstone-Yeager views boils down to whether the presence of fixed-exchange rate rules increases or decreases the likelihood of credible domestic monetary rules. Schwartz's case against the usefulness of fixed exchange rates to this end seems weak in light of pre-World War I experience, and in light of the fact that the post-World War I era— from which her pessimism is derived—is one that failed to establish, or test, rules for maintaining fixed exchange rates. The relatively successful experiences of the EPU and the EMS add to the case for feasible fixed exchange rate coordination when rules are explicit.

In a sense it is not surprising that the early-to-mid twentieth century should have witnessed relatively many failures to coordinate. The sequence of large disturbances of the early-to-mid twentieth century—World War I, the Great Depression, and World War II—motivated coordination, but at the same time made the establishment and implementation of rules unlikely. While the perceived needs for coordinated, credible action were great, political and economic instability operated against the establishment of credible rules. Perhaps the most important historical lesson to draw from the failures of this period is that arrangements made in haste in an atmosphere of crisis, with little thought for long-run credibility, are doomed from the start.

Anna Schwartz's paper is extremely useful in outlining the pitfalls that must be avoided if rules produced in calmer times are likely to be successful. Monetary authorities must have clear, observable goals and rules for conduct. Vagueness and secrecy cannot be part of a credible policy. There should be coordination among countries that assign specific responsibilities for specific actions based on specific observable events to maintain fixed exchange rates. The underlying reserve asset must be governed by a rule that ensures long-run international price stability. Deviating from rules must be costly to individual countries. I would add to this list the need to avoid shared responsibility for policy among different regulators. Multiple regulators, like committees, can serve as convenient means to avoid responsibility for decision making. So long as the Fed and the Treasury, for example, share responsibility for foreign currency intervention, it is difficult to know who to blame for policy errors. As Alexander Hamilton recognized over 200 years ago, centralized decision making provides reputational consequences for individuals in ways that decisions by Congressional committees do not. This provides a strong argument for vesting the power to implement rules in the hands of identifiable individuals.

References

Bordo, Michael D. and Finn Kydland, 1989, "The Gold Standard as a Rule," mimeograph.

Calomiris, Charles W. 1990, "The Motives of U.S. Debt-Management Policy, 1790–1880: Efficient Discrimination and Time Consistency," forthcoming, *Research in Economic History.*

Eichengreen, Barry, 1990, *Golden Fetters: The Gold Standard and the Great Depression, 1919–1939,* mimeograph.

Helms, Lloyd Alvin. 1939, *The Contributions of Lord Overstone to the Theory of Currency and Banking,* Urbana, University of Illinois Press.

McKinnon, Ronald I. 1979, *Money in International Exchange: The Convertible Currency System,* New York: Oxford University Press.

McKinnon, Ronald I. 1984, *An International Standard for Monetary Stabilization,* Washington, D.C.: Institute for International Economics, March.

Yeager, Leland B. 1976, *International Monetary Relations: Theory, History, and Policy,* second edition. New York: Harper and Row.

Debt, Deflation, the Great Depression and the Gold Standard

by Ronald W. Batchelder and David Glasner

Introduction

This paper proposes a revised interpretation of the prolonged deflation and monetary contraction in the United States and most of the world during the Great Depression. Contrary to modern Monetarist explanations, we argue that the monetary contraction of 1929–33 was the consequence of U.S. adherence to the gold standard; that the sequential return to gold convertibility by most countries during the 1920's increased the world's monetary demand for gold which induced a worldwide deflation. Further, we believe the U.S. maintained its commitment to a fixed dollar parity of gold over a longer period than most other countries did, because America's politically powerful, domestic creditor interests successfully opposed increasing the dollar parity of gold. While the role of the gold standard in causing the Great Depression was recognized by several economists at the time, most notably Hawtrey, Cassel, and Warren and Pearson, recent monetary explanations have *incorrectly* identified the operation of the U.S. monetary system under the gold standard with the price-specie-flow mechanism and quantity theory of money.

Why the Federal Reserve permitted a dramatic contraction of the money stock between 1929 and 1933 when the Federal Reserve Act of 1913 authorized actions that apparently enabled the Federal Reserve to prevent the contraction remains a puzzle to many economists. The conventional Monetarist explanation, as developed by Friedman and Schwartz (1963), is that the monetary contraction was caused by the Federal Reserve's passive response to a series of domestic banking panics (late 1930, early 1931, and early 1933), which in turn caused the public to switch from bank deposits to currency.

278   DEBT, DEFLATION, THE GREAT DEPRESSION

They argue that even though the policies for avoiding a monetary contraction were well-known, the Federal Reserve System fell under the control of inept governors and that their ineptitude was reinforced by a lack of informed criticism from outside the system (Friedman and Schwartz, pp. 407–19). Friedman and Schwartz concede that the system had performed very well before 1929, and attribute the inept policy after 1929 to a "shift in power within the System and the lack of understanding and experience of those individuals to whom the power shifted" (p. 411). Benjamin Strong, the "enlightened" governor of the New York Federal Reserve Bank, was the dominant figure in the system until his death in 1928. Without the wisdom and leadership of this "great man," the system failed to take the measures that would have averted the catastrophe.[1]

Friedman and Schwartz go on to argue that the monetary contraction of 1929–33 caused the Great Depression, so that the misguided monetary policy followed by the Federal Reserve was ultimately responsible for the output contraction.[2] This monetary explanation was contrary to the generally accepted Keynesian interpretation of the Depression which emphasized a collapse in private investment and suggested that monetary policy would be ineffective during a Depression. In fact, the Keynesian explanation of the Great Depression dismissed the monetary contraction as irrelevant. In response to Friedman and Schwartz, Temin (1976) has challenged the Monetarist interpretation of the Depression by arguing that the contraction in the money stock was caused by a decrease in money demand, which in turn was the result of the decline in income during the period. Temin points out that the real money balances actually increased slightly during the Depression.

The Keynesian-Monetarist debate over the cause(s) of the Great Depression was at bottom an argument about whether government intervention is necessary to stabilize an inherently unstable private sector, or whether government intervention is itself the primary source of instability in a market economy. The Monetarist argument that monetary mismanagement was largely to blame for the prolonged contraction during the Depression was also part of the earlier Austrian explanation of the Depression to which Keynes was in large measure responding. The key policy difference between the Austrians and Monetarists is that the Austrians asserted that the error in policy was an overly expansionary monetary policy in the

1920's, particularly in 1927 and 1928,[3] while the Monetarists contend the mistake was an unnecessary policy-induced monetary contraction beginning in 1928 and continuing almost without interruption until 1933.

Not all interpretations of the Great Depression fit easily into the Keynesian or the Monetarist paradigms. According to some, the Great Depression was a historically unique episode that cannot be fully explained within any single theoretical approach. One exponent of this approach (Kindleberger, 1973) argues that while shifts in spending patterns and monetary mismanagement by the Federal Reserve played a part in the Depression, deflationary trends in commodity prices, the cessation of foreign lending by the United States in the late 1920's, and a lack of international policy coordination all contributed to the magnitude of the catastrophe. Even Irving Fisher, who helped develop the theoretical foundations of what is now called Monetarism, adopted an eclectic approach (*Booms and Depressions,* 1932).

Unfortunately, the monetary theory of the Great Depression developed by Hawtrey (1932, 1947) and Cassel (1932, 1936) and supported by the empirical studies of Warren and Pearson (1933), which preceded the Austrian, Keynesian, and Monetarist theories of the Depression has fallen into an undeserved obscurity. The theory was displaced by the Austrian theory in the early 1930s, so that by the time of the Keynesian Revolution, it had already been dismissed. This early monetary explanation focused on the deflationary forces inherent in the restoration of the prewar gold standard during the 1920's and specifically on how the actions of the French monetary authorities and the Federal Reserve in 1928–1929 triggered a deflationary collapse in late 1929.[4]

In reviewing a monetary explanation of the Great Depression, Friedman and Schwartz generously acknowledged the contributions of Clark Warburton and of the previous generation of Chicago monetary theorists. But they made no reference to the monetary theory of the Great Depression suggested by Hawtrey and Cassel, or to the empirical work of Warren and Pearson. In discussing the background to his approach, Friedman (1976) took great pains to distinguish his approach from that of Robbins and others in the Austrian tradition, as if Chicago and Vienna (transplanted to the London School of Economics) produced the only pre-Keynesian monetary explanations of the Depression.

Although Friedman and Schwartz (1963, pp. 360–61) did attempt to evaluate the role of the gold standard in causing the Depression, they never made clear what specific hypothesis they were rejecting, not even mentioning the explanation advanced by Hawtrey and Cassel. The discussion of the role of the gold standard contained in *The Monetary History* is based on a simple application of the price-specie-flow mechanism which fails to capture the essential problem of resorting the international gold standard that Hawtrey and Cassel had in mind when they linked the Great Depression to the gold standard. The point Hawtrey and Cassel addressed was how restoring the international gold standard triggered a general decline in the international price level. But the price-specie-flow mechanism can at most explain the effect of national disturbances around an undetermined international price level.

The defects in the price-specie-flow mechanism as an explanation of international price movements have been emphasized by Thompson (1974, 1978), who independently restated the essential elements of the Hawtrey-Cassel theory of the Great Depression within a more formal theoretical framework than they had originally used and by the McCloskey and Zecher (1976). This work has encouraged a further re-examination of the behavior of the gold standard within a framework different from the price-specie-flow mechanism (Fremling, 1985; Glasner, 1985, 1989a,b).

We begin by explaining the critical role that restoration of the gold standard played in the monetary contraction and deflation during the Depression under the Hawtrey-Cassel-Thompson model of the gold standard. This theory easily incorporates many of the special factors, such as inter-allied war debts, war reparations and trade conflicts, that are often cited as independent contributory factors to the Depression. In our view, these factors all helped to intensify an inherently deflationary situation under the gold standard by adding to the international demand for gold. Given that the U.S. adherence to the gold standard was causing an unprecedented economic catastrophe, we are led to ask why the U.S. chose to remain on the gold standard for so long, especially when other countries had begun economic expansion immediately after they suspended convertibility (Warren and Pearson 1933). We shall argue that the shift in the international creditor-debtor position of the United States and the political dominance of domestic creditors are essential elements of an answer to this question. Finally, we offer some comparisons of the empirical implications of our approach with those of competing theories of the Great Depression.

The International Price Level Under the Gold Standard

Before World War I, most industrialized countries were adhering to the gold standard as it evolved in England in the eighteenth and early nineteenth centuries. The essential characteristics of the gold standard were that (1) a country's currency unit is legally defined in terms of a fixed weight of gold of specified fineness and (2) this fixed parity is maintained by the monetary authority's statutory obligations to redeem and issue currency for gold in unlimited amounts; moreover, (3) if the monetary authority temporarily suspends convertibility, as may occur during a wartime emergency, the presumption is that convertibility will be restored at the prewar parity. The essential characteristics of the gold standard do not include adherence to what are often referred to as "the rules of the game." Under "the rules of the game," the domestic money supply of a country adhering to the gold standard is supposed to vary in proportion to the reserves held by the country's monetary authority. Although the tight correlation between gold reserves and the total supply of money prescribed by the rules of the game dominates theoretical and popular expositions of the gold standard (Barro, 1979), such a correlation is neither necessary theoretically nor observed empirically (McCloskey and Zecher, 1976).

The "rules of the game" (*monetary reserve*) gold standard implies that a country's currency supply is strictly determined by the amount of gold reserves held by the *monetary authority*. The benchmark for this system is the behavior of a system in which all money consisted of a gold coinage which could be freely minted or melted down. In principle, a paper currency could be used if the monetary authority issued paper notes (or deposits) that were fully covered by gold reserves. (An example of transferrable, gold-backed deposits is the Bank of Amsterdam, founded in 1609.) Thus, a country's currency (or note) supply was determined by the quantity of the *monetary authority's* gold reserves. In turn, the country's *monetary* gold reserves were assumed to be determined by international gold flows that occur when there was an imbalance in the international exchange of commodities. Under this gold reserve version of the international gold standard, a country's domestic price level is determined according to the relation between the quantities of money and of the domestic output, while the quantity of money is determined through international gold flows that occur when a country's domestic price level differs from the one consistent with equilibrium in the balance-of-payments.

The supposed necessity for the rules of the game to be observed follows from the assumption that international monetary equilibrium is maintained by operation of the price-specie-flow mechanism. Under this view, if a tight correlation between domestic gold reserves and domestic money supplies is not maintained (by the appropriate behavior of the monetary authorities), domestic price levels could diverge considerably for extended periods, eventually either causing a financial crisis or jeopardizing the maintenance of convertibility. But in fact, operation of the price-specie-flow mechanism is theoretically irrelevant to the maintenance of international monetary equilibrium (Samuelson, 1980) and there is no evidence that the pattern of gold flows and price-level movements under the gold standard was at all similar the pattern that would have been observed had international monetary equilibrium been maintained by the price-specie-flow mechanism (McCloskey and Zecher, 1976).

A common equilibrium price level among countries adopting fixed gold parities when there are no restrictions upon either the import or the export of gold obtains without the price-specie-flow mechanism, because the *gold* prices of internationally traded commodities are determined in the *world* market. Thus, the prices of these commodities in terms of currencies fixed to gold are also determined simultaneously. Thus, an individual country's domestic price level is determined by arbitrating the real exchange rate between goods and gold on the world market. Domestic monetary conditions, apart from the balance-of-payments constraint, cannot affect these world prices of goods in terms of *gold*. Perhaps domestic monetary conditions could affect the prices of non-tradable goods, but since international trade tends to equalize the quality-adjusted prices of immobile factors of production, international arbitrage will tend to equalize even the prices of non-tradeable goods independently of a balance-of-payments constraint on the domestic monetary authorities (Frenkel and Johnson, 1976).

Since the world stock of gold is virtually fixed in the short run, the combined world monetary and non-monetary demands for gold imply a determinate worldwide value of gold in relation to all other commodities. Because the cost of transporting gold is low compared to its value, the value of gold cannot differ significantly across countries in the absence of controls on the international shipment of gold. This internationally determined value of gold (in relation to all other goods) is the worldwide price level (in terms of gold). Given this (worldwide) "international" gold price level, the national *nominal money* price levels within each of the gold standard countries are dictated by the conversion rates of their national currencies into gold (Thompson, 1974; Glasner, 1985). The quantity of *convertible* paper currency actually issued by issuing banks plus the total of convertible monetary deposits of commercial banks simply adjusts to the demand for money at the price level consistent with equilibrium in the international gold market. Only insofar as the gold-reserve accumulations of banks affects the world demand for gold can banks affect the price level (in terms of gold).

The crucial implications of this (English) convertibility version of the international gold standard is that domestic monetary authorities cannot affect the domestic price level. Central banks can only control the rate at which they accumulate gold or equivalent foreign-exchange reserves. For example, suppose monetary authorities in one country adopt a gold-accumulation policy. They will not affect its internal price level except insofar as this increased demand for gold reserves causes gold to appreciate relative to other commodities worldwide thereby causing money prices to fall in all other gold-standard countries. Conversely, gold decumulation by one country will not imply any domestic inflation except insofar as the reduction in the demand for gold is sufficient to cause gold to decrease in worldwide exchange value. Certainly no small country *adhering* to convertibility under the international gold standard has the ability to control its domestic price level.

There is no essential monetary role for monetary gold reserves under this gold convertibility standard. The supply of currency in the nation does not vary with the *monetary authority's* gold reserves. The so-called "automatic regulation of the supply of means of payment" operates independently of any adjustment to changes in official gold reserves. Maintaining convertibility at the gold parity is simply a policy of changing one nation's amount of money along a perfectly elastic supply of money to match the fluctuating demand for money at an *exogenously determined gold price level.*

In fact, because of national legislation that required that some fraction of gold cover be held against certain categories of monetary liabilities (usually the banknotes issued by central banks), some correlation may have in fact existed between money supplies and reserves. However, the causal relation was in the opposite direction of that normally assumed. Fluctuations in money supplies created a derived demand for gold reserves to meet the legal reserve requirements. Thus, the quantity of money determined the level reserves rather than the other way around. We conjecture that while there was no operational significance of *legally* imposed gold-reserve or cover requirements under this gold-parity system, their existence contributed to a confusion in understanding the difference between the pure logic of the gold standard and its supposed performance under the rules of the game and the price-specie-flow mechanism in which the note issue fluctuated in response to fluctuations in the gold reserves of the monetary authority.

An examination of the statutes which established the U.S. gold standard strongly supports our interpretation of the intended basis for the U.S. gold standard. The procedures the U.S. monetary authorities were to follow in maintaining the gold standard were specified in two important statutes. First, the Gold Standard Act of 1900 required that "all forms of money issued or coined by the United States shall be maintained at a parity of value with this standard and it shall be the duty of the Secretary of the Treasury to maintain such parity." The Act required the Treasury to establish and maintain a redemption fund of $150 million in gold coin and bullion. Also, the redemption fund was given a priority claim on all the Treasury's other gold reserves, and, in the event that the redemption fund itself fell below $100 million and the Treasury's gold reserves were exhausted, the Secretary of the Treasury was *required* to restore the fund by issuing Treasury bonds payable in gold coin. The issue of gold bonds to obtain gold bullion to maintain convertibility was unlimited; in effect, the entire world's gold stock served as backing for the U.S. convertibility commitment. The Treasury was also authorized to issue gold certificates upon the presentation of gold coins or bullion to the Treasury.

Second, the Federal Reserve Act of 1913 created the Federal Reserve System and specified its role in maintaining the convertibility of an *"elastic"* supply. The purpose of the Federal Reserve Act was to provide an elastic currency supply and a means whereby national banks could rediscount commercial paper to obtain currency. The Federal Reserve System was authorized to issue Federal Reserve notes which were to be (a) "receivable by all national and member banks and the Federal reserve banks and for all taxes, customs, and other public dues," and (b) "were to be redeemed in gold on demand at the Treasury Department of the United States—or in gold or lawful money at any Federal reserve bank." The final section of the Federal Reserve Act protected the gold parity of the dollar by stating that nothing in the Federal Reserve Act was to be interpreted as a repeal of the gold-parity provision of the Gold Standard Act of 1900. These Acts established a mechanism whereby the entire world's gold stock could be used to discharge a commitment to maintain the convertibility of the U.S. currency.

The requirement that Federal Reserve banks maintain a gold-redemption fund at the Treasury to ensure the redemption of Federal Reserve notes should not be viewed as an essential part of the U.S. version of a gold standard. In fact, this gold reserve (or cover) requirement, which had tied up a large part of the U.S. gold stock, was overcome by the passage of the Glass-Steagall Act in February 1932, and was always revised when it was about to become a binding constraint on issuing additional notes.

Monetary Disorder After World War I and the Restoration of the Gold Standard

The gold standard, as an international institution, was relatively short-lived, lasting about only 40 years from the early 1870's to the eve of World War I, when the expectation of imminent hostilities was sufficient to cause the individual countries to renege on commitments to maintain full convertibility. The 40 years preceding World War I were a period of unprecedented prosperity and economic growth, and although concerns about fluctuation in the value of gold were common at the time, in retrospect the period now stands out as one of impressive stability in the overall price level.

The international scope of the gold standard broke down even before the first shots were fired, because of uncertainty about whether commitments under the gold standard would be honored once the war broke out (Kindleberger, 1984). But it soon became clear that there were even more fundamental reasons why the gold standard could not continue to function—the demands of the belligerent countries for wartime finance were incompatible with the maintenance of the gold standard. To be able to pay for the necessary imports of war materiel, countries mobilized their internal gold coinage, replacing gold coins with paper and token coins. The gold accumulated by governments was then exported to pay for needed imports or simply added to emergency reserves. Thus, although central bank gold reserves increased sharply during the war, so much of that gold was shifted from monetary to non-monetary use that the value of gold in relation to commodities dropped sharply during the War. Thus, even those countries, like the United States and Sweden, that remained on the gold standard for a long time after the war broke out, underwent a sharp inflation as the value of gold to which their currencies remained tied fell sharply. Because the inflation was the result of a general depreciation in the value of gold in international markets, sterilizing gold inflows would not have prevented inflation from occurring, it would merely have speeded up the inflow.

Of course, in the belligerent countries, inflation was even more rapid than in the U.S. and Sweden, since the belligerents abandoned the gold standard in substance if not in form, so that domestic prices were determined by domestic monetary conditions. In these circumstances, monetary expansion was almost always resorted to as an additional source of revenue and domestic price levels were determined by domestic monetary and financial conditions.

At the end of the war, there was widespread support among countries previously on the gold standard for a return to convertibility at the pre-war parities under the international monetary and financial system that had collapsed in 1914. But by the end of the war, gold had lost about half of its pre-war value in relation to commodities. Thus, at the pre-war parities of national currencies into gold, money prices were about twice as high as they were before the war broke out. Of course, as already noted, money prices in most countries had risen by far more than gold had depreciated, so that the restoration of pre-war parities was often not a politically acceptable alternative.

The return to the pre-war gold standard after the war presented gold standard countries with two serious problems:

(1)   The basic reason for the wartime doubling of the worldwide gold value of goods was that national governments had demonetized their gold coinages and used the proceeds to purchase non-gold goods. The resulting increase in the demand for these goods relative to gold drove down the value of gold relative to other commodities. Therefore, if restoring the gold standard was not to trigger a corresponding deflation of prices in terms of gold, it was necessary to prevent the restoration from increasing the monetary demand for gold and thus driving up the value of gold in relation to commodities.

(2)   In addition to this problem, a further complication was that of selecting the appropriate parities at which to reestablish the gold standard for those countries which had depreciated their temporarily non-gold-backed currencies too drastically to make restoration of the pre-war parities politically feasible. In such cases, there could easily be a temptation to select a parity that would initially undervalue the currency relative to gold which might induce a temporary inflow of gold to the government, thereby adding to the world's *monetary* demand for gold.

As early as 1919, R.G. Hawtrey (1919/1923) recognized the inherent instability of the post-war international price level and the deflationary risk the world faced in attempting to reconstruct an international monetary order based on the gold standard. Recognition of this problem was widespread enough to occasion an international monetary conference in Genoa in 1922. The Genoa Conference produced no agreements on parity adjustments, but it did produce a general understanding that central banks ought to moderate their demands for gold reserves in seeking to re-establish the gold standard nationally. The conference explicitly endorsed the idea of a gold-exchange standard under which countries would join the gold standard not by making their currencies formally convertible into gold coin on demand, but would maintain a fixed parity between their own currency and other currencies (in particular the dollar) which were already convertible into gold. Operating in the foreign-exchange markets, using dollars as reserves, instead of gold, would limit at least one source of demand for gold reserves.

The understanding worked reasonably well for most of the decade, and a steady stream of countries rejoined the gold standard. Prices remained virtually stable for most of the decade until late 1929, falling only slightly on average between 1923 and 1928. But the potential for deflation was widely recognized and the possibility of a "gold shortage" (i.e., increased demand for gold) and its deflationary implications was a widely discussed and controversial issue during the 1920's (Nelson, 1990). For example, Gustav Cassel, in particular, wrote extensively during the 1920's about the deflationary implications of the gold standard without a mechanism for limiting the growth of the world's demand for gold for *monetary* reserve purposes.

The critical fact about the international gold market in the 1920's was that, after importing massive amounts of gold during the war, the United States owned about 40 percent of the gold held by the world's *monetary* authorities. The United States government, by itself, could to a large extent control the value of gold. A willingness by the U.S. government to tolerate an outflow of gold could counteract the deflationary pressures inherent in the international monetary system. On the other hand, as the dominant economic power in the world, the United States government was also capable of powerfully intensifying those pressures by pursuing a policy of gold accumulation.

The uneasy balance of the world economy on the edge of deflation was first threatened in 1926–27 by the French stabilization of the franc under the national-unity government of Poincare. After a series of ineffectual governments had permitted a deterioration of the fiscal situation and a loss of confidence in the franc, causing the franc to depreciate to a dollar exchange rate only a tenth of its pre-war parity (from about 20 cents to 2 cents), Poincare became premier and finance minister in 1926 and initiated a series of reforms that led to a rapid doubling in the franc's dollar exchange rate to almost 4 cents in December 1926. The 3.92 cent parity chosen for the stabilization undervalued the franc and induced a continuing gold inflow and balance-of-trade surplus for France.

The usual, and we believe, erroneous presumption is that French real wages had been eroded by the rapid inflation of the previous year, so that the new parity did not restore French real wages to their earlier level. It is not clear from discussions about the behavior of French wages why they were so slow to respond to purely monetary changes. That slowness raises at least the possibility that real (nonmonetary) factors were reducing French real wages. Under a gold standard, one would normally have expected French prices and wages to adjust rapidly to the international levels dictated by the gold standard and the chosen conversion rate. A more plausible (to us) explanation for the continuing gold inflow was offered by Hawtrey (1932).

He observed that the French law stabilizing the exchange rate also severely restricted the kinds of assets other than gold that the Bank of France could hold. As the French economy expanded rapidly after the restoration of confidence by the Poincare economic reforms, the Bank of France could supply the public with the bank notes demanded only by accumulating additional gold reserves. A continuing export surplus of non-gold goods was the only means by which the French could obtain the additional gold reserves the government desired.

Before 1928, when the stabilization law was passed, the Bank of France had been accumulating foreign exchange reserves rather than gold to "support" its increased note issue. The French, on balance, did not exert a major contractionary force on the world economy until late in 1928. Nevertheless in 1927, a slowdown in economic activity occurred. The slowdown was counteracted by an expansive U.S. Federal Reserve monetary policy under the direction of Governor Benjamin Strong of the Federal Reserve Bank of New York. The expansionary policy caused an outflow of gold from the United States that helped to meet the growing demand for gold elsewhere in the world. This prompt expansionary response of the Federal Reserve to the early signs of deflation and recession helped to allay the continuing concerns at that time that the restoration of the gold standard would eventually cause deflation.

As fears of deflation began to recede, optimism about future business conditions increased and fueled the stock market boom of 1927-29. The Austrian interpretation of this episode is particularly misguided, yet, despite the general disfavor into which the Austrian explanation of the Great Depression has fallen, it remains influential since, in this single respect, it reinforces popular prejudices about stock-market speculation. According to the Austrian explanation, the Federal Reserve, instead of properly allowing the natural forces of recession to cleanse the economy of the inflationary excesses that had been built up between 1922 and 1927, artificially expanded credit and prolonged the boom beyond its capacity to sustain itself. The excess "credit" which the Federal Reserve used to sustain the boom was largely diverted to the stock market where it was used to finance a speculative boom in stocks. That commodity prices remained stable or fell slightly from 1927 to 1929 hides the inflationary pressures which were primarily manifested in the stock market. In the end the stock-market boom proved unsustainable and collapsed in 1929 when the Federal Reserve could no longer sustain an artificial inflationary boom and maintain the gold parity of the dollar.

But even if the stock-market boom could not be justified by expected real increases in earnings, there is no reason to believe it was inflationary. Even if the stock-market boom were a speculative bubble, inflationary financing by the Fed had nothing to do with it. Inflationary expectations could have generated an increase in stock prices only if those expectations were reflected only in increased earnings forecasts but not increased discount rates. It is hard to understand what could have caused expectations of inflation to be reflected in earnings forecasts but not in the discount rates that convert the forecasts into present values (see Hawtrey, 1932). Indeed, the stock-market boom itself probably increased the demand to hold money as the volume of stock-market transactions increased rapidly (Field 1984).[5] Thus, far from being a manifestation of inflation that had to be suppressed by tight money, the stock-market boom had deflationary implications *if* the money supply did not expand to match the increased demand.

In any event, the Federal Reserve interpreted the stock-market boom in accordance with the Austrian view and attempted to counteract it by reducing the monetary expansion and raising short-term interest rates in 1928. The tightening coincided with an increasing French demand for gold as its stabilization law forced the Bank of France to convert its foreign-exchange holdings into gold, drastically increasing the inflow of gold into France. The steady or slightly falling trend in commodity prices broke early in 1929 as the impact of the increasing demand for gold began to be felt. However, the boom in the stock market continued until the fall, even after the recession had started and deflationary trends were becoming increasingly apparent. The delayed response by the stock market may have reflected a continuing belief that the Federal Reserve would, as it had in 1927, ease monetary supply conditions in time to avert a serious recession. However, this time the Federal Reserve was determined to break the stock-market boom and did not relent at all until stock prices collapsed.

A full understanding of the deflationary forces affecting the world economy at the outbreak of the Great Depression requires consideration not just of the effects of monetary policy, but also the role of war debts, reparations, and trade policy in unleashing deflation. We turn to these features in the following section.

War Debts, Reparations, Tariffs, and the Demand for Gold

Monetary disorder was not the only legacy of World War I. The war also left a huge burden of financial obligations in its wake. The European allies had borrowed vast sums from the United States to finance their war efforts, and the Treaty of Versailles imposed on Germany the obligation of paying heavy reparations to the allies, particularly to France.

We need not enter into the controversial question of whether the burden imposed on Germany was too great to have ever been discharged. The only relevant question for our purposes is what means existed for paying the reparations and war debts, or, at least, carrying them forward without causing a default on the obligations. To simplify the discussion, we concentrate on the relationship between the U.S. and Germany, since many of the other obligations of the allies to the U.S. were offset by those of Germany to the allies.[6]

The debt to the U.S. could be extinguished either by a net payment in goods reflected in a German balance-of-trade surplus and a U.S. balance-of-trade deficit, or by a transfer of gold from Germany to the U.S. Stretching out of the debt would have required the U.S., in effect to lend Germany the funds required to service its obligations.

For most of the 1920's, the U.S. did in fact lend heavily to Germany, thereby lending Germany the funds to meet its financial obligations to the U.S. (and its European creditors). U.S. lending was not explicitly for that purpose, but on the consolidated national balance sheets, U.S. lending offset German financial obligations, obviating any real transfer.

Thus, to avoid a transfer from Germany to the U.S. in goods or specie required continued U.S. lending. But the shift to a tight money lending policy by the Federal Reserve in 1928 raised domestic interest rates and curtailed lending abroad as U.S. interest rates rose and discouraged many foreign borrowers from seeking funds in the U.S. capital market. Short of default, avoiding a transfer from Germany to the U.S. was no longer possible. To accomplish a transfer in goods, Germany would have to shift resources from its non-tradable goods sector to its tradable goods sector, which would require a reduction on spending on goods in the nontradable sector, and perhaps in their relative prices as well. Thus, Germany began to slide into a recession in 1928.

In 1929 the United States began making the transfer even more difficult when the newly installed Hoover administration reaffirmed the Republican campaign commitment to raising U.S. tariffs, thus taxing the goods transfer that would allow Germany to discharge its obligations. Although the bill to increase tariffs that became the infamous Hawley-Smoot Act was not passed until 1930, the commitment to raise tariffs made it increasingly unlikely that the U.S. would allow the debts owed it to be discharged by a transfer of goods. The only means left to discharge the debt was a transfer of gold. Thus, anticipating the need for gold to discharge obligations to the U.S., Germany undoubtedly increased its demand for gold to be able to meet its obligations. The increased demand for gold was reflected in its tight monetary policy that raised domestic interest rates in an attempt to reduce spending and to induce an inflow of gold into Germany.

Thus, we now have an explanation of how the Hawley-Smoot tariff was macroeconomically destructive and deflationary, a proposition that is still controversial. Given the huge debts owed to the United States, the tariff imposed a deflationary monetary policy on all U.S. debtors as they attempted to accumulate sufficient gold to be able to service their debt obligations to the U.S. But, under the gold standard, the United States could not insulate itself from the effects of the deflationary monetary policies its trade policy was imposing on its debtors.[7]

The U.S. could have counteracted these pressures by adopting a sufficiently expansive monetary policy and satisfying the demand of other countries for gold. This, in effect, would be continuing the policy of lending to its debtors to allow them to extend their obligations. But preoccupation with the stock-market boom seems to us to have blinded U.S. monetary authorities to the impossible alternatives that were being forced on U.S. debtors by the combination of a tight U.S. monetary policy and a protectionist trade policy.

As it became more likely that protectionist legislation would pass, and that U.S. monetary policy would not be eased, the deflationary signs became increasingly clear and alarming. The panic of October 1929 was not so much the breaking of a speculative bubble as the market's realization that monetary and trade policies were combining to produce a deflation.

And once the deflation took hold, the nature of the gold standard with a *fixed* price of gold was such that gold could only appreciate relative to paper, because the probability of the devaluation of weak currencies began increasing. This led to a speculative increase in the demand for gold that further intensified the building deflationary pressures (Hamilton, 1988). Moreover, devaluation by one country at a time increased the deflationary pressure in other countries. A uniform all-around devaluation might have had some chance of quickly completing the deflationary process, but piecemeal deflation could only prolong the deflationary pressure on nations that remained on the gold standard.

The Role of the Federal Reserve System In the Great Depression

Although in contrast to Friedman and Schwartz, we have emphasized that the monetary forces that produced the Great Depression were international in origin and scope and were not at first confined to the United States, nothing in our argument implies that the United States did not play a central role in causing the Depression. Nor by focusing on events outside the narrow purview of the Federal Reserve do we mean to slight the importance of the Federal Reserve as a contributor to the catastrophe. As holder of over 40 percent of the gold reserves of the world's monetary authorities, the Federal Reserve had ample power to have prevented the disastrous appreciation of gold and the corresponding price deflation from having started or, once started, from having continued as long and as far as it did.

However, for the Federal Reserve to have followed such a policy at the time would have required it to violate widely accepted views about the obligations of the monetary authorities *under the gold standard.* A leading precept of behavior under the gold standard was that a central bank was obligated to reduce credit availability in the face of a continuing loss of gold. While this precept may have led to the correct responses under more or less normal conditions, the conditions in the 1920's, when the U.S. held so vast a share of the world's monetary reserves and when there were so many other reasons for other countries to want to increase their holdings of gold, were not normal. For the Federal Reserve to have violated the precept would have required considerable statesmanship and courage. Perhaps Friedman and Schwartz as well as Hawtrey, Cassel, and Fisher were correct in speculating that Benjamin Strong, had he not died in 1928, would have had the courage and insight to avoid the mistakes made by his successors. But speculation on that question can lead to no definite conclusions.

Given the policy decisions of the Federal Reserve Board, the United States still could have avoided catastrophe if it had abandoned the gold standard, a course which was eventually followed by Great Britain in 1931 along with what became known as the sterling bloc, and by Sweden (Jonung, 1981). By abandoning the gold standard, those countries were able to moderate the impact of the Depression and begin recovering a year before the United States did (after President Roosevelt effectively suspended U.S. adherence to the gold standard).

Friedman and Schwartz agree that abandoning the gold standard helped Britain and Sweden cushion the impact of the Great Depression. However, they contend, as we understand their argument, that the Depression began in the United States and was transmitted by the gold standard to the nations remaining on the gold standard. Friedman and Schwartz distinguished between the initial phase of the decline (which they regarded as severe but not unprecedented) from the later declines beginning in late 1930 with the failure of the Bank of United States. The later shocks, in their view, all resulted from banking panics that the Federal Reserve could have prevented or curtailed, but chose not to. It is less clear to what extent they believe the initial deflationary shocks of 1928–29 originated in the U.S.

We view the bank failures as incidental to a deflationary process that would have continued in more or less the same fashion even if the U.S. had a well-developed system of branch banking that would have avoided most of the bank failures that took place (as was true in Canada). More important to the analysis, the price level was determined in a *global* setting, and it was the shifts in the demand for gold that primarily determined the behavior of the price level. Bank failures may have had a role in causing people to want to hold gold, which would intensify deflationary pressures. But a decline in the quantity of money supplied to the public was not the critical *exogenous* change to which all other economic variables were adjusting.

As long as the Federal Reserve was constrained by its statutory obligation to maintain the gold standard, it could only have stemmed the deflationary tide (after helping to start it in 1928–1929) by tolerating a massive outflow of gold. A gold outflow large enough to have counteracted the deflation would have been difficult to justify under traditional conceptions of the gold standard that were then widely accepted.

An important and thus far unanswered question that arises is why the U.S. was so committed to the gold standard, especially when the attachment of the United States to the gold standard before World War I, particularly in deflationary periods, had been equivocal at best? We try next to answer this question.

The Politics of Debt, Deflation, and the Gold Standard

Perhaps the most important immediate effect of unexpected deflation (inflation) is to redistribute wealth from (to) monetary debtors to (from) creditors. Although there are many other reasons to favor or oppose unexpected price-level changes, distributional effects are obviously an important if not overriding factor in determining one's attitude to such changes. Our thesis is that the political dominance of domestic creditor interests prevented the U.S. from abandoning the gold standard before 1933. The wealth of creditors was obviously enhanced by deflation and the expectation that gold would appreciate made attachment to the gold standard a prescription for deflation, at least until insolvency among debtors became widespread.

The political dominance of the creditors was manifested by the Hoover Administration's communicated commitment to veto any legislation that would have invalidated the gold-parity provision in the statutes that defined and mandated the U.S. obligation to adhere to the gold standard, and by the inability of the Senate to override a presidential veto on this issue. It is noteworthy that while most countries attempted to rejoin the gold standard after World War I, only the two major international creditor countries, the United States and England, returned at their *pre-war* parities. All other countries depreciated the gold content of their currencies, thus writing down the real value of all debts denominated in their currencies.

Changes in the international investment position of the United States also help to explain the strength of the U.S. commitment to the gold standard in the face of the catastrophic deflation between 1929 and 1933. The United States had shifted from being a net debtor in 1914 to being the world's largest net creditor by 1919, and added significantly to its creditor position during the 1920's. At a percentage of nominal U.S. GNP, the U.S. net creditor position increased from 7.6 percent in 1919 to 14.8 percent in 1930. From 1919 to 1930, the governmental and private foreign dollar capital issues publicly offered in the United States totalled $12.1 billion (*Handbook on American Underwriting of Foreign Securities*, 1930, pp. 10–11). The foreign debts owed the U.S. were payable to fixed nominal amounts of U.S. dollars. For 1929, Warren and Pearson (1933, p. 237) estimated total public and private debts in the U.S. to be $203 billion, while the national wealth was estimated at $362 billion. Total debts were thus equal to 56 percent of national wealth. The net U.S. investment abroad totalled approximately $15 billion, or roughly 7.5 percent of the total U.S. creditor-debtor position.

According to Warren and Pearson (1933, p. 360), most outstanding debts in the U.S. in 1929 had been contracted during the period 1922–1929 when the price level was 50 percent above the pre-war price level. In contrasting the situation in the U.S. in 1929 to earlier panics, Warren (Testimony Before the Senate Banking and Currency Committee, May 12, 1932, p. 63) argued that the panics of 1815, 1865, and 1920 were not similar to the 1929 episode, because the earlier panics each followed a relatively short period of high prices in which most public and private debts were not generally expressed in terms of the higher price levels of those short periods that preceded the panics.

While the net external creditor position of the United States grew substantially during the 1930's, the real wealth transfer from our foreign net creditor position during the Depression was small, especially in comparison with the country's loss of output in the Depression. It is possible that the credit expansion during the 1920's was predicated upon the ability of creditor interests to defend the gold standard, and that rational expectations were formed on that presumption. U.S. creditor interests would have had to develop significant political power compared to their economic position in the country. The significant growth of the United States as an international creditor country was concentrated in large U.S. banks, and it was the large banks that became the strongest defenders of the gold standard during the Great Depression.

Several attempts were made in the 1920's and early 1930's to eliminate or repeal the statutory provisions for maintaining the convertibility of the dollar into gold. Such legislation was first introduced in the House of Representatives in 1922 after the Depression of 1920–1921; the last attempt was in May 1932 when the House passed the Goldsborough bill described in the following paragraph. In each instance, the legislation was introduced as an amendment to the Federal Reserve Act of 1913, and directed the Federal Reserve to operate its monetary policy to stabilize the value of the dollar rather than maintain the parity of gold. For our purposes, what is of interest in this series of failed attempts to abandon the gold standard is the transparent political power of the domestic creditor interests to prevent enactment of the legislation. Furthermore, the debates show that the participants had a very clear understanding of the operation of the gold standard, and that many participants identified the quantity theory of money as relevant to a different system from (and, for some, a more desirable system than) the gold standard.

In early 1932, legislation to amend the Federal Reserve Act was introduced by Representative T. Alan Goldsborough that would have forced the United States to abandon the fixed convertibility of the dollar into gold by directing the Federal Reserve System to take actions to raise the wholesale commodity price level as fast as possible to the average level prevailing during the period 1921 to 1929. With gold appreciating, the Federal Reserve could either maintain the gold parity of the dollar or raise the dollar price level of goods, but not both. The Goldsborough bill, which passed the House overwhelmingly with 289 in favor and just 60 opposed on May 2, 1932, later died in the Senate Committee on Banking and Currency. It was the final section of the bill which was especially controversial, stating that any other "Acts and parts of acts inconsistent with this act are hereby repealed." This provision would have eventually forced the United States to abandon the gold parity of the dollar, since maintaining the gold parity of the dollar would have been inconsistent with reflating the dollar to reestablish the wholesale price level that prevailed in 1926.

The chief opponent of the Goldsborough bill was Senator Carter Glass, the co-author and chief architect of the Federal Reserve Act (the Glass-Owen bill). The Goldsborough bill was never reported from the Senate Committee on Banking and Currency for consideration by the Senate because of a threatened veto by President Hoover, and the insufficient number of votes in the Senate to override a veto. In fact, the essential provisions of the Glass-Steagall Act had originally been introduced as part of the Goldsborough bill. It was alleged that Senator Glass had authored these provisions into a separate bill in an attempt to narrow the scope of the original Goldsborough bill and then separately defeat the price-stabilization provisions that would have been incompatible with maintaining the gold content of the dollar. For our purposes, the significance of the Goldsborough bill is first, that the House and Senate hearings and debates reveal that the central issue regarding the maintenance of the gold standard was primarily the protection of creditors, and second, that its defeat demonstrated the political dominance of U.S. creditors.

Representative Goldsborough had first introduced a purchasing-power-stabilization bill in 1922, following the Depression of 1920–21 in which the U.S. wholesale price level fell by 50 percent. The stated purpose of the bill was to protect the economy from price level fluctuations and the redistribution of wealth between debtors and creditors. The original bill sought to stabilize the purchasing power of the dollar by varying the amount of gold that was convertible into the dollar, an idea that Goldsborough attributed to Irving Fisher. In 1926 and 1928, Representative Strong, the Chairman of the House Banking and Currency Committee, introduced bills that directed the Federal Reserve System to stabilize the purchasing power of the dollar. In fact, the original draft of the Federal Reserve Act had directed the powers of the Federal Reserve System to be used by promoting a stable price level. Senator Glass was responsible for removing the stabilization provision, adding the final section of the Act which restated the adherence of the gold-parity provision and the primary provision of unlimited authority of the Treasury to issue bonds in order to purchase gold if necessary to maintain the gold parity.

According to Irving Fisher (1932, pp. 149–52), the opposition to the Goldsborough bill rested mainly upon the fear that it would force the United States off the gold standard and the cause inflation. Even Fisher seemed confounded by the fears of inflation when the country's problem was the severe deflation from 1929 to 1932. Responding to an amendment to his bill introduced by Senator Glass in the Senate Banking and Currency Committee, a move which Senator Glass himself stated was an attempt to defeat the bill, Goldsborough, in a speech before the House on June 8, 1932, showed his frustration that a relatively small group could prevent enactment of his bill. He stated that when his bill was sent to the Senate, "the administration came out in advance and said that if the Senate passed the bill and it was put up to the executive he would veto it." He continued, "I will call your attention to the fact that the Democratic Party does not control the Senate, and call your attention to the further fact, that if this stabilization legislation had the support of the administration it would pass the Senate without five dissenting votes, and I know exactly whereof I speak." Later in his speech, Goldsborough referred to the role of the banks in blocking his proposal: "It has been impossible for me, in the very serious, prolonged, and trying study I have made of this matter, to disassociate the action of the great bankers of this country from the point of view of the executive branch of this Government" (*Congressional Record*—House June 8, 1932, pp. H123454-5).

Evaluating the Evidence on the Great Depression

Evidence for and against competing theories of the Great Depression has not been conclusive. However, the reasons for believing that monetary sources predominated are powerful. First, we know of no episode of severe deflation that was not caused by monetary forces. Second, the severity and longevity of the Depression in various countries was closely related to the nature of the monetary regime. Countries on the gold standard suffered most, and no country recovered before leaving the gold standard. Countries like Britain and Sweden and later the United States began to recover very soon after abandoning the gold standard.

China, which was on a silver standard, at first escaped the ravages of the Depression. However, the subsequent silver-purchase policy adopted by the United States to raise silver prices at the behest of domestic silver interests after 1933 inflicted a severe deflation on China from 1933 onwards (Kindleberger, 1973). This episode is particularly noteworthy because it demonstrates that shifts in the international supply of or demand for a precious metal used as a monetary standard can cause inflation or deflation in countries without first altering the domestic *quantity* of money.

Spain had an inconvertible currency with a flexible exchange rate. Choudri and Kochin (1980) present evidence showing that Spain was only mildly affected by the Depression and attribute this fact to Spain's flexible-exchange-rate monetary regime.

Few economists would deny that monetary factors played some role in the Depression. Most critics of a monetary explanation are content to assert that monetary forces could not have been the whole story, that the Depression was too complex a phenomenon to be a result of a single causal relationship (Hughes, 1981; Kindleberger, 1973). Temin (1966, 1981) has argued that the changes in the money supply identified by Friedman and Schwartz were purely passive responses to a decline in income and prices that was taking place for other reasons. His argument rests on the failure of interest rates to rise, as they would have been expected to within a standard IS–LM framework in response to an excess demand for money, and on the fact that the real quantity of money rose rather than declined between 1929 and 1933. He also points out that the reduction in the nominal quantity of money in 1929 and 1930 was relatively small, so that it is difficult to believe that a small downward adjustment in the money growth path of the previous two years could have produced the cataclysmic downturn of 1929–1930.

It should be noted that Temin's criticisms only apply to the quantity-theoretic explanation of Friedman and Schwartz, but are irrelevant to the Hawtrey-Cassel-Thompson theory of the value of *gold-money* given here. There was no *quantity* of money-income causality in the sense that exogenous changes in the *quantity* of money preceded changes in income and other variables. Changes in the value of gold in the world market determine the international price level without first affecting national money supplies. The monetary aggregates are the wrong place to look for an exogenous monetary shock. National money supplies later responded to changes in the international price level events centered in the international gold market.[8]

Moreover, the argument that a decline in the quantity of money should have led to rising nominal interest rates may be valid only if increased expectations of deflation were not depressing nominal interest rates. Our interpretation of events after World War I suggests that the risk of deflation was widely recognized and that the events of 1928–1929 were widely understood at the time to have increased those risks (Nelson, 1990).[9] It might be objected in reply that if deflation had been widely expected, then the increase in unemployment and the decline in output associated with the deflation are difficult to explain since workers should then have been willing to accept wage reductions sufficient to allow them to retain employment. While theoretically correct, the significance of the point is not overwhelming, since there was obviously a great deal of dispersion of expectations.[10] Thus, many workers may not have been forecasting deflation and therefore resisted the cuts in wages that might have prevented unemployment from rising as rapidly as it did. Furthermore, as long as employers expected greater deflation than workers did, expected deflation would still have a net contractionary effect, since the wage cuts acceptable to workers would be less than those required by employers to maintain output. Finally, even if workers and employers were correctly anticipating deflation on average, rapid expected deflation implies that the return to holding money exceeds the return to holding real capital, so that investment in new capital goods will cease until enough existing capital wears out to raise the expected return to holding capital goods as high as the expected return to holding money. The cessation of investment implies the shutdown of capital goods industries and requires workers employed in those industries to find employment elsewhere. A sectoral shift of that magnitude cannot fail to have a severe negative impact on output and employment.

The high anticipated return to holding money easily accounts for the increase in the real quantity of money, quite apart from the well-confirmed cyclical tendency of velocity to decline in a downturn. Moreover, whether the real value of the money supply increased or decreased in the Depression is not a test of our theory of the Depression. From our perspective there is no reason to assume that the stock of money balances held by the public was ever less than the amount the public wanted to hold. The decline in the price level was generated by an excess demand for gold, not by an excess demand for deposits or for currency.

Nor can Temin's contention that the Great Depression was caused by an unexplained reduction in consumption spending be evaluated in a systematic way, since the fall in consumption cannot be derived from a more general model. Moreover, similar fluctuations in consumption do not seem to have had as powerful an impact on output as Temin asserts it did after 1929, so not only the cause of the change but the effect of the change remains unexplained (Gandolfi and Lothian, 1977).

Kindleberger cited a variety of contributing factors to the Depression. Commodity prices were under downward pressure because of increased supplies. Meanwhile, the U.S. closed off its markets to those commodities, increasing pressures on commodity prices elsewhere and forcing more primary producers to default on their loans. This also forced countries dependent upon primary commodities for income to devalue their currencies to avoid internal price deflation. We would not disagree with much of Kindleberger's argument. It increases the theoretical coherence and explanatory power of our argument, since most of the factors he discussed can be interpreted as factors that increased the demand for gold and reinforced the existing deflationary trends. However, Kindleberger largely ignored the inherently deflationary monetary conditions of the 1920's, and his discussion of the monetary forces behind the Depression did not go very far beyond his dismissal of bank runs as the crucial element in the Depression. Moreover, Kindleberger offered no theory of an international price level. International considerations were introduced only insofar as he asserted that the series of devaluations to which the Depression gave rise were on balance deflationary.[11]

In arguing that U.S. bank runs rather than international monetary conditions were the crucial exogenous monetary shock that precipitated the acceleration of the decline in 1931, Friedman and Schwartz (1963, pp. 360–61) rely on the fact that the U.S. was importing gold between 1929 and 1932. If the monetary shock had been outside the U.S., they assert, the U.S. should have been exporting gold rather than importing it. An inflow of gold into the U.S. indicates that the U.S. was the source of the monetary disturbance.

But in making this argument, Friedman and Schwartz overlook the even greater inflow of gold into France at the same time. From December 1928 to December 1929, the United States imported $154 million of gold, and France imported $389 million. From December 1929 to December 1930, the United States imported $325 million of gold, and France imported $467 million (Cassel, 1936, p. 60). Thus, by their own standard of judgment, France was an even more serious source of deflationary pressure than the U.S. Moreover, as Fremling (1983, p. 1183) points out, the increase in U.S. gold holdings during the Great Depression was proportionately less than the growth in total world reserves of gold, so that the test Friedman and Schwartz use to determine whether the U.S. was the source of the disturbance in the international economy is inappropriate.

In our view, however, the fault of the United States government was that with 40 percent of the world's gold reserves it could easily have accommodated the French demand for gold. Instead, it followed policies that induced even more gold to flow into the U.S. when we believe it should have been tolerating an outflow to the rest of the world.

Moreover, as we have already observed, international gold *flows* do not capture the degree of increased demand for gold in the world. With a fixed stock of gold, redistributions of gold among countries occurred in response to changes in their *relative* demands for gold. Changes in relative demands tell us nothing about what was happening to the *absolute* demand for gold, which is what determines the world price level under the gold standard. It is our contention that it was increasing rapidly. However much it increased, a uniform increase in gold demand would not cause any redistribution of existing stocks, so that looking at changes in gold holdings misses an important part of the story. A more appropriate measure of the increase in the demand for gold is the increase in the percentage of world gold held in central bank assets (accounted for by gold). In his study of the interwar gold standard, Ragnar Nurske (1944) showed the enormous increase in the share of world gold held as monetary reserves during the Depression. Nurke calculated the reserves held by 24 central banks, not including the Federal Reserve. Between 1928 and 1932, the gold holdings of the banks increased by nearly $2.4 billion while their holdings of foreign exchange fell by $2 billion. That shift in demand from financial instruments to gold reflected the serious deflationary pressure the world's monetary authorities other than the Federal Reserve were exerting during the Depression.

Other recent attempts to test the role of the gold standard in causing the Great Depression (Meltzer 1976, 1981; Gordon and Wilcox, 1981) also suffer from a similar preoccupation with the operation of the price-specie-flow mechanism. Indeed, Gordon and Wilcox rightly dismissed Meltzer's argument the price-specie-flow mechanism had an important role in propagating the Depression by noting that the mechanism implies a relative shift in expenditure patterns, not the absolute shift required to explain the monumental impact of the Depression. However, having made that observation, Gordon and Wilcox incorrectly concluded that they disposed of the question of whether the gold standard led to the Depression.

Finally, the importance of bank failures seems to be diminished when one observes that while no other country experienced bank failures on the scale that they occurred in the United States, the Depression in the United States was not more serious than in a number of other countries. Adherence to the gold standard seems to be a better predictor of the seriousness of the Depression in a given country than the number of bank failures, a fact which supports our belief that the attempt to restore the gold standard is the most important factor explaining the Great Depression.

It may be that the attempt to restore the gold standard was not inevitably destined to produce the catastrophic deflation and economic contraction that occurred. As we have argued, attempts by the world's central banks to accumulate gold reserves, which were what actually triggered the deflation, were not required by the theory or practice of the gold standard. However, the world's experience in trying to revive the gold standard after World War I surely justifies the overwhelming reluctance of the public and of almost all economists to consider seriously any proposal for re-establishing the gold standard.

Notes*

*We wish to especially thank Armen Alchian for many helpful comments and discussions; we also benefited from discussion with Earl Thompson and Malcolm Fisher. Responsibility for any errors in the paper is ours. The views expressed in this paper do not necessarily reflect the views of the Federal Trade Commission or of individual commissioners.

1. This argument is based in part upon the earlier work of Chandler (1958). This view was also supported by Irving Fisher (Fisher, 1934, p. 151): "I thoroughly believe that if he (Strong) had lived and his policies had been continued, we might have had the stock market crash in a milder form, but after the crash there would not have been the great industrial depression."

2. Anderson, Shughart, and Tollison (1988) have recently proposed the alternative thesis that Federal Reserve policy may have ben motivated by the desire of large banks to force the failure of smaller banks.

3. The Austrian theory is no longer widely held and concerns us here primarily of its role in the development of modern macroeconomics. It first displaced the purely monetary theory of the Great Depression of Hawtrey and Cassel with a theory of how monetary policy affected relative prices and caused misallocations of resources only to become a casualty of the Keynesian

revolution. The theory was eventually repudiated by some of its staunchest adherents at the time (e.g., Haberler, Machlup, and Robbins); and even its principal exponent, Hayek, ultimately conceded that though theoretically correct it was not relevant to the conditions prevailing at the time. However, the Austrian preference for letting the Depression run its course was so pronounced that modern Monetarists have distinguished their own monetary theory of the Depression from the Austrian theory at least as sharply as they have from the Keynesian theory.

4. A recent contribution by Hamilton (1988) emphasizes the workings of the gold standard in propagating the Depression. Although implicitly recognizing the importance of the gold market, the focus is primarily on the deflationary implications for monetary policy of countries that were expected to devalue their currencies in terms of gold. While we do not disagree with the substance of Hamilton's analysis, we believe that his analysis is not usefully carried out as an application of the general approach we are suggesting.

5. This is the grain of truth in one popular prejudice against stock-market speculation which holds that speculation in the stock-market diverts capital from productive to unproductive uses and forces up interest rates. Since speculation simply transfers funds from one party to another, there is no net loss of capital available for "productive" investments. However, if the stock-market boom increases the demand to hold money and the money supply does not respond accordingly, the increased demand to hold money may crowd out some capital spending to support increased demands for liquidity.

6. The United States, as a matter of law, always resisted such a comparison, contending that the war debts were commercial obligations in no way comparable to the politically imposed reparations. However, as a final matter, there was obviously a strict correspondence between the two sets of obligations. The total size of German obligations was never precisely determined. However, those obligations were certainly several times the size of the war debts owed the United States. Focusing simply on the U.S.-German relationship therefore is simply a heuristic device.

7. Viewed from a different perspective, the tariff was a policy aimed at transferring wealth from the U.S. foreign debtors to the U.S.. government by taxing debt payments on debt already fixed in nominal terms. Moreover, deflation from whatever source increased the real value of the fixed nominal debts owed the U.S. This way of looking at the impact of the tariff will be important for our discussions in Section VI.

8. See Glasner (1989a, pp. 222–25) for a discussion of how the inflation following the Australian gold discoveries could have caused changes in national money supplies rather than, as it usually assumed, the other way around.

9. Gordon and Wilcox (1981, pp. 54–58) dismiss a purely monetary explanation of the 1929–30 downturn precisely because they contend that a shift in price-level expectations in 1929 is "inexplicable" given the previous eight years

of relative price-level stability. We do not regard that shift as inexplicable, given the disparity between the pre-war price level measured in gold and the obvious increase in the world demand for gold as a result of French monetary policy, the U.S. shift towards protectionism, and the shift by the Federal Reserve to a tighter monetary policy to counter stock-market speculation when a sharp easing of policy was necessary to offset the other factors. As we have already pointed out, the dangerous potential for deflation under a resurrected gold standard was identified as early as 1919 by Hawtrey and was widely enough understood to have prompted the international conference at Genoa in 1923 to seek to avoid just that outcome. That deflation was avoided until 1929 does not mean that people had ceased to be concerned about it.

10. Moreover, on *a priori* grounds there is more reason to expect bond traders to devote resources to predicting the future price level than to expect workers to do so. Thus, we might expect participants in the bond markets to predict inflation or deflation more accurately than we should expect workers to do so.

11. Thus while we agree with Eichengreen and Sachs (1985) that devaluations were on balance helpful, we do not believe their stimulative impact came from the profits enjoyed by the devaluing central banks with which they could then finance a more expansive policy. Rather, devaluation had an immediate impact in raising nominal prices in comparison with prevailing prices measured in terms of gold.

References

Anderson, Gary M., William F. Shughart II, and Robert D. Tollison. 1988 "A Public Choice Theory of the Great Contraction." *Public Choice.* 59 (October): 3–23.

Barro, Robert J. 1979. "Money and the Price Level Under the Gold Standard." *Economic Journal.* 89 (March): 13–33.

Brown, William A. 1940. *The International Gold Standard Reinterpreted, 1914–1934.* (2 Vols.) New York: NBER, Number 37.

Cassel, Gustav. 1932. *Crisis in the World's Monetary System.* Oxford: The Clarendon Press.

Cassel, Gustav. 1936. *The Downfall of the Gold Standard.* Oxford: The Clarendon Press.

Chandler, Lester V. 1958. *Benjamin Strong, Central Banker,* Washington, D.C.: Brookings.

Choudhri, Eshan U. and Levis A. Kochin. 1980. "The Exchange Rate and The International Transmission of the Business Cycle Disturbances," *Journal of Money, Credit, and Banking.* 12 (November): 565–574.

Congressional Record. 72nd Congress, Vol. 75, Part 9, May 2, 1932. Washington: U.S. Government Printing Office.

Eichengreen, Barry and Jeffrey Sachs. 1985. "Exchange Rates and Economic Recovery in the 1930s," *Journal of Economic History* 45 (December): 925–46.

Field, Alexander J. 1984. "Asset Exchanges and the Transactions Demand for Money, 1919–1929," *American Economic Review* 74 (March): 43–59.

Fisher, Irving. *Booms and Depressions.* New York: Adelphi Co., 1932.

Fisher, Irving. "Discussions by Professor Irving Fisher," *The Annals of the American Academy of Political and Social Science.* Philadelphia, January 1934, pp. 150–51.

Frenkel, Jacob A. and Harry G. Johnson. "The Monetary Approach to the Balance of Payments: Essential Concepts and Historical Origins." In *The Monetary Approach to the Balance of Payments,* edited by Jacob A. Frenkel and Harry G. Johnson, pp. 21–45. London: Allen and Unwin, 1976.

Friedman, Milton. "Comments on the Critics." In *Milton Friedman's Monetary Framework,* edited by R.J. Gordon, pp. 132–85. Chicago: The University of Chicago Press, 1970.

Friedman, Milton and Anna J. Schwartz. *A Monetary History of the United States, 1867–1960.* Princeton, N.J.: Princeton University Press, 1963.

Fremling, Gertrude. "Did the United States Transmit the Great Depression to the Rest of the World?" *American Economic Review* 75 (December) 1985: 1181–85.

Gandolfi, A.E. and J.R. Lothian. 1977. "Did Monetary Forces Cause the Great Depression: A Review Essay," *Journal of Money, Credit and Banking.* 9 (November): 679–91.

Glasner, David. 1985. "A Reinterpretation of Classical Monetary Theory," *Southern Economic Journal.* 52 (July): 46–67.

Glasner, David. 1989a. "On Some Classical Monetary Controversies." *History of Political Economy* 21 (Summer): 201–29.

Glasner, David. 1989b. *Free Banking and Monetary Reform.* New York: Cambridge University Press.

Gordon, Robert J. and James A. Wilcox. 1981. "Monetarist Interpretations of the Great Depression: An Interpretation and Critique," in *The Great Depression Revisited,* edited by Karl Brunner, pp. 49–107. The Hague: Martinus Nijhoff, 1981.

Hamilton, James D. 1988. "The Role of the International Gold Standard in Propagating the Great Depression," *Contemporary Policy Issues* 6 (April): 67–89.

Hawtrey, Ralph G. 1919. "The Gold Standard," *Economic Journal* 3 (December): 428–42. Reprinted in Hawtrey, *Monetary Reconstruction,* pp. 48–65. London: Longmans, Green and Co., 1923.

Hawtrey, Ralph G. 1932. *The Art of Central Banking.* London: Longmans, Green, and Co.

Hawtrey, Ralph G. 1947. *The Gold Standard in Theory and Practice,* Fifth Edition. London: Longmans, Green, and Co.

Hughes, J.R.T. 1984. "Stagnation Without 'Flation: The 1930s Again," in *Money in Crisis,* edited by Barry N. Siegel, pp. 137–56. Cambridge, MA: Ballinger Press.

Jonung, Lars. 1981. "The Depression in Sweden and the United States: A Comparison of Causes and Politics," in *The Great Depression Revisited,* edition by Karl Brunner, pp. 286–315/ The Hague: Martinus Nijhoff.

Kindleberger, Charles. 1973. *The World in Depression, 1929–39.* Berkeley: University of California Press.

Kindleberger, Charles. 1984. *A Financial History of Western Europe.* London: George Allen and Unwin.

McCloskey, Donald N. and J. Richard Zecher. 1976. "How the Gold Standard Worked, 1880–1913," in *The Monetary Approach to the Balance of Payments,* edited by J.A. Frenkel and H.G. Johnson, pp. 357–85. London: Allen and Unwin.

McCloskey, Donald N. and J. Richard Zecher. 1984. "Purchasing-Power Parity," in *A Retrospective on the Classical Gold Standard, 1821–1931,* edited by Michael D. Bordo, and Anna J. Schwartz, Chicago: The University of Chicago Press.

Meltzer, Allan H. 1976. "Monetary and Other Explanations of the Start of the Great Depression," *Journal of Monetary Economics* 2:455–73.

Meltzer, Allan H. "Comments on 'Monetarist Interpretations of the Great Depression,'" in *The Great Depression Revisited,* edited by Karl Brunner, pp. 148–64. The Hague: Martinus Nijhoff, 1981.

Mills, Frederick C. 1932. *Economic Tendencies in the United States,* New York: NBER, Number 21.

Nelson, Daniel. 1990. "Was the Deflation of 1929–1930 Anticipated? The Monetary Regime as Viewed by the Business Press." Manuscript, The University of Chicago Graduate School of Business, January.

Nurske, Ragnar. 1944. *International Currency Experience, Lessons of the Interwar Period.* Princeton, NJ: League of Nations.

Samuelson, Paul A. 1980. "A Corrected Version of Hume's Equilibrating Mechanisms for International Trade," in *Flexible Exchange Rates and the Balance of Payments,* edited by J.S. Chipman and C.F. Kindleberger, Amsterdam: North Holland.

Temin, Peter. 1976. *Did Monetary Forces Cause the Great Depression?* New York: Norton.

Temin, Peter. 1981. "Notes on the Causes of the Great Depression," in *The Great Depression Revisited,* edited by Karl Brunner, pp. 108–24. The Hague: Martinus Nijhoff, 1981.

Thompson, Earl A. 1974. "The Theory of Money and Income Consistent with Orthodox Value Theory," in *Trade, Stability, and Macroeconomics,* edited by G. Horwich and P.A. Samuelson, pp. 427–53. New York: Academic Press.

Thompson, Earl A. 1978. "A Reformulation of Macroeconomic Theory." Working Paper, UCLA Department of Economics.

Thompson, Earl A. 1987. "Currency and Government Finance in a Competitive Money Economy." Working Paper, UCLA Department of Economics.

Thompson, Earl A. 1990. "A New Theory of Government Money. Emergency Finance and Economic Ideology." Working Paper, UCLA Department of Economics.

United States Statutes at Large. December 1889 to March 1901, Vol. XXXI. Washington: Government Printing Office, 1901.

Warren, George F. and Frank, A. Pearson. 1933. *Prices.* New York: John Wiley and Sons.

Table 1
The Restoration Sequence of the International Gold Standard

Country	Date of Restoration (or establishment) of Gold Standard	Date of Restoration of Stability of Exchange on New York
United States[a]	June 1919	
Lithuania	Aug. 1922	Aug. 1922
Latvia	Nov. 1922	Mar. 1922
Austria*[b]	Jan. 1923	Sept. 1922
Sweden	Apr. 1924	Aug. 1922
Germany*	Oct. 1924	June 1924
Switzerland*	Nov. 1924	Nov. 1924
Netherlands	Apr. 1925	Nov. 1924
United Kingdom	May 1925	May 1925
Australia	May 1925	May 1925
New Zealand	May 1925	May 1925
Union of South Africa	May 1925	May 1925
Hungary*[c]	May 1925	Jan. 1925
Finland*	Dec. 1925	Mar. 1924
Chile*	Jan. 1926	Oct. 1925
Czechoslovakia*	Apr. 1926	Feb. 1923
Canada	July 1926	July 1924
Belgium*	Oct. 1926	Oct. 1926
Bulgaria*	Jan. 1927	Jan. 1924
Denmark	Jan. 1927	Mar. 1926
British India*	Mar. 1927	May 1925
Argentina	Aug. 1927	Mar. 1927
Poland*	Oct. 1927	Nov. 1926
Italy*	Dec. 1927	Dec. 1927
Estonia*	Jan. 1928	Nov. 1924
Norway	May 1928	Sept. 1927
Greece*	May 1928	Jan. 1927
France	June 1928	Dec. 1926
Rumania*	Feb. 1929	Feb. 1929

*Redemption permitted in gold exchange.
[a]Restrictions on export of gold removed.
[b]National Bank under obligation to keep its notes at gold par.
[c]Stabilized with reference to the British pound, Aug. 1924.
Source: Mills, *Economic Tendencies in the United States*, p. 319.

Comment

Debt, Deflation, the Great
Depression and the Gold Standard

by Michael D. Bordo

In this interesting paper Batchelder and Glasner join the ranks of Peter Temin (1989) in his new book, and Barry Eichengreen in his recent work (1989), in attributing the Great Depression to the gold standard. Unlike the other two authors who focus on the flaws of the gold exchange standard and the failure of national monetary policy by the U.S., Great Britain, France, and Germany, these authors hark back to the earlier tradition of Hawtrey and Cassel based on the classical commodity theory of money. According to this view deflation and depression resulted solely from a worldwide excess demand for gold. Batchelder and Glasner distinguish their product from Temin and Eichengreen and downplay the importance of national policy failures, by following a strict version of the monetary approach to the balance of payments in which perfect arbitrage, perfect substitution between traded and non-traded goods, and perfect offset between domestic credit and foreign reserves prevails.

According to this story the source of imbalance in the world gold market begins with World War I when the belligerents diverted sufficient monetary gold to non-monetary uses to reduce the real price of gold to one-half its prewar level by 1918. After the war a return by the world to the gold standard without massive deflation required instituting mechanisms to prevent increases in the demand for monetary gold. Such an equilibrium was produced under the gold exchange standard until 1928. After that point several forces created a strong worldwide excess demand for monetary gold: a) France returning to gold at an undervalued parity and a central bank law requiring gold backing for marginal note issue (a point made by Eichengreen, 1989; b) tight money in the U.S. in response to the stock-market boom

(Field, 1984); c) reparations and war debts which in the face of tight U.S. policy and expectations of increased tariffs required the Germans to accumulate gold to make the necessary transfers.

Once deflation began in earnest, expectations of a flight from national currencies to gold worsened it. The authors dismiss on two grounds Friedman and Schwartz's (1963) view that the worldwide depression spread to the rest of the world from the U.S., where it was produced by massive banking failures. First, other countries had similar experiences to the U.S. with deflation and depression without experiencing massive banking failures. Second, following Fremling (1985), although the U.S. experienced gold inflows from 1929 to 1931, world gold reserves increased in the same period. According to the authors had the U.S. authorities violated the rules of the game and allowed sufficient gold outflows the depression could have been allayed. Furthermore, according to the authors, the U.S. did not leave the gold standard in 1931, although it was widely recognized by contemporaries that it was the cause of the depression, because she had become a net creditor nation in the 1920's. Large banks and other politically powerful creditor interests opposed to devaluation and inflation, blocked several attempts at such legislation. My criticism will focus on both theory and history.

Theory

I believe the treatment of the gold standard in Section II of this paper is too black and white to adequately explain the salient facts of the interwar economy. In following a strict interpretation of the classical commodity theory of money the paper does not distinguish between the short run and the long run. The price level under a mixed fiduciary coin gold standard such as prevailed in the interwar period, according to recent models by Barro (1979) and McCallum (1988), depends on both the money market and the market for gold as a commodity. The issue of fiduciary money or alternatively a change in the ratio of the money stock to the monetary gold stock in a closed economy context, or by a large open economy, will affect the price level directly through a simple quantity theory mechanism. The rise in the price level will in time decrease the real price of gold. In the long run, production and shifts between monetary and non-monetary gold stocks will restore the real price of gold, and the price level, to its original level.

Similarly, banking panic-induced declines in the money supply will produce short run deflationary effects. In turn, falling prices will be associated with declining real output. Indeed, Triffin (1964) argued that a massive increase in the world ratio of money to the monetary gold stock after 1870, to offset deflationary effects of a world excess demand for gold, was a source of increased fragility for the pre World War I gold standard.

In addition, in the international gold standard, national monetary policies, especially for large countries, are important in the short run. Neither the world of today nor that of the 1920's and 1930's was characterized by perfect arbitrage in traded goods, perfect substitution between traded and non-traded goods, and perfect offsets between domestic credit and international reserves. The implications of these points is that for the 1928–1932 period national monetary policies should not be dismissed as they are in the discussion in the paper, and indeed in the historical treatment in this paper of the role of U.S. and French monetary policy they are not.

History

I believe alternative explanations for the record can be given on a number of points: 1) Three alternative scenarios to that given by the authors on what World War I did to the price level might be worth considering: First, the export of gold by the belligerents to the non belligerents (especially the U.S.) which remained on the gold standard, raised the monetary gold stock of the greatly diminished gold standard world and hence the price levels in terms of gold; second, the total world gold stock continued its rapid rise, resulting from the big discoveries in South Africa and Alaska in the 1890's, until 1920; third, World War I required a rise in the real rate of interest to induce a shift of resources from the future to the present. The rise in real interest rates reduced both the demand for money and the demand for non-monetary gold, in turn raising the price level.

2) The authors argue that tight U.S. monetary policy in 1928 ended capital flows to Germany, in turn requiring a deflationary transfer in goods and/or gold. Recent evidence by Stephen Schucker (1988) suggests that this did not happen until 1930.

3) The authors argue that U.S. banking panics were inconsequential for the Great Depression. Recent convincing evidence by Bernanke (1990) shows that for a sample of over 20 countries in the

period under consideration, that both staying on the gold standard and the presence of banking panics were important determinants of deflation and depression. Moreover, Bernanke shows that U.S. banking panics had negative effects on the world price level.

More fundamentally, however, the banking panics were important for the rest of the world because they reduced the world price level more than would otherwise have been the case. In other words, other countries had falling prices and output because of what had been happening in the United States.

Glasner in his recent book (1989) argues that the banking panics of 1930–1933 should be interpreted in the same way as those in 1893 or earlier—as just a mechanism by which the U.S. money supply adjusted to maintain external equilibrium. However, there are three key differences between 1893 and 1929–1933 which should be stressed:

a) The U.S. was a much bigger player in the world in the 1930's and was not just reacting to events in the rest of the world; b) in 1893 as in earlier episodes bank panics were quickly ended by private lender of last resort arrangements or by suspensions of payments. This was not the case in the 1930's because the Fed was now lender of last resort and private arrangements no longer existed, and, as Friedman and Schwartz point out, the Fed failed to stop the panics from spreading, leading to massive declines in the money supply, in the price level, in output, and via the gold standard, in these variables in the rest of the world; c) in 1893 the U.S. was losing gold, in the early 1930's it was gaining gold.

4) The authors as well as Gertrud Fremling may be correct in stating that world international reserves increased from 1929 to 1931, but the distribution of reserves among countries was still important. U.S. gold reserves were increasing and these reserves were coming from somewhere. The countries losing gold to the U.S. were subject to deflationary pressure.

Finally, I believe the paper would have been improved by including some empirical evidence. With the exception of some figures on the U.S. net creditor position in the 1920's, there is nothing tangible to back up the interpretation given.

References

Barro, R.J. 1979, "Money and the Price Level Under the Gold Standard," *Economic Journal* 89 (March), 13–34.

Bernanke, B. 1990, "The Gold Standard, Deflation, and Financial Crisis in the Great Depression: An International Comparison." Princeton University (Mimeo).

Eichengreen, B. 1989, *Elusive Stability: Essays in the History of International Finance, 1919–1939*. Cambridge: Cambridge University Press.

Field, A. 1984, "Asset Exchanges and the Transactions Demand on Money, 1919–29." *American Economic Review*, 74, 43–59.

Fremling, G. 1985, "Did the United States Transmit the Great Depression to the Rest of the World?" *American Economic Review* 75 (December), 1881–85.

Friedman, M. and A.J. Schartz. 1963. *A Monetary History of the United States 1867–1963*. Princeton: Princeton University Press.

Glasner, D. 1989, *Free Banking and Monetary Reform*. New York: Cambridge University Press.

McCallum, B. 1988, *Monetary Economics: Theory and Policy*. New York: MacMillan.

Shucker, S. 1988, "American 'Reparations' to Germany, 1919–33: Implications for the Third-World Debt Crisis," *Princeton Studies in International Finance* No. 61. July.

Temin, P. 1989, *Lessons of the Great Depression*. Cambridge: MIT Press.

Triffin, R. 1964, "The Evolution of the International Monetary System: Historical Reappraisal and Future Perspectives," *Princeton Studies in International Finance*, No. 12.

Comment

Debt, Deflation, the Great
Depression and the Gold Standard

by Mark Toma

Recently, monetary theories of the business cycle have been challenged by economists who use a classical framework as their starting point. This new classical approach denies that a change in the money supply growth rate is an important factor explaining real income fluctuations. Instead, the new classical approach highlights the role of real factors in the business cycle. With respect to the most pronounced cycle of this century, the Great Depression, real business cycle theorists have pointed to changes in government policy (for example, trade legislation) and the breakdown of the financial intermediation process (Bernanke, 1983) as important non-monetary factors.

The Glasner and Batchelder paper attempts to rehabilitate a monetary theory of the Great Depression. They point to a monetary theory of the Great Depression that is older than the monetary theory popularized by Friedman and Schwartz. While Friedman and Schwartz (1963) emphasized the 1929–1933 drop in the United States money supply, earlier work by Hawtrey and Cassel argued that the Great Depression was caused by the "deflationary forces inherent in the restoration of the pre-war gold standard." In particular, the gold standard environment of the later 1920's triggered an increase in the worldwide demand for gold and therefore a decline in the international (gold) price level.

I shall argue that the Glasner and Batchelder interpretation of the Hawtrey and Cassel hypothesis contributes significantly to our understanding of the deflation experienced during the Great Depression. Glasner and Batchelder ask us to shift our attention away from the United States money supply over the 1929–1933 period toward how the (international) rules of the monetary game changed in the years preceding the Great Depression. In other words, the Glasner and Batchelder analysis focuses on a change in the monetary regime as the cause of the Great Depression while the Friedman and Schwartz analysis was conducted in the spirit of a change in current monetary policy within a given monetary regime.

Instead of criticizing the details of the Glasner and Batchelder interpretation of Hawtrey and Cassel, I shall show why a "policy regime" approach is critical to understanding an episode like the Great Depression where the time series behavior of key macroeconomic variables changed quickly and dramatically. In the process I shall argue that the Glasner and Batchelder interpretation provides a convincing explanation of the time series behavior of the price level during 1929–1933. With respect to the fall in output, however, I argue that Glasner and Batchelder are less successful.

1. Policy Regimes and Deflation

The Friedman and Schwartz monetarist theory of the 1930's deflation asserts that the unprecedented drop in the money supply from 1929 to 1933 was the causal factor. A simple money demand function underlies the monetarist hypothesis. Either money demand is assumed to be independent of inflation expectations, or, if it does depend on inflation expectations, these expectations are fixed at some level determined outside of the model. Accordingly, the rate of inflation (deflation) over any period is directly related to the rate of money growth over the same period.

The Friedman and Schwartz hypothesis can be contrasted to what I refer to as a new classical/rational expectations approach. The assumption that the public forms their expectations rationally is the foundation of the new classical approach. In particular, the new classical approach is forward-looking. People's demand for money depends on forecasted rates of inflation and these forecasts are adjusted as new information becomes available.

The rational expectations approach has an interesting implication for the time series behavior of the general price level. Assume that the equilibrium price level in any period is the level that makes people willingly hold the actual amount of money supplied by the monetary authority. With rational expectations, this implies that the price level in period t depends not just on the period t money stock (as in the monetarist analysis), but, through money demand, also on the expected price level in period $t + 1$. Moreover the expected $t + 1$ price level depends on the expected $t + 1$ money supply and on the price level expected for the subsequent period. Continuing this line of reasoning leads to the conclusion that today's price level (period t) depends not only on today's money supply, but on the expected money supplies into the indefinite future.

Given rational expectations, expected future money supplies depend critically on the monetary regime. If the rules governing how money is produced do not change, then the public will have little reason to change their expectations about future money supplies. In other words, the public's expectations, and therefore the current price level, may be relatively insensitive to changes in current monetary policy.

Alternatively, if government announces a new set of rules (a new monetary regime), then the public will take these new rules into account in forming their inflation expectations. A regime change that causes people to anticipate lower rates of money growth in the future results in a lower inflation rate today. In this case today's inflation rate falls even if current monetary policy does not become more deflationary. The rational expectations approach warns of the danger of placing too much weight on current money supply changes.

2. *The Gold Standard as a Monetary Regime*

The Glasner and Batchelder description of the monetary regime that prevailed throughout much of the pre-Depression period differs significantly from the description offered by Friedman and Schwartz. Under the pre-1914 gold standard, or the gold exchange standard of the 1920's, Friedman and Schwartz argue that a nation could influence its price level in the short run by manipulating the domestic money supply. In contrast, Glasner and Batchelder argue that, as a first approximation, a (small) country must take the price level as given by international conditions. The global supply and demand for gold (money) determines the international price level. Whether a country pursues an expansionary or contractionary monetary policy primarily affects the rate at which that country acquires gold reserves.

While the Glasner and Batchelder characterization of the pre-Depression monetary regime is an important issue, I would like to focus attention on another dimension of their analysis. Even if Glasner and Batchelder agreed with Friedman and Schwartz about the operation of the pre-Depression gold standard, their analysis would still be distinctive because they perceive the fundamental cause of the early 1930's deflation to be a change in policy regimes. They argue that the international monetary regime was changing in the late 1920's in a way that tended to increase the global demand for gold. For example, France under Poincaré initiated a series of fiscal reforms that promised an end to government budget deficits and a return to the gold standard (by stabilizing the franc's exchange rate against the dollar). At about the same time the Federal Reserve tightened the United States money supply. Glasner and Batchelder conclude that since these policy actions, and other less direct forces, increased the worldwide demand for gold in 1929, they triggered the deflation of the Great Depression.

While I think that the Glasner and Batchelder discussion provides the framework for identifying the fundamental cause of the 1930's deflation, the problem is that they do not go far enough. They do not explicitly address the issue of whether the French fiscal policy reforms and the Fed's 1929 monetary policy were temporary policy changes or signaled well understood changes in policy regimes. If they were only temporary changes, then the rational expectations approach suggests they would have little impact on the international price level.

First, consider the French experience. What if the French public was not convinced by government's fiscal policy reform measures? That is, the public perceived that current budget surpluses would be followed by persistent budget deficits in the future. Under these circumstances, the public would have anticipated that government would resort to inflationary finance at some future date. This expectation would tend to undermine the French government's stated intent to return to the gold standard.

Alternatively, what if in the 1920's the United States public foresaw large budget deficits for subsequent decades? Then the public would have anticipated that monetary tightness in the late 1920's would be followed by monetary expansion later. The international price level, which presumably is based not just on current demands for gold but on current and prospective demands, might have risen instead of fallen.

My point is not to argue that the French and American public in the 1920's anticipated large future deficits. At least with respect to the French episode, a strong case can be made that the French reform measures were credible (see Sargent, 1986). I do not want to argue, however, that this is the issue that Glasner and Batchelder should emphasize. A fundamental explanation of deflation must identify more than just changes in current monetary and fiscal decisions. A fundamental explanation must identify a change in (international) policy regimes. To their credit, Glasner and Batchelder have at least pointed us in this direction.

3. Deflation and Depression

Glasner and Batchelder, however, are under the impression that they have offered more than simply an explanation for the deflation of this period. They seem to think that once they have provided a plausible explanation for deflation (that is, a new monetary regime), they need search no further for the explanation of the output drop. There is only one passage where they pause to consider more carefully the connection between deflation and depression: "Of course, it might be argued that expectations of deflation should have increased labor supply and thus moderated unemployment. While correct, the significance of the point is not overwhelming, since there was obviously a great deal of dispersion of expectations. Thus many workers may not have been forecasting deflation and therefore resisted the cuts in wages that might have prevented unemployment from rising as rapidly as it did. Furthermore, if employers generally expected greater deflation than workers, there would still be a net contractionary effect, since the wage cuts acceptable to workers were less than required to maintain output by employers" (p. 28).

One troubling aspect of the Glasner and Batchelder arguments is that it seems to fly in the face of rational expectations. While it may be true that some workers underestimated the deflation associated with the new monetary order, others may have overestimated the fall in prices. The latter group would have accepted nominal wage cuts that entailed falling real wages. Moreover, there is no obvious reason why the expectations of workers as a group should systematically differ from the expectations of employers. Note finally that recent work by Cecchetti (1989) implies that the deflation during the Great Depression was not unanticipated.

In fairness to Glasner and Batchelder, their emphasis on the dispersion of expectations may provide a rational expectations type connection between deflation and the fall in output. In abandoning the old international monetary order there may have been a great deal of uncertainty about the new rules of the game. How many countries would return to the gold standard? At what rates of exchange would the gold standard countries return? To the extent that these questions were unsettled, the future monetary policies of countries throughout the world would be uncertain. An extreme case would be where future policies are so uncertain that people were unable to rationally form their expectations. This comes close to saying there were no well understood rules of the game. Since rules of the game tend to be welfare-enhancing, it follows that the absence of a monetary regime tends to be destructive of the general welfare. Therefore, one general class of explanations for the Great Depression would conjecture that the rules of the (international) monetary environment deteriorated in the late 1920's. In this special sense, the Great Depression might be attributed to monetary forces.

Glasner and Batchelder, however, should seriously consider another possibility. Though the monetary regime was changing in the late 1920's, perhaps the nature of this change was well understood. In this case there need to be no adverse output effect, even if the new monetary order created the expectations of future budget surpluses, and therefore deflation, in a number of countries throughout the world.

According to this argument, the depression may have been a result of some "real" factor that is independent of any monetary regime change. As one possible candidate, perhaps the Hawley-Smoot tariff bill led to a fall in output worldwide because it reduced exchange opportunities worldwide. If not for this protectionist legislation, the world economy might have experienced a period of deflation but not necessarily a depression.

4. Conclusion

In the conclusion of their paper Glasner and Batchelder summarize their reasons for believing that monetary forces were important in the Great Depression. "First, we know of no other episode of severe deflation that was not caused by monetary forces. Major inflations and major deflations are primarily monetary events. More specifically, the severity and longevity of the depression in various countries was closely related to the nature of the monetary regime.

Countries on the gold standard suffered most and no country recovered before leaving the gold standard."

I have argued that the Glasner and Batchelder emphasis on "monetary events" as regime changes represents a significant improvement over the Friedman and Schwartz approach in explaining the deflation of the 1930's. But why a deflationary policy regime shift necessarily leads to a depression is not so clear. Furthermore, the evidence for this proposition is sketchy at best. In order for this implication of the Glasner and Batchelder argument to be convincing, they must be more careful, both conceptually and empirically, in developing the connection between a policy regime change and the time series behavior of output.

References

Bernanke, Ben. 1983, "Nonmonetary Effects of the Financial Crisis in the Propagation of the Great Depression," *American Economic Review* 73, 257–76.

Cecchetti, Stephen. 1989, "Prices During the Great Depression: Was the Deflation of 1930–1932 Really Unanticipated?" National Bureau of Economic Research Working Paper number 3174.

Friedman, Milton and Anna Schwartz. 1963, *A Monetary History of the United States, 1867–1960*, Princeton University Press.

Sargent, Thomas. 1986, "Stopping Moderate Inflations: The Methods of Poincaré and Thatcher," in *Rational Expectations and Inflation*, edited by Thomas Sargent, 110–57, New York: Harper and Row.

A New Perspective on George Wingfield and Nevada Banking, 1920-1933

by Larry Schweikart*

The collapse of the twelve-bank chain of Nevada banks owned by George Wingfield in 1933 has been viewed as both contributing to the nation's banking troubles and a microcosm of them. Wingfield, revered and feared in Nevada politics and finance in the 1920's, headed a banking empire that by 1930 commanded more than half of all the state's banking assets. When this chain failed, he personally bore most of the blame.

Many of Wingfield's critics contended the collapse was due to his poor management. Due to allegations that Wingfield had an earlier instance of involvement in a political/financial scandal, other critics thought that Wingfield banks had not been regulated properly. Wingfield's supporters, most notably Clel Georgetta, saw the collapse of the chain as a manifestation of the political battles between the Republican Wingfield and the Democratic administration of Franklin Roosevelt. They especially pointed to the Reconstruction Finance Corporation's denial of a last minute loan that would have allowed Wingfield to reorganize his chain and save his banks—a denial that they contend Roosevelt ordered. James Olsen, who interpreted the collapse of Wingfield's chain as symptomatic of the Reconstruction Finance Corporation's inability to deal with the crises of the era, argued that falling livestock prices destroyed the banks' collateral. Wingfield was not a bad manager, according to Olsen; rather his chain was caught up in events beyond anyone's control. Finally, though not specifically referring to Wingfield, many historians of banking, pointing to the advantages of both intra- and interstate banking, by implication suggest that either form of branch banking may have saved

Wingfield and Nevada banks.[1] None of those earlier writers had the advantage of seeing George Wingfield's papers, which reside at the Nevada Historical Society. Those papers originally placed under a 50 year restriction, have been opened recently. They suggest that none of the previous explanations account for the demise of the Wingfield chain in a satisfactory manner.

George Wingfield (b. 1876) arrived in Tonopah in 1902 after working as a cattle drover. He dealt cards at the Tonopah Club and with his winnings organized the gambling concession of the club. With the profits from gambling, Wingfield acquired rich Goldfield mining properties along with George S. Nixon, a Winnemucca banker (and a future U.S. Senator), and the two men controlled much of the Goldfield Consolidated Mines Company, one of the richest mining properties in Nevada. Wingfield eventually bought out Nixon for $3 million; by the time the mines closed the company had paid out over $29 million in dividends. He later established with Nixon the Nixon National Bank (renamed the Reno National Bank in 1922).[2]

As expected with any powerful individual, Wingfield made a number of enemies. His reputation as a political "kingmaker" also left him open to charges of corruption at the slightest irregularity in his banks. One of the most famous episodes of a bank/political scandal occurred in George Wingfield's Nevada banking chain when one of his cashiers, H.C. Clapp of the Carson Valley Bank, became involved in fraud with the state highway department.[3]

On April 27, 1927, George Cole, the former Nevada State Controller, and Ed Malley, the current state treasurer, met with George Wingfield in Reno.[4] They disclosed that $516,322 in state funds was missing from the Carson Valley Bank, which Wingfield owned, and that they and Clapp had taken the money, which they had sunk into speculative oil venture. Wingfield had recently discharged Clapp for sloppy work related to the cashier's drinking, and no doubt Clapp wished to get even. It is also clear, though, that a year before the confession by Cole and Malley, Wingfield suspected the cashier was a risk (although he apparently never suspected him of criminal activity). In a letter to Wingfield dated well before the news of the defalcations became public, Clapp admitted he had fallen into heavy debt covering the overdrafts of a friend (as he claimed) when the two of them invested in stocks.[5] Wingfield may have doubted the existence of the "friend,"and he certainly had no sympathy for such activities on the part of one of his cashiers.

Wingfield demanded weekly reports from Clapp "explaining the details of every loan made through the week . . . ."[6] The Reno banker received similar reports from his other cashiers, which already exceeded the information most bank presidents would receive, so he had not singled out Clapp. But it was clear Wingfield had his eye on the Carson Valley cashier.

Cole, Malley, and Clapp had worked their scam on the state as well as the bank and had successfully perpetrated their crime since 1919, issuing fraudulent cashier's checks that Clapp paid out a little at a time. Regardless of the incremental disappearance of funds, the *Reno Evening Gazette* found it astonishing that "one-half million dollars of the peoples' money could be lifted . . . and replaced by paper which may prove worthless."[7] Of course, that was not the case, as Wingfield responded by personally depositing $600,000 in the Carson Valley Bank to prevent a run, and his dollars were as green as the state's.[8] Clapp turned state's evidence following his arrest, making Cole and Malley's chances for acquittal nil, despite the strained attempts by the weasely defense attorney (and political boss) Fat McCarran. In an ironic twist, McCarran's defense of Cole and Malley hinged on implicating the bank—especially Wingfield—but in the process McCarran exposed the *unrelated* corruption of the bank examiner who had investigated the Carson Valley Bank, Gilbert Ross.[9] Even under severe questioning, Clapp acknowledged that the bank allowed Ross some $6,900 in overdrafts, not because he was in on the plot but simply because *he was the examiner.* Wingfield's bank eventually agreed to pay 50 percent more than the law required— almost $155,000 against the required bond of $100,000—yet he earned the enmity of redistributionists who thought he should have covered the entire amount. It is ironic that while some historians (McCarran's biographer, for example) thought Wingfield schemed to avoid paying for the state's losses by not going beyond what the law required, the Reno banker won praise from other financiers, including important bankers outside Nevada who correctly understood that he had prevented a major panic. Frederick Kiesel of the California National Bank praised Wingfield's "magnanimous action" that protected the Carson Valley Bank.[10]

The Carson Valley Bank exposed several problems with which Western regulators had not yet come to grips. First, the public had increasingly taken a less active role as a regulatory force as the emphasis instead shifted to investigations by "impartial" examiners. In some ways, that tended to make bank activities more than ever a "secret" business "understood" by only a few "experts." Thus, ironically, regulations designed to make banks more open to public scrutiny actually removed the banks even further from view, because the new wave of regulations—especially after 1900—tended to reinforce the perception that now the regulators were watching the banks. Second, the process of public regulation inevitably made banking more political than ever before, especially in the west. Regulators and examiners, as political appointees, could not help but be influenced by party bosses. Third, the regulators added yet another level to the gradually expanding layers of bureaucracy that separated the public from the bankers—a layer that itself proved in need of policing, as Ross showed. Yet examiners could no more expect to police successfully all banks in the 1920's than they had in the 1890's. The North Dakota Banking Board, for example, admitted in 1917 that reports to the examiners showed that many banks were "grossly violating" state banking laws.[11]

One could also apply Richard Hofstadter's more esoteric assessment of the trends in government at the time: regulators and examiners joined academics as the new "experts" whose special "knowledge" of a bank's condition further added to the inability of the public to decipher bank reports.[12] In the citizen's mind, the bank reports took on an aura of mystery, further convincing depositors to leave them in the hands of the specialists. If the experts vouched for the institution's safety, then who would doubt it? So as the law required increased public access to banks' information, the process also had the unintended effect of making that very information increasingly less useful. Moreover, new temptations arose for examiners, depending on the current political winds, to find troubled banks solvent or vice versa. These factors combined to make the reports of examiners in the 1920's and 1930's suspect, and the procedures instituted on the basis of those reports questionable.

Perhaps more than any other single Western banker, George Wingfield embodied the cumulative effects of those forces in the late 1920's and the Great Depression. By the 1920's, the Wingfield chain had already started to feel the brunt of the agricultural problems that had plagued the West for a decade. His chain's collapse, called by the historian of the Reconstruction Finance Corporation, James Olson, the "rehearsal for disaster," not only provides a remarkable case study of the dynamics of the R.F.C.'s lending to banks, but it also offers a unique opportunity to explore the largest Western chain failure of the Depression and to examine the view that chain banking was an effective substitute for branch banking.[13]

Wingfield fit the image of a Westerner held by most Americans of the day. When the International Workers of the World (Wobblies) once tried to suppress distribution of a local paper that carried an anti-IWW editorial by Wingfield's friend, editor L.C. Bramson, Wingfield strapped on two Colts and paraded the streets with the newsboys, riding "shotgun" on their deliveries.[14] As a banker, Wingfield soaked up huge quantities of detail about his operations, demanding weekly reports from his cashiers. He returned those with considerable analysis of the loans, collateral behind them, and bank balance sheets. At times, Wingfield's comments suggest that he knew each borrower personally, and he certainly identified problem debtors.[15] At one time, for example, Wingfield thought the Carson Valley Bank's livestock loans needed improvement, so he brought in D.P. Malloy of Lake View, Oregon, a livestock expert, to evaluate all of the bank's livestock loans.[16] (At that time Wingfield may have sensed that something was wrong at the Carson Valley Bank—where cashier Clapp was embezzling—but likely thought the problem stemmed from poor banking practices, not dishonesty.) And Wingfield had no reluctance when it came to collection: Of one borrower, for example, Wingfield instructed Clapp to "get right after the Heinicke Construction Co. & make them [sic] settle up their balance . . . as I don't like the way that thing looks."[17] On another occasion, the Reno banker urged Clapp's successor to hire a new collector "who has no political friends to reward by going easy on them . . . ."[18] Wingfield also kept a close eye on cash accounts, ordering Clapp to reduce cash by $100,000 on one occasion.[19] Examinations of the bank's taxes paid to the U.S. suggest that the bank usually did an accurate job of reporting, and the examiners even noted that loopholes existed that Wingfield had not exploited.[20] When another of Wingfield's banks underpaid its taxes, Wingfield strongly suggested that the bank finish them early and forward the forms to Wingfield's accountants and tax advisors for inspection.[21] More important, earnings sheets for banks such as the Carson Valley Bank showed constant profits during the 1920's.

Indeed, nothing of Wingfield's management smacks of incompetence. He knew the position of all of his investments, most of which in the 1920's produced regular profits. He insisted on uniform reporting—right down to standardized forms for his weekly cashier's memos—and demanded competence and loyalty from his employees. To a request for a vacation from the superior of one assistant cashier, Wingfield in exasperation replied that he would give all employees a "permanent vacation" if they did not "pep up."[22]

Given the meticulous attention Wingfield lavished on his banks, it is interesting that many scholars have assumed that mismanagement caused the collapse of Wingfield's chain in 1933.[23] Certainly warning signs had appeared: The Carson Valley Bank's net earnings had plunged by an average of $20,000 over a two-year period from 1926 to 1928.[24] In 1929, Wingfield owned outright or held a controlling interest in twelve banks spread through nine cities, and by 1932 these 12 banks (of Nevada's 41) held 65 percent of the state's deposits and made 75 percent of the state's commercial loans.[25] During the 1920's, even the weakest of the banks made noteworthy profits. The Carson Valley Bank, where the corrupt Clapp was cashier, reported a profit of $9,344 to the Internal Revenue Service in 1920, and earnings for the yearly period ending in 1921 totaled $18,000.[26] A year later, net earnings passed $20,000 and profit reached $17,396, all from a bank whose cashier had engaged in embezzling and which had not collected $6,000 owed by the previous examiner Ross.[27] Although earnings dropped through 1927, when net earnings only totaled $3,597, losses charged off also fell by 95% from 1926 to 1927. White collar crime again struck the bank, however, this time at the hands of Irma Emmitt, an employee whose embezzling was discovered by an internal audit.[28]

While one might contend that Wingfield should have known of those problems, Wingfield operated as thorough an auditing procedure as any other bank, and probably more standardized than most chains or even some branch operations. He displayed constant concern with costs, especially items such as company autos (the cashiers frequently wanted luxury cars, while Wingfield demanded they use no-frills passenger cars), yet he never hesitated to pay high wages. Once, he admonished the cashier of the Churchill County Bank to hire a "better class of help than you have . . . even if you have to pay them a little more."[29] The evidence suggests that Wingfield always suspected trouble well before it appeared in internal audits or external examinations. Wingfield cautioned the inexperienced Churchill County Bank cashier E.W. Blair that banking was "somewhat a new line for you. After staying in a mining camp for 20 years, it is hard to break in as a farmer banker."[30]

All Nevada's economy had developed trouble spots, with unemployment in the mining countries reaching 75 percent. The state suffered from overbanking, even under normal conditions. Elko, a town of fewer than 5,000 people, had two banks.[31] Moreover, "the banks in Nevada in general and the Wingfield banks in particular, suffered from a chronic inability to diversify their loans."[32] Wingfield especially had a soft spot for the Nevada sheepmen and farmers, hundreds of whom he kept in business. During the 1920's, few questioned the Reno banker's strategy, as sheep worth $18–20 a head secured the sheepmens' loans taken at $4 a head. But when the wool market collapsed, the price of wool fell from $.30 per pound to $.08 by 1932.[33] The drastic plunge in wool prices placed a huge demand on Wingfield's banks for renewals of existing loans or additional funds to keep the sheep alive. In 1932 alone, defaults in the Wingfield chain amounted to more than $3.5 million, and the sheepmen still pressed for more loans. To refuse these requests not only ensured the demise of the sheep ranches but also would have forced the banks to take the sheep as settlement and attempt to sell them in a slow market. Even in a good market, the banks lacked the ability to sell livestock on a regular basis. Yet Wingfield personally knew many of the ranchers, and compassion compelled him to extend their loans as much as possible. He could have permitted his weaker banks to fail, thus saving the bulk of his banking empire and his entire non-bank-related fortune, including his own ranches and hotels.

Ironically, a rejected loan may have sent the listing ship under. In July 1932, E.W. Blair noted that a disgruntled borrower had spread rumors about the bank's stability, and by October, "the run . . . had become a 'stampede.' "[34] That year, Wingfield applied for a loan from the Reconstruction Finance Corporation (R.F.C.) of $2 million for the Reno National Bank, and he soon followed that request with a request for another $1 million. In addition, Wingfield's other banks received over $2.1 million in 1932.[35] Those R.F.C. loans temporarily helped the Wingfield chain, but introduced several long-term harms as well. The R.F.C. made the loans at relatively high interest rates (six percent) and only allowed six month maturity dates, meaning that the banks no sooner got a loan than they had to scramble to pay it back. Worse, the R.F.C. claimed the best assets of the banks as collateral, claiming, for example, $3 million of Reno National's best securities for a $1.1 million loan in April 1932.[36] The Henderson Banking Company, which received its first R.F.C. loan in May 1932, for $150,000, asked for $55,000 in June, $200,000 in July, and $220,000 in September. For the May and September loans alone, the R.F.C. demanded $1.3 million in securities. Banks had to liquidate their best assets just to keep the R.F.C. happy. And the R.F.C. undervalued the assets it accepted. For livestock held as security by the Wingfield chain valued at $15 million in 1928, the face value had plummeted to under $8 million in 1932. But the R.F.C. valued it at only $3 million.[37]

It is important to note that Wingfield indeed took the loans, and that without them the system may have collapsed. On the other hand, the crisis may have brought immediate help, either from the California banks or the state government had the chains not accepted the R.F.C. loans. Had it not done so, it would have at least retained some of its valuable securities for bargaining purposes.

Wingfield appealed to Governor Fred B. Balzer for a bank holiday to allow the liquidation of some of Wingfield's personal assets for application to the banks' capital structures.[38] Balzar met with President Herbert Hoover on October 30, 1932, and the following day, after talking to R.F.C. officials, Balzar telephoned his Lieutenant Governor, Morley Griswold, instructing him to enact a "business holiday" the following day, since the Nevada constitution did not permit, in his opinion, a specific bank holiday. Indeed, under the business holiday edict, not all banks closed, with Wingfield's competitor in Reno, the First National Bank, remaining open. (Balzar had a special interest in Wingfield's banks, as they held all the state's public funds.) But Wingfield shut his banks' doors on November 1.

During that period, T.E. Harris, the chief bank examiner for the San Francisco district of the Federal Reserve, warned J.G. Moore, the cashier at the First National Bank of Winnemucca, to "carefully review your assets and determine whether your capital structure is sound."[39] The examiner noted his "experience with closed banks, as distinguished from banks operating under a holiday ... [was that] the estimate [of the bank's ability to meet depositor demands] is usually too low and I advise you to be very careful . . . to see that your capital is intact and that you have sufficient liquidity to meet withdrawals . . . ."[40]

Appeals to Crocker First National Bank of San Francisco, to whom Wingfield already owed $850,000, received a by-then standard rejection. Crocker officials in fact had already loaned Wingfield his limit and without hesitation Crocker Bank offered to participate in the reorganization plan in which a syndicate of San Francisco banks and businesses planned to lend Wingfield between $.5 million and $1 million.[41] However, by that time the R.F.C. had already gobbled up the best securities. Depositors, nevertheless, remained confident: according to the cashier Moore, "the worst element we have to contend with are those who have little or nothing in the bank. Their chief diversion is to stand around the corners and hang crepe."[42] On the other hand, one depositor offered as a loan the contents of her safe deposit box—$2,000 in government bonds.[43] Federal examiners, meanwhile, actively inspected the books and loans of the national banks, and determined that the banks no longer had enough collateral to guarantee their solvency.[44]

As ever, politics figured into the banks' immediate condition. Wingfield's opponents in Stroey County presented county drafts during the business holiday, contending that the governor did not have the authority to close the banks.[45] After extensive examinations by both state and federal regulators, the banks then formally closed down on December 14, 1932. Cashier Moore reported to Wingfield that he would make a final check of the books "and then join the 'army of the unemployed'."[46]

On January 6, 1933, the deteriorating condition of the Wingfield chain led the Comptroller of the Currency to levy an assessment of $700,000 on the stockholders of the Reno National Bank.[47] Depositors committees, which had already started to meet, demanded that any reorganization plans give the depositors sole claim to the banks' assets.[48] Wingfield asked for depositors to sign waivers on their deposits in which they waived the right to withdraw 75 percent of their deposits immediately, giving Wingfield and the other owners the authority to reorganize the banks. At that time, the Comptroller would have to agree to the plan. Rumors spread wildly, with a "non-signing depositor"—believed to be Graham Sanford, editor of the anti-Wingfield *Reno Evening Gazette*—raising a list of unanswerable questions and asking for "guarantees" that no banker could make.[49] By February, Wingfield had agreed to a plan worked out with "a group of San Francisco financiers" that included formation of a mortgage company to take over the twelve closed banks, along with a $1.5 million RFC loan; a promise by the California bankers not to withdraw their deposits for three years; and an agreement (contained in the waivers) by which the depositors would accept 25 percent of their deposits in stock in the new bank.[50] All the stockholders had to agree to the plan, and most of the major stockholders expressed their approval. Of the 27,000 depositors, the majority of them held deposits of less than $200, and the ready cash would be used to pay them before other depositors. The plan did not state that Standard Oil and the Southern Pacific Railroad rejected calls for $500,000 in new outside capital. The potential investors did not want the RFC's stringent credit restrictions.

According to the plan, only one director would be named by the existing stockholders, twelve by the depositors, and three by the California bankers. Still, hatred of Wingfield by some was so strong that the *Santa Barbara Daily News* reported the plan with the comment that "thousands of people in [Nevada] regard [Wingfield] with high affection and esteem [but] Thousands hate him."[51] A week after that editorial, W.J. Henly, cashier at the Virginia City Bank, observed that "the majority of the larger depositors here are all for reorganization . . . . [but there are] some who are very bitter and do a lot of shouting . . . ."[52] The *Reno Evening Gazette* continued to paint the situation in the darkest of colors, arguing that Wingfield had already lost everything, agitating depositors' committees to lobby for his total exclusion from the new bank.[53]

The Nevada legislature had introduced a bill that would have turned over all the closed banks to the depositors, essentially confiscating Wingfield's investments. Although the house passed the bill, the Nevada senate bottled it up in committee, reporting out a substitute bill allegedly written by Wingfield's attorney George Thatcher, and the legislation passed this bill instead.[54] It allowed depositors with over 50 percent of the majority stock to reorganize an insolvent bank, giving the original stockholders Class B nonvoting stock and retaining for themselves Class A voting stock. As soon as possible, the bank was to purchase the A stock and retire it, leaving the B stockholders in control after all the depositors received their money.

However, conditions for Nevada banks (as for banks throughout the West) had deteriorated since the submission of the reorganization plan, and on March 1, 1933, the governor declared another business holiday. Without the authority to declare a bank holiday, Balzar requested a bill to give him authority, then mysteriously sat on a slightly altered bill that contained essentially similar provisions. After considerable political pressure by both pro- and anti-Wingfield forces, Balzar signed the measure. The legislature immediately convened a joint committee to investigate all closed banks in the state, and the committee's report concluded that the livestock loans had broken the Wingfield banks. The report also condemned the State Banking Board and the Bank Examiner for permitting the ongoing livestock loans.[55]

Wingfield, in accordance with the provisions of the new law, revised his reorganization plan with a mortgage company containing individual trust funds for each of the twelve banks, specifically to hold the slow-liquidating sheep loans. This plan required depositors to also take some of their deposits in mortgage company stock as well as bank stock. This, plus a $2 million loan from the R.F.C., would ease the immediate cash problems until the sheep loans could be liquidated.[56] A projected distribution of deposit liability per $1,000 in each of the 12 banks showed the Riverside Bank, the Wells State Bank, the Bank of Sparks, and the United Nevada Bank to have the lowest levels of unacceptable loans (all below $255 per thousand), while Wingfield's Reno National, Virginia City Bank, Bank of Nevada Savings and Trust, and the Tonopah Banking Corporation all had over $500 per thousand in unacceptable loans.[57] But Wingfield had assumed the worst and the balance sheet of the proposed bank reflected huge write-offs, while he could point to some of the newly acquired banks as indicators that he could gradually restructure with newer, more profitable banks.[58] By late March, six banks had received enough waivers to enable them to reorganize, including the Tonopah Bank, the Virginia City Bank, Sparks Bank, Henderson Bank, Carson Valley Bank, and the First National Bank of Winnemucca. By the beginning of May, only the stockholders from the Riverside Bank, United Nevada Bank, and Churchill County Bank had not approved the plan. Ultimately, all but the depositors in the latter bank signed the waivers.

Still, a number of hurdles remained. First, Wingfield faced a deadline of June 17, 1933, that appeared on the waivers. Wingfield applied for the $2 million R.F.C. loan on June 13 and filed articles of incorporation on June 15, leaving virtually no room for error. He contended all the while with a lawsuit alleging mismanagement, and in subsequent suits the plaintiffs requested an opinion from the Comptroller of the Currency, J.F.T. O'Connor, as to whether the Comptroller's office would approve of the plan. O'Connor replied that his office would not approve any plan under which a depositor who had not signed a waiver was co-opted into the reorganization of the bank, thus effectively removing the two national banks from the entire reorganization proposal. Wingfield also received a setback from the courts, which ruled the Nevada Bank Act of 1933, under which Wingfield had proposed to reorganize the banks, unconstitutional.[59]

A final attempt at reorganization, with enough cash to buy out the non-signing depositors, followed a two-month trial in which a Nevada district court agreed with the Comptroller that non-signing depositors could not be forced into the reorganization. The court dealt another blow to reorganization when it added that state and county governments would not be permitted to hold stock in the banks, thus adding the public deposits to the "non-signers."[60] In desperation, Wingfield obtained yet additional support from the San Francisco financiers, but the R.F.C. refused any additional loans, and in November the Nevada District Court, seeing the reorganization plans stalled, ordered a receivership for the state banks following the lead of the Comptroller, who had already appointed a receiver for the national banks. Wingfield's personal liability on the national banks alone totalled over $450,000, and the demands forced him to involuntary bankruptcy.[61] Sheep prices later returned, and the depositors, by hindsight, would have fared better under the reorganization than under the receiverships.

Did this mean that the premier banker in Nevada's history was a poor manager? Or was he, as Clel Georgetta claimed, a victim of Franklin Roosevelt's manipulations of the R.F.C. in Washington?[62] The best evidence that Wingfield's *long term* prospects were good can be found in the eagerness with which other corporations and banks rushed to grant him loans. In 1929, for example, Continental Illinois Bank and Trust offered Wingfield a substantial line of credit to help him acquire the Washoe County Bank.[63] California bankers' willingness to lend Wingfield a total of $1.85 million in 1933 clearly reflected their estimation of his managerial and banking abilities. Had they not viewed him as a solid risk, or his sheep loans as ultimately recoverable, they would have abandoned him well before 1932. The banks' own weakened internal position also probably contributed to their reluctance to support the plan after 1935. Standard Oil and the Southern Pacific only refused funds once the R.F.C. got involved. Wingfield's reorganization plan was an ingenious attempt to keep the banks afloat, and would have restored them to solvency after the sheep prices rose. Even in forced liquidation, all his banks paid approximately 90 cents on the dollar and the Riverside Bank paid 100 percent to depositors.[64]

Free market advocates might well ask why any well-managed bank would need a "bailout," and posit that the consumer might be better served by allowing the banks to fail. In Wingfield's defense, however, the condition of banks across the country had made government aid commonplace, and the R.F.C. existed for the purpose of extending such aid. What is so striking about this episode is the ease with which the banks got "hooked" on government support, which by its very conditions became addicting unto death. The ultimate culprit—Nevada's undiversified economy and the crippling conditions of the R.F.C. loans—eluded even Wingfield's brilliant attempt to introduce a quasi-branching system.

Other economists have pointed to the advantages of branching, arguing that even intrastate branching diversified portfolios and made the state systems that permitted branching far more stable and secure than other regimes.[65] Charles Calomiris, for example, has argued that from the standpoint of desirability of outcomes during the 1920's, the various regulatory regimes could be ranked in order of preference as follows: "full statewide branching, limited branching, uninsured unit banking, voluntary insurance unit banking, and compulsory insurance unit banking."[66] Eugene White has similarly seen nationwide branch banking as potentially derailing the Great Depression had the states implemented it. According to White, "Branching was a viable policy alternative to deposit insurance, and it appears that banks might have been strengthened and the number of failures decreased if there had been more branching in the 1920's."[67] While statewide branching could have strengthened an undiversified economy, it could not save it. As matters stood, ultimately only the wool prices could have saved Wingfield.

Interstate banking, from California's banks, however, could have absorbed the losses until prices rose, and the influence of the California bankers in the reorganization plan suggested that Wingfield appreciated the advantages of interstate branch banking. The records of the R.F.C. suggest that this was exactly the case when the California banks not only absorbed parts of Wingfield's chain but paid off the depositors. Likewise, the R.F.C. changed some of its policies, lending beyond the collateral offered by banks. But that all came too late for Wingfield's banks.

The situation in Nevada shocked neighboring California and triggered similar developments elsewhere in the West. The ripples spread rapidly: M.S. Cravath, a director of the Stockmen's National Bank in Rushville, Nebraska, was at his vacation resort in Long Beach when he reported "the Seaside National Bank of Long Beach closed its doors last Tuesday . . . we had our money in the bank . . . ."[68]

Although it was too late for Wingfield, Nevada joined Idaho in 1933 to correct its system by permitting branching. With the exception of the Idaho chain, which reopened with an R.F.C. loan, branching and chain banking had demonstrated considerable more flexibility than unit banking. Ironically, a branch banking holding company ended Nevada's woes related to Wingfield's failed chain. Unfortunately, regulators in the West aimed some of the rearrangement in policies after the turbulent twenties at propping up the unit bank systems. Only an interstate branch banking system would have saved the Nevada banks.[69] But A.P. Giannini in California had already came up against a stone wall with the government regulators on that issue. Indeed, fellow westerner, Marriner Eccles, in his capacity as chairman of the Federal Reserve Board, ended Giannini's dream of an interstate system. It took more than 40 years for the country to pass even regional interstate banking laws of the type that might have rescued Nevada and the Wingfield banks. By that time the Nevadan had lost his fortune, made another in mining, and died.

Notes

*The author wishes to thank the University of Dayton Research Institute and the Earhart Foundation for research support. This article is exerpted from a forthcoming book, *Banking in the American West,* Oklahoma University

Press, co-authored with Lynne Pierson Doti. This paper expresses only the views of the author.

1. Thomas F. Cargill and Kerry Sullivan. "An Historical Perspective of Nevada Banks," *Journal of the West*, XXIII, April 1984, pp. 21–28; Clel Georgetta, *Golden Fleece in Nevada* (Reno, NV: Venture Publishing Co., 1972); James S. Olson, "Rehearsal for Disaster: Hoover, the R.F.C., and the Banking Crisis in Nevada, 1932-1933," *Western Historical Quarterly*, April 1975, pp. 149–161; Eugene N. White, *Regulation and Reform of the American Banking System, 1900–1929* (Princeton University Press, 1983).

2. "George Wingfield" in Lamar, ed., *Readers Encyclopedia*, p. 1275; C. Elizabeth Raymond, "George Wingfield," in *The Encyclopedia of American Business History, Banking and Finance, 1913–1986* (Columbia: Broccoli Clark Layman, 1990); Russell Elliott, *History of Nevada* (Lincoln: University of Nebraska Press, 1973), pp. 286–287; Thomas Cargill and Kerry S. Sullivan, "An Historical Perspective on Nevada Banking," *Journal of the West*, XXIII, April 1984, pp. 21–28.

3. Jerome E. Edwards, *Pat McCarren: Political Boss of Nevada* (Reno: University of Nevada Press, 1982), p. 36.

4. *Ibid.*, p. 33.

5. George Winfield to H.C. Clapp, March 6, 1926, Series VII, box 108, "Carson Valley Bank, 1926," George Wingfield Papers, Nevada Historical Society (henceforth abbreviated as GW, NHS).

6. George Wingfield to H.C. Clapp, March 6, 1926, Series VII, box 108, "Carson Valley Bank, 1926," GW, NHS.

7. Reno *Evening Gazette* quoted in Edwards, *Pat McCarran*, p. 36.

8. Edwards, *Pat McCarran*, p. 36.

9. *Ibid.*

10. Frederick W. Kiesel to George Wingfield, May 9, 1927, Series VII, box 108, Carson Valley Bank, 192," GW, NHS.

11. North Dakota Banking Board memo, October 25, 1917, box 27, "Banking and Home Building," Isaac Post Baker Papers [IPB], NDHS.

12. Richard Hofstader, *The Age of Reform: From Bryan to FDR* (New York: Vinage, 1955), *passim.*

13. Olson, "Rehearsal for Disaster," pp. 149–161.

14. Georgetta, *Golden Fleece in Nevada*, pp. 383–425.

15. See, for example, George Wingfield to H.C. Clapp, January 20, 1926; "Carson Valley Bank, 1926," to H.C. Clapp, June 17, 1921; "Carson Valley Bank, 1921," to F.P. Strasberg, September 20, 1916; "Churchill County Bank, 1916," to L.W. Horton, January 9, 1930; "Carson Valley Bank, 1930," all in Series VII, box 10E; to E.W. Blair, January 22, 1927; "Churchill County, Bank, 1927," in Series VII, Box 109; and to E.W. Blair, February 28, 1929; "Churchill County Bank, Jan.-Apr. 1929," Series VII, Box 109, all in GW, NHS.

16. George Wingfield to H.C. Clapp, June 23, 1921, "Carson Valley Bank, 1921," Series VII, box 108, GW, NHS.

17. George Wingfield to H.C. Clapp, August 16, 1923, "Carson Valley Bank, 1923," Series VII, box 108, GW, NHS.

18. George Wingfield to L.W. Horton, July 23, 1928, "Carson Valley Bank, Apr.–Dec. 1928," Series VII, box 108, GW, NHS.

19. George Wingfield to H.C. Clapp, October 7, 1925, "Carson Valley Bank, 1925," Series VII, box 108, GW, NHS.

20. Treasury Department Report, February 19, 1923, "Carson Valley Bank, Taxes, 1923," Series VII, box 108, GW, NHS.

21. George Wingfield to C.W. Foote, January 17, 1918, "Churchill County Bank, 1918," Series VII, box 108, GW, NHS.

22. George Wingfield to E.W. Blair, August 10, 1927, "Churchill County Bank, 1927," Series VII, box 108, GW, NHS.

23. See, for example, Cargill and Sullivan, "Nevada Banking," p. 26, and Elliot, *History of Nevada*, pp. 286–7.

24. "Carson Valley Bank," net earnings, 1919–1931, Series VII, box 8, "Carson Valley Bank, Jan.–July, 1932, GW, NHS.

25. See the minutes of the R.F.C., July 30, 1932, National Archives, Record Group, 234, Secretarial Division, Washington, D.C.; Olson, "Rehearsal for Disaster," p. 150.

26. Income Tax Forms, "Carson Valley Bank, Taxes," Series VII, box 108, GW, NHS.

27. H.C. Clapp to George Wingfield, December 11, 1922, "Carson Valley Bank, 1922," Series VII, box 108, GW, NHS.

28. Audit, March 31, 1928, "Carson Valley Bank, 1928, Special Audit," Series VII, box 108, GW, NHS.

29. E.W. Blair to George Wingfield, February 28, 1929, "Churchill County Bank, Jan.–Apr. 1929," Series VII, box 109; George Wingfield to E.W. Blair, September 6, 1927; "Churchill County Bank, 1927," Series VII, box 108, all in GW, NHS.

30. See George Wingfield to E.W. Blair, February 26, 1929, "Churchill County Bank, Jan.–Apr. 1929," Series VII, box 109; and "Churchill County Bank, Audit, 1929," *ibid.*, all in GW, NHS.

31. Olson, "Rehearsal for Disaster," p. 151.

32. *Loc. cit.*

33. See Georgetta, *Golden Fleece*, pp. 403–404.

34. E.W. Blair to George Wingfield, July 28, 1932, "Churchill County Bank, July–Dec. 1929," Series VII, box 109, GW, NHS.

35. Olson, "Rehearsal for Disaster," p. 153.

36. *Los. cit.*, p. 154.

37. *Los. cit.*, pp. 154–155.

38. *Los. cit.*, p. 155.

39. Georgetta, *Golden Fleece*, p. 405; memo to Reconstruction Finance Corporation, n.d. [1932], "Reno National Bank, Feb.–July, 1932," Series VII, box 113, GW, NHS.

40. T.E. Harris to J.G. Moore, n.d., "First National Bank of Winnenucca, Aug.–Dec. 1932," Series VII, box 111, GW, NHS.

41. *Loc. cit.*

42. F.G. Willis to George Wingfield, August 11, 1932, Series VII, box 113, "Reno National Bank, Aug. 1932," GW, NHS.

43. J.G. Moore to George Wingfield, November 6, 1932, "First National Bank of Winnemucca, Aug.–Dec. 1952," Series VII, box 111; William J. Henley to George Wingfield, November 5, 1932, "Virginia City Bank, 1932," Series VII, box 115, both in GW, NHS.

44. J.G. Moore to George Wingfield, November 6, 1932, Series VII, box 111, "First National Bank of Winnemucca, Aug.–Dec., 1952," GW, NHS.

45. *Loc. cit.*

46. W.J. Henley to J. Sheehan, November 15, 1932, Series VII, box 115, "Virginia City Bank, 1922," GW, NHS.

47. J.G. Moore to George Wingfield, December 16, 1922, Series VII, "First Natural Bank of Winnemucca, Aug.–Dec. 1932," GW, NHS.

48. F.G. Awalt, "Assessment Upon the Shareholders," January 6, 1933, Series VII, box 112, "Reno National Bank, 1933," GW, NHS.

49. "To the Depositors of the Riverside Bank," January 25, 1933, Series VII, box 113, Riverside Bank, 1933," GW, NHS.

50. "Bank Depositors . . .," reprint in "George Wingfield Correspondence," re: Banking Reorganization, 1933," Series I, box 40, GW, NHS.

51. "Wingfield's Future," *Santa Barbara Daily News,* February 14, 1933, clipping in *loc. cit.*

52. *Loc. cit.*

53. W.J. Henley to George Wingfield, February 21, 1933, Series VII, box 715, "Virginia City Bank, 1933," GW, NHS.

54. Georgetta, *Golden Fleece,* pp. 406–407.

55. *Ibid.,* p. 407.

56. *Ibid.,* pp. 410–411.

57. "Proposed Balance Sheet, Wingfield Banks," *Reno, Evening Gazette,* February 22, 1933: "The Plan for Reorganization and Reopening of Nevada's Closed Banks," in "George Wingfield Correspondence re: Banking Reorganization, Printed Matter," Series 1, box 40, GW, NHA.

58. "Proposed Balance Sheet."

59. *Loc. cit.*

60. Georgetta, *Golden Fleece,* pp. 414–416.

61. *Ibid.,* p. 420.

62. *Ibid.,* pp. 421–422.

63. *Ibid.,* p. 421.

64. George Wingfield to James G. Wakefield, July 5, 1929. Series VII, box 113, "Reno National Bank, June–Dec. 1929," GW, NHS.

65. See Lynne Pierson Doti, "Banking in California: the First Branching Era," *Journal of the West,* April 1984, pp. 65–71; White, *Regulation and Reform:* Charles W. Calomiris, "State Deposit Insurance: Lessons From the Record,"

342   A NEW PERSPECTIVE

Economic Perspectives, Federal Reserve Bank of Chicago, May–June 1989, pp. 10–30.

66. Charles W. Calomiris, "Do 'Vulnerable' Economies Need Deposit Insurance?: Lessons from the U.S. Agricultural Boom and Bust of the 1920's," Unpublished paper, Federal Reserve Bank of Chicago, 1989, in author's possession, p. 53.

67. White, *Regulation and Reform,* p. 218.

68. Georgetta, *Golden Fleece,* p. 422; M.D. Cravath to C.T. Smith, February 8, 1932, Series I, Box 1, Folder 3, MS 3987, Stockmen's National Bank-Rushville, NE, Nebraska State Historical Society. Also see Cravath to Jereme Wadd, February 8, 1932. *Loc. cit.*

69. See Richard W. Nelson, "Optimal Banking Structure: Implications for Interstate Banking," *Contemporary Policy Issues,* April 1988, pp. 13–23; Bernard Shull, "Interstate Banking and Antitrust Laws: History of Public Policies to Promote Banking Competition," *ibid.,* pp. 24–40; Larry A. Frieder, "The Interstate Banking Landscape: Legislative Policies and Rationale," *ibid.,* pp. 41–66; and Lynne Pierson Doti, "Interstate Banking: Past, Present and Future: Some Lessons From the West," unpublished paper presented at the Economic and Business History Society meeting, April 26–28, 1990, in author's possession. One frequently used comparison of a state with a similar undiversified economy to Nevada's was South Carolina, which had intrastate branching. Charles Calomiris argues that intrastate branching kept South Carolina banks reasonably resiliant despite horrific agricultural conditions. Yet the comparison may not be as applicable as it appears: South Carolina's branch systems did not really expand until the late 1920's. Of the three branch systems with more than two branches in 1929, the largest—Peoples State Bank, with 44 branches, really emerged when Robert Rhett combined several small banks in 1926. Virtually all branches were acquired by merger, not created *de novo,* and Peoples, along with the other two significant branch systems, all failed. Consequently, rather than vindicating branching, South Carolina survived the 1920's with few branch banks, then saw widespread failure when mergers tried to put great numbers of banks together. What that proved is that branching—especially intrastate branching in an undiversified economy undertaken at a poor moment—cannot itself save the banking system. Had true widespread branching with South Carolina existed from 1920 on, even then it is doubtful that the state's banks would not have still suffered. However, it is also plausible that the large branch systems would have survived. See John G. Sproat and Larry Schweikart, *Making Change: South Carolina Banking in the Twentieth Century* (Columbia, S.C.: South Carolina Bankers Association, 1990), pp. 56–57, 78. Compare with Calomiris, "State Deposit Insurance," pp. 6–27 *passim.*

Comment

A New Perspective on George Wingfield and Nevada Banking, 1920–1933

by Dwight R. Lee

Professor Schweikart has written a well researched and nicely organized paper on an interesting episode in the U.S. banking crisis of the early 1930's. Certainly the run on Wingfield's Nevada Banks in 1932 and the collapse of his Nevada banking chain in 1933 constitute an important part of the 1933 banking panic and the perpetuation of the depression of the 1930's. Schweikart has been able to make use of Wingfield's papers, only recently made available, to examine the reasons behind the collapse of Wingfield's banks. Was the collapse due to poor management on the part of Wingfield; the political repercussions of a financial scandal which involved some of Wingfield's banks in the 1920's; the harsh terms on loans to Wingfield imposed by the Reconstruction Finance Corporation (R.F.C.); falling livestock prices; or legal restrictions on branch banking?

Based on his research, Schweikart clearly rules out poor management on Wingfield's part as an explanation for the collapse of his banks. Also, given the lack of diversity in the Nevada economy at the time, Schweikart does not seem to believe that intrastate branch banking would have been sufficient to have saved Wingfield's banking system. Schweikart does seem to believe that if interstate banking had been legally possible Wingfield would have been able to save his banks. The real villains, though, according to Schweikart, are Western regulators and the Reconstruction Finance Corporation.

As Schweikart sees the problem with the Western regulators and the Reconstruction Finance Corporation, "the public had increasingly been squeezed out as a regulatory force, and the emphasis instead on investigations by 'impartial' examiners had made bank activities more than ever a 'secret' business 'understood' by only a few 'experts.' Thus, ironically, regulations designed to make banks more open to public scrutiny actually removed the banks even further from view, while at the same time citizens reassured themselves that 'someone' was 'watching' the banks."

While I am in complete agreement with Schweikart on the pernicious effect of much state banking regulation, his discussion does leave some important questions unanswered. First, it is far from clear that regulations were even ostensibly aimed at making banks more open to public scrutiny. Regulations of all kinds are typically implemented in response to organized groups which are far less concerned with the public's advantage than with their own advantage. Some discussion by Schweikart of the interest groups which were in the best position to shape banking legislation in Nevada and how their interests were advanced by particular regulations would be useful. And while it is no doubt true that many consumers feel less need for being vigilant in their choice of banks when they have been assured that they are being protected against bad choices by government experts, it is hard to see this as a particularly important factor in the Nevada case. At least as early as the so called "free banking" laws of pre-Civil War vintage, state governments were certifying bank notes. Such certification continued after the Civil War with the National Banking Acts. If the lack of due diligence on the part of bank customers was a problem in Nevada during the 1930's it certainly was not a new problem or one peculiar to Nevada. And there is no indication that this problem was any worse in the early 1930's than it was earlier.

The chief villain pointed to in Schweikart's paper is R.F.C. loans. According to Schweikart, "those R.F.C. loans actually harmed the Wingfield chain in several ways. The R.F.C. made the loans at relatively high interest rates (six percent) and only allowed six month maturity dates, . . . Worse the R.F.C. claimed the best assets of the banks as collateral, ..."

One does not have to be a fan of the R.F.C., or believe that it did more good than harm to banks and their customers generally, to question Schweikart's view that Wingfield's banks were themselves harmed by the R.F.C. loans, at least harmed *ex ante*. Clearly the R.F.C. offered Wingfield an option he otherwise would not have had. Given this option, why would Wingfield have decided to take advantage of it and borrow from the R.F.C. if he thought it would harm his chain? Wingfield was obviously aware of the interest rate being charged, the collateral being demanded, and the duration of R.F.C. loans being extended. Wingfield must have also been aware (as Friedman and Schwartz point out in their *Monetary History,* p. 325) that "the inclusion of a bank's name on the list [of R.F.C. loans] was correctly interpreted as a sign of weakness, and hence frequently led to runs on the bank." The fact that Wingfield took the R.F.C. loans is compelling evidence that he thought they would benefit him and his chain of banks compared to a policy of refusing R.F.C. loans. The fact that Wingfield may have been mistaken *ex post,* or that the benefit may not have been sufficient to save his banks, does not prove that Wingfield was somehow victimized by the R.F.C., or that the R.F.C. loans imposed "crippling conditions" on Wingfield's banks.

Schweikart also argues that Standard Oil and the Southern Pacific refused loans to Wingfield as soon as the R.F.C. got involved. The reason why these businesses were frightened off by the R.F.C. loans is not explained in Schweikart's paper, but it could have been for the reason pointed to in the Friedman-Schwartz quote above. But again, if obtaining an R.F.C. loan reduced the opportunity of obtaining loans from other sources (increasing the interest rate demand on other sources), then Wingfield should have recognized this as a cost of R.F.C. loans. Once this cost, as well as all other costs, was taken into consideration, the cost of a loan from R.F.C. must have been seen by Wingfield to have been lower, at the margin, than the cost of alternative loans.

Although I believe Schweikart overstates the role of the R.F.C. in the collapse of Wingfield's banks, it does seem to me that the R.F.C. was a poor substitute for market initiatives and structures precluded by government prohibitions. Schweikart is no doubt correct in believing that even if state-wide branch banking had been allowed it would not have saved Wingfield's banks given the lack of diversification in the Nevada economy. However, as Schweikart argues, if interstate banking had been allowed, it is quite possible that the losses from the temporary drop in wool prices could have been absorbed with extra flexibility in the allocation of funds that would have existed.

Let me conclude my comments on Schweikart's paper by congratulating him on a richly researched and well written paper on a very interesting episode in U.S. banking history. But let me also criticize him for being so bold as to reach a conclusion from his research that differs from the conclusion I reach. According to Schweikart, "the ultimate culprit—Nevada's undiversified economy and the crippling conditions of the R.F.C. loans—eluded even Wingfield's brilliant attempt to introduce a quasi-branching system." I would argue that the real culprits were the government restrictions against branch banking that prevented Wingfield's brilliance from being subjected to a far more accurate market test than was possible under the regulatory environment of the 1930's.

Index

and pressure against dollar,
247–251
turmoil caused by 1971 U. S. efforts to devalue dollar, 251–255
United States domestic needs v.,
231, 237, 238, 260
"Iron Triangle", 72, 74

Jackson, Andrew, 89, 106
Jacksonian democrats, 38, 106
Jefferson, Thomas, 95, 96
on denominational restrictions,
104
and First National Bank of the
United States, 69–70
Julliard v. Greenman, 42–44, 50, 57,
60–61, 71

Knox v. Lee, 40–42, 49, 57, 60–61

Legal Tender Act of 1862, 52, 208,
222, 225
as Civil War measure, 34, 51
constitutionality of tested, 32,
38–42, 52, 57, 60–61
criticism and analysis of test cases,
41–42, 44–50
economists' debate over, 47–50
'necessary and proper' clause and,
35, 41–42
passage of, 33–37, 41–42, 51–52
Legal tender United States notes in
California, 210
See also: Legal Tender Act of
1862; Treasury notes, United
States.; Greenbacks
Legal tender cases
See: *Hepburn v. Griswold,
Julliard v. Greenman, Knox v.
Lee, McCulloch v. Maryland,
Parker v. Davis*
Liability insurance, 107–109
antebellum experience, 17–18,
107–109
early 20th Century schemes,
18–19
effect of National Banking
System on, 18

in midwest, 17, 107–109, 124
mutual insurance systems, 17
in New York, 17, 107–108, 110,
113, 123–125, 127–128
in northeast, 17, 107–108
and principal-agent problem, 124
problems caused by, 16–17
public interest theory and, 124,
125–126
safety fund systems, 17
state sponsored, 5, 23–24, 101
unit banking lobby and, 18
Lincoln, Abraham, 135, 143, 144
Long Island central bankers conference of 1927, 238

Macroeconomics
and German reunification,
165–166
warfare, 164–166
Madison, James, 69–71, 74, 96
Marshall, Chief Justice John in
McCulloch v. Maryland, 3–4,
70–71, 74, 96
McCulloch, Hugh, 37, 41
greenback retirement policy of, 38
on *Julliard v. Greenman*, 43–44
and resumption, 209
McCulloch v. Maryland, 3–4, 35, 45,
70–71, 74, 96
McFadden Act (1927), 19
Medium of exchange, 53
Memminger, Christopher G.,
150–156
and conversion of Southern monetary system to war basis,
136–138
Minimum legal denomination restriction
See: Denominational restrictions
Mint Ratio (1792–1811), 90
Mint Ratio Adjustment of 1834,
57–60, 64
Monetary forces
as contributing factor in Great
Depression, 277–278, 299–301,
305–306, 312–313, 318, 322

About the Authors

Ronald W. Batchelder

Ronald W. Batchelder is a professor of economics at Pepperdine University. Dr. Batchelder has published widely in both professional and trade journals.

Michael David Bordo

Dr. Bordo is a professor of economics at Rutgers University and research associate for the National Bureau of Economic Research. Dr. Bordo's most recent book is *Money, History, and International Finance: Essays in Honor of Anna J. Schwartz.* He has published scores of essays, reviews, and articles in professional journals, and is a contributor to the *New Palgrave: A Dictionary of Economic Theory and Doctrine* and to the *Encyclopedia of Business Cycles, Panics, Crises, and Depressions.*

Charles Calomiris

Charles Calomiris is an assistant professor of economics at Northwestern University and consultant to the Federal Reserve Bank of Chicago. Dr. Calomiris has published dozens of essays in economics in various academic journals.

Gregory Christainsen

Dr. Christainsen is a professor of economics with the California State University at Hayward. Prof. Christainsen has published dozens of academic papers in economics and acted as a consultant to many organizations, including the Organization for Economic Cooperation and Development and the Pacific Research Institute.

Tyler Cowen

Tyler Cowen is an associate professor of economics at George Mason University. Dr. Cowen has authored many essays in economics for academic journals, and is the co-author of *Explorations in the New Monetary Economics.*

James A. Dorn

Dr. Dorn is vice president of academic affairs at the Cato Institute, editor of the *Cato Journal,* and professor of economics at Towson State University. He has co-edited several books on economics.

Kevin Dowd

Kevin Dowd is a lecturer in economics at the University of Nottingham, author of *Free Banking: The Route to Monetary Stability* (1988) and *The State and the Monetary System* (1989). Dr. Dowd is an advisor to the Bruges Group.

David Glasner

David Glasner is a staff economist with the Federal Trade Commission. Dr. Glasner's most recent book is *Free Banking and Monetary Reform* (1989). He has written dozens of articles for both the academic and popular press, and has taught at several colleges and universities.

Robert Greenfield

Dr. Greenfield is a professor of economics and finance and director of the Master of Business Administration Program, College of Business Administration at Fairleigh Dickinson University. Dr. Greenfield has published widely in both the academic and popular press.

Jeffrey Rogers Hummel

Mr. Hummel is publications director for the Independent Institute. He is the author of many essays for both the professional and popular press and an instructor in the Department of Economics, Golden Gate University.

Dwight R. Lee

Dr. Lee is a professor of economics at the University of Georgia (Athens). Prof. Lee is the author of dozens of essays for both popular and professional journals, contributor to several books, and the author of textbooks on microeconomics, macroeconomics, and constitutional economics.

Huston McCulloch

Huston McCulloch is a professor of economics at Ohio State University, and editor of the *Journal of Money, Credit and Banking*. Dr. McCulloch published *Money and Inflation: A Monetarist Approach* in 1982 and has written dozens of essays, reviews, and articles for professional, trade, and popular journals.

Ron Paul

Dr. Paul is a practicing physician and lecturer. He is a former Member of Congress from Texas, co-authored The Case for Gold (with Lewis Lehrman) and author of several other books, including *Ten Myths About Paper Money*. Dr. Paul offered the legislation in the House of Representatives that created the Gold Commission of 1981–1982. He is presently host of the talk show "At Issue" on the Discovery Channel.

Gary M. Pecquet

Gary Pecquet is an assistant professor of economics at Southwest Texas State University. Dr. Pecquet has published several articles on money and finance in the Confederacy, and is a contributor to the *Encyclopedia of American Business History and Biography*.

Hugh Rockoff

Dr. Rockoff is a professor of economics at Rutgers University. Prof. Rockoff published *The Free Banking Era: A Re-Examination* in 1975 and is the author of *War and the Growth of the Federal Government*, as well as numerous essays and reviews for professional journals.

Joseph T. Salerno

Joseph Salerno is an associate professor in the Department of Economics at Lubin Graduate School of Business, Pace University. Dr. Salerno has also taught at Rutgers University and Stockton State College, has published many essays in both professional and popular journals, and has contributed to several books.

Anna J. Schwartz

Dr. Schwartz is a research associate with the National Bureau of Economic Research and adjunct professor of economics at City University of New York. Prof. Schwartz is a member of the Board of Editors of the *Journal of Money, Credit and Banking* and the *Journal of*

Monetary Economics, past president of the Western Economic Association, and the author of scores of essays, reviews, and books in the field of money and banking.

Larry E. Schweikart

Larry Schweikart is an associate professor of History at the University of Dayton. Prof. Schweikart is the author of several books about banking in the South and Southwest, including *Banking in the American South from the Age of Jackson to Reconstruction* (1987). He has published scores of essays and reviews in both professional and popular journals.

George Selgin

Dr. Selgin is an assistant professor of economics at the University of Georgia and a Durell Fellow. Prof. Selgin is the author of *The Theory of Free Banking: Money Supply Under Competitive Note Issue* (1988). He has published many essays and reviews in the area of money and banking.

Hans F. Sennholz

Hans Sennholz is chairman of the economics department at Grove City College. Dr. Sennholz is the author of several economics books, including *Money and Freedom* (1985), and hundreds of essays and reviews in both professional and popular journals.

Richard Sylla

Dr. Sylla is a professor of economics and business at North Carolina State University and research associate for the National Bureau of Economic Research. Prof. Sylla is the author of two books, contributor to several more, and has published dozens of reviews and essays in professional and popular journals.

Clifford F. Thies

Clifford F. Thies is the Durell Professor of Money, Banking and Finance at Shenandoah University. Dr. has taught at several colleges and universities and is the author of dozens of reviews, articles and essays in scholarly journals. His most recent book, *Macroeconomics for Managers,* was published in 1990.

Richard H. Timberlake, Jr.

Richard Timberlake was a professor of economics at the University of Georgia before retiring. Dr. Timberlake has had a distinguished career as a teacher and author of several books, including *Origins of Central Banking in the United States (1978) and Gold, Greenbacks, and the Constitution* (1991). Prof. Timberlake has also published dozens of articles on money and banking in academic journals and acted as a consultant to various organizations.

Mark Toma

Dr. Toma is an associate professor of economics at the University of Kentucky. He has co-edited *Central Bankers, Bureaucratic Incentives, and Monetary Policy,* and is the author of a score of essays and reviews in economic journals.

Eugene White

Eugene White is an associate professor at Rutgers University. Dr. White is the author of *The Regulation and Reform of the American Banking System, 1900–1929,* the co-editor of *Crashes and Panics in Historical Perspective,* and the author of many reviews and articles in professional and popular journals.

Lawrence H. White

Dr. White is an associate professor of economics at the University of Georgia. Prof. White has authored scores of essays and reviews in money and banking. His most recent book is *Competition and Currency: Essays on Free Banking and Money.*